THE FRENCH REVOLUTION

Recent debates and new controversies

Second Edition

Edited by
Gary Kates

Routledge
Taylor & Francis Group

NEW YORK AND LONDON

First published 1998
by Routledge
270 Madison Avenue, New York, NY 10016

Simultaneously published in the UK
by Routledge
2 Park Square, Milton Park, Abingdon, Oxon OX14 4RN

Reprinted 2001

Second edition, 2006

Reprinted 2007, 2009

Routledge is an imprint of the Taylor & Francis Group

Typeset in Palatino by
RefineCatch Ltd, Bungay, Suffolk
Printed and bound in Great Britain by the
MPG Books Group

British Library Cataloguing in Publication Data
A catalogue record for this book is available from
the British Library

Library of Congress Cataloging in Publication Data
The French Revolution : recent debates and new controversies /
edited by Gary Kates. – 2nd ed.
   p.   cm. – (Rewriting histories)
Includes bibliographical references and index.
ISBN 0–415–35832–9 (hardback) – ISBN 0–415–35833–7 (pbk.)
   1. France – History – Revolution, 1789–1799 – Influence.   2. France
– History – Revolution, 1789–1799 – Historiography.   3. Historians
– Political and social views.   4. Civilization, Modern – French
influences.   I. Kates, Gary, 1952–   .   II. Series.
DC148.F727 2005
944.04–dc22
2005013088

ISBN 10: 0–415–35832–9 (hbk)
ISBN 10: 0–415–35833–7 (pbk)

ISBN 13: 978–0–415–35832–3 (hbk)
ISBN 13: 978–0–415–35833–0 (pbk)

THE FRENCH REVOLUTION

The latest in the successful *Rewriting History* series, Gary Kates' fascinating second edition studies all aspects of the French Revolution from its origins, through its development, and examines the consequences of this major historical event.

Completely updated with new research and articles, the book brings together key texts at the forefront of research and interpretation. It challenges orthodox assumptions concerning the origins, development and long-term historical repercussions of the Revolution.

The volume includes an updated introduction by the editor that contextualizes the historiographical controversies, and articles which include contributions from major figures in the debate, such as Lynn Hunt and François Furet. These articles are woven into a sophisticated narrative which covers areas including the intellectual connection and the feminist dimension. This new edition also includes articles discussing colonialism and family legislation, emphasizing approaches that focus on class, gender, and race.

This engaging collection on a crucial turning point in history is presented in a new, student-friendly format and is a perfect reader for anyone studying the French Revolution.

Gary Kates is Dean of the College and Professor of History at Pomona College, California. His other books include *Monsieur d'Eon Is a Woman* (2001) and *The Cercle Social, the Girondins, and the French Revolution* (1985).

REWRITING HISTORIES
Series editor: Jack R. Censer

CONTENTS

CONTENTS

LIST OF ILLUSTRATIONS

FIGURES

TABLES

CONTRIBUTORS

Keith Michael Baker is The J. E. Wallace Sterling Professor of Humanities at Stanford University. He is the author of *Condorcet: From Natural Philosophy to Social Mathematics* (Chicago, 1975), and *Inventing the French Revolution: Essays on French Political Culture in the Eighteenth Century* (Cambridge, 1990).

Suzanne Desan is Professor of History at the University of Wisconsin, Madison. She is the author of *Reclaiming the Sacred: Lay Religion and Popular Politics in Revolutionary France* (Ithaca, NY, 1990), which won the Herbert Baxter Adams Prize, and most recently, *The Family on Trial in Revolutionary France* (Berkeley and Los Angeles, 2004).

Laurent Dubois is Associate Professor of History at Michigan State University. He is the author of *A Colony of Citizens: Revolution & Slave Emancipation in the French Caribbean, 1787–1804* (Chapel Hill, NC, 2004) and *Avengers of the New World: The Story of the Haitian Revolution* (Cambridge, MA, 2004).

François Furet (1927–1997) taught at the Etude des Haute Etudes in Paris and the University of Chicago. He is best known for *Interpreting the French Revolution* (Paris, 1978; Cambridge, 1981).

Lynn Hunt is Eugen Weber Professor of Modern European History at the University of California, Los Angeles. Among other works, she is the author of *Politics, Culture, and Class in the French Revolution* (Berkeley and Los Angeles, 1984), and *The Family Romance of the French Revolution* (Berkeley and Los Angeles, 1992). In 2002 she was President of the American Historical Association.

Colin Jones is Professor of History at the University of Warwick, where he was Chair of the History Department from 1998 to 2001. He is the author of *The Great Nation: France 1715–99* (London, 2002). In 2003, he was a visiting professor at the Collège de France.

Gary Kates is Vice President for Academic Affairs, Dean of the College, and Professor of History at Pomona College. He is the author of *The Cercle Social, the Girondins, and the French Revolution* (Princeton, 1985), and *Monsieur d'Eon is* *a Woman: A Tale of Political Intrigue and Sexual Masquerade* (1995; Baltimore, 2001).

Sir Colin Lucas is former Master of Balliol College and Vice Chancellor of the University of Oxford, where he taught history for many years. He is currently Chief Executive of the Rhodes Trust and Warden of the Rhodes House. Among other works, he is the author of *The Structure of the Terror: The Example of Javogues and the Loire* (Oxford, 1973).

John Markoff is Professor of Sociology, History, and Political Science and Research Professor, University Center for International Studies, at the University of Pittsburgh. He is the author of *The Abolition of Feudalism: Peasants, Lords and Legislators in the French Revolution* (University Park, PA: The Pennsylvania State University Press, 1997), and with Gilbert Shapiro, *Revolutionary Demands: A Content Analysis of the Cahiers de Doléances of 1789* (Stanford, CA: Stanford University Press, 1998).

Sarah Maza is the Jane Long Professor in the Humanities and Professor of History at Northwestern University. She is the author of *Private Lives and Public Affairs: The Causes Célèbres of Pre-Revolutionary France* (Ithaca, NY, 1993), which won the David Pinkney Prize of the Society for French Historical Studies, and *The Myth of the French Bourgeoisie: An Essay on the Social Imaginary, 1750–1850* (Cambridge, MA, 2003).

Albert Soboul (1914–82) taught for many years at the Sorbonne and was Director of the Société des Etudes Robespierristes and coeditor of the journal *Annales historiques de la Révolution française*. Among his important works are *Les Sans-culottes parisiens en l'an II* (Paris, 1958).

Timothy Tackett is Professor of History at the University of California, Irvine. Among other works, he is the author of *Becoming a Revolutionary: The Deputies of the National Assembly and the Origins of the French Revolution* (Princeton, 1996), and *When the King Took Flight* (Cambridge, MA, 2003).

SERIES EDITOR'S PREFACE

Rewriting history, or revisionism, has always followed closely in the wake of history writing. In their efforts to re-evaluate the past, professional as well as amateur scholars have followed many approaches, most commonly as empiricists, uncovering new information to challenge earlier accounts. Historians have also revised previous versions by adopting new perspectives, usually fortified by new research, which overturn received views.

Even though rewriting is constantly taking place, historians' attitudes towards using new interpretations have been anything but settled. For most, the validity of revisionism lies in providing a stronger, more convincing account that better captures the objective truth of the matter. Although such historians might agree that we never finally arrive at the 'truth', they believe it exists and over time may be better approximated. At the other extreme stand scholars who believe that each generation or even each cultural group or subgroup necessarily regards the past differently, each creating for itself a more usable history. Although these latter scholars do not reject the possibility of demonstrating empirically that some contentions are better than others, they focus upon generating new views based upon different life experiences. Different truths exist for different groups. Surely such an understanding, by emphasizing subjectivity, further encourages rewriting history. Between these two groups are those historians who wish to borrow from both sides. This third group, while accepting that every congeries of individuals sees matters differently, still wishes somewhat contradictorily to fashion a broader history that incorporates both of these particular visions. Revisionists who stress empiricism fall into the first of the three camps, while others spread out across the board.

Today the rewriting of history seems to have accelerated to a blinding speed as a consequence of the evolution of revisionism. A variety of approaches has emerged. A major factor in this process has been the enormous increase in the number of researchers. This explosion has reinforced and enabled the re-testing of many assertions. Significant ideological shifts have also played a major part in the growth of revisionism. First, the crisis of Marxism, culminating in the events in Eastern Europe in 1989, has given rise to doubts about explicitly Marxist accounts. Such doubts have spilled over into the entire field of social history which has been a dominant subfield of the discipline for several decades.

Focusing on society and its class divisions implied that these are the most important elements in historical analysis. Because Marxism was built on the same claim, the whole basis of social history has been questioned, despite the very many studies that directly had little to do with Marxism. Disillusionment with social history simultaneously opened the door to cultural and linguistic approaches largely developed in anthropology and literature. Multi-culturalism and feminism further generated revisionism. By claiming that scholars had, wittingly or not, operated from a white European/American male point of view, newer researchers argued that other approaches had been neglected or misunderstood. Not surprisingly, these last historians are the most likely to envision each subgroup rewriting its own usable history, while other scholars incline towards revisionism as part of the search for some stable truth.

Rewriting Histories will make these new approaches available to the student population. Often new scholarly debates take place in the scattered issues of journals which are sometimes difficult to find. Furthermore, in these first inter-actions, historians tend to address one another, leaving out the evidence that would make their arguments more accessible to the uninitiated. This series of books will collect in one place a strong group of the major articles in selected fields, adding notes and introductions conducive to improved understanding. Editors will select articles containing substantial historical data, so that students – at least those who approach the subject as an objective phenomenon – can advance not only their comprehension of debated points but also their grasp of substantive aspects of the subject.

Few historical topics have been subjected to more reconsideration than the French Revolution. Not so long ago a Marxist interpretation prevailed that employed an emphasis on class struggle to explain both the causes and con-sequences of the Revolution. Although one or another version of this view dominated for better than half a century, it was upstaged in the 1980s by a focus upon politics and ideas – the very factors that the revolutionaries themselves would have tended to emphasize. Many have embraced the new concepts. But this book identifies and defines a challenge to this recent opinion. This collection concentrates both upon feminist criticisms as well as a retort from a neo-Marxist view in which class interests still figure prominently. Whatever their differences – and they are large – they oppose the most recent view. Will one of these two views displace the others? For now, this book of essays suggests more, rather than a narrowing, debate.

Jack R. Censer

ACKNOWLEDGMENTS

All extracts and articles published in this volume have already been published. We would like to thank the following copyright holders for permission to reproduce their work:

Chapter 1   Reprinted in an abridged format from Albert Soboul, *Understanding the French Revolution*, trans. April Ane Knutson (New York: International Publishers, 1988): 274–299.

Chapter 2   Reprinted in an abridged format from *Past and Present* 60 (August 1973): 84–126.

Chapter 3   Reprinted from *Government and Opposition* 16:2 (Spring 1981): 200–218.

Chapter 4   Reprinted by permission of the publisher from *A Critical Dictionary of the French Revolution*, ed. François Furet and Mona Ozouf, trans. Arthur Goldhammer (Cambridge, MA: Harvard University Press, 1989 by the President and Fellows of Harvard College): 479–493.

Chapter 5   Reprinted in an abridged format from *The French Revolution and Social Change*, ed. Colin Lucas (Oxford: Oxford University Press, 1990): 69–118.

Chapter 6   Reprinted in an abridged format from the *Journal of Modern History* 69 (June 1997): 199–229.

Chapter 7   Reprinted from the *American Historical Review* 94 (April 1989): 271–301.

Chapter 8   Reprinted from the *American Historical Review* 100 (April 1995): 360–386.

Chapter 9   Reprinted from *Eroticism and the Body Politic*, ed. Lynn Hunt (Baltimore: Johns Hopkins University Press, 1991): 108–130.

Chapter 10   Reprinted in an abridged format from *French Historical Studies* 20 (1997): 597–634.

Chapter 11   Reprinted in an abridged format from *The William and Mary Quarterly*, 3rd Ser., 56 (April 1999): 363–392.

INTRODUCTION

Gary Kates

"What? You have something *new* to say about the
French Revolution?"

That was the reaction of one of my graduate school professors when he heard
that I intended to write a doctoral dissertation on the French Revolution. Indeed
it is a sensible reaction. After all, whole forests have been cleared to make way
for the historical literature on the French Revolution, as a trip to any decent
university library will demonstrate. There, the casual stroller will discover stacks
and stacks of books on every conceivable topic. Perhaps no other event in history
has attracted so much attention.

Much of the problem with studying the French Revolution involves sorting
through what others have said about it. Ever since Edmund Burke and Thomas
Paine first argued about the Revolution's meaning, the debate on it has seemed
almost as interesting as the event itself. That debate, of course, has spilled over
into neighboring disciplines: political scientists, philosophers, sociologists,
literary critics, and art historians have all given the French Revolution prominent
weight in their fields. The French Revolution is perhaps the closest thing
historians have developed to a litmus test: One's stance on the French Revolution inevitably reveals much about one's deepest ideological and political
convictions.

This book deals only with a small, but significant, part of that debate: the
quarrels that have captivated professional historians primarily since the Revolution's 1989 bicentennial celebration. After all, since historians devote their entire
careers to developing an expertise by way of its archives and bibliographies, they
are perhaps in the best position to comment on the Revolution's significance and
meaning.

The study of the French Revolution by professional historians (as opposed to
philosophers, writers, or journalists) is hardly a century old, barely half the
temporal distance from the Revolution itself. It began with the centennial
celebration of 1889, when the Paris City Council awarded its first Chair of the
History of the French Revolution at the Sorbonne to Alphonse Aulard (1849–
1928). Since then, the holder of this Chair has been acknowledged as the dean of
French Revolutionary studies.

Aulard's writings promoted democratic republicanism buttressing left-wing political parties of the Third Republic. Aulard had no sympathy for the monarchy. In his view, the despotic abuses of the Ancien Régime justified the violent uprising of 1789. Aulard admired the courage of the Constituent Assembly deputies, but in the end he thought that they sheepishly balked from confronting a recalcitrant king and treasonous queen. The Constitution of 1791, a flawed document in Aulard's eyes that allowed the monarchy too much power, was weakened by the king's flight to Varennes in June 1791. The courage of Georges Danton and the other Paris militant activists pushed the Revolution beyond the halfway point. Aulard praised their efforts which culminated in the insurrection of August 10, 1792 and the declaration of France's first democratic republic based upon universal male suffrage. For Aulard, the establishment of a republic under the National Convention marked the zenith of the Revolution.[1]

After World War I, Aulard was challenged by his most gifted student, Albert Mathiez (1874–1932). Influenced both by the recent victory of Bolshevism in Russia, as well as by the awesome legacy of French socialist leader Jean Jaurès (himself an important historian of the Revolution), Mathiez rejected Aulard's beloved Danton as a corrupt bourgeois politician, and instead defended whole-heartedly Robespierre's efforts to save France through the Terror. Mathiez's Marxism was pragmatic rather than dogmatic; but his defense of the Terror was nonetheless passionate and had great influence upon a generation of historians from Europe and the United States. In perhaps his most brilliant book, *La vie chère et le movement social sous la terreur* ('The Cost of Living and Popular Movements During the Terror' [1927]), Mathiez argued that the cost of living for ordinary Parisians improved more during the Terror than at any other time. In Mathiez's view, Robespierre was not a dictator hungry for arbitrary power, but a democratic politician responding to popular pressures from Parisian workers. Unfortunately, the gains of those sans-culottes were temporary; and while the Revolution counted on their support, its bourgeois leaders turned against Robespierre and renounced sans-culottes participation and demands.[2]

Mathiez's influence was especially great because of the Société des Etudes Robespierristes (Society of Robespierrist Studies), the organization he founded that published documentary collections, books, and most importantly, the scholarly journal *Annales historiques de la révolution française*. By Mathiez's early death in 1932, the *Annales* had established itself as the premier journal of record for French Revolutionary historiography. Mathiez's successors closely followed the master: Georges Lefebvre (1874–1959), Albert Soboul (1914–1982), and Michel Vovelle (1933–   ) all combined the Sorbonne's Chair of the History of the Revolution, and the editorship of the *Annales historiques*, with a commitment to Marxism usually demonstrated by membership in the French Communist Party. Consequently, in the century since the founding of Aulard's Sorbonne Chair, the academy of French Revolutionary scholars has been dominated by left-wing socialists committed to a particular way of seeing the Revolution and to a special set of contemporary political values.

As it solidified into its own sort of orthodoxy, this Marxist interpretation could be summarized in the following manner: The French Revolution was not simply a political struggle from [evil] absolute monarchy to [good] democratic republicanism, but represented a deeper shift from feudalism to capitalism. The Revolution was led by an alliance between a bourgeois elite [owners of liquid capital], and popular classes [artisans and peasants], against the land-owning nobility. The greatest success of such an alliance occurred in 1789, but after that it began to show signs of strains. By the summer of 1791, revolutionary events were marked by class conflict between the capitalist bourgeoisie and the popular classes. This struggle produced an urban political movement led by the sans-culottes, whose vision of a truly social revolution influenced nineteenth-century radicalism. The Terror represented the pinnacle of the sans-culottes movement, in which the Jacobins established (albeit temporarily) the first modern democracy in a major European state. Thus the French Revolution was essentially a class struggle in which one class was destroyed (the nobility), one class was awakened (the sans-culottes), and one class won control of the state (the bourgeoisie).

Outside France, England and the United States, there was less of a commitment to Marxism among French Revolutionary scholars. Historians such as J. M. Thompson (1878–1956) or Louis Gottschalk (1899–1975) were not known for their political activism or party labels. Still, it is remarkable how easily a watered-down version of French Marxism spread throughout Anglo-American college texts between 1930 and 1970. Just as Gottschalk championed Mathiez's work in the 1930s, so R. R. Palmer (1909–2002) translated Lefebvre's most accessible book into English shortly after World War II.[3]

To be sure, there were some important differences between the Anglo-Americans and the French. During the 1930s, for example, Harvard historian Crane Brinton (1898–1968) adopted a skeptical position in his influential *Anatomy of Revolution*. In his view, the French Revolution was achieved by "moderates" who bravely fought the forces of the Ancien Régime, and busily tried to construct a regime based upon the noble virtues of liberty and equality. Such "moderates" were unable to halt the Revolution's surge toward war and anarchy, and the result was "the accession of the extremists," whereby freedom turned sour. Thrown off course by Danton, Robespierre and the Jacobins, the Revolution toppled from liberty to tyranny.[4]

Outside of the historical academy there was a rich tradition stemming from Edmund Burke that viewed the Revolution itself as wholly unnecessary, and in fact counterproductive for the establishment of liberty. Among scholars, their voices were isolated and ignored.

But no longer. During the past thirty years, there has been a transformation of enormous magnitude in the scholarship on the French Revolution. This change – one is tempted to call it a revolution – has been marked by the almost total collapse of the orthodox Marxist interpretation, and a range of sharp attacks on virtually all of its major points and approaches. The broad teachings of Mathiez, Lefebvre, and Soboul are today, even in France, discredited. Considering how monolithic orthodox Marxist interpretations of the Revolution had become since the 1920s, some sort of challenge within academia was inevitable – but if the attack was anticipated, the complete collapse of the Marxist paradigm was a surprise.

Alfred Cobban (1901–1968), a distinguished professor at the University of London, deserves credit for breaking the first window (if not throwing the first stone) in the Marxist house. During a 1954 lecture, Cobban questioned whether the Revolution was led by a rising bourgeoisie. Analyzing those leaders of the Third Estate who opposed king and aristocracy in the Estates General, Cobban noted that only 13 percent were merchants, manufacturers, or financiers. This revolution was not, in fact, made by a capitalist bourgeoisie. Rather, Cobban argued that the greatest number of leaders came from the ranks of local, petty public officials: administrators, prosecutors, judges, and the like: hardly capitalists, and hardly people who had no connection to the Ancien Régime. Cobban agreed with the Marxists that the French Revolution was a social revolution; but it was one of "notables" not of capitalists.[5]

Beyond Cobban's graduate students, few colleagues paid much attention to his insights until his research was reworked into a book in 1964. By that time, his efforts were helped greatly by George Taylor of the University of North Carolina, whose important articles in mainstream journals added much empirical ammunition to the revisionist stockpile. Just as Cobban had robbed the Revolution of an angry revolutionary bourgeoisie, Taylor demonstrated how the investment patterns by bourgeois and noble families were remarkably similar.[6] By the seventies, when Colin Lucas published his now-classic article reprinted in this volume, the Revisionist school had become an entrenched minority among French Revolutionary scholars.

No matter what is written about the French Revolution in England or the United States, it is really only France that counts. Revisionists would thus remain an iconoclastic minority until they could mount a beachhead in France. That occurred dramatically with the 1978 publication of François Furet's *Penser la Révolution française* (translated into English as *Interpreting the French Revolution*). Despite its turgid prose, the absence of new archival material, and an idiosyncratic structure, no other book has shaped the current research agenda for French Revolutionary scholarship more than this one.[7]

Furet (1927–1997) attacked the Marxist "catechisme," but he did much more than translate Cobbanite Revisionism for a French audience. Until Furet's book, most Revisionist attacks had come from social and economic historians who disputed the Marxist version of class struggle. Furet, on the other hand, hoped to restore "to the French Revolution its most obvious dimension, the political one, and of focusing attention . . . in the ways of legitimating and representing historical action."[8] In Furet's hands, this meant a return to political theory and intellectual history. By studying more carefully the meaning of revolutionary rhetoric, historians could recapture the profound ideological change that occurred in how Frenchmen thought about politics. Furet ignited new interest in the cultural history of the Revolution, which had diminished into an isolated corner by the mid-1970s. Almost overnight that oldest of problems – the relationship of the Enlightenment to the French Revolution – was resurrected into a burning issue for debate and controversy.

Furet argued that advanced democratic ideas of certain Enlightened philosophers such as Jean-Jacques Rousseau became the heart and soul of the French Revolution. Democracy here did not mean governing by consent, or even respecting individual human rights. Rather, wrote Furet, the Revolution embraced a radical ideology of popular sovereignty so that any abuse of power could be excused so long as it was achieved in the name of *the people*. In short, Democracy meant the power of a national state to defeat those who opposed its will. Consequently, Furet argued that the trajectory of the Revolution from its first day was toward the state using democratic ideology to rule in a despotic manner; that is, without regard for human rights. That process culminated, of course, in the Terror, which was the pinnacle of revolutionary democracy and dictatorship.

Just as Furet interpreted the early years of the Revolution as a kind of prologue to the Terror, so he viewed the Napoleonic Empire as its epilogue. Napoleon did not so much turn against the Revolution as consolidate its radical principles. Like the Jacobins of the Year II, Napoleon abused the rights of the people while acting in their name, and he continued the Revolution's bent towards administrative unity and political centralization. While he led the army to new glories, the campaigns he waged and the armies he championed had their roots in the war begun by the Jacobins in 1792 and 1793. For Furet, the Empire was but a late stage of the Revolution, with few fundamental differences.[9]

Furet's attitude toward the revolutionary era is profoundly conservative. France becoming a democracy did not mean that its people became free; it meant that the collective French People was sovereign, and that each individual was subservient to it. Politicians who thought of themselves as democratic claimed to speak in the name of the whole people. Dissent was at best distrusted, since it could lead to factional strife that undermined unity. For Furet, the Terror was not an accidental phase of the Revolution, but rather emblematic of the entire Revolution. Unlike Crane Brinton, who believed that circumstances had thrown the Revolution off course after a moderate phase filled with notable achievements, Furet argued that the Revolution was radical from the start, and its early achievements were only a mirage.

During the 1980s, as the bicentennial celebration approached, Furet followed up this suggestive essay with a series of more solid historical works. Many of them were joint projects from conferences and colloquiums, where he and his allies presented their approach to the Revolution in a more comprehensive but rarely systematic fashion. By 1989 Furet had become arguably the most important historian of the French Revolution in the world.[10]

Furet's ascendancy not only furthered the demise of Marxist historiography, but also gave greater visibility in France to Anglo-American scholarship. Furet was perhaps the first major historian of the French Revolution to speak fluent English and the first to accept a permanent appointment at an American university – for much of the 1980s and early 1990s he had a regular visiting appointment at the University of Chicago.

It is no wonder then that many of Furet's earliest and strongest supporters came from scholars working in the United States. Among them is Keith Baker, who introduced Furet to Chicago. In a series of brilliant articles, Baker has done much to revitalize the intellectual history of the Revolution by carefully tracing how certain Rousseauian strands of Enlightenment political ideology mutated into revolutionary Jacobinism. For him, as for Furet, the key conduit was the Constituent Assembly deputy, priest, and pamphleteer Emmannuel-Joseph Sieyès, "the theorist who had done more than anyone to interject Rousseauian notions of national sovereignty into the assembly's debates."[11]

The influence of Rousseau upon the French Revolution has been among the most heated debates in eighteenth-century studies, and no one has discussed this problem with more sensitivity and erudition than Baker. In 1762, Rousseau had set forth his theory of the general will in his small but difficult book, *The Social Contract*. In contrast to other Enlightenment thinkers such as John Locke, David Hume, or Thomas Jefferson, Rousseau believed that politics was largely the process of discovering the will of the nation. If a member of that nation was found in a small minority of citizens who were dissenting from the national will, Rousseau advised the citizen to drop such views and gladly yield to the majority of citizens. No citizen, argued Rousseau, had a right to go against what a nation wants for itself. Such a doctrine may be democratic (in the sense of being populist), but it clearly poses serious problems for protecting the civic rights of minority groups.

According to Baker, the Revolution's free-fall into Rousseauian democracy was not the product of 1792–3 when the nation was at war, but was the result of deliberate decisions made by the National Assembly as early as the summer of 1789. At the end of one well-known lecture delivered as part of a bicentennial commemoration in 1989, Baker argued that by accepting Rousseau's theory of the general will as the basis for rejecting an absolute royal veto, the Constituent Assembly "was opting for the Terror."[12]

Like Furet, Baker placed the Terror squarely at the center of the revolutionary process. The Terror was not some detour away from the Revolution's true goal; it was the outcome of the Constituent Assembly's repeated adoption of Rousseauian political principles. After reading Furet and Baker, it seemed impossible to condemn the Terror as a temporary deviation from some political norm. In Furet's and Baker's view, the terror occurred not only because of what happened in 1792 or 1793, but because of the way in which politics was reconceptualized in 1789.

Furet and his collaborators opened the door to even more conservative views of the Revoluton among academic historians. Since the early nineteenth century, most historical writing was done by those who championed the great event. Liberals, or Whigs, believed that the French Revolution, when taken as a whole, was necessary to move France and Europe from a pre-modern to a modern society. For Liberals, the Ancien Régime had become so ossified and paralyzed by its own internal contradictions that only revolutionary change could resolve France's grave problems. By the mid-twentieth century, the notion of the Revolution as an agent of progress, despite its great faults, was shared by virtually all of the academic historical community, from Cobban to Soboul. If Anglo and American historians often accepted the views of French Marxists, it was because they shared fundamental attitudes about the nature of the Revolution as an agent of liberty.[13]

At the center of the Liberal approach to the Revolution is a periodization that separates a moderate and constructive early phase of the Revolution (1789–92) from the more radical and violent period that followed (1792–4). Liberal historians typically point to the great achievements of the early phase (passage of the *Declaration of the Rights of Man and Citizen*, abolition of feudalism, reorganization of the judiciary and administration, freedom for Protestants and Jews, etc.) as demonstrating the virtues of revolutionary change. Correspondingly, they typically explain away the excessive violence of the Terror by noting the grave circumstances that led to its establishment: war, economic dislocation, and counter-revolution.

To declare that the Terror was conceptualized or originated in 1789 is to say that the Revolution never went through a "moderate" phase: the entire political dynamic from the Tennis Court Oath through the death of Robespierre can be viewed as one great era in which the state wielded unprecedented authority in the name of the people, but usually not to their benefit. Indeed, in the hands of some Revisionists who go beyond Furet and Baker, the entire Revolution is viewed as one gigantic imposition forced on the backs of the peasants, who, of course, made up more than three-quarters of the population. "The violence was all rather senseless," remarks historian Donald Sutherland.[14] The French Revolution wasn't worth the trouble.

This conclusion would have surprised Alfred Cobban, the British historian who began Revisionism forty years ago. For Cobban, the Ancien Régime was so beset with contradictions and structural problems that nothing short of revolution could reform the country; nor was the Revolution itself all senseless violence. The construction of a liberal political order, based upon respect for human rights and religious toleration would have been impossible without the clashes of 1789 and the achievements of the Constituent Assembly. For Cobban, the Third Republic was unthinkable without the first, even if the original model had its defects.[15]

The turn of recent French Revolutionary historiography against its Liberal foundations is startling. Certainly the ascendancy of Neo-Conservative ideas in England and the United States has provided the context for the warm reception of Revisionism. Usually former Liberals themselves, Neo-Conservatives in the 1960s and 1970s turned against the whole idea of revolutionary change as itself illiberal. Associating the revolutionary process with fanaticism (read Bolshevism and later Islamic fundamentalism), Neo-Conservatives gave up their Rousseau for copies of Burke and Tocqueville: progressive change occurs, they now argued, slowly and outside of institutions controlled by the state. Any efforts by the state to push through large-scale social or political programs were bound to lead to violations of property and civil liberties.[16]

Since the early 1950s, Neo-Conservative thinkers have had their own pet history of the French Revolution. In his 1952 classic, *The Origins of Totalitarian Democracy*, Jacob Talmon argues the French state became a "totalitarian democracy" during the Terror in the sense that its social programs were designed to alter the course of every citizen's life, producing a secular version of a messianic age. In Talmon's view, such a state would become a harbinger for twentieth-century experiments on both the political right and left. Talmon traced the idea of totalitarian democracy back through Sieyès to certain key Enlightenment figures, Rousseau most prominent among them. While Talmon's history was attacked by Liberal historians – even his own Ph.D. advisor Alfred Cobban dismissed his argument – the book succeeded in associating Rousseau with the Terror.[17]

Talmon's intellectual history has much in common with the newer approach of Furet. Both Talmon's and Furet's approach privilege political theory and the spread of ideas; both see a direct line from Rousseau through Sieyès to Robespierre; both associate Rousseauian democratic ideas with a collectivism that quickly turned oppressive; both, in short, see the Terror as the essence of the Revolution and view it as a harbinger of Bolshevism and Fascism. Talmon's methodology is primitive in comparison to Furet and Baker, whose perceptive investigations into discourse theory have significantly advanced the field. In contrast, Talmon's method tends to distort Enlightenment ideology by projecting twentieth-century meanings onto eighteenth-century ideas. Only the most extreme historians writing today, such as Raynald Sécher, extend Talmon's view by arguing that the Terror culminated in a genocidal campaign in the Vendée resembling twentieth-century horrors.[18]

Whether in its older form from Talmon, or its more sophisticated version from Furet, Revisionism had clearly become the dominant interpretation of the historical establishment in England, France, and the United States by the 1989 bicentennial celebration. In France, despite Michel Vovelle's semi-official position, it was Furet whom the media annointed "King of the Revolution," and who seemingly made an appearance at every academic conference and on numerous French television shows.[19] In the United States, the best illustration of Revisionism's popularity was the enormous success of Simon Schama's mega-history of the Revolution, *Citizens*, which exaggerated Furet's arguments into slogans that at times echoed Margaret Thatcher if not Burke:

> ... the Revolution did indeed invent a new kind of politics, an insti-
> tutional transference of Rousseau's sovereignty of the General Will
> that abolished private space and time, and created a form of patriotic
> militarism more all-embracing than anything that had yet been seen
> in Europe. For one year, it invented and practiced representative
> democracy; for two years, it imposed coercive egalitarianism. ... But
> for two decades its enduring product was a new kind of militarized

state. . . . The notion that between 1789 and 1791, France basked in some sort of liberal pleasure garden before the erection of the guillotine is a complete fantasy. . . . The terror was merely 1789 with a higher body count.[20]

Since the bicentennial celebration, the most important developments in the historiography of the Revolution have been challenges to the position laid out by Furet and his colleagues. In this volume, we have selected articles by four historians – Colin Jones, Timothy Tackett, John Markoff, and Sarah Maza – that seek to critique Furet's approach to the Revolution. While each of the authors approaches the Revolution differently, and while none would regard themselves in any kind of formal school with the other, we can nonetheless see the beginnings of a shared set of attitudes. First, unlike Revisionists, these recent interpretations do not minimize the oppressive character of the eighteenth-century nobility. The aristocracy is seen as a distinct political group with interests separate and opposing those of commoners. Second, these four historians would agree that the period of the Constituent Assembly was substantively different (i.e., more moderate and more constructive) than the Jacobinism of the Terror. Third, they would accept the claim, most forcefully made by Markoff, that the collective violence of the Revolution's early years was often purposeful and necessary to the establishment of a liberal and free state.

Perhaps most important, these historians challenge the view that the Revolution was primarily a failure. A rising bourgeoisie may not have started the Revolution, but the revolutionaries successfully destroyed the Ancien Régime and refashioned a society that made a nineteenth-century liberal state possible. Some scholars, such as Colin Jones, are even willing to resurrect the notion that the Revolution did indeed involve a transition to capitalism. Still, the new approach to social cleavages seems different than Marxism, if only because these recent scholars define class more in terms of specific professions and occupations with varied social interests than in terms of a solid group with political interests. There is little idealization among recent scholars of either the sans-culottes or the Committee of Public Safety. More orthodox responses to Revisionism have not yet made much of an impact.[21]

Alongside this challenge to Revisionism, another significant recent trend in French Revolutionary scholarship has been the maturation of women's and gender history. Until the 1970s, few general histories or document collections on the Revolution included much information about women, feminism, or gender. This omission changed in the 1970s with the rise of a contemporary feminist movement; and it was clearly American feminists who set the pace toward a new history that took into account the fate of women and used gender as an analytical tool. One of the first articles in a major journal to deal with the topic was authored not by an established scholar, but by a female American graduate student obviously inspired by the women's movement.[22] When in 1979 three American feminist historians published a collection of primary documents devoted to French Revolutionary women, a new research agenda was established for the field.[23]

Unfortunately, that research did not filter down into college classrooms with any great speed, perhaps because of the traditional nature of much of the historical profession. Of course, the new research made us realize that women participated in every major event in the Revolution. We learned more about the movements of street women during the great events of the Revolution (such as the October Days), as well as the influence of elite women in the clubs and presses of Paris. Unfortunately however, that did not necessarily mean that this feminist-driven research changed the way that other specialists or college teachers approached the Revolution. Curiously, by classifying the new research as "women's history," it became possible for many historians to ignore or marginalize such research, and continue teaching their subject along the same old lines. Some professors muttered that knowing about women's participation was one thing; discovering how that participation changed the fundamental character of the Revolution was quite another. This kind of attitude seems to have been especially true in France, where Furet's recent general text as well as his and Mona Ozouf's *Critical Dictionary* ignore women, feminism, and gender.[24]

Since at least the 1980s, feminist-inspired historians have addressed this challenge by exploring how gender might be used fruitfully as an analytical tool. Instead of identifying women as the primary subject, recent feminist historians have widened the scope to include revolutionary discourse, policies, events, culture – interpreted through the lens of gender. Benefiting from advances made in other fields, such as literary criticism and gay and women's studies, historians have become interested in how the Revolutionaries refashioned gender roles for both men and women, and, correspondingly, how ideas regarding manhood and womanhood influenced the way revolutionary statesmen conceived of the new regime.

For example, historians have long known that women were formally excluded from organizing political clubs by the National Convention during the fall of 1793. But it has been too easy to see Jacobin attitudes as prejudicial, old-fashioned, and out of character with their more democratic political beliefs. Nonetheless, recent work shows that Jacobin ideas about women may not have been simply old-fashioned; they may have been part of an effort to articulate a new and daring view of democratic politics, in which both "men" and "women" are redefined in contrast to looser aristocratic gender roles: "Each sex is called to the kind of occupation which is fitting for it," the Jacobin deputy Amar declared on behalf of the Convention. "Man is strong, robust, born with great energy, audacity, and courage;" while women are destined for "private functions." Historians who use gender as an analytical tool teach us that Amar is not simply echoing old prejudices, but repositioning an ancient idea into a modern cornerstone of republican politics.[25]

If we are to make sense of Amar's political program, we must learn how Jacobins like him used gender to differentiate one group of citizens from another. No one has pioneered this path more successfully than Lynn Hunt. In a study from the early 1980s, Hunt explored why the Jacobins replaced Marianne with Hercules as the anthropomorphic symbol of the French nation. What did it mean for the French nation to be represented by a man instead of a woman? In the article on Marie-Antoinette reprinted in this volume, Hunt demonstrates how attitudes towards the French queen reveal much about the ways in which French revolutionary leaders hoped to shape sexual roles in the new republic.[26]

Suzanne Desan's innovative research into the once-arcane and difficult area of inheritance law reform is a prime example of how attention to gender can change our understanding of the Revolution. Through consistent legislation from 1789 that attempted to apply an unusually egalitarian standard to the application of inheritance laws, French Revolutionaries altered fundamental relationships within the family, potentially giving daughters far more authority over inherited property than had been the case in the Ancien Régime. Through dramatic archival examples, Desan is able to get an up-close view of precisely how ordinary women made use of a set of new laws passed by the National Assembly. The result is a view of the Terror ignored by Simon Schama: not women rioters battling the authorities, but women suing their brothers – literally their own siblings – in family law courts established throughout the country precisely to hear their complaints.[27]

This volume ends with Laurent Dubois's compelling analysis of how the French Revolution was refracted 3000 miles away on the Carribean island of Guadeloupe. Dubois reminds us that the French Revolution occurred precisely when the Atlantic slave trade system was at its zenith, bringing incredible wealth to Europe and America, and untold misery for the African slaves working the colonial plantations. The French revolutionaries could not avoid addressing themselves to what was certainly the greatest man-made evil in their eighteenth-century world. After all, the French Revolution was always about more than just France. As Tom Paine argued in *Rights of Man* (1791 and 1792), echoing most of his Jacobin colleagues, the French Revolution – even more than its American counterpart – was a beacon of liberty setting an example for the rest of Europe and indeed the world. But Guadeloupe's leaders would not simply let it imitate France. A sugar colony for over a century, Guadeloupe's slave economy provided the motherland with more wealth than any other colonial possession. And there was the rub: destroying slavery in the colonies might further the aims of the rights of man, but it could ruin the French economy, raise bread prices for the common people, and undermine political stability and the Revolution itself. Dubois's article gives us a good sense of the limitations of French notions of liberty.

Sometimes new students of the Revolution – and veteran scholars as well – grow weary at the noisy debates over its meaning and place in history. Most historians choose their field not because of a fondness for theory or political polemics, but usually because of a love to study the documents themselves. Yet, the historiography of the French Revolution is so monumental that it often threatens to intimidate the young researcher. Is it really necessary to pay close attention to the polemics among historians and other partisans? Why isn't it possible to simply ignore the various schools of historical thinking, and to study the Revolution without becoming embroiled in its historiography?

Without historiography scholars would not know how to go about their business. We would be like travelers lost in the forest without a map – all the trees might look alike, and we would not know which path to travel. Instead of thousands of trees, we have primary source documents. And the first problem confronting the historian is deciding which document to investigate and what questions to ask about it. Without a rigorous historiography that compels us to think critically about our approaches, our political views, and our rhetorical strategies, we would have only our our prejudices and our passions on which to rely. As in the nineteenth century, history without historiography might still be worth reading as literature, but it would rarely be considered part of the social sciences.

François Furet is right that "the French Revolution is over." We live in another age, and the problems of the late eighteenth century are no longer our own. Nevertheless, the legacy of the achievements and failings of that age are still with us. The French Revolutionaries dreamed of a world (like ours) dominated by democratic republics. They tried to work out what duties a democratic government had towards its citizens; and what responsibilities it had towards its neighbors. Our era may not be theirs but surely how we choose to write about their early efforts will help shape how our readers think about our own political problems.

NOTES

1 Paul Farmer, *France Reviews Its Revolutionary Origins: Social Politics and Historical Opinion in the Third Republic* (New York, 1944), pp. 61–66; James L. Godrey, "Alphonse Aulard," *Some Historians of Modern Europe*, ed. Bernadotte E. Schmitt (Chicago, 1942), pp. 45–65.
2 James Friguglietti, *Albert Mathiez, historien révolutionnaire* (Paris, 1974).
3 Georges Lefebvre, *The Coming of the French Revolution*, trans. R. R. Palmer (Princeton, 1947). Because of his popular college text, *A History of the Modern World*, Palmer is probably the most influential American historian of the French Revolution. Palmer's highly sympathetic view of the Terror is presented in *Twelve Who Ruled: The Year of the Terror in the French Revolution* (Princeton, 1941).
4 Crane Brinton, *The Anatomy of Revolution* (New York, 1965 [originally published 1938]).
5 *The Social Interpretation of the French Revolution* (Cambridge, 1964). The 1954 lecture was reprinted in Cobban's *Aspects of the French Revolution* (New York, 1970), pp. 90–111.
6 George V. Taylor, "Types of Capitalism in Eighteenth-Century France," *English Historical Review* 79 (1964): 478–497; "Noncapitalist Wealth and the Origins of the French Revolution," *American Historical Review* 72 (1967): 469–496.
7 François Furet, *Interpreting the French Revolution*, trans. Elborg Forster (Cambridge, 1981).
8 Ibid., p. 27. The quote below also comes from this page.
9 See his "Napoleon Bonaparte," in *A Critical Dictionary of the French Revolution*, eds. François Furet and Mona Ozouf, trans. Arthur Goldhammer (Cambridge, MA, 1989): 273–286.

10 For his most concisely doctrinaire statement see the introduction to *Les Orateurs de la révolution française, tome 1: Les Constituents*, ed. François Furet and Ran Halevi (Paris 1989). See also *L'Héritage de la révolution française*, ed. Françoise Furet (Paris, 1989); *Terminer la révolution: Mounier et Barnave dans la révolution française*, ed. François Furet and Mona Ozouf (Grenoble, 1990); *La Gironde et les Girondins*, ed. François Furet and Mona Ozouf (Paris, 1991); *Le siècle de l'avènement républicain*, ed. François Furet and Mona Ozouf (Paris, 1993); *Dictionnaire critique de la révolution française*, ed. François Furet and Mona Ozouf (Paris, 1988; English trans. Arthur Goldhammer Cambridge, MA., 1989); François Furet, *La Révolution* (Paris, 1988; trans. Antonia Nevill, Oxford, 1992 as *Revolutionary France 1770–1880*). See also the series of conference proceedings organized by Keith Baker, Colin Lucas, and Furet, *The French Revolution and the Creation of Modern Political Culture*, 4 vols (Oxford 1987–93), which include several important articles by Furet and his colleagues.

11 Keith Michael Baker, *Inventing the French Revolution: Essays on French Political Culture in the Eighteenth Century* (Cambridge, 1990), p. 295.

12 Ibid.

13 On the Liberal foundations of Marxist historiography, see George Comninel, *Rethinking the French Revolution: Marxism and the Revisionist Challenge* (London, 1987).

14 Donald Sutherland, "The Revolution in the Provinces: Class or Counterrevolution?," in *Essays on the French Revolution: Paris and the Provinces*, ed. Steven G. Reinhardt *et al.* (College Station, TX, 1992), p. 116. But even Sutherland doesn't descend into the more extreme antics of, say, Raynauld Sécher.

15 For Cobban's more liberal views see his *In Search of Humanity: The Role of the Enlightenment in Modern History* (New York, 1960), esp. Parts 4 and 5. For all his liberalism, however, Cobban was certainly no cheerleader for the Revolution and sometimes adopted a more critical posture. See, for example, "Local Government During the French Revolution," in *Aspects of the French Revolution* (New York, 1968), p. 130.

16 Irving Kristol, *Neo-Conservativism: Selected Essays 1949–1995* (New York, 1995); Gertrude Himmelfarb, *The Roads to Modernity: The British, French, and American Enlightenments* (New York, 2004).

17 J. L. Talmon, *The Origins of Totalitarian Democracy* (London, 1952). The book has been reprinted several times in paperback and has been translated into French, German, Hebrew, and Japanese. For Cobban's criticisms, see his *Rousseau and the Modern State*, 2nd edn (London, 1964), pp. 29–31, and *In Search of Humanity*, pp. 182–185.

18 Raynauld Sécher, *A French Genocide: The Vendée*, trans. George Holoch (South Bend, Indiana, 2003). See Hugh Gough, "Genocide and the Bicentenary: The French Revolution and the Revenge of the Vendée," *Historical Journal* 30 (1987): 977–988.

19 Steven Lawrence Kaplan, *The Historians' Feud* (Ithaca, 1994).

20 Simon Schama, *Citizens: A Chronicle of the French Revolution* (New York, 1989), pp. 184, 436, and 447.

21 Neo-Marxist works include Comninel, *Rethinking the French Revolution*; E. J. Hobsbawm, *Echoes of the Marseillaise: Two Centuries Look Back on the French Revolution* (New Brunswick, 1989); and Morris Slavin, *The Left and the French Revolution* (Atlantic Highlands, NJ, 1995).

22 Jane Abray, "Feminism in the French Revolution," *American Historical Review* 80 (1975): 43–62.

23 *Women in Revolutionary Paris, 1789–1795*, ed. Darline Gay Levy, Harriet Branson Applewhite, and Mary Durham Johnson (Urbana, 1979).

24 Furet, *Revolutionary France; Critical Dictionary*, ed. Furet and Ozouf. For more general reflections on women's historiography see Joan Wallach Scott, *Gender and the Politics of History* (New York, 1988), pp. 15–50; and Karen Offen, "The New Sexual Politics of French Revolutionary Historiography," *French Historical Studies* 16 (1990): 909–922.

Ozouf has responded to critics in *Women's Words: Essay on French Singularity*, trans. Jane Marie Todd (Chicago, 1997).

25 Amar's speech is reproduced in *Women in Revolutionary Politics*, pp. 213–217. See also Christine Fauré, *Democracy Without Women: Feminism and the Rise of Individualism in France*, trans. Claudia Gorbman and John Berks (Bloomington, Indiana, 1991), and Geneviève Fraise, *Reason's Muse: Sexual Difference and the Birth of Democracy*, trans. Jane Marie Todd (Chicago, 1994), and Dena Goodman, *The Republic of Letters: A Cultural History of the French Enlightenment* (Ithaca, 1994).

26 Lynn Hunt, "Hercules and the Radical Image in the French Revolution," *Representations* 1 (1983): 95–117, and included in her *Politics, Culture, and Class in the French Revolution* (Berkeley, 1984), pp. 87–119.

27 See also Suzanne Desan, *The Family on Trial in Revolutionary France* (Berkeley and Los Angeles, 2004).

Part I

THE OVERTHROW OF THE MARXIST PARADIGM

Danton, Robespierre, Saint-Just, Napoleon, the heroes as well as the parties and the masses of the old French Revolution, performed the task of their time in Roman costume and with Roman phrases, the task of unchaining and setting up modern bourgeois society.

Karl Marx
The Eighteenth Brumaire of Louis Bonaparte

1

THE FRENCH REVOLUTION
IN THE HISTORY OF THE
CONTEMPORARY WORLD

Albert Soboul

Born in 1914 to small farmers, Soboul won scholarships to France's most prestigious schools and decided upon a career teaching history. In 1932 he joined the Communist Party, and after World War II he combined his innovative historical research with a commitment to Marxist politics. His most important book, Les sans-culottes parisiennes de l'an II *(1958), a study of Parisian workers during the Terror, established a new standard of scholarship for the social history of the Revolution. Along with British historians E.P. Thompson and George Rudé, Soboul was part of a group of social historians who hoped to reconstruct the lives of ordinary workers and activists during the revolutionary era. During the 1960's, their "history from below" approach influenced a younger generation of historians on both sides of the Atlantic. In 1967, Soboul was appointed to the Sorbonne's prestigious chair of the History of the Revolution. He died in 1975.*

The following article, originally published in 1969, is a digest of Soboul's Marxist approach to the Revolution. The first sentence encapsulates Soboul's entire perspective: the Revolution was much more than a political transformation; it was also essentially social and economic. Socially, it was a bourgeois revolution in the sense that political power moved from landed aristocrats to the bourgeoisie – that is, middle-class business-men, professionals, and civil servants who claimed to represent the nation. Economically, it was a capitalist revolution in which this new bourgeois class transferred the source of wealth from land to more liquid forms of capital. The peasants and urban artisans (sans-culottes) began as the partners of the bourgeoisie against the nobility, but by 1792 had become its victims. The bourgeoisie consolidated victory between the Thermidorean Reaction that followed the Terror and the ascendancy of Napoleon Bonaparte. In this way, Soboul argues, France did not actually become a democracy, because genuine political power was simply transferred from one élite group to another.

* * *

The Revolution of 1789–1794 marked the advent of modern society – bourgeois and capitalist – in the history of France. Its essential characteristic is to have effected the national unity of the country on the base of the destruction of the seigniorial regime and the privileged feudal orders; according to Tocqueville in *The Ancien Régime and the Revolution*, its "particular object was to abolish everywhere the remnants of the institutions of the Middle Ages."[1] Its historical significance is further clarified by the fact that the French Revolution in the end succeeded in establishing a liberal democracy. From this double point of view, and the perspective of world history which concerns us here, it deserves to be considered as a classical model of a bourgeois revolution.

The comparative study of the French Revolution thus poses two series of problems.

Problems of a general nature: those concerning the historical law of the transition from feudalism to modern capitalism. To take up again the question posed by Marx in book III of *Capital*, this transition is carried out in two ways: by the total destruction of the old economic and social system – that is, the "really revolutionary way" – or by the preservation of large sectors of the old mode of production in the heart of the new capitalist society – that is, the way of compromise.[2]

Problems of a special nature: those that bear on the specific structure of French society at the end of the Ancien Régime and that take into account the particular characteristics of the French Revolution in regard to the various types of bourgeois revolutions.[3]

From this double point of view, the history of the French Revolution cannot be isolated from that of Europe. In all the European countries, the formation of modern society is drafted in the very heart of the old economic and social system with its vestiges of feudalism, then forged at their expense. In all the European countries, this evolution was made with varying degrees to the advantage of the bourgeoisie. The French Revolution was not the first to benefit the bourgeoisie; before it, the revolution in Holland in the sixteenth century, the two revolutions of England in the seventeenth century, the American Revolution in the eighteenth century paved the way for this revolution. Once again it is a question of recognizing the specific traits of the French Revolution.

At the end of the eighteenth century, France and the major part of Europe were subject to what has been called the Ancien Régime.[4] This was characterized on the social plane by aristocratic privilege, on that of the State by monarchial absolutism of divine right.

The aristocracy, whose role had not ceased to diminish since the Middle Ages, nevertheless remained in the first ranks of the hierarchy.[5] The social structure of France was always essentially aristocratic; it conserved the character of its origin in the period when land constituted the only form of social wealth, and thus conferred on those who possessed it power over those who cultivated it. The Capetian monarchy had indeed, with great effort, stripped the feudal lords of their royal rights and the nobles and high clergy of all political influence. Having become subjects, the nobles and clerics had nonetheless remained the privileged;

the feudal lords had kept their social and economic privileges, the seigniorial rights always underscoring the subjection of the peasants.

Socially privileged, but politically diminished, the aristocracy did not pardon the absolute monarch for having stripped it of all political authority; it denounced despotism and demanded liberty; it intended to have a share in the power. Its ideal of a *tempered* monarchy fitted into the framework of the theory of historic right. It had been expressed from the end of the reign of Louis XIV, particularly by Fénelon, whose political ideas were not only conveyed in the allegories of the *Adventures of Télémaque* (1699), but were more explicitly clarified in *The Projects of Government . . . to be proposed to the Duke of Burgundy*, published in 1711 under the title *Tables of Chaulnes*.[6] This anti-absolute aristocratic reaction was diversified, from the first half of the century on, in two currents: one of feudal reaction corresponding to the interests of the nobility of the sword, whose principal representative was the count of Boulainvillers;[7] the other of parlementary reaction corresponding to the nobility of the robe, declaring itself by the publication in 1732 of the *Judicium Francorum*.[8] The theories of the parlementary and feudal reaction were taken up again in the middle of the century, no longer by obscure pamphleteers, but by Montesquieu, with the publication in 1748 of *The Spirit of the Laws*.[9] This aristocratic demand for liberty, in the face of monarchial absolutism, was only, as Georges Lefebvre remarked, a "relic of the past."

However, the rebirth of commerce and the development of craft production since the tenth and eleventh centuries had created a new form of wealth, personal and moveable, and thus given birth to a new class, the bourgeoisie, whose importance was established by admission to the Estates General in the fourteenth century. In the framework of the feudal society, the bourgeoisie had continued to expand to the very rhythm of the development of capitalism, stimulated by the great discoveries of the fifteenth and sixteenth centuries and the exploitation of the colonial worlds, as well as the financial dealings of a monarchy always short of money. In the eighteenth century, the bourgeoisie were leaders in finance, commerce, and industry; they provided the monarchy with administrative cadres as well as the resources necessary to operate the State. Thus, even while the aristocracy was becoming ossified in its caste, the bourgeoisie was expanding in number, in economic power, in culture and in consciousness. The progress of the Enlightenment had undermined the ideological foundations of the established order, at the same time that it was expressing the class consciousness of the bourgeoisie, and its good conscience. As a rising class, believing in progress, it was convinced that it was representing the general interest and assuming responsibility for the nation; as a progressive class, it offered a decisive attraction for the popular masses as well as for dissident sectors of the aristocracy. But bourgeois ambition, prompted by the social and economic reality, collided with the aristocratic order of laws and institutions.[10]

The bourgeoisie, like the aristocracy, hoped to have a share of the power and demanded liberty from the monarch. But rather than justifying this demand by historic right, as the aristocracy did, the bourgeoisie proclaimed natural right: society is founded on the free contract between its members; government, on the free contract between that one who governs and those who are governed, such that power is conceived only to benefit the community and to guarantee the rights of the citizens.[11] In 1724 the French translation of Locke's *Treatise on Civil Government* (1690) appeared, a work that inspired the whole century. Theoretician of the English Revolution of 1688–9, Locke expressed the ideal of the bourgeoisie, transforming (one might say) "an historical accident into an event dictated by human reason." His political ideal – and this explains his profound influence – coincided with that of a bourgeoisie in full expansion, presenting a complex mixture of empiricism and rationalism: defend the established social order and property, but appeal to morality; concern with effective power, but necessity of consent; individualism, but recognition of majority rule.

Political freedom was certainly important, but even more so was economic freedom, that of enterprise and profit. Capitalism required freedom because freedom was necessary to assure its development, freedom in all its forms: freedom of the person, a condition for hiring labor; freedom of property, a condition for its mobility; freedom of thought, a condition for research and scientific and technical discoveries.

Unlike the aristocracy, the bourgeoisie did not demand only power and freedom; it meant to suppress privilege and acquire equal rights. In the second half of the eighteenth century, the bourgeoisie in effect found itself battling against the aristocracy. For centuries, the bourgeoisie had dreamed of becoming noble; the venality of offices had provided the means to this end. From the sixteenth century on, the French monarchy had put bourgeois wealth to good use by putting some public offices up for sale along with the added attraction of accompanying privileges and personal or hereditary nobility. Thus, while many bourgeois families were directly infiltrating the nobility, a nobility of the robe was being established, which, although sustaining ever closer relations with the aristocracy, nevertheless remained bourgeois, especially in the administration of its wealth. But in the eighteenth century, the nobility of the robe was tending to close its ranks, even while the bourgeoisie remained too numerous to be able to hope to be admitted.[12] "In one way or another," Sieyes wrote in his brochure *What is the Third Estate?*, "all the branches of executive power have fallen to the caste that supplies the Church, the robe and the sword. A sort of spirit of co-fraternity makes the nobility prefer themselves to the rest of the nation. The usurpation is complete; they truly reign."[13] The bourgeoisie demanded the suppression of privilege, and equal rights.

In France, therefore, in the second half of the eighteenth century, the development of the capitalist economy, on the base of which the power of the bourgeoisie was erected, was checked by the feudal framework of society, by the traditional and regulated organization of property, production and trade. "It was necessary to break these chains," the authors of the *Communist Manifesto* wrote – "they were broken." In this way the problem is posed of the passage from feudalism to capitalism. It did not escape the most perceptive men of the period. Far from being inspired by an abstract individualism, as Taine would have it, the revolutionary bourgeoisie had a clear understanding of the economic reality that produced its strength and determined its victory. Barnave was the first to formulate, more than half a century before Marx, the theory of the bourgeois revolution. In his *Introduction to the French Revolution*, written in 1792, Barnave set down the principle that property *influences* institutions. "The reign of the aristocracy lasts so long as the farm population continues to ignore or neglect the arts, and landed property continues to be the only wealth. . . . Once the arts and commerce succeed in penetrating the people and create a new means to wealth to aid the laboring class, all is ready for a revolution in political laws: a new distribution of wealth produces a new distribution of power. Just as the possession of land elevates the aristocracy, industrial property elevates the power of the people; they obtain their freedom." When Barnave writes "people," he means the bourgeoisie.[14]

The Dutch and English revolutions had already shown that the deep causes of the bourgeois revolution are to be sought in the feudal vestiges and contradictions of the old society. But this aspect does not explain all the characteristics of the French Revolution. The reasons why it constituted, by its very violence, the most resounding episode in the class struggles that carried the bourgeoisie to power must be sought in certain specific traits of the French society of the Ancien Régime.

Without a doubt, the bourgeoisie would have been content with a compromise that would have given it a share of the power, similar to the English oligarchy of the eighteenth century. The aristocracy stubbornly refused, since all compromise stumbled against feudalism. The peasant masses could not tolerate the preservation of this system; the nobility as a whole could not envisage its suppression, which would mean their decline. On the basis of the economic and social compromise represented by the repurchase of feudal rights decreed in principle on the night of 4 August (1789) and systematized by the law of 15 March 1790, the Constituent bourgeoisie for a long time tried desperately to reach a political compromise with the aristocracy.[15] The obstinate resistance of the bulk of the small nobility that lived for the most part from landed income, the stubborn and aggressive will of the peasants to end all vestiges of feudalism, were reason enough for this policy of compromise and conciliation. In order to triumph, the bourgeoisie had to resolve to form an alliance with the popular masses.

The popular masses bore all the weight of the Ancien Régime: they could no longer tolerate it.

The popular urban masses, artisans and shopkeepers, journeymen and apprentices, service workers, to a lesser degree manufacturing workers, were pushed to revolt by the worsening of their living conditions. These have been exposed by the works of C.-E. Labrousse.[16] From 1726–41 to 1785–9, the long-term rise in prices brought about a 62 per cent increase in the cost of living. On the average, bread accounted for about half of the popular budget; the seasonal variations in the price of grain raised the price of bread by 88 per cent in 1789.

This price increase forced the wealthy categories to economize; it overwhelmed the poor. The nominal increase in wages, 22 per cent on the average, did not come close to compensating the increase in prices. As usual, wages followed prices, but without catching up; more precisely, real wages were lowered by about 25 per cent. This worsening of living conditions of the popular masses did not escape the better observers of the period: as early as 1766, Turgot first formulated the "iron law" of wages, in his *Reflections on the Formation and Distribution of Wealth*. More than to the demands for liberty, the popular urban masses were sensitive to the demand for daily bread; they placed up front the question of subsistence. They countered the demand for economic freedom with the right of survival, very specifically price controls and regulation. They countered the equal rights that the bourgeoisie claimed from the aristocracy with "equal enjoyment."[17]

The popular urban masses, soon to be designated by the term sans-culotterie, properly speaking, lacked class consciousness. Scattered in numerous workshops, neither specialized – as a result of limited technological development – nor concentrated in large enterprises or industrial districts, often poorly differentiated from the peasantry, the wage-earners were no more capable than the peasants of conceiving effective solutions to their misery; the weakness of the guilds vouched for that. Hatred of the aristocracy and unmitigated opposition to the "fat" and the rich provided the ferment of unity for the laboring masses. When the poor harvests and the resulting economic crisis set them in motion, they lined up, not as a distinct class, but as part of the craft industry, behind the bourgeoisie. In this way, the most effective blows were struck against the old society. But this victory of the popular masses could be only a "bourgeois victory"; the bourgeoisie accepted the popular alliance against the aristocracy only because the masses remained subordinate. In the opposite case, the bourgeoisie would have renounced, as in Germany in the nineteenth century and to a lesser degree in Italy, the support of allies deemed too dangerous.

The peasant masses constituted the bulk of the French population, doubtless 22 to 23 million out of about 28 million.[18] In 1789, the great majority of the peasants had been free for a long time, serfdom surviving in only a few regions, Nivernais and Franche-Comté in particular. The feudal relations of production nonetheless dominated the countryside, as is evidenced by the seigniorial fees and ecclesiastical tithes. Certain historians tend to minimize the weight of feudalism at the end of the Ancien Régime. Tocqueville had already answered them in a chapter of *The Ancien Régime and the Revolution*: "Why feudal rights had become more odious to the people in France than anywhere else." If the French peasant had not possessed the land, he would have been less sensitive to the burdens that the feudal system placed on landed property.[19] It would even be appropriate, in order to better define the problem, to specify quantitatively the feudal imposition; for the three subdivisions of Aurillac, Mauriac and Saint-Flour, according to fiscal documents, it would be about 10 per cent of the taxed product (that is, the average net product), not taking into account the *lods et ventes* (fees received by the lord on the price of sold inherited property), the *banalités* (exclusive rights of lord to maintain a mill, an oven or a winepress) and the *dîme* (ecclesiastical tithe).[20] Yet it is the total weight that tenure supported in relation to production that we would have to determine in order to have an idea of the relative burden imposed by the whole of the *feudal complex*. In these same subdivisions of Haute-Auvergne, a third of the revenues of the seigniory, in round numbers, came from feudal rights. This percentage would in a large measure account for the resistance of the Auvergne nobility to the abolition of feudalism, for their refusal of all compromise, and in the last analysis for the agrarian troubles as counter-revolutionary endeavors from 1789 to 1792 and 1793. "Imagine," writes Tocqueville regarding the French peasant of the eighteenth century, "the condition, the needs, the character, the passions of this man, and calculate, if you can, the store of hate and desire amassed in his heart."[21]

To the hatred of feudalism, let us add the hunger for land that tormented the peasant, made still sharper by the demographic upsurge that characterized the eighteenth century. While about 130,000 members of the clergy shared 10 per cent of the land among themselves, very unequally moreover, the nobility (about 350,000 persons) held about 20 per cent; while the bourgeoisie held for themselves about 30 per cent, the portion for the 22 to 23 million peasants was only 35 per cent.[22] We cannot stress enough the importance of the peasant question in the heart of the bourgeois revolution. For Gramsci, Jacobinism, the very essence of the French Revolution, is characterized by the alliance of the revolutionary bourgeoisie and the peasant masses.

The popular masses, peasant or urban, had a social ideal corresponding to the economic conditions of the times: conception of a limited right to property, protest actions against concentration of farming and industrial concerns. In order to freely dispose of their persons and their labor, peasants and artisans first had to break their enforced allegiance, whether attached to the land or prisoners of the corporation. These conditions explain their hatred of the aristocracy and the Ancien Régime and the fact that the popular classes were the driving force of the bourgeois revolution. But, whether they were immediate producers or dreaming of attaining that state, peasants and artisans understood property to be based on individual work and dreamed of a society of small independent producers; in a confused way, they intended to prevent the establishment of a monopoly of wealth along with a dependent proletariat.[23] These profound aspirations account for the social and political struggles during the Revolution, of their turns and progression. From 1789 to 1793, we saw a deepening of the struggle of the bourgeoisie against the aristocracy, marked by the growing role of the middle layers and the popular masses, not by a change in the nature of the social struggles. In this sense, it is possible to speak of a "change in the front" of the bourgeoisie after the fall of Robespierre: before and after 9 Thermidor, since that aristocracy had not been disarmed, they remained the basic enemy. This was proved by the law of 29 November 1797, inspired by Sieyes, that reduced the former nobles to the state of foreigners. The French Revolution is indeed "a bloc": antifeudal and bourgeois throughout its various ups and downs.

23

This rooting of the Revolution in French society, this continuity and unity, were underscored by Tocqueville with his customary lucidity, while noting their necessity. "What the Revolution was least of all was an accidental event. It is true that it took the world by surprise, and yet it was only the complement of a much longer work, the sudden and violent termination of an undertaking on which ten generations of men had worked.[24]

If the French Revolution was the most dazzling of the bourgeois revolutions, eclipsing by the dramatic character of its class struggles the revolutions that preceded it, this was due to the obstinacy of the aristocracy rooted in its feudal privileges, refusing all concessions, and to the opposing determination of the popular masses. The bourgeoisie had not sought the ruin of the aristocracy, but the refusal of compromise and the counter-revolution obliged them to pursue the destruction of the old order. But they only achieved that by forming an alliance with the rural and urban masses, to whom they were forced to give satisfaction: the popular revolution and the Terror made a clean sweep; feudalism was irremediably destroyed and democracy established.

The French Revolution took the "truly revolutionary path" from feudalism to capitalism. By wiping the slate clean of all feudal vestiges, by liberating the peasants of seigniorial rights and ecclesiastical tithes, and to a certain degree from community constraints, by destroying the trade monopolies and unifying the national market, the French Revolution marked a decisive stage on the path to capitalism. Suppressing feudal landed property, it even freed small direct producers, making possible the differentiation of the peasant mass and its polarization between capital and wage labor. This led to entirely new relations of production; capital, once under feudal domination, was able to make the value of work mercenary. In this way, the autonomy of capitalist production was finally assured in the agricultural domain as well as the industrial sector. Two conditions appeared necessary in this passage to capitalist society, in the light of the French Revolution: the breaking up of feudal landed property and the emancipation of the peasants. The agrarian question indeed occupies "an axial position" in the bourgeois revolution.

The active element of this revolution was less the commercial bourgeoisie (to the extent that they remained solely commercial and intermediary, they accommodated themselves to the old society – from 1789 to 1793, from the "Monarchiens" to the "Feuillants," then the Girondists, they generally supported compromise) than the mass of small direct producers from whom the feudal aristocracy exacted overwork and overproduction with the support of the judicial apparatus and the means of constraint provided by the State of the Ancien Régime. The political instrument of change was the Jacobin dictatorship of the small and middle bourgeoisie, supported by the popular masses, social categories whose ideal was a democracy of small autonomous producers, independent peasants and artisans, freely working and trading. The peasant and popular revolution was at the heart of the bourgeois revolution and pushed it forward.[25]

The victory over feudalism and the Ancien Régime did not, however, mean the simultaneous appearance of new social relations. The passage to capitalism is not a simple process, by which the capitalist elements develop in the womb of the old society until the moment when they are strong enough to break through its framework. A long time would still be needed before capitalism would assert itself definitively in France; its progress was slow during the revolutionary period, the dimension of enterprises often remaining modest, with commercial capital dominating.[26] The ruin of feudal landed property, and the corporative, regulated system, by assuring the autonomy of the capitalist mode of production, also uncompromisingly paved the way for bourgeois relations of production and trade – revolutionary transformation par excellence.

Overturning economic and social structures, the French Revolution at the same time shattered the state apparatus of the Ancien Régime, sweeping away the vestiges of old autonomies, destroying local privileges and provincial particularisms. It thus made possible, from the Directory to the Empire, the establishment of a modern State responding to the interests and requirements of the new bourgeoisie.

The French Revolution holds a singular place in the history of the contemporary world.

As a revolution for liberty, it invoked natural right, as did the American Revolution, and conferred upon its work a universal character that the English Revolution had ignored. But who could deny that the Declaration of 1789 affirmed this universality with much more force than the American Declarations? Let us add that the French Declaration went much further on the road to freedom, affirming freedom of conscience and admitting Protestants and Jews into the "city"; but by creating the civil state, on 20 September 1792, it also recognized the right of the citizen to adhere to no religion. It liberated the white man but by the law of 4 February 1794, it also abolished "Negro slavery in all the colonies."

As a Revolution for equality, the French Revolution went far beyond the revolutions that preceded it. Neither in England nor in the United States was emphasis placed on equality, as the aristocracy and the bourgeoisie were partners in power. The resistance of the aristocracy, the counter-revolution and the war forced the French bourgeoisie to push the struggle for equal rights to the first rank. In this way it could rally the people and win. But what was drafted in 1793–4 was a regime of social democracy characterized by a compromise between bourgeois conceptions and popular aspirations. The popular masses realized what fate awaited them: that's why they demonstrated hostility to the economic freedom that opened the way to concentration and capitalism. At the end of the eighteenth century, the ideal of the people was that each peasant would be a landowner, each artisan independent and each wage earner protected against the all-powerful rich.

After 10 August 1792, when the throne was overturned, and the revolutionary bourgeoisie had instituted universal suffrage and sealed its alliance with the sans-culottes, it was indeed necessary to go beyond theoretical equality of rights and move toward that "equality of enjoyment" that the people demanded. This led to the management of the economy to set prices in harmony with wages and assure daily bread for all: price controls and regulation were instituted by the law of the "general maximum" on 29 September 1793, and war manufacturing and foreign commerce were nationalized. There was also the endeavor to establish public education accessible to all by the law of 19 December 1793. In addition, there were also the beginnings of social security with the law of national charity of 11 May 1794. This egalitarian republic filled the propertied bourgeoisie with indignation and dread; after 9 Thermidor, it was banned forever. But the conviction remained in the consciousness of the people that freedom without equality meant only privilege for some, that liberty and equality are inseparable, that political equality by itself can be only a façade when social inequality asserts itself. "Liberty is but a vain phantom when a class of men can starve others with impunity," the *enragé* Jacques Roux had declared to the gallery of the Convention on 21 June 1793. "Equality is but a vain phantom when the rich, through their monopolies, exercise the right of life and death on their fellow men."[27]

Finally, as a revolution for unity, the French Revolution made the nation one and indivisible.[28] Certainly the Capetian monarchy had established the territorial and administrative framework of the nation, but without completing this task; in 1789, national unity remained imperfect. The nation was still divided territorially by the incoherence of administrative divisions and the persistence of the "feudal parcelling"; the diversity of weights and measures and interior customs posed obstacles to the formation of a national market. Moreover, the nation was socially divided, for the Ancien Régime was organized into a hierarchy and partly into guilds. (As Georges Lefebvre remarked, whoever says "guild" implies "privileges.") Everywhere inequality reigned in a nation created by a unitary government, whose cohesion had been reinforced in the eighteenth century through the multiple bonds woven by material progress, the expansion of the French language, the development of culture and the brilliance of the Enlightenment.

Once the orders, states, and guilds were abolished, the French people were free and equal under the law, constituting a nation, one and indivisible. The rationalization of institutions by the Constituent Assembly, the return to centralization by the revolutionary government, the administrative exertions of the Directory, the reconstruction of the State by Napoleon – all completed the work of the monarchy of the Ancien Régime, destroying autonomies and particularisms, putting in place the institutional framework of a unified State. At the same time, the consciousness of a unified nation was awakened and strengthened by civil equality, the 1790 federations movement, the development of the network of Jacobin societies, and the antifederalism and the congresses or *central meetings* of the popular societies in 1793. The advances of the French language went in the same direction. New economic ties reinforced the national consciousness. Once the feudal parcelling was destroyed, and the tolls and interior customs abolished, the "withdrawal of barriers" to the political frontier tended to unify the national market, which was, moreover, protected from foreign competition by a protectionist tariff. The French Revolution gave a strength and effectiveness to the national sovereignty that up till then it had not had.

A new public international law was expressed. Seeking to define its principles, during the affair of the German princes who owned land in Alsace, Merlin de Douai in effect posited the nation conceived as a voluntary association against the dynastic State. Speaking on 28 October 1790, he said, "There is between you and your Alsacian brothers no other legitimate title of union than the social pact formed last year between all old and modern French people in this Assembly" – an allusion to the decision of the Third Estate on 17 June 1789 to proclaim itself a National Assembly, and to that of the Assembly on the following 9 July to declare itself a Constituent Assembly, and to the *federative pact* of 14 July 1790. One sole question, "infinitely simple," remained: that of knowing "if it is to these diplomatic parchments that the Alsacian people owe the advantage of being French ... What do these conventions matter to the people of Alsace or the people of France, when in the times of despotism, they had as their object to unite the first to the second? The Alsacian people joined the French people because they wanted to; it is their will alone, and not the treaty of Münster, that legitimized the union."[29] This will had been demonstrated by participation in the Federation of 14 July 1790. The international public law was revolutionized as the interior public law was – nations now had the right to self-determination.

After ten years of revolution, the French reality appeared to be radically transformed. The aristocracy of the Ancien Régime was ruined, its privileges and social domination stripped away with the abolition of feudalism. We should not stretch this point, however; many nobles did not emigrate and succeeded in safeguarding their landed patrimony; the Napoleonic consolidation restored their social prestige; the squire replaced the feudal lord. The fusion of this landed aristocracy and the upper bourgeoisie constituted the dominant class in the new society.

At the other extreme of the social scale, the popular urban classes had not drawn any positive advantage from the Revolution. In fact, by proclaiming economic freedom, and by prohibiting unions and strikes by the Le Chapelier law of 14 June 1791 – a truly constituent law of free-trade capitalism (the prohibition persisted until 1864 for the right to strike and until 1884 for the right to unionize) – the bourgeois revolution left the popular urban classes defenseless in the new economy. Liberalism, founded on the ideal of an abstract social individualism, profited the most. Economic freedom accelerated the concentration of industrial enterprises, transforming the material conditions of social life, but at the same time altering the structure of traditional popular classes: how many artisans, working their way up in industry, were reduced by capitalist concentration to the rank of proletarians?

The peasantry were split up, in the end. The abolition of the ecclesiastical tithe and real feudal rights profited only the land-owning peasants; farmworkers and sharecroppers gained only from the abolition of serfdom and personal feudal rights. The national lands were sold in such a way that peasant property was increased to the advantage of those who already owned land: the *laboureurs*, or big farmers from the regions with large areas of cultivation. In the Nord department from 1789 to 1802, their share of the land rose from 30 to 42 per cent (that of the bourgeoisie rose from 16 to 28 per cent, while the percentage held by the nobility decreased from 22 per cent to 12 per cent, that of the clergy from 20 per cent to 0). From that time on, a powerful minority of proprietary peasants, attached to the new order, rallied around the bourgeoisie in its conservative proposals. In this way is the social work of the French Revolution measured in the countryside, an accomplishment further clarified by comparative study. While the French peasant increased his share of the land, the English peasant, freed from serfdom and feudal obligations from the beginning of modern times, was expropriated in the course of the vast movement of regrouping and enclosure of lands, and was reduced to the ranks of a wage-earning day laborer – free, certainly – but without land. In Central and Eastern Europe, serfdom persisted; the great landowning nobles exploited their lands by means of statute labor owed to them by the peasants. Serfdom was not abolished until 1807 in Prussia, 1848 in Bohemia and Hungary, and 1861 in Russia. And the liberated peasant did not receive any land; the aristocracy maintained its landed privilege until the revolutions of the twentieth century. By comparison, as far as the society resulting from the French Revolution goes, Jaurès was able to speak of "rural democracy."

Upon seizing power in November 1799, Bonaparte declared, "the Revolution is over." He thus assigned an end point to the task of demolishing the Ancien Régime. But it was not in the power of a single man, no matter how brilliant, to change the characteristics of the new society that had already been clearly sketched. The actions of the First Consul, then the Emperor, whatever his evolution may have been, essentially belonged to the line of the revolutionary heritage. The desire for order on the part of both old and new property owners facilitated the stabilization efforts of the Consulate. The social hierarchy was re-established, with the administration reorganized according to the wishes of the "notables"; but control of the government eluded them. In 1814, the Charter allowed them to believe that they would see themselves in power: the aristocratic reaction, once again, contested their claim. In this sense, the Restoration represents the epilogue of the drama. The Revolution in 1789 did not really end until 1830 when, having brought a king to power who accepted their principles, the bourgeoisie took definitive possession of France.[30]

The characteristics that we have just sketched account for the repercussions of the French Revolution and its value as an example in the evolution of the contemporary world. Without a doubt, the armies of the Republic and then of Napoleon knocked down the Ancien Régime in the European countries they occupied, more by force than by ideas. By abolishing serfdom, by freeing the peasants of seigniorial fees and ecclesiastical tithes, by putting in circulation the wealth of *mainmorte*, the French conquest cleared the path for the development of capitalism. If nothing remained of the continental empire that Napoleon had had the ambition to found, it nevertheless destroyed the Ancien Régime everywhere it had time to do so. In this sense, his reign prolonged the Revolution, and he was indeed its soldier, a fact for which the sovereigns of the Ancien Régime never ceased reproaching him.[31]

After Napoleon, the prestige of the Revolution did not vanish. With the passage of time, it appeared both as the daughter of reason and the daughter of enthusiasm. Its memory evoked a powerful emotion, the storming of the Bastille remaining the symbol of popular insurrection and *La Marseillaise* the battle song for liberty and independence. In this sense, the French Revolution indeed has mythical value, in the sense Georges Sorel intended: it seduced the imagination and the heart; announcer of better times, it incited people to action. Beyond this revolutionary romanticism, its ideological attraction was no less powerful; the French Revolution affirms itself as an immense effort to set society on a rational foundation.

The French Revolution is consequently situated in the very heart of the history of the contemporary world, at the crossroads of the diverse social and political currents that divided nations and still divides them. A classical bourgeois revolution, it represented – by the uncompromising abolition of feudalism and the seigniorial regime – the starting point for capitalist society and a liberal representative system in the history of France. A peasant and popular revolution, it tried twice to go beyond its bourgeois limits: in year II an attempt that, despite the inevitable failure, still served for a long time as a prophetic example; and, at the time of the Conspiracy for Equality, an episode that stands at the fertile origin of contemporary revolutionary thought and action. This explains these vain but dangerous efforts to deny the French Revolution its historic reality or its social and national specificity. But this also explains the shaking felt throughout the world and the way the French Revolution still stirs the consciousness of the people of our century.

Tocqueville, in *The Ancien Régime and the Revolution*, recalls the "two principal passions" of the French at the end of the eighteenth century: "one, deeper and coming from farther back, is the violent and inextinguishable hatred of inequality"; "the other, more recent and not so deeply rooted, led them to wish to live not only as equals, but free." That was 1789: "a time of inexperience, without a doubt, but also of generosity, enthusiasm, virility and grandeur, a time of immortal memory, which men will turn to regard with admiration and respect. . . . Thus the French were proud enough of their cause and themselves to believe they could be equal in liberty."

Equality in freedom: an ideal never attained, but always pursued, that never ceases to inflame men's hearts.

NOTES

Source Reprinted in an abridged format from Albert Soboul, *Understanding the French Revolution*, trans. April Ane Knutson (New York: International Publishers, 1988), pp. 274–99.

1 *L'Ancien Régime et la Révolution*, book II, chap. I, ed. 1952, with an introduction by G. Lefebvre, p. 99.

2 *Capital.* vol. III, chap. XX, "Historical view of merchant capital." On the problem of the transition from feudalism to capitalism, cf. *The Transition from Feudalism to Capitalism, A Symposium* by P.M. Sweezy, M. Dobb, H.K. Takahashi, R. Hilton, C. Hill, London, 1954. R. Hilton, "Y eut-il une crise générale de la féodalite?." *Annales, E.S.C.*, 1951. no. 1; G. Procacci, G. Lefebvre and A. Soboul, "Une discussion historique: du feudalisme au capitalisme." *La Pensée*, 1956, no. 65.

3 These are problems posed in particular by G. Lefebvre, "La Révolution française dans l'histoire du monde," *Annales, E.S.C.*, 1948, reprinted in *Etudes sur la Révolution française*, 1954, 2nd edition, 1963, p. 431.

4 The expression *Ancien Régime* appeared at the end of the year 1789; naturally it is charged with emotional content: there is almost a repudiation in this alliance of words (F. Brunot, *Histoire de la Langue française*, vol IX, *La Révolution et l'Empire*, p. 621). The expression, consecrated by its use, is historically valid; we understand poorly the obscure reasons why certain historians currently are tending to reject it.

5 On the problems of the French nobility in the eighteenth century, we will content ourselves with citing one old article: M. Bloch, "Sur le passé de la noblesse française: quelques jalons de recherche," *Annales d'histoire économique et sociale*, 1936, p. 336; and a recent article: A. Goodwin, "The Social Structure and Economic and Political Attitudes of the French Nobility in the Eighteenth Century;" International Committee of Historical Sciences, XII Congress, Vienna, 1965, *Rapports. I. Grands thèmes*, p. 356; by the same author, "General Problems and the Diversity of European Nobilities in the Modern Period," *ibid.*, p. 345. We refer to the critical bibliography of J. Meyer. *La Noblesse bretonne au XVIIIᵉ siècle*, Paris, 1966, vol. I, P. XXI.

6 See B. Mousnier, "Les Idées politiques de Fénelon," *XVIIᵉ siècle*, 1951–52.

7 Boulainvilliers (1658–1722), *Histoire de l'ancien gouvernement de la France, avec XIV lettres historiques sur les parlements ou Etats généraux* (1722), *Essai sur la noblesse de France contenant une dissertation sur son origine et son abaissement* (1732).

8 *Le Judicium Francorum* reprints an anti-absolutist pamphlet from the time of the Fronde, *Les vertiables maximes du gouvernement de la France justifiées par l'ordre des temps depuis l'établissement de la monarchie jusqu' aux temps présents* (1652). See also, in the same line, a writing circulated in manuscript copies, *Essai historique concernant les droits et prérogatives de la Cour des pairs de France*.

9 See basically book XXX. Cf. L. Althusser, *Montesquieu. La politique et l'histoire*, 1959.

10 We can only refer here to general works: J. Aynard, *La bourgeoisie française*, 1934; B. Groethuysen, *Origines de l'esprit bourgeois en France*, vol. I: *L'Eglise et la Bourgeoisie*, 1927; F. Borkenau, *Der Uebergang vom feudalen zum burgerlichen Weltbild. Studien zur Geschichte der Philosophie der Manufakturperiode*, 1934; see the remarks of L. Febvre, "Fondations économiques. Superstructure philosophique: une synthèse," *Annales d'histoire économique et sociale*, 1934, p. 369. Of precise documentary interest are the studies relating to the bourgeoisie in *Assemblée générale de la Commission centrale . . .*, 1939. Commission d'histoire économique et sociale de la Révolution, 1942, vol. I. p. 33; P. Léon, "Recherches sur la bourgeoisie française de province au XVIIIᵉ siecle," *L'Information historique*, 1958, no. 3. p. 101. On the current orientation of research, E. Labrousse, "Voies nouvelles vers une histoire de la bourgeoisie occidentale aux XVIIIᵉ et XIXᵉ siècles," *X Congresso internazionale di scienze storiche . . . 1955. Relazionei*, Florence, 1955, vol. IV, p. 365.

11 On natural right, an ample bibliography will be found in R. Derathé, *Jean-Jacques Rousseau et la Science politique de son temps.* Paris, 1950. Natural right was developed in the seventeenth century by Protestant authors, principally jurists – Grotius, Althusius, Hobbes, Pufendorf – certain of whom were then translated and commented on by Barbeyrac et Burlamaqui. The authors of the seventeenth century were criticized

by Rousseau who drew the logical consequences from natural right, by formulating the theory of inalienable and indivisible popular sovereignty.

12 See J. Egret. "L'Aristocratie parlementaire à la fin de l'Ancien Régime," *Revue historique*, July–September 1952, p. 1. Essential are the works of J.-Fr. Bluche, *L'Origine des magistrats du Parlement de Paris au XVIIIe siècle*, 1956, *Les magistrats du Parlement de Paris au XVIIIe siècle, 1715–1771*, 1960.

13 *Qu'est-ce que le Tiers Etat?* by Em. Sieyes, critical edition by Ed. Champion, Paris, 1888, p. 35.

14 *Oeuvres de Barnave*, published by M. Bérenger de la Drôme, 1843, vol. I, p. 12 and p. 13. The *Introduction à la Revolution française* has been republished by F. Rude, Paris, 1960. In fact, this important text is still awaiting a critical edition. Having forcefully affirmed the necessary connection between political institutions and the movement of the economy, Barnave attaches to it the educational movement, "To the degree that the arts, industry and commerce enrich the laboring class of people, impoverish the great landowners and bring the classes closer together by fortune, the progress in education brings them closer by custom and recalls, after a long oblivion, the primitive ideas of equality."

15 The important problem of repurchase of feudal rights and of their abolition has been definitively tackled by Ph. Sagnac, *La Législation civile de la Révolution française*, 1898; in a still valuable sketch, A. Aulard, *La Révolution française et le Régime féodal*, 1919; M. Garaud, *La Révolution et la Propriété foncière*, 1959. But only local or regional monographs would permit the drawing up of a true and complete picture of the partial survival, the vicissitudes and the final disappearance of the feudal regime during the Revolution: let us indicate two classical works, A. Ferradou, *Le Rachat des droits féodaux dans la Gironde. 1790–1793*, 1928: J. Millot, *L'Abolition des droits seigneuriaux, dans le département du Doubs et la région comtoise*, 1941. Likewise, on the agrarian riots and the jacqueries which, from the Great Fear to the definitive abolition of feudal rights (1793 July 17), marked the revolutionary history of the peasantry, we have only fragmentary local studies at our disposal. This history remains to be written.

16 C.-E. Labrousse, *Esquisse du mouvement des prix et des revenus en France au XVIIIe siècle*, Paris, 1933, 2 vol.; *La Crise de l'économie française à la fin de l'Ancien Régime et au début de la Révolution*, Paris, 1944.

17 On the social aspirations of the popular masses, see A. Soboul, *Les sans-culottes parisiens en l'an II*, Paris, 1958, part II, chap. 2.

18 On the peasant question, the works of Georges Lefebvre are essential: *Les Paysans du Nord pendant la Révolution française*, 1924. *Questions agraires au temps de la Terreur*, 1932, *La Grande Peur de 1789*, 1932, and the articles appearing and regrouped in *Etudes sur la Révolution française*, 1954, 2nd edition, 1967; "Répartition de la propriété et de l'exploitation foncières à la fin de l'Ancien Régime," 1928, p. 279; "La Vente des biens nationaux," 1928, p. 307; "La Révolution française et les Paysans," 1932, p. 338.

19 *Op. Cit.*, p. 99, "The effect of the Revolution has not been to divide the soil but to liberate it for a moment. All the small landowners were, in effect, severely hampered in the exploitation of their lands and endured many constraints that they were not allowed to deliver themselves from." (p. 102) "If the peasant had not owned the soil, he would have been insensitive to several of the burdens that the feudal system laid on landed property. Of what importance was the tithe to one who was not a farmer? It was imposed on the product of cultivation" (p. 105).

20 M. Leymarie, "Les Redevances foncières seigneuriales en Haute-Auvergne," *Annales historiques de la Révolution française*, 1968, no. 3.

21 *L'Ancien Régime et la Révolution*, p. 106.

22 G. Lefebvre, "Répartition de la propriété et de l'exploitation foncières à la fin de l'Ancien Régime".

23 The petition of the Parisian section of Sans-Culottes of 2 September 1793 intended to not only limit "the profits of industry and commerce" by general price controls, and

limit the extent of agricultural exploitations ("Let no one be able to hold more land to rent than what is needed for a determined quantity of plows"), but to also impose a maximum on wealth. What would it be? The petition does not specify, but makes it clear that it would correspond to the small artisan and shopkeeper property: "Let no one have more than one workshop, or one shop." These radical measures, concludes the Sans-Culottes section, "would make the too great inequality of wealth disappear gradually and increase the number of property owners" (*Bibliothèque nationale*, Lb 40 2140, imp. in-8°, 6 p.).

24   *L'Ancien Régime et la Révolution*, p. 96.

25   On the theoretical aspects of these problems, see M. Dobb, *Studies in the Development of Capitalism*, London, 1946. H.K. Takahashi, *Shimin Kakumei-no kozó* [Structure of the bourgeois revolution], Tokyo, 1951, reviewed by Ch. Haguenauer, *Revue historique*, no. 434, 1955, p. 345.

26   We must however stress the progress of the economy in the course of the Napoleonic period which was tightly bound to the revolutionary period. See E. Labrousse, "Le Bilan du monde en 1815. Eléments d'un bilan economique la croissance dans la guerre." Comité international des sciences historiques, XIIth Congress, Vienna, 1965. *Rapports I Grands thèmes*, p. 473.

27   *Adresse présentée à la Convention nationale au nom de la section des Gravilliers*, by J. Roux (Archives nationales, W 20, d. 1073, imp in-8°, p. 12).

28   On this problem in its totality, see A. Soboul, "De l'Ancien Régime à l'empire problème nationale et réalités sociales." *L'Information historique*, 1960, pp. 59–64 and 96–104.

29   *Moniteur*, vol. VI, p. 239.

30   See above for the comparison that must be established between the French Revolution of 1830 and the "respectable" English Revolution of 1688. Both ended up replacing one king with another, without attacking the social structure in any way. In July, 1830, it was a matter of a sort of legal insurrection punishing the violation of the Charter. But the fundamental difference to which the Anglo-Saxons are especially sensitive, is that the Revolution of 1688 was "respectable" because it was provoked by the leaders of the social hierarchy and carried out without the intervention of the popular masses. In France, Charles X was expelled not by a William of Orange, but by the people of Paris, armed behind barricades. See in this line the review by G. Lefebvre, in the *Annales historiques de la Révolution française*, 1955, p. 176 of the book by L. Pinkham. *William III and the Respectable Revolution*. Cambridge, Mass., 1954.

31   *Lendemains*, no. 12, November, 1978.

2

NOBLES, BOURGEOIS, AND THE ORIGINS OF THE FRENCH REVOLUTION*

Colin Lucas

This 1973 article by a then relatively young Oxford professor quickly became one of the most important weapons in the Revisionist arsenal – and its author went on to become Master of Oxford's Balliol College. The reason for its success lies in its bold attack upon the Marxist view of the Revolution as characterized by a class struggle between an ascending bourgeoisie and ossified nobility. Using an array of empirical evidence, Lucas shows that by the end of the Ancien Régime, the bourgeoisie and the nobility were both part of a "homogeneous" ruling élite. Lucas shows that by this time privileges that were once perhaps monopolized by the nobility had become shared between the two groups. Lucas finds many bourgeois commoners who were privileged from taxes, who acted as lay seigneurs on landed estates, and who added the particle "de" to their name. In short, he finds bourgeois everywhere whose authorities overlapped with noblemen, and whose lifestyle imitated noblemen – indeed, bourgeois who were even confused by contemporaries as noblemen.

But such an analysis, however novel and challenging, begs the question of why the Revolution occurred in the first place. If an embittered bourgeoisie did not cause the Revolution, who did? The last part of the article deals with this fundamental question, in which Lucas proposes what might be called a non-Marxist class analysis: the political crisis from 1786–88 convinced the sector of privileged bourgeois commoners that their social pathway to full landed noble status was now being barred, and that Ancien Régime social structure was about to become much more closed. The fear of being shut out, rather than any kind of revolutionary class consciousness or genuine class difference, is what in the end motivated them to revolt.

After almost twenty-five years, Lucas's remarkable article continues to stimulate much debate among historians because of its imaginative web of social and political analysis.

* * *

Once upon a time, the historians of the French Revolution labored fraternally in the vineyards of the past. They were united in simple yet satisfying beliefs. In the eighteenth century, the French bourgeoisie had become aware of the increasing disparity between its wealth and social usefulness, on the one hand, and its social prestige and opportunities, on the other. Its way was blocked and recognition of its worth denied by a decaying class of parasitic, hereditarily privileged, noble landowners. Its vitality was further jeopardized by a monarchy not only committed to antiquated aristocratic values, but also incapable of giving the country that firm yet benignly restrained direction under which the initiative of men of business might flourish. The conflict of these elements produced the French Revolution. It was, furthermore, a deeper conflict between the progressive capitalist-orientated classes and the retrograde aristocratic classes. The French Revolution was won by the bourgeoisie, despite some interference from below, thus establishing the framework for the emergence of the capitalist economy and a class society and – *eureka* – the modern world. This, in capsule form, was the interpretation of the revolutionary crisis of the late eighteenth century favoured by the great authorities of the first half of this century from Jaurès to Soboul, each one giving to it a more or less explicitly Marxist tone according to his personal convictions.[1] But Marxist or non-Marxist, we were all united in the belief that we could not escape this groundswell of history.

This interpretation has been the subject of increasing debate among Anglo-Saxon historians ever since the publication in 1964 of the attack launched upon it by the late Professor Cobban in his Wiles Lectures of 1962.[2] A parallel, though apparently unrelated, debate has also been developing in France, where Monsieur Furet and Monsieur Richet in particular have been attempting to elaborate a more theoretical schema than Cobban's yet on basically the same lines.[3] Cobban's essential contribution to the historiography of the French Revolution was to question the notion of the bourgeoisie as a capitalist or even proto-capitalist class. He thereby questioned the whole nature of the Revolution. Cobban was a brilliant polemicist and his book displays both the qualities and the defects of this type of writing. He had an unerring eye for the weaknesses in the arguments of others; but they tended to capture his attention to the exclusion of all other considerations. His book, therefore, remained a very piecemeal affair, concerned primarily with destroying what he took, rightly or wrongly, to be a number of commonly accepted fallacies with only a relatively loose thread connecting them. Cobban made no attempt to produce any systematic construction to replace the whole edifice of interpretation, which he was very conscious of having undermined.[4] At most, he carved a few stones for a new façade. Thus, for example, he proposed a new definition of the revolutionary bourgeoisie, which he saw as a declining class of venal office-holders, yet he did not attempt to work out the structure of social conflict implied in such a view. He presumably believed this group to be but one element of the Ancien Régime bourgeoisie and he also suggested that the nature of the bourgeoisie was altered during the Revolution, yet he did not try to examine what the bourgeoisie was before the Revolution nor what the relationship was between the various component parts that he perceived. Above all, Cobban does not seem to have questioned the notion that a noble-bourgeois class conflict was the fundamental element in the genesis of the Revolution. He merely sought to alter one part of that proposition. In this sense, therefore, he retained a class interpretation of the French Revolution which did not stray too far from the classic mould.

Nevertheless, Cobban's remarks on the nature of the revolutionary bourgeoisie, together with Professor Taylor's fundamental work on French capitalism in the eighteenth century, have in fact brought into question the whole schema of the Revolution as the product of a conflict between nobles and bourgeois, as Taylor himself has pointed out.[5] For such an interpretation is necessarily based on the premise that there existed in eighteenth-century France two distinct and antagonistic classes of bourgeois and nobles. If, however, in our attempt to define the eighteenth-century bourgeoisie we can discover no such clear division, then it becomes extremely difficult to define a class conflict. But, in that case, we have to decide why, in 1788–89, groups which can be identified as non-noble combatted and defeated groups which can be identified as noble, thereby laying the foundations of the political system of the nineteenth-century bourgeoisie; and why they attacked and destroyed privilege in 1789, thereby destroying the formal organization of eighteenth-century French society and preparing a structure within which the socio-economic developments of the nineteenth century might blossom.

The orthodox approach to the upper strata of eighteenth-century French society has always been to stress exclusively the elements of disparity and division within them and to split them into two clearly defined and clearly antagonistic classes of nobles and bourgeois. Such an approach ignores all the elements that conferred on these strata a degree of homogeneity in some important respects. We may understand this without difficulty if, instead of peering so closely at the top of society, we stand back and attempt to view it as a whole. Whatever the distinctions and whatever the striking differences in wealth levels inside these strata, they achieved a certain common identity as a minority with disproportionate wealth in relation to the mass of poor Frenchmen. The primary articulation in Ancien Régime society was not the distinction between the privileged and the Third Estate; rather, it was between those for whom manual labour provided their livelihood and those for whom it did not.[6] Clearly, this division, in common with all those in this society, was neither rigid nor absolute. It did not have the character of a boundary, but more that of a frontier with its attendant no-man's-land formed by transitional categories. The inhabitants of this zone were the artisans – the sans-culottes in Paris – the degree of whose penetration into the ranks of the lesser bourgeoisie can be determined by the extent to which trading activity had become preponderant in the combination of trade and manual production which characterized their state.[7] Moreover, some trades were more prestigious than others, either inherently so or because of local factors, and allowed those who exercised them to reconcile status with manual labour more easily than in the majority of cases.[8] For example, those engaged on luxury articles, such as the goldsmiths (*orfèvres*) or the wig-makers (*perruquiers*), derived status either from the value of their raw material or from the nature of their clientele.[9] This was a highly permeable frontier: the passport was basically the acquisition of a modest capital.[10]

There was, then, an important and real sense in which all levels of the bourgeoisie and nobility attained in very general terms a community of interest in face of the vulgar mechanic classes and of the vile and abject poor.[11] At the other end of the scale, the apparent simplicity of the distinction between privileged and unprivileged is misleading. In reality no such absolute, horizontal division existed. Certainly trade was definitely inferior; certainly the hereditary noble was evidently superior. But between the two the permutations, the nuances, the ambiguities were infinite. The pursuit of ennoblement remained a realistic enterprise for the bourgeoisie of the eighteenth century.[12] The king continued to concede Letters of Nobility to honorable, successful and well-connected men.[13] Venal offices which carried nobility – particularly the office of *secrétaire du roi*, certain judicial posts, and municipal office in nineteen towns – could be purchased throughout the century. Privilege, which, in its origin, was the most tangible expression of noble social superiority, had long since been infiltrated by non-nobles. Fiscal exemption, the commonest form of privilege, could be acquired without particular difficulty by men of substance and even, in a partial way, by men of very little substance.[14] On the other hand, the eighteenth-century noble always paid some taxes – more indeed than the wealthy bourgeois of certain towns favored by a history of bargains with the Crown – while, in practice, rich commoners benefited as much as nobles from the complaisance, deference or laxity of administrators and collectors of taxes.[15] Similarly, seigneurial rights were certainly not restricted to the nobility. They had become a merchandise possibly more readily obtainable than venal office. Fiefs and rights had been divided, subdivided, and shared out to such an extent that in some places it was impossible to know their origin. In 1781, 22 per cent of the lay seigneurs in the *Election* of Le Mans were non-nobles.[16] Just before the Revolution, the Duc de Chaulnes sold his seigneury and viscounty of Amiens to a certain Colmar, a Jew and therefore definitely not noble, while the Polignacs' alienation of their seigneuries in the Velay around the beginning of the century was a veritable godsend for the socially ambitious wealthy of that region.[17] In sum, between the privileged noble and the unprivileged commoner stood an important transitional category of indeterminate social mutants. They were neither nobles nor commoners. Indeed, almost everywhere except in Normandy, the appellation "noble" really meant a superior sort of non-noble; hence the birth certificate of the future Director Larevellière-Lépeaux stated that he was the son of "nobleman Jean-Baptiste de la Revellière, bourgeois of the town of Angers".[18] How noble was a man whose office conferred on him personal nobility but who had not yet served the twenty years necessary to obtain the *lettres d'honneur* which declared that nobility now hereditary in the family?[19] Was a man privileged or not when he possessed a fief, where he paid no taxes and levied seigneurial dues, and also non-noble land, where he paid both taxes and dues? Of course, it had been stated as early as the Ordinance of Blois (1579) that possession of a fief in no way made a man noble. But, when taken with a certain lifestyle and other similar attributes, it was an important element in helping to make a man appear noble. And in social promotion in this period, appearances were the first step towards reality. In the 1780s an authority on jurisprudence complained that the usurpation of rank had got quite out of hand with men ennobled (*anoblis*) styling themselves in a manner reserved to lords of early fifteenth-century extraction, and commoners of good standing having themselves addressed as *marquis, comte, vicomte*, or *baron*, and even passing themselves off as such in legal documents.[20] More modest, but more commonplace, were the eighteenth-century families which had added the particle to their name,[21] and had acquired over a number of generations a surreptitious accumulation of partial recognitions of privileged status which allowed them to establish as a fact exemptions and privileges to which they had no real documented right. Provided that such a family was of some wealth, conformed to the standards of noble behavior, and married advantageously, it was sufficient for its members to claim indefatigably enough and for long enough a customary privileged position in order to obtain ultimately the Intendant's tacit acquiescence to their inclusion in some list of privileged persons, thus achieving irrefutable evidence of privileged status. A sustained effort of this kind by succeeding generations could finally be crowned either by the grant of Letters of Nobility or by an official decision ratifying explicitly or implicitly a claim to nobility.[22]

Purchasing office.

Jaurès sought to explain these anomalies as "a hybrid social force at the junction of the Ancien Régime and the new capitalism."[23] Obviously, such an interpretation alone was capable of safeguarding the concept of two distinct and antagonistic classes. In fact, however, it does not seem possible to discern a fundamental cleavage at this time between the bourgeoisie and the nobility. The middle class of the late Ancien Régime displayed no significant functional differences from the nobility, no significant difference in accepted values and above all no consciousness of belonging to a class whose economic and social characteristics were antithetical to those of the nobility.[24] The commercial middle class of France at this time was not capitalist in one vital respect. The business of making money was subordinated to a non-capitalist social ideal, and social classifications and values did not depend upon a notion of productive force. The middle class accepted really without debate aristocratic values and sought to gain social approval by adhering to these standards. Social promotion required the abandonment of trade as soon as was financially possible. The consistent pattern of the eighteenth century, as of the seventeenth, was that commercial families placed their capital in land, in government and private annuities (*rentes*), and in venal office, all of which gave returns on investment in the order of 2 to 4 per cent, instead of seeking the higher returns on commercial investment.[25] These men were dominated by the social motive, not by the capitalist profit motive. They accepted that trade was by definition ignoble and dishonorable. If the corn merchant speculated on the misery of the times or if the cloth merchant risked his all in the chance of large profits from army contracts, it was in order that their progeny might the more quickly retreat into the social respectability of professional status and that, hopefully, they might themselves retire to live the life of noble idleness on revenues from land, government stock, and private loans.[26] Thus, in economic terms, nobles and bourgeois resembled each other to the extent that both sought to secure the greater part of their fortune in non-capitalist forms; at the same time, nobles indulged quite as much as wealthy commoners in proto-capitalist industrial and financial activities.[27] It seems difficult to perceive here the representatives of significantly different stages "in a complex set of socio-economic relationships, the one feudal, the other capitalist".[28] Such fundamental divisions and their ensuing antagonisms did not properly begin to appear in France until the nineteenth century, possibly during the reign of Louis-Philippe, and even then the socio-economic pattern described in this paragraph remained predominant among the entrepreneurial group.[29]

Hence, in the upper reaches of French society the great articulation was not between noble and commoner which, as I have tried to show, is an almost impossible division to demonstrate. It was between those who traded and those who did not. Of course, this dividing line, like all the others in this society, was neither absolute nor drawn horizontally across society. Each family made its own calculation of the amount of fortune necessary before severing its connection with the generating source of wealth in trade.[30] In the few great cities and seaports, with their opportunities for massive accumulation of wealth, oligarchies of trading families appeared, of such great wealth that social respect and even noble status could not be denied them.[31] Clearly, such men may be adduced as evidence of a capitalist haute-bourgeoisie in the classic sense; but the extent to which their careers are typical of the middle class as a whole is highly debatable and we shall refer later in this essay to other senses in which their situation may have been significant in the structure of this society. Moreover, in most cases, despite having been able to rise so high socially while in trade, even they quickly sought to take root among the landed nobility and retreated behind the discretion of intermediaries if they continued their business interests.[32]

In general it would appear true to say that above this frontier of trade – and always provided the possession of a level of wealth sufficient not to live meanly – there stood an élite whose internal distinctions could not destroy a common identity between its component elements.[33] It was united, in the first place, by its control of landed property, both directly as the landowning class and indirectly through the exercise of seigneurial rights. In the second place, the tangible manifestations of social superiority – essentially fiscal and seigneurial privilege – were becoming increasingly accessible during the century to the majority of its members without regard to their nobility or lack of it. This is very clearly the message of the difficulties which one encounters in trying to distinguish between noble and rich commoner. The third major element of unity is that *in origin* the nobility of the late eighteenth century was no different from those members of the élite who had not yet achieved noble rank. Already in 1660 an observer estimated that hardly 5 per cent of noble families could trace their lineage back to the medieval feudal age.[34] The great majority of the nobility of France dated from the sixteenth, seventeenth, and eighteenth centuries.[35] They were the product of that very same patient acquisition of social pre-eminence upon which the non-noble élite of the later eighteenth century was so ardently engaged.[36] Most of the élite shared a common origin in that, in the first instance, it was some measure of wealth which had given them access to land and office.[37] From that base, there began the slow ascension through the devious channels of a careful accumulation and permutation of a succession of progressively prestigious offices, of advantageous marriage alliances, of inheritances, and so on.[38]

What I have said does not necessarily deny the existence of a "middle class" that was within the élite and that did not merely consist of the trading elements – these latter both stood outside the élite and played little direct part in the genesis of the Revolution. But until considerably more detailed research which does not postulate a "bourgeoisie" separate from and in contradiction with the élite has been accomplished, it is difficult to define it exactly. Above all, one may debate whether such a definition would be of major significance when there is little evidence that it possessed either a "class consciousness" or an alternative social structure. This argument does, however, deny the notion of two clearly defined and clearly antagonistic classes of nobles and bourgeois in eighteenth-century France and therefore denies the existence of a class conflict in the classic sense. It does not deny – and is not intended to deny – the existence of very real distinctions, divisions and antagonisms within this élite. Nor does it deny the existence of a social crisis, for, as H.R. Trevor-Roper remarked in quite a different context, "social crises are caused not by the clear-cut opposition of mutually exclusive interests but by the tug-of-war of opposite interests *within one body*".[39] It is quite wrong to consider that the upper reaches of late Ancien Régime society were static and decaying. Any analysis confined to only a few decades will inevitably project a static image unless that period be one of actual crisis or revolution. A wider context of a couple of centuries suggests that, on the contrary, this élite was the product of a process of evolution and that it was still evolving.

It is evident from the preceding pages that the nature of the nobility had been undergoing tremendous change since the end of the fifteenth century. Indeed, the historian of the later Valois would not find unfamiliar our description of the ambiguity of the frontier between nobles and commoners, with its references to the escape from trade, venal office, usurpation, the adoption of the particle, ennoblement, and the purchase of fiefs, of elements of privilege, and of nobility itself. Noble complaints about the debasement of their estate sound very much the same whether written in the 1780s or the 1580s. The combined action of three major factors seems to have been responsible for this development: first, the financial difficulties of the late medieval and Renaissance nobility; second, the attempts of the emergent absolute monarchs to secure their power upon a service nobility; third, the financial difficulties of these monarchs which prompted them to abandon ennobling offices into the possession of their incumbents and subsequently to resort to the downright sale of privileges and offices. The great period of the transformation of the élite was unquestionably the seventeenth century. It was in this period that the monarchy expanded its power and the business of its government enormously, and thus multiplied its officials and the machinery for the enforcement of its will; it was also the period when a great series of wars, undertaken on an unprecedented scale and in a time of economic instability, obliged the monarch to exploit office and privilege for revenue purposes.[40] This double process, reaching its apogee under Louis XIV, accelerated the infiltration of the nobility by wealthy commoners which had been taking place during the sixteenth century. More important perhaps, by encouraging its generalization, it finally rendered irrevocable the sixteenth-century encroachment on characteristically noble attributes by wealthy non-nobles.[41] Louis XIV in particular exploited every financial opportunity provided by office and privilege.[42] He even resorted several times to the direct sale of nobility, whereas neither of the eighteenth-century kings did more than sell the confirmation of nobility acquired in the normal ways. His extensive warfaring allowed commoners to enter the officer corps in relatively large numbers.[43] A man with wits enough to discover profit in the ruins of the economy and intelligence enough to further the extension of royal power could rise rapidly. In this sense, we may restore a dimension to Saint-Simon's much abused description of the Sun King's rule as the "reign of the vile bourgeoisie." Early in the seventeenth century, the famous jurist and political theorist Loyseau still based his work on the concept of a society divided into three separate estates. In the last decade of that same century the theorist Domat, whose writings influenced jurists for the next ninety years, was dividing society on a functional basis: the first rank, with honor, dignity, and authority, he accorded to the prelates, high magistrates, and military commanders; and in the second rank, endowed with honor but not dignity, he placed without differentiation – and this is significant in the context of this essay – the *avocats*, the doctors, the members of the liberal and scientific professions generally and also the "gentlemen" (*gentilhommes*).[44]

This, then, had been the heyday of social promotion and, as a result, not merely was the composition of the nobility altered but also its traditional attributes diffused and its traditional functions adulterated. The situation in the later eighteenth century was simply the development of conditions already apparent in the second half of the seventeenth.[45] By the end of the Ancien Régime, the distinction between the Robe nobility and the Sword nobility, which had appeared so vital during the preceding two centuries, had become largely meaningless. Similar lifestyles, intermarriage, the parallel pursuit of military, judicial and administrative careers by the different sons of the same Sword or Robe family had abolished the distinction.[46] Some old provincial nobles still attached a significance of prestige to the profession of arms, but found rich commoners among their brother officers for most of the century. After 1750 the most important distinction inside the nobility was that between the men of noble descent (*noblesse de race*) and those ennobled (*anoblis*). But since, as we have seen, the vast majority of noble families had originally been ennobled, noble "purity" was essentially a biological question of survival while successive generations of nobles left the family origins behind. With all other things being equal, the *anobli* family of the sixteenth century was, in 1780, more prestigious than that of the seventeenth century, which was in turn more prestigious than that of the eighteenth century.[47]

But all these distinctions, by whose shifting complexities Frenchmen sought to keep abreast of social evolution, mask from us as they did from contemporaries the fact that the fundamental effect of these changes was to alter nobility over a long period of time from being the expression of certain hereditary virtues to being the crude expression of great wealth and powerful connections.[48] At the end of the Ancien Régime this evolution was not complete, it was only implied. There existed a hybrid situation in which men sought to express complex social realities in symbols and language whose connotations referred to a qualitatively different structure.[49] The tension of the later eighteenth century was produced in no small measure by a problem of definition and perception. Frenchmen still accepted that nobility was the purest expression of social superiority. They accepted, as the medieval world had accepted, that it reflected virtue. Echoing three centuries of noble spokesmen, not to mention such figures as Boileau and La Bruyère, one obscure Poitevin count began his memoirs in the 1790s with the statement that "the titles of nobility contain no merit unless they reside upon virtue without which they can only be considered as useless baubles".[50] But ever since the sixteenth century they had debated what was this virtue, testifying by their debate to the presence of the evolutionary trend.[51] By the eighteenth century, the notion of virtue had clearly been extended to include both the chivalric concept of "without fear and without reproach" and also the notion of great political, administrative, diplomatic, and judicial talents such as render signal service to the honor and power of the monarch. Much of the debate continued to revolve, as it always had done, around the degree to which such forms of virtue were hereditary or due to environment and education, that is to say whether nobility was in the blood or in the mind.[52] Most writers sought some compromise to accommodate both. But, as the century wore on, a new notion of virtue came to challenge these and to change the nature of the debate, thus reflecting more accurately the increasing departure of the élite from its old standards and its old composition. This was a notion culled by the highly educated professional groups from their reading of the Latin authors such as Cicero, Livy, Sallust, and Tacitus, upon whom the eighteenth-century schools laid increasing emphasis.[53] It was the Roman Republican definition of virtue as civic virtue – the interest in, the care for, and the adeptness at the defence of the *res publica*. This radical notion implying that nobility belonged only to those capable of administering, and by extension ultimately of ruling, looked forward in a real sense to the Revolution. The Montagnard Laignelot was to exclaim in 1793: "Virtue is simply the love of the Republic: the Romans were great only because they were virtuous."[54]

[*In the next section, Lucas argues that while French society did not exhibit a classic class conflict between nobility and bourgeoisie, it did experience "stress zones" of genuine*

*social conflict. Such zones included urban landowners, military officers, and adminis-
trative office holders. Here social mobility may have lessened during the 1780s,
producing a social crisis that led to the Revolution.*]

Should one, therefore, agree with one recent historian in seeing the outbreak of
revolution in France as essentially a political event?[55] In this context, the importance of the decision by the Parlement of Paris in September 1788 (largely
endorsed by the second Assembly of Notables) that the Estates-General should
meet in its form of 1614 has never been ignored.[56] But the nature of its significance has not perhaps always been exactly recognized. This decision polarized
the component elements of the élite and crystalized their latent tensions by
reintroducing from the early seventeenth century concepts of French society
which, already obsolescent at that time, were by now totally erroneous.[57] The
conditions demanded for entry into the noble electoral assemblies were far more
rigorous than any that had been imposed for noble gatherings and lists during
the preceding century.[58] The electoral procedure thus took on the aspect of
a seventeenth-century type inquiry into nobility. The frontier between noble
and non-noble, which had been of diminishing importance, was suddenly and
artificially reimposed. The decision to separate the nobility from the Third Estate
pushed the central and lower echelons of the élite down into the Third Estate.
It rent asunder what was essentially by now a homogeneous social unit, and
identified quite gratuitously a section of that unit as irremediably inferior and
to be confused not merely with the trading classes but also with the manual
laborers and the vile and abject poor. It is in this context that one must understand the apparent paradox of the fact that the leading voices at the national level
against this decision in late 1788 were those of "liberal" nobles.[59] As far as those
who were directly affected by these measures are concerned, it needs no temerity
to suggest that the *anobli* Le Chapelier, for instance, discovered his revolutionary
vocation when he was excluded, despite his bitter protests, from the electoral
assembly of the Breton nobility.[60] But, in general, the position of the *anobli* was
naturally somewhat ambivalent. It was men further down in the channels of
promotion who reacted most categorically to the situation. At Rennes, to use
examples from Brittany again, it was the *procureurs* of the *Présidial* who led the
attack on the oligarchy of *anoblis* in the Municipality for refusing to endorse a
demand for vote by head, and it was the *avocats* who organized the electoral
campaign there, while at Saint-Malo and in most of the other Breton towns
except Nantes the professional groups again took the initiative in the agitation.[61]
This was the situation in most of France. In Provence, however, although the
same direct effects of the decisions relating to the calling of the Estates-General
are visible, the situation was somewhat different in that the polarization
was already well under way by this time.[62] But, at root, a similar catalyst had
operated, for the conflict took shape in the debate during the later months of
1787 over whether the provincial Estates of Provence should be re-established in
the form of their last meeting in 1639, a debate which the Third Estate lost. Once
again, the lawyers had taken a leading part and continued to do so in 1788.

It was their experience of problems in social promotion which rendered many of the people thus implicitly demoted by the Parlement's decision so sensitive to such distinctions.[63] This helps to explain why the traditional liberal professions provided so many of the leaders of the Third Estate movement at the local level during the winter of 1788–9. This decision was all the more critical because it seemed to arbitrate definitively between two contradictory trends in recent comparable situations: it was all the more of a shock because the Estates-General were supremely more important than any of those situations and because this decision ran counter to the conceptions which the government had apparently been favoring. In 1787, following an earlier experiment by Necker in the Berry and a plan submitted to the Assembly of Notables by Calonne, Loménie de Brienne had established a three-tier structure of municipal, intermediary, and provincial assemblies to handle some aspects of local government.[64] Although a proportion of seats in all these bodies was reserved to the privileged orders, the system called for elections to the lowest assembly among the men of property on a tax franchise and for each assembly to designate to the one above it. Above all, there was to be no distinction by Order, voting was to be by head, and the Third Estate had double representation. Moreover, the events at Vizille in the Dauphiné in July 1788 seemed to confirm this trend towards the unity of an élite of comfortable men of property. On the other hand, the decision of September 1788 echoed the most exclusive and antiquated formulas of representation which the government had conceded, by omission at least, to the renewed Estates of Provence. Together these two events, reinforced in December 1788 by the widely read and extremely reactionary *Mémoire des Princes présenté au roi*, could appear as the final implementation of a threat long expressed. We do not yet possess a close study of the disputes between nobles and commoners during the years preceding the Revolution. But it is possible to argue that they usually arose because the nobleman acted in such a way as to suggest not merely that the respectable commoner was inferior socially, which in relative terms within the élite he obviously was, but that he was on a par with the vulgar mass. The nobleman who insisted on his precedence in church would certainly mortify the pride of the well-to-do commoner; but the nobleman who thrashed the son of a bourgeois was treating him as he would treat a domestic servant or a street porter – it was even worse when he had the job done for him by his lackeys.[65] This is of course an extreme example. The propagandists of the Third Estate in Brittany still remembered the reception of the demand formulated ten years previously that the provincial Estates authorize commoners to be admitted to the charitable institution for poor gentlemen, which they indeed had helped to subsidize.[66] "What, do they not have the poorhouses (*hôpitaux*), the workhouses (*maisons de force*), and the prisons?" a nobleman had inquired, thereby implicitly excluding all commoners from the élite and consigning them without distinction to those institutions which catered not merely for the honest though humble poor, but also for the vagabonds and beggars who stood outside society altogether. Of course, all this was very tame when compared with noble behaviour during the previous two centuries.[67] It is significant of the changing situation of the commoner elements of the élite that their sensitivity to this kind of attitude should have been such as to make them often the aggressors in violent quarrels.

This, then, was what Mallet du Pan was expressing in his oftquoted observation – "The nature of the debate has completely changed. King, despotism, and constitution are now very secondary questions; the war is between the Third Estate and the other two Orders."[68] In this sense, the doubling of the representation of the *Tiers* was a wholly irrelevant concession. The revolt of the Third Estate was a revolt against a loss of status by the central and lower sections of the élite with the approval of those elements of the trading groups which were on the threshold of the élite. It was this social group which became the "revolutionary bourgeoisie." The abbé Sieyes became such an influential personality because he expressed precisely their aspirations.[69] Under the rhetoric of his most celebrated pamphlet, *Qu'est-ce que le Tiers-état?* he was not in fact pressing the social and political claims of all those he defined as the Third Estate in the first chapter, but only those of the group which he called "the available classes of the Third Estate."[70] In all his political writings, Sieyes conceived of society as composed essentially of two peoples, the property owners and the "work machines," and demanded the union of the property owners in defence of property against the poor. He militated against the privileged orders because their existence prevented that union; from the beginning to the end of the Revolution he extolled the notables as a homogeneous social and political élite. In 1789, the system of elections served this revolt for, whereas the direct election procedure for the First and Second Estates produced a faithful reflection of the stress zones within them, the indirect elections of the Third Estate not only eliminated the non-élite groups (and therefore the stress zones that their relations with the élite constituted), but also brought in a solid and unified group of professional men, that is to say precisely those who were the most directly affected by the contraction of the traditional channels of promotion. Once the Third Estate had taken control in July 1789, the National Assembly abandoned the Ancien Régime structure of privilege with reluctance and considerable reservations in August. It was hardly the act of an assembly of bourgeois liberating themselves from the restricting fetters of feudalism. Indeed, the abbé Sieyes did all he could to reverse it.[71] These men became the champions of an attack on privilege in part by the force of the logic of revolutionary politics in the context of the popular revolt of 1789. But they also did so as a consequence of a number of confusions. Obliged to become the leaders of the Third Estate, they presented their own grievances as those of the whole of the Third Estate. Certainly, they expressed hostility to the nobility, but their grievance was one of political and social definition in the precise context of 1788–9. However, the mere fact that they did express this hostility encouraged the peasantry, initially at least, to identify privilege predominantly with the nobility rather than with the élite as a whole and to confuse the grievances of the "revolutionary bourgeoisie" with its own.[72] It was this which enabled the revolutionary behavior of the representatives of the Third Estate to find support among the protest movements of the vile and abject sections of the community, which were not their natural allies. Furthermore, in 1788–9 the circumstances and background which have been elaborated in this essay allowed the "revolutionary bourgeoisie" to identify, erroneously and in general terms, the Ancien Régime nobility as an exclusive group threatening its social position, while the political developments of the early days of the Estates-General incited it to confuse this conception of the nobility with the system of absolute monarchy, and to see the two as interdependent and as allies. But such a thought-process necessarily imposed the identification of the nobility as a distinct social group, which, as we have seen, was an unrealistic enterprise; the easiest solution to this paradox was to indulge in another confusion and to identify the nobility by the traditional system of privileges which had originally been specifically noble attributes. Thus, spokesmen of the Third Estate could quite happily refer to the first two Estates as the "privileged Orders", forgetting that they themselves were in many cases at least partially privileged. It was for this reason that the attachment of the "revolutionary bourgeoisie" to that system of privilege, in which they themselves participated, was weakened. In mid-1789 the combination of the counter-offensive of the Ancien Régime and anti-privilege pressure from below brought the revolutionary leaders to jettison privilege.

However, the true sense of the rejection of the Ancien Régime system of privilege by the "revolutionary bourgeoisie" was revealed by the Constitution of 1791. In this document, this assembly of men from the Ancien Régime élite redefined that same élite in such a way that it could never be divided again by artificial distinctions within it. The characteristic of élite status was recognized to be the control of landed property. The tangible attribute of élite status was defined as access to public office and the political control of the country. This is the sense of a Constitution which made every public position elective and largely confined eligibility to men of some substance expressed in property. The Thermidorians and the Directorials reasserted these same conceptions of politics and society far more explicitly and successfully, as the surviving Jacobins, not to mention Babeuf, clearly understood.[73] The Constitution of 1791 in no way implied a rejection of the Ancien Régime nobility, for it was comprised within this definition as much as were wealthy non-nobles. It was merely because some noble elements chose rather vociferously not to participate that the Revolution was made to appear as a revolt against the nobility as a social class. In the same way, the technical detail of the ordering of the Estates-General, while crystalizing the tensions of the Ancien Régime, also forced them to be expressed in terms which can easily be taken as those of a conflict between nobles and bourgeois, a conflict which did not exist in any very meaningful sense in the eighteenth century. Nevertheless, the redefinition of the élite by the Revolution was indubitably of fundamental importance. Although nobility as an institution was only momentarily abolished and Napoleon was indeed to reinforce it in a certain sense, the revolutionary crisis did result in the emergence of an élite defined in terms of landholding and function, with the hereditary element confined to the simple passage of wealth and its advantages from one generation to another in a family. The Revolution did therefore provide a social framework within which the acquisition of nobility was to be increasingly irrelevant and which allowed élite status to develop into the attribute of men of wealth however acquired and however expressed. In this sense, we may say that the Revolution made the bourgeoisie even if it was not made by the bourgeoisie.

NOTES

Source Reprinted in an abridged format from *Past and Present*, 60 (August 1973): 84–126.

* *Acknowledgement* I would like to thank Dr John Roberts and my colleague Dr I. Prothero for their perceptive criticisms of this essay in its final stages.

1 Perhaps the clearest statement of this schema is to be found in A. Soboul, "Classes and Class Struggles during the French Revolution," *Science and Society*, xvii (1953), 238–57: e.g., "The essential cause of the Revolution was the power of a bourgeoisie arrived at its maturity and confronted by a decadent aristocracy holding tenaciously to its privileges."

2 A. Cobban, *The Social Interpretation of the French Revolution* (Cambridge, 1964).

3 D. Richet, "Autour des origines idéologiques lointaines de la Révolution française: élites et despotismes," *Annales: Economies; Sociétés, Civilizations* (hereafter *Annales E.S.C.*), xxiv (1969), 1–23; F. Furet, "Le catéchisme de la Révolution française," *Annales E.S.C.*, xxvi (1971), 255–89; C. Mazauric, *Sur la Révolution française* (Paris, 1970), 21–113.

4 A. Cobban, "The French Revolution, Orthodox and Unorthodox," *History*, lii (1967), 149–59.

5 G.V. Taylor, "Types of Capitalism in Eighteenth-Century France," *English Historical Review*, lxxix (1964), 478–97, and "Non-Capitalist Wealth and the Origins of the French Revolution," *American Historical Review*, lxxii (1967), 469–96, esp. 490.

6 Cf. E.G. Barber, *The Bourgeoisie in Eighteenth-Century France* (Princeton, 1955), 15; M. Couturier, *Recherches sur les structures sociales de Châteaudun* (Paris, 1969), 221–2; A. Daumard and F. Furet, *Structures et relations sociales à Paris au milieu du XVIIIème siècle* (Paris, 1963), 68.

7 In this point resides the weakness of using professional categories as social categories. Not only can there be significant wealth differences between two carpenters or two stonemasons, but also significant functional differences. Cf. M. Thoumas-Schapira, "La bourgeoisie toulousaine à la fin du XVIIème siècle," *Annales du Midi*, lxvii (1955), 315, 318.

8 One can suggest that the inferiority of surgeons (*chirurgiens*) to doctors (*médecins*), although clearly connected with their barbering, may also be imputable in part to the predominantly manual nature of their profession.

9 Note how Chaumette, terrorist *agent national* of Paris, seems to have tried to substitute "jeweller" (*bijoutier*) for "shoemaker" (*cordonnier*) as his father's profession on his birth certificate: *Papiers de Chaumette*, ed. F. Braesch (Paris, 1908), 12.

10 A calculation of the fortunes of the joiners (*menuisiers*) of Toulouse reveals an average of 1,000 *livres* for the masters, 600 for those companions who subsequently became masters, and 470 for those who did not: J. Godechot, "L'histoire économique et sociale de Toulouse au XVIIIème siècle," *Annales du Midi*, lxxviii (1966), 371.

11 Richet, "Autour des origines idéologiques lointaines de la Révolution française."

12 E.g. H. Carré, *La noblesse de France et l'opinion publique au XVIIIème siècle* (Paris, 1920), 3, 12–14, and F.L. Ford, *Robe and Sword* (New York, 1965), 208–9. Cf. J.G.C. Blacker,

"Social Ambitions of the Bourgeoisie in Eighteenth-Century France and their Relation to Family Limitation," *Population Studies*, xi (1957), 46–63, and P. Goubert, *L'Ancien Régime*, 2 vols (Paris, 1969), i, 145 ff.

13 E.g. J. Meyer, *La noblesse bretonne au XVIIIème siècle*, 2 vols (Paris, 1966), i, 321–442.

14 E.g., out of a total of 1,715 names on the tax rolls of Montargis in 1789, 852 were marked either as being exempt or privileged, or else as having a special status: B. Hyslop, "Les élections de la ville de Montargis en 1789," *Ann. hist. Rév. fr.*, xviii (1946), 125; cf. G. Bouchard, *La famille du conventionnel Basire* (Paris, 1952), 91–2.

15 C.B.A. Behrens "Nobles, Privileges, and Taxes in France at the end of the Ancien Régime," *Econ. Hist. Rev.*, 2nd ser., xv (1962–3), 451–75; M Marion, *Histoire financière de la France depuis 1715*, 3 vols (Paris, 1914–28), i, 10–12.

16 P. Bois, *Les Paysans de l'Ouest* (Le Mans, 1960), 378. But the regional variations were great; around Dieppe there was only one non-noble for thirty-six noble fief holders: M. de Bouard (ed.), *Histoire de Normandie* (Toulouse, 1970), 339.

17 A. Young, *Travels in France*, (ed.) C. Maxwell (Cambridge, 1950), 8; G. Sabatier, "L'Emblavès au début du XVIIIème siècle", in P. Léon (ed.), *Structures économiques et problèmes sociaux du monde rural dans la France du Sud-Est* (Paris, 1966), 88–90. Cf. M. Bouloiseau (ed.) *Cahiers de doléances du Tiers-Etat du bailliage de Rouen* (Paris, 1957), i, xxix, on the dispersion of the seigneuries in the duchy of Longueville during the same period.

18 A. Brette, "La noblesse et ses privilèges pécuniaires en 1789," *La Révolution française*, xxvi (1906), 102.

19 Note, for example, how one inhabitant of Saint-Etienne, who at the beginning of the Revolution certainly considered himself, and was considered by others, to be a noble, was able to vote in the Year VI by arguing that his father had been a *secrétaire du roi* for only fourteen years and that therefore he himself could not possibly be noble: Archives Départmentales (hereafter A.D.), Loire, L. 276, proceedings of electoral assembly at Saint-Etienne, Year VI.

20 Quoted by Carré, *La noblesse de France*, 14.

21 160 signatures on the Tennis Court Oath had the particle: Brette, *op. cit.*, 104.

22 E.g. V.R. Gruder, *The Royal Provincial Intendants* (Ithaca, 1968), 130; F. Bluche, *Les Magistrats du Parlement de Paris au XVIIIème siècle* (Besançon, 1960), 95; G. Lefebvre, *Etudes Orléanaises*, 2 vols (Paris, 1962–3), i, 165–70.

23 J. Jaurès, *Histoire socialiste, 1789–1900*, 12 vols (Paris, 1900–8), i, p. 40.

24 Taylor, "Non-Capitalist Wealth and the Origins of the French Revolution," *passim*. Cf. Godechot, "L'histoire économique et sociale de Toulouse", 363–74; Barber, *The Bourgeoisie in Eighteenth-Century France*, 62–3; J. Sentou, *Fortunes et groupes sociaux à Toulouse sous la Révolution* (Toulouse, 1969), 79–322, esp. 182–3. P. Léon ("Recherches sur la bourgeoisie française de province au XVIIIème siècle", *L'Information historique*, xxi (1958), 101–5) believes that the division between the nobility and the bourgeoisie can be seen in the tax registers, provided that one recognizes a number of "enclaves" and operates a selection among the office-holders on the fringes of the Robe nobility. This sort of categorization (which is a fairly common approach to the problem) seems unrealistic in view of what we know about tax exemption; it is also extremely arbitrary, as indeed the author admits.

25 But there were variations: both F. Bluche (*Les Magistrats du Parlement de Paris au XVIIIème siècle* (Besançon, 1960), p. 170) and R. Forster (*The Nobility of Toulouse* (Baltimore, 1960), 104, find returns of 5 per cent for the Parlements they study, while the government annuities (*rentes*) paid 5 per cent at most, as did private ones under the law at least.

26 Cf. M. Vovelle and D. Roche, "Bourgeois, rentiers, propriétaires: éléments pour la définition d'une catégorie sociale à la fin du XVIIIème siècle," in *Actes du 84ème congrès national des sociétés savantes* (Paris, 1959), 419–52; also Sentou, *op cit.*, 191–2 and 253 on the connection between the *rentier* and professional groups.

27 Taylor, *op. cit.*; G. Richard, "Les corporations et la noblesse commerçante en France au XVIIIème siècle," *L'Information historique*, xx (1957), 185–9; Meyer, *La noblesse bretonne*, i, 151–8.

28 J. Kaplow, "On 'Who intervened in 1788?' ", *American Historical Review*, lxxii (1967), 498.

29 D.S. Landes, "French Entrepreneurship and Industrial Growth in the Nineteenth Century," *Journal of Economic History*, ix (1949), 45–61.

30 There are of course countless individual examples, each with its own, different permutation of the elements contributing to such a promotion; Taylor (*op. cit.*) presents some, as does O. Hufton (*Bayeux in the Late Eighteenth Century* (Oxford, 1967), 61). A very clear example of a family in the act of transferring – marrying profitably, buying land and office, yet hesitating to abandon trade altogether – is provided by the future revolutionary Laurent LeCointre and his brother in the 1770s and 1780s: T. Lhuillier, "Laurent LeCointre (de Versailles)," *La Révolution française*, xv (1895), 234–56.

31 E.g. G. Richard, "A propos de la noblesse commerçante de Lyon au XVIIIème siècle," *L'Information historique*, xxii (1959), 156–61. A royal decree of 1767 accorded the wholesale merchants (*négociants en gros*) the reputation of "living nobly" and some privileges.

32 E.g. the complaint from Toulouse in 1773 that the moment a merchant obtained the ennobling office of *capitoul*, "he considers trading to be a thing very much beneath his dignity": M. Marion, *Dictionnaire des institutions de la France aux XVIIème et XVIIIème siècles* (Paris, 1968), v. "noblesse".

33 The notion of an élite was first examined in general terms by D. Richet, "Autour des origines idéologiques lointaines de la Révolution française". See also H. Luethy, *La banque protestante en France*, 2 vols (Paris, 1959–61), ii, 15–25, and Goubert, *L'Ancien Régime*, i, 235. Cf. the interesting comment on such a view in Mazauric, *Sur la Révolution française*, 107.

34 D. Bitton, *The French Nobility in Crisis* (Stanford, 1969), 98.

35 A. Goodwin, "The Social Structure and Economic and Political Attitudes of the French Nobility in the Eighteenth Century," in *XIIème congrès international des sciences historiques*, 5 vols (Vienna, 1965), i, 356–65; Gruder, *The Royal Provincial Intendants*, 177–80. Cf. Bayeux in 1789, where five-sixths of the noble families could not claim nobility before 1500; the nobility of the majority of them was acquired during the seventeenth and early eighteenth centuries: Hufton, *Bayeux in the Late Eighteenth Century*, 41.

36 E.g. the interesting comparison established by R. Bouscayrol, "Les origines familiales et sociales de Romme et de Soubrany," in *Gilbert Romme et son Temps* (Publications de l'Institut d'Etudes du Massif Central, Paris, 1966), 23–42.

37 Cf. Lefebvre, *Etudes Orléanaises*, i, 171–3; Sentou, *Fortunes et groupes sociaux à Toulouse*, 253–4; M. Bloch, *Les caractères originaux de l'histoire rurale française*, 2 vols (Paris, 1961–4), i, 142–3.

38 E.g. Bosher, *French Finances*, 61–2, 69–71, 178, 278–84; Gruder, *op. cit.*, 136–9, 142–66; Meyer, *La noblesse bretonne*, i, 171–422, esp. 349–61; Lefebvre, *op. cit.*, i, 175–6. A few spectacular careers are detailed in Forster, *The Nobility of Toulouse*, 24–6. Cf. Couturier, *Recherches sur les structures sociales de Châteaudun*, 236 ff.

39 H. R. Trevor-Roper, "Trevor-Roper's 'General Crisis': Symposium," repr. in Trevor Aston (ed.), *Crisis in Europe, 1560–1660* (London, 1965), 114.

40 Note how the concession of hereditary nobility to the members of the great law courts of Paris and the provinces coincided with moments of acute financial embarrassment – 1644–5, 1691 and 1704; there is a similar pattern in the sales of nobility: Marion, *Dictionnaire des institutions de la France*, v. "noblesse".

41 R. Mousnier, *La vénalité des offices sous Henri IV et Louis XIII* (Rouen, 1946), *passim*.

42 Ford, *Robe and Sword*, 12.

43 E.G. Léonard, "Le question sociale dans l'armée française au XVIIIème siècle", *Annales E.S.C.*, iii (1948), 139–40.

44 R. Mousnier, *La société française de 1770 à 1789*, 2 vols (Paris C.D.U., 1970), i, 11–15.

45 Cf. R.B. Grassby, "Social Status and Commercial Enterprise under Louis XIV", *Econ. Hist. Rev.*, 2nd ser., xiii (1960–1), 19–38.

46 Ford, *op. cit., passim.* Cf. Bluche, *op. cit.*, 116 and 303; Forster, *op. cit.*, 26 and 103; Carré, *La noblesse de France*, 34 ff.; Berthe, *op. cit.*, genealogy facing 56.

47 Bluche, *op. cit.*, 87–92; Meyer, *op. cit.*, i, 362.

48 Cf. Lefebvre, *op. cit.*, i, 171–3.

49 Possibly, we should ascribe the maintenance of old forms partly to the action, or inertia, of the socially conservative Sully and Richelieu at a time when the composition of the social èlite was undergoing radical change, partly to the consequences of their policies: cf. R. Mousnier, "Sully et le Conseil d'Etat et des Finances," *Revue historique*, cxcii (1941), 68–86; O. Ranum, "Richelieu and the Great Nobility," *French Historical Studies*, iii (1963), 184–204; F.E. Sutcliffe, "Agriculture or Industry: a French dilemma at the period of Henry IV," *Bull John Rylands Library*, liv (1972), 434–48. I am grateful to Professor Sutcliffe for discussing several of these points with me.

50 P.A. Pichot and F. Masson (eds) *Un Vendéen sous la Terreur: mémoires inédits de Toussaint-Ambroise de la Cartrie* (Paris, 1910), p. 87; cf. Ford, *op. cit.*, 9, n. 9.

51 Bitton, *The French Nobility in Crisis*, pp. 77–91; Richet, "Autour des origines idéologiques lointaines de la Révolution française".

52 M. Reinhard, "Elite et noblesse dans la seconde moitié du XVIIIème siècle", *Rev. d'hist. mod. et contemp.*, iii (1956), 5–37. Cf. an anonymous pamphleteer at Orléans in 1789; "nobility does not reside in parchments . . . it is to be found in the heart, in the mind, in the way of thinking of those of our Order": Lefebvre, *Etudes Orléanaises*, i, 187.

53 H.T. Parker, *The Cult of Antiquity and the French Revolutionaries* (Chicago, 1937), *passim*; F. Delbèke, *L'action politique et sociale des avocats au XVIIIème siècle* (Louvain, 1927), 9, 11, 19 and 23. The clearest expression of this is J-P. Brissot, *Un Indépendant à l'ordre des avocats, sur la décadence du Barreau en France* (Berlin, 1781).

54 C.L. Chassin, "La mission de Lequinio et Laignelot," *La Révolution française*, xv (1895), 133.

55 Taylor, "Non-Capitalist Wealth and the Origins of the French Revolution," 491.

56 E.g. Lefebvre, *Quatre-vingt-neuf* (Paris, 1939), 58.

57 Sée, "Le rôle de la bourgeoisie bretonne à la veille de la Révolution, *Annales de Bretagne*, xxxiv (1920)," 410: "The really active campaign of the Third Estate begins in October (1788)".

58 Brette, "La noblesse et ses privilèges pécuniaires en 1789," 97 and 124.

59 Cf. Eisenstein, "Who intervened in 1788?" *American Historical Review*, xxi (1965), 77–103. Note also that only ten of the *General Cahiers* of the Third Estate thought that its representatives were sovereign and should ignore those of the privileged Orders: Hyslop, *French Nationalism in 1789* (New York, 1967), 69. The liberal noble Gouy d'Arcy wrote at the end of 1788, "What is an Order in an Empire? It is an essential portion of the governrnent, it is a fundamental class of society, and in both of these respects, there are only two Orders in France, the patricians and the plebeians": quoted by A. Decouflé, "L'aristocratie française devant l'opinion publique à la veille de la Révolution", in R. Besnier (ed.), *Etudes d'histoire économique et sociale du XVIIIème siècle* (Paris, 1966), 37.

60 Meyer, *La noblesse bretonne*, i, 436–8; Cf. Egret, *La Pré-révolution française* (Paris, 1962), 353.

61 Sée, *op. cit.*

62 J. Egret, "La Pré-révolution en Provence", *Ann. hist. Rév. fr.*, xxvi (1954), 195–213.

63 See the instruction given by the electoral assembly of the Third Estate of the Forez to its deputies to refuse to admit any of the distinctions of nobility which might humiliate the Third Estate. Note also the great protests against the imposition of

distinctively different costumes on the three Estates in April 1789; the Forezian deputies argued, significantly enough, that "the Third Estate's interest is that nothing should be *innovated*" (my italics). G. Lefebvre and A. Terroine (eds) *Receuil de documents relatifs aux séances des Etats-Généraux*, 2 vols (Paris, 1953–62), i, 69, 76–82.

64 P. Renouvin, *Les assemblées provinciales de 1787* (Paris, 1921), 79 ff.

65 Already in 1700 a wealthy merchant resented being described by any formula that might also be used of his tailor: Grassby, "Social Status and Commercial Enterprise," 27–8. Note also the agitation over the militia during the century and Barbier's comment that it put the son of the wholesale merchant on the same level as servants, workers and shopboys: E.J.F. Barbier, *Journal historique et anecdotique du règne de Louis XV*, ed. A. de Villegille, 4 vols (Paris, 1857–75), ii, 353–4. Daniel Mornet, *Les origines intellectuelles de la Révolution Française* (Paris, 1933), p. 436, cites some cases of such quarrels, but they are very uninformative, although army officers (and I have referred to their stress zone situation) figure rather prominently in the examples he has chosen.

66 Meyer, *La noblesse bretonne*, ii, 1,114.

67 E.g. E. Fléchier, *Mémoires sur les Grands-Jours d'Auvergne*, ed. M. Chéruel (Paris, 1856), *passim*.

68 Lefebvre, *Quatre-vingt-neuf*, 58.

69 E. Sieyes, *Qu'est-ce que le Tiers-état?*, ed. R. Zapperi (Geneva, 1970), esp. 27–43.

70 *Ibid.*, 143: "les classes disponibles du Tiers-état".

71 *Ibid.*, 31–3.

72 Cf. Lefebvre, *Etudes Orléanaises*, i, 73: "The wealthy peasants (*laboureurs*) and the artisans only spoke out frankly against the seigneur. . . . The hostility towards traders and members of the liberal professions, and more generally towards all town dwellers, which indubitably existed, does not transpire . . ."

73 Cf. I. Woloch, *Jacobin Legacy* (Princeton, 1970), especially pp. 155–6. But note the social assumptions expressed by the Jacobin Garnerin in the middle of Year II when he denounced speculation by the Jews; "There are some among them rich to the tune of fifteen or twenty millions' worth of assignats, and who do not have a sou's worth of landed property": Véron-Réville, *Histoire de la Révolution française dans le département du Haut-Rhin* (Paris, 1865), 194. R. Marx, *Recherches sur la vie politique de l'Alsace pré-révolutionnaire et révolutionnaire* (Strasbourg, 1966), *passim*, contains interesting illustrations of the practice of this situation at all levels throughout the Revolution. Cf. Cobban, *Social Interpretation of the French Revolution*, 81 ff.

Part II

THE REVISIONIST
ORTHODOXY

I shall show how a government, both stronger and far more autocratic than the one which the Revolution had overthrown, centralized once more the entire administration, made itself all-powerful, suppressed our dearly bought liberties, and replaced them by a mere pretense of freedom; how the so-called "sovereignty of the people" came to be based on the votes of an electorate that was neither given adequate information nor an opportunity of getting together and deciding on one policy rather than another; and how the much vaunted "free vote" in matters of taxation came to signify no more than the meaningless assent of assemblies tamed to servility and silence.

Alexis de Tocqueville
foreword to *The Old Regime and the French Revolution*

3

THE FRENCH REVOLUTION REVISITED

François Furet

In this lecture, originally given at the London School of Economics in December 1980, François Furet distills in a lighter style many of the ideas that are elaborated in his monumental book, Interpreting the French Revolution. *Furet begins the talk by trying to come to terms with the fierce and partisan historiography that has dominated the study of the Revolution. His explanation is twofold. First, France's own nineteenth-century political history of revolving regimes and political instability meant that the legacy of the Revolution continued to live on in the fiery speeches and idealistic plans of French statesmen (some of whom were important historians). Second, the outbreak of the Bolshevik Revolution in 1917 made any interpretation of its French precursor a loaded political act. Not until the 1970s, when militant Bolshevism had decayed beyond repair, was it possible to look at the Revolution from a truly fresh perspective.*

This new viewpoint involves relating Tocqueville's idea regarding the growth of the centralized state with a sophisticated understanding about the birth of modern democracy. In his 1856 classic, The Old Regime and the French Revolution, *Alexis de Tocqueville argued that the French Revolution did not so much mark the overthrow of the Ancien Régime as its culmination. By abolishing feudalism, guilds, economic regulation, and noble privilege, the Revolution continued trends begun under the absolute monarchy. Once the noble privilege and institutions were gone, nothing stood between the individual citizen and the all-encompassing power of the centralized state.*

Furet's work is concerned with explaining how this transformation came about. He suggests that by undermining the traditional social order of the Ancien Régime, the monarchy created, in Furet's words, a kind of "empty space" that weakened the monarchy's sense of legitimacy. Rather suddenly, the idea of "the people" moved into this void, creating a 'mobilized society' that 'disarmed the state.' The Revolution, then, is seen as 'the torrential birth of democratic politics and ideology' in which the centralized state is refashioned with far more power and authority than dreamed possible by the eighteenth-century monarchs.

* * *

I should like to start with an extremely simple statement about the French Revolution. This is that there are many historical arguments among historians on many subjects, but that none of these arguments is so intense and so heated as the one which takes place in every generation about the French Revolution. It is as though the historical interpretation of this particular subject and the arguments of specialists directly reflect the political struggles and the gamble for power. It is true that we are all aware today that there are no unbiased historical interpretations: the selection of facts which provide the raw material for the historian's work is already the result of a choice, even though that choice is not an explicit one. To some extent, history is always the result of a relationship between the present and the past and more specifically between the characteristics of an individual and the vast realm of his possible roots in the past. But, nevertheless, even within this relative framework, not all the themes of history are equally relevant to the present interests of the historian and to the passions of his public. The subject of Clovis, for example, and of the Frankish invasions, was of burning interest in the eighteenth century, because historians of that era thought that the Frankish invasions were the source of the division between the nobility and the common people: the conquerors having evolved into the nobility and the conquered having become the commoners. Today, the Germanic invasions are no longer considered to contain or reveal any secret about French society: they have become once again a subject for historiography, left to scholars and to the arguments of specialists.

To be convinced that the French Revolution, in contrast, is not like any other historical subject, one has only to look at the particular violence of the polemics engendered by its study: it is as though the Revolution had prolonged the original conflict for two hundred years and as if the main function of its history was to renew and to maintain it.

This specific historiographic situation appeared with particular clarity in the nineteenth century, as it was linked at that time to the long survival of the revolutionary phenomenon. In fact, the French from 1815 to 1880 were perpetually enacting the same historical drama, the elements of which had been given once and for all between 1789 and 1799. First of all, they 'restored' their former kings, but not the former kingship, in order to re-enact against them in 1830 what they imagined to be an English 1688, that is, a successful 1789, with a new monarchy linked to a new political and social order. But the revolutionary process which they believed that they had exorcised à l'anglaise by the change of dynasty remained the symbol of their national destiny. The year 1848 saw a constituent assembly, a legislative assembly, a Bonaparte. The second Republic found actors for all the roles in the great revolutionary repertory, Lamartine as Brissot, Ledru-Rollin as Robespierre, the nephew Bonaparte as his uncle. The same combination of parliamentary impotence and Jacobin nostalgia which had led to 18 Brumaire brought a second Bonaparte to power under the aegis of memory. The Second Empire collapsed like the first because it was defeated in war, but only to open the way first to the new Jacobin resurrection, which was the Paris Commune, and afterwards to the final attempt to restore the former monarchy in the guise of the 'moral order.' Then began, almost one hundred years after the explosion which we call the French Revolution, the apparently terminal struggle which was to found the Third Republic on the victory of the principles of 1789.

[*Between 1815 and 1940, France experienced the following regimes: The Bourbon Restoration of Louis XVIII and Charles X (1815–30); The July Monarchy of Louis-Philippe (1830–48); The Second Republic (1848–52); The Second Empire of Napoleon III (1852–70); The Third Republic (1870–1940).*]

Thus, the French of the nineteenth century lived on a repertory of political forms which was rich and yet limited: rich because it allowed for a very rapid rhythm of change of regime; limited because all the characters in the repertory had been invented in the last decade of the eighteenth century, within the period which we call the French Revolution in the strict sense of the word. It is, therefore, not surprising that the Frenchmen of the nineteenth century felt that they were living in a sort of indefinitely prolonged French Revolution: every episode in the political history of the country offered them, through its duplicating character, all the elements of identification with (or rejection of) the primordial event. Chateaubriand, Tocqueville, Michelet, Quinet continued to relive the Revolution through their own experiences.

This explains why the point of reference of the whole of politics, of the thought and of the history of the nineteenth century and particularly of romantic politics, thought, history, was centered around the Revolution. The Revolution represents the moment when the old world tipped over towards the new and thus also the abolition of the former and the arrival of the latter: it is the Revolution which holds the title-deeds of the national legitimacy, recognizes the claimants, defines the political families and their share in the legacy. The royalist Right detested the Revolution, but all its thoughts were directed against it and related to it. The liberal bourgeoisie endorsed the Revolution, in part at least. The Bonapartists derive all their ancestors from it. The Republican Left adopted it as its standard. But if the Revolution offered to all of them the reasons for remembering their origins (happy or unhappy), it was because it enveloped them in the civilization which it had created and which made all of them, friend or foe, its sons. The Revolution was thus written only in its own words.

One could illustrate the intellectual constraints of this kind of closed circuit with the example of the historiographical treatment reserved for that particular episode in the Revolution, which is the Terror, particularly in the form it took of a system of repression carried out by the state. The counter-revolutionary Right had no difficulty in including the Terror in its general condemnation of the Revolution and even in making it the very symbol of revolutionary perversion because of the highly spectacular violence which it implied. But in doing so, it is led to attribute the Terror either to the intentional villainy of the historic actors (the theory of the plot) or to the exemplary design of Providence (as in Joseph de Maistre). The link between the Revolution and the Terror is only seen through the ineluctability of evil, under its psychological or theological form: but this is merely to beg the question.

For the Terror embarrasses even more deeply the supporters of the French Revolution, regardless of which branch of the 'Left' they belong to. The liberals, indissolubly linked to 1789, reject 1793. This was Guizot's problem and also that of his friend, Mignet. Even before the problem appeared in reality, in July 1830 (they were to solve it then by resorting to Louis Philippe), they had encountered it historically: 1793, they claimed, was not contained in 1789; it was, on the contrary, an unhappy deviation which must not be repeated. Everything of value in the French Revolution was already there in 1789.

Farther to the Left, and a generation later, Edgar Quinet rediscovered the same question: an intransigent republican, with an unbreakable attachment to the legacy of 1789, this exile from the Second Empire was forced to pick and choose from the revolutionary legacy. Just as Robespierre, so the Second Empire was strong, in his view, only because of Jacobin goodwill. He set his face therefore against everything in the Revolution which weakened liberty, the dictatorship, the Terror of 1793–4, the harbinger of the coup d'état of Brumaire. By the same token, the Terror, far from being consubstantial with the Revolution became, on the contrary, the emergence of its antithesis from within the Revolution, its anti-principle, the resurrection of the Ancien Régime within the new and the corruption of the new by the old. If Robespierre was to be blamed, it was not because he wanted to force the future: it was because he reincarnated Richelieu and absolutism.

The Jacobin Republicans of the same period, who polemicized against Quinet, accepted the Terror as part and parcel of the revolutionary legacy. But they excused it rather than explained it. What I am saying is that their interpretation of the terrorist dictatorship – in Louis Blanc, for example – was a circumstantial one. If the Revolution resorted to coercion and to the guillotine, it was because it was constrained to do so by its internal and external enemies. Within this line of argument – which resembles the plea of 'extenuating circumstances' in our courts – the Terror is no longer thought of as inseparable from the Revolution. It was one of its risks, not one of its component parts. And if 1793–4 was a particularly heroic period, it was because it was victorious rather than because of the means it used to achieve victory. In other words, the difference between Mignet, Quinet and Louis Blanc is not that one or the other tried to conceptualize the Terror as an intrinsic element in the mechanics of revolution: on the contrary, all three of them, distant though they might be from each other on the political chessboard, thought of the Terror as external to the Revolution and independent of it. The first said of the Terror that it was a regrettable deviation in relation to 1789. The second that it was a resurgence of absolutism. The third that it was a necessity imposed by the enemies of the Revolution. These interpretations imply different and even contradictory value judgments on the revolutionary phenomenon – within a general agreement with 1789 – and a common dissociation, at the analytical level, of the pair Revolution–Terror. In other words, they defined themselves or rather they differentiated themselves by the way in which they identified themselves with the revolutionary heritage, rather than by the way in which they understood or analyzed it.

At this stage of the argument, it could be objected that this type of historiographical identification with the French Revolution should have died out with the final triumph of the Revolution: it should not have been able to survive for long the victory of the Third Republic. But it was the opposite that happened: the revolutionary historiography of the twentieth century is just as passionate, partisan, and exclusive as that of the nineteenth century, although the real political stakes linked with the French Revolution have gradually disappeared and no one any longer contests, at least since 1945, the values of 1789 and their legitimacy.

This is because something very simple has happened: the polemics about the conflict between Monarchy and Republic have been replaced by the intellectual and political polemics engendered by the socialist revolution. In fact, the socialists of the second half of the nineteenth century visualized their activity as something at once allied to and distinct from that of the democrats. Allied because democracy is in their eyes the essential condition of socialism; distinct from, because it is a historical stage of the social organization destined to be overtaken, and because 1789 is for them a stage in a historical process in which the socialist revolution does the overtaking. But in reality these two struggles for democracy and for socialism are two successive manifestations of a dynamic of egalitarianism which has its roots deep in the events of the French Revolution.

Thus a linear history of the progress of mankind was composed, of which the first stage was the flowering and the diffusion of the values of 1789 and the second stage was to fulfill all the promises of 1789 by means of the socialist revolution. It is basically a two-handled mechanism of which the pre-1917 great socialist authors had not yet, and rightly, set the second stage, since the second stage had not yet arrived. Jaurès, for example in his *Histoire socialiste de la Revolution française*, built the narration of the French Revolution around what was still only a hope and surrounded the Jacobin epic with a kind of great halo which proclaimed a more decisive liberation of mankind. The French Revolution was pregnant with hope which had a name but which had not yet a face.

Everything changed in 1917. The socialist revolution acquired a face; the French Revolution ceased to be a matrix of probabilities on which another liberating revolution could and should be modeled. It was no longer the field of possibilities, discovered and described by Jaurès; it had become the mother of a real event, dated, fixed, which had taken place and which was the Russian Revolution of October 1917. In 1920, in a little book, an academic historian of the French Revolution, Albert Mathiez, emphasized the kinship between the government of the Mountain and the Bolshevik dictatorship of the civil war period, that is, of the heroic period of the Russian Revolution. I quote:

> Jacobinism and Bolshevism are two dictatorships born of civil war
> and of war, two class dictatorships operating through the same means:
> terror, requisitioning and taxes; and having, in the last resort, the same

goal: the transformation of society and not only of the Russian or French society, but of the universal society.

Moreover, as Mathiez underlined, the Russian Bolsheviks have always had in their minds the example of the French Revolution, especially of its Jacobin period. The Russian revolutionaries were obsessed by the presence in history of the French Revolution which had preceded them. This was one of the great differences between the two revolutions, since by definition the French men of 1789 had no model.

We know, for example, that after the seizure of power by the Bolsheviks, and especially after Lenin's death, all the Russian revolutionaries, from Trotsky to Zinóvyev, including Bukharin, feared a Thermidor, since Thermidor was supposed to have brought the French Revolution to an end. Thus, Thermidor, with all its pejorative connotations, was a threat to the Russian Revolution. And again Thermidor was the harbinger of Bonaparte. In the imagination of the triumvirate Stalin–Zinóvyev–Kamenev, it was Trotsky who represented Bonaparte. The former head of the Red Army re-embodied, for a time, and this was to be fatal to him, the main risk that the Revolution would be liquidated. In other words, the example of the French Revolution was a source of permanent contamination of the Russian Revolution. This contamination played upon the minds of the actors in that revolution; but it also existed in the opposite sense in the minds of many historians of the French Revolution who sympathized instinctively with both revolutions.

The 'overtaking' of the French Revolution by the Russian Revolution has thus displaced the stress and interest in contemporary historiography from the period of 1789 to the period of 1793, from the founding period of the French Revolution to the Jacobin period; this has had some positive effects upon scholarship: to the extent that for thirty or forty years the stress has been laid on the role of the popular masses in the French Revolution, the subject has become one which is reasonably well studied.

But if this telescoping of the history of the two revolutions has had positive effects, it is nonetheless true that the projection of the vision of 1917 upon the narration of the events of 1789 has been the source, at the interpretative level, of grave inconveniences. In the first place a simplified and simplifying Marxism has taken the place of the sometimes contradictory but valuable analyses of the French Revolution left to us by Marx and Engels themselves. There is often in this history, as it has been written after the Bolshevik Revolution, a sort of linear perspective in which the bourgeois revolution, rallying behind it the peasantry and the urban popular masses, enables the transition from the feudal 'mode of production' to the capitalist 'mode of production' to be made. In this interpretation, the dictatorship of the Mountain is singled out as the most popular episode in the process, and is endowed at the same time with the most progressive significance, namely that of accomplishing through war and terror the tasks assigned previously to the bourgeois revolution as well as the task of announcing the liberations to come, notably the Russian Revolution. As a result, the French Revolution was pushed more and more out of kilter in relation to its own chronological reality, drawn from 1789 towards 1793, then suddenly interrupted at the moment of Robespierre's fall, without anyone realizing the inherent contradictions in calling a historical process a 'bourgeois revolution' and in bringing it to an end just when its nonbourgeois period had ceased and its bourgeois period had reached its culmination.

If these contradictions, to which I shall return, in a history which has become a sort of lay teleology dominated by two successive visions which overlap each other, if these contradictions are not more often perceived, this is surely because the history of the French Revolution is not merely something to be studied or an academic discipline: it has also social significance. What gives it its pre-eminent status among all the other subjects in French history is less the discussion of a Marxist schema – which is a kind of feedback from the Soviet revolution – than a far more powerful, political and emotional appeal which is nothing less than the interpretation of the French Revolution through itself, at once as the keystone of a great nation and as the liberator of universal society.

The history of a founding event is for every collectivity a ceremony, a commemoration of its origins as well as an understanding of its meaning and as everyone knows, the magic of commemorations is created more by the quarrels of the heirs over the legacy than by any critical discussion of the inheritance. There are royalist commemorations in which the misfortunes of the king, the loss of legitimacy are mourned. There are bourgeois commemorations in which, on the contrary, the new national contract of 1789 is celebrated. There are revolutionary commemorations which stress the dynamic of the founding event and the promises it brings with it of a more egalitarian future. But no matter what the nature of the commemoration, behind these quarrels over the legacy, the heirs share the same vision, the same reference back to the origins. In this sense, it is probably inevitable that every history of the Revolution should be up to a point a commemoration. But I would suggest that if it is not possible to reduce completely the Shamanistic part in every history of the Revolution, it has become absolutely necessary for the historian to preserve an acute awareness of it and to try to reduce or to control it, in making as clear as possible his own intellectual standpoint as well as the problems with which he is trying to deal, through this mass of events of every kind which is called the French Revolution.

In order to illustrate and to develop my argument, I shall start with the work of Tocqueville which I shall use to test one of the fundamental concepts which the French Revolution has given rise to and which in consequence dominates its whole history: this is the concept of the 'before' and the 'after,' separated by a radical break.

If the revolutionary conscience can be defined by an idea, it is indeed this one: the Revolution severed the web of history between an old and a new, a before and an after; this is what I have called the zero point. The men who made the Revolution felt that by their action something was irretrievably destroyed and that something new was set in its place or, as Goethe said at Valmy, a new era had begun. The revolutionary world was characterized in fact by an exceptional mobilization of the habitually inert social forces and by a highly developed ideological capital in politics. If I use the expression 'ideology' here, it is to express two ideas: first of all that all the intellectual, moral, and social problems of mankind had become politicized and that, therefore, there was no human misfortune that could not be blamed on politics. Second, that the revolutionary militants identified their lives with the defense of their ideas, and there was thus an essential intolerance in the revolutionary ideology similar to that of religious ideology in its heyday. In other words, politics has become for the revolutionary conscience the realm of good and evil of the old and the new. It is politics that draws the dividing line between the good and the bad, the patriots and the counter-revolutionaries, thus creating a historical universe which is entirely new compared with the 'normal' periods in history.

Now it is this awareness, this revolutionary ideology which, since 1789, had defined what the Revolution had brought to an end: the Ancien Régime has since become a central concept in our national historiography; it feeds our textbooks; it is the cornerstone of our chronological constructs. The Ancien Régime is the before, marked by the minus sign of what has been destroyed: the Revolution is the 'after,' the new, the point of the break, the take-off of a new history.

This spontaneous conception of the revolutionary ideology cannot, however, be that of the historian, since the craft of a historian consists in dominating the whole of temporal continuity; but it can influence him and cause him to overestimate the part played by the break and by the new in the revolutionary phenomenon. It is here that the work of Tocqueville remains very actual because it is characterized by a critique of the revolutionary phenomenon, by a critique of what can be called the illusion of the Revolution about itself. What Tocqueville said to his contemporaries was: 'The Revolution was not the beginning of a new history of France: it is the flowering of our past.' You know the argument. At the heart of this analysis there lies the problem of the formation of the centralized state and of the domination of the communities and the civil societies by that state. Taking this as his starting point, Tocqueville shows that the Revolution was the crowning point of the work of the kings of France and that Robespierre and even more Bonaparte were the true heirs of Louis XI and Louis XIV. The Revolution therefore did not represent a break but, on the contrary a continuity, contrary to its own idea of itself.

Tocqueville's interpretation could be extended to fields other than that of state, for example to the foreign policy of the Revolution which multiplied, magnified, dramatized, but which in the end espoused the great conflicts of the French kings. One can equally show without difficulty to what extent the Revolution was the heir of the Ancien Régime in the realm of thought: it preserved for example the superstitious belief in military values, in honor and glory, which are values typical of nobility, values which the Revolution democratized but without changing their significance. This appeared clearly under the Empire: the post-revolutionary army, formerly the monopoly of the nobility, became the arena for the promotion of commoners. But in both cases, the army remained *par excellence* the bearer of the highest social prestige. In other words, the Revolution changed everything but by preserving everything.

But I want to limit myself to the central point in Tocqueville's analysis in which he suggests that the main characteristic of the French Revolution was the strengthening of the domination of society by the administrative state. Tocqueville starts in fact from the premise of what I call the Revolution as process or the Revolution as balance-sheet (in contrast with the Revolution as event) and this process is one of continuity: the Revolution extends, consolidates and perfects the twinned pair which was in his eyes the administrative state and the egalitarian society of France and which had both been developed characteristically by the monarchy. Therefore, if one takes seriously, as one should, this historical judgment, there is a complete divorce between the objective history of the Revolution, its significance or its balance-sheet and the awareness which the actors in the Revolution had of their own action. They thought that they were breaking with the past, while in reality they were bringing it to fruition; in holding up to obloquy the despotism of Louis XIV, they were preparing the triumph of Bonaparte. In other words, how can one think simultaneously of the Revolution as a radical rupture and as an essential continuity? What kind of process of continuity is it which takes the road of revolution?

There is at least one aspect from which this apparent paradox is not difficult to understand. It is that of the objective process through which the Revolution, by destroying the traditional forms of the former society, creates the conditions for the omnipotence of the centralized state. In fact, the society of the Ancien Régime neglected the individual; it recognized only the *corps*, such as the orders, the corporations, the associations around the possession of a profession or an office, the communities of people, etc. This explains why what we call the Ancien Régime worked by means of a perpetual process of bargaining – especially fiscal bargaining – between the central state in the hands of bureaucracy at Versailles and society, organized into *corps* and communities, resisting the encroachment of the absolute monarchy in the name of its 'privileges,' that is, of its traditional liberties. Now the Revolution realized in practice the simplifying promise of the philosophy of the eighteenth century: it destroyed all the *corps* root and branch in order to leave only individuals confronting the state under the name of citizens, whose task it now was to renegotiate a new social contract, based on their rights. Hence the opportunity (which does not mean the necessity) for the state to extend its powers and its control over society. Already Mirabeau, in his secret letters to the court in 1790 and 1791, was advising Louis XVI to draw strength from the destruction created by the Revolution and to build up a stronger state than the former one, a state which he called the 'national monarchy.' What! said he to the king of the Ancien Régime, you no longer have any nobility, clergy, or Parliament, nor any of those *corps* which spent their time in defying your authority and yet you complain. You should, on the contrary, take advantage of these circumstances to realize the dream of your ancestors and establish at least a really strong royal authority, which would be the monarchy of the Revolution. As it happened, ten years later, Bonaparte was to follow his advice.

But if the process by which the Revolution created the conditions for the increased power of the administrative state is relatively easy to analyze, that process was nevertheless the embodiment of the exact opposite of what the revolutionaries had wanted to do and had believed that they had done: that is, to free the individual from despotism and to give him back his liberty with his rights. Now, Tocqueville says almost nothing about this second aspect of the revolutionary paradox. He was obsessed by the analysis of the causes and of the effects, and he never analyzed – or had time to analyze – what had actually taken place between the causes and the effects, between 1789 and 1799. This was quite simply the French Revolution as an event, as the event which, on the contrary, embodied the radical will to extirpate the past.

There are in the third volume of *L'Ancien Régime* some answers to these questions, such as the replacement of the politicians by the intellectuals in eighteenth-century France or the spread throughout all classes of society of a democratic state of mind: but the extraordinary dynamism of the egalitarian ideology in the years 1789–93 remains for Tocqueville a kind of sacrament of evil, a kind of inverted religion. Nowhere in his work is there any conceptual connexion between his theory of the French Revolution and revolutionary action, as it was experienced, in the way characteristic of the period – as, for example, the Jacobin phenomenon. Tocqueville makes us wonder if one can ever establish such a connexion; he forces us to disconnect, at least for a while, the two parts of this confused amalgam which makes up the 'history of the Revolution' and to cease juxtaposing the analysis of homogeneous discourse, the one following from the other.

This is not only because these 'events', which are of a political and ideological nature, could not be causally analyzed in terms of economic or social contradiction. It is because even if conducted on the level of the political system and its legitimacy, such an analysis could not take into account what was radically new in the speedy development of the Revolution. There is in the concept of revolution, taken in this sense, something which belongs only to its history as it was lived and which does not conform to the logical sequence of cause and effect: this is the appearance on the stage of history of a practical and ideological mode of action which differs entirely from everything which went before. A given type of political crisis renders this mode possible but not necessary and the revolt itself does not offer any precedent since it is by definition part and parcel of the old political and cultural system.

There is, thus, in the French Revolution a new type of historical praxis and conscience which are linked to a type of situation but are not defined by it. It is this ensemble which must be explained in detail if one wants to interpret rather than to proceed as though the revolutionary conscience, the normal product of legitimate discontent, was the most natural thing in human history. In fact, the Marxist popular interpretation of the history of the French Revolution turns the world upside down: it situates the revolutionary break on the economic and social level while nothing more resembles French society under Louis XVI than that same society under Louis-Philippe. And as that interpretation is at one with the revolutionary conscience and shares its illusions and values, it is unable to see what is most radically new and mysterious in the French Revolution and, on the contrary, perceives it as a normal product of circumstances and a natural chapter in the history of the oppressed. For neither capitalism nor the bourgeoisie had any need for revolutions in order to appear in and to dominate the history of the major European countries in the nineteenth century. But France is the country which, through the Revolution, invented democratic culture, and which revealed to the world one of the fundamental meanings of historical action.

Let us first look at the circumstances. What matters here is not the problem of poverty or of oppression, but the problem of the relation between freedom on the social plane and on the political plane. If the Revolution was invention, dis-equilibrium, if it set in motion so many unexpected forces that the traditional mechanisms of politics were transformed thereby, it was because the Revolution took over an empty space or rather that it proliferated in the hitherto forbidden and suddenly conquered sphere of power. In this dialogue between the societies and their states, which is one of the most profound threads of history, every-thing, because of the Revolution, tilts towards society and away from the state. For the Revolution mobilized society and disarmed the state: this is an exceptional situation which opens up for society a field of action which is nearly always barred to it. From 1787 the kingdom of France was a society without a state. Louis XVI continued to gather around his person the consensus of his subjects, but behind his façade of tradition, there was confusion within the gates; the royal authority, nominally respected, no longer extended its legitimacy over its agents. 'The King had bad Ministers, perfidious advisers, evil *intendants*.' It had not yet been realized that the meaning of this perennial refrain of the monarchy when times were hard was no longer to exalt the royal authority, but to institute the control of the citizens. It was a way of saying that civil society, in which the example is set by those above to those below, freed itself from the symbolic power of the state at the same time as from its rules.

The year 1789 arrived: for the highest nobleman as for the humblest peasant the 'revolution' was born at the coming together of several series of events, very different in kind, since an economic crisis (itself complex, being at once agricultural and 'industrial,' meteorological and social) emerged alongside the political crisis which had existed openly since 1787. It is in this coming together of a heterogeneous series of events which gave unpredictability to the situation, a situation which, viewed retrospectively in the light of the illusions of spring 1789, was to be transformed into a necessary consequence of the bad government of men and hence as the stake in the struggle between the patriots and the aristocrats. For the revolutionary situation is not characterized solely by this power vacuum into which the new forces swept and by the 'free' activity of the social body. The revolutionary situation is inseparable from a kind of hypertrophy of the historical conscience and from a system of symbols shared among the social actors. From 1789, the revolutionary conscience was the illusion of conquering a state which no longer existed in the name of a coalition of well-meaning people and forces which prefigured the future. From the beginning, the revolutionary conscience constantly outbid real history on behalf of an idea, as if its function was to reconstruct through the imagination the whole social edifice which had fallen to pieces. The outcry against repression began when that repression collapsed. The Revolution was the historical interlude which separated one power from another power and in which the concept of human action in history replaced what existed.

In this unforeseeable and accelerated drifting, this concept of human action borrows its aims from the reverse of the traditional principles of the social order. The Ancien Régime was in the hands of the king, the Revolution was the accomplishment of the people. The old France was a kingdom of subjects, the new France was a nation of citizens. The old society was one of privilege, the Revolution established equality. There developed an ideology of the radical break with the past, a formidable cultural dynamism of equality. Everything from then – economy, society, politics – bent to the impetus of ideology and of the militants who were its bearers; every line, every institution was merely provisional, faced with this unimpeded torrent.

The word ideology is used here to describe two things which I think form the bedrock of the revolutionary conscience. First of all, that all individual problems, all moral or intellectual problems have become political and there is no human misfortune which is not susceptible to a political solution. Then, to the extent that everything can be known and everything can be transformed, action depends on knowledge and ethics; the revolutionary militants therefore identified their private lives with their public life and with the defense of their ideas; this was a formidable logic which reconstituted in a secular form the psychological certainties of religious belief. If politics had become the realm of what was true and what was false, if it was politics that drew the line separating the good from the bad, then we are faced by a historical universe with an entirely new dynamic. As Marx saw clearly in his early works, the Revolution embodies the illusion of politics: it transforms that which has been experienced into that of which one is conscious. It ushered in a world in which every social change could be imputed to known living forces, with their parts to play; like mythical thought, it clothed the objective universe in subjective wills, in those who were either responsible agents or scapegoats according to the standpoint. Action no longer met with obstacles or restrictions, but only with adversaries, preferably traitors; by the frequency of these mental images one recognizes the moral universe which characterizes the revolutionary explosion.

Freed from the bonds of the state and from the constraint of the sovereign power which were masking its disintegration, society re-formed itself on the ideological plane. This world populated by wills, which recognized only the faithful or the enemy, possessed an incomparable capacity for integration. It opened up what has since been called 'politics,' namely a language at once common and contradictory of debates and action revolving around the issue of power. Not that, naturally, the French Revolution invented politics as an autonomous realm of knowledge: to take only Christian Europe, the theory of political action as such dates from Machiavelli, and learned discussion on the historical origins of social institutions was at its height in the seventeenth century.

But the example of the English Revolution shows that the spiritual background or collective mobilization and activity remained religious. What the French launched at the end of the eighteenth century was not politics as the secular and distinct field of critical reflection, but democratic politics as a national ideology. The secret, the message, the radiance of 1789 lies in this discovery which had no precedent and was to have such vast consequences. And if, out of all the traits which, although they are separated by a hundred years in time, are common to the English Revolution and the French Revolution, there is not one which could give the former the role of a universal model which the second has played since it first appeared on the stage of history, it is precisely because what was missing in Cromwell's Commonwealth, all wrapped as it was in religion and frozen in the return to before the Fall, was what transforms Robespierre's language into the prophecy of new times: democratic politics, which had become the arbiter of the destiny of men and of peoples.

The expression 'democratic politics' does not mean here the collection of rules or procedures destined to organize the working of the public authorities starting from the electoral consultation of the citizens. It describes a system of beliefs which constitutes the new legitimacy, born of the Revolution, and according to which 'the people,' in order to establish the liberty and the equality which are the aims of collective action, must break the resistance of its enemies. Politics, having become the supreme method by which these values are achieved and the inevitable test of wills, good or bad, has only one public actor, who incarnates these values and whose enemies are hidden, since their design cannot be avowed. The 'people' is defined by its goals, and is an amorphous mass of the well intentioned. It is through this oblique approach, which excludes representation, that the revolutionary conscience reconstructs an imaginary society in the name of and starting from, the individual will. This is also how it solves the great dilemma of the eighteenth century which was to think of the social in terms of the individual. If the individual is to be defined in terms of the aims of his political action, it is enough for these aims to be as simple as those of ethics, for the Revolution to be able to found both a language and a society, or rather to found a society through a language: what is called a nation. This was the Feast of the Federation.

This type of analysis has the double advantage of restoring to the French Revolution its most obvious dimension, which is of a political nature, and to place at the centre of our reflections the true solution of continuity by which it separates the before and the after, that of legitimation and the staging of historical action. The action of the sans-culottes of 1793 was not important because it was the action of a 'popular' social group (impossible by the way to define in socio-economic terms) but because it expressed in its chemically pure state that revolutionary staging of political action, the obsession with betrayal and plot, the rejection of representation, the will to punish, etc. And nothing enables us or will ever enable us to explain those dramatizations starting from a social situation, made up of contradictory interests. It seems to me that the first task of revolutionary historiography is to rediscover the analysis of the political as such. But the price to be paid is twofold: we must, on the one hand, stop seeing the revolutionary conscience as a quasi 'natural' product of oppression and discontent; and on the other hand we have also to conceptualize this strange 'child' – at least in a chronological sense – of philosophy.

Thus in order to write the page left blank by Tocqueville on the period which runs from 1789 to 1799, between the origins of the Revolution and its outcome, the period which was the Revolution itself, any historical reflection must inevitably embark on an analysis that Tocqueville himself never undertook, of what constituted the specificity of the revolutionary phenomenon and of its radical novelty in the history of the world, namely the torrential birth of democratic politics and ideology. The French Revolution is the period in which social and political legitimacy suddenly tilted away from the divine right of kings towards the sovereignty of the people and in which society as a whole was continually reformed by the permanent celebration of the democratic contract in the name of the will of the people.

If this system of beliefs excludes the normal functioning of a representative regime, it is because the French of that period experienced collectively the paradox of democracy explored by Rousseau: there can be no intermediate structure, in terms of the representation of the citizens, between the general will and the individual wills which go to make the former. Because a disposition of this kind, by transferring some wills to others by the mechanism of the delegation of sovereignty, would establish a screen of particular interests which would shatter the balance necessary between the liberty of the individual and his subordination to the law. In order to be free and to found a free people, each citizen should at all times take part in the formation of the general will.

The practical experience of this logical impasse of democracy is to be found in the conception that the French Revolution held of power, and more generally of politics: power, which had at all times to reflect the people and to absorb symbolically in this identification the whole of the social sphere. This explains, moreover, not only a phenomenon like the Terror, the role of which is symbolically to re-establish this identity of power and people by means of the punishment/expulsion of plotters, and the villains. But above all this experience of 'pure' democracy which absorbs power and society into the same abstract vision of the people, restores, without knowing it is doing so and by reversing it, the image of the old monarchical power, that of the 'absolute' king. In the old society, the seat of power was occupied by divine right by the king: it was never vacant except at the price of an act which was both heretical and criminal; the king was the owner of society, encompassing it completely and embodying the people. The Revolution exorcised the curse which surrounded this incarnate monarchy by means of an inverted consecration: it was no longer power which was the people – it was the people which was the power. Here is where we discover, at the level of imaginary symbolism, the secret of what Tocqueville had perceived at the level of objective processes: if the Revolution succeeded in establishing an administrative state infinitely stronger than the monarchy of Louis XIV, it was because it carried in it and with it an image of 'absolute' power: in other words, it absorbed society in the name of the people. This is the reverse side of the image of Ancien Régime – it places the people in the place of the king – which is what gives the whole dimension to the revolutionary break. But that image also subordinates the social to the symbolic representation of the state, which explains why 'pure democracy' was finally embodied in a king of democracy: Robespierre and then Bonaparte.

Pure democracy culminated in the government of the Terror. And if Bonaparte was able "to put an end" to the Revolution, it was because he himself is the plebiscitary version of the Revolution: that is to say, the form discovered, at last, by which society establishes a power which derives everything from itself and yet remains independent of it and above it, like the Terror, but which offers to a new king what it had looked for in vain since 1789, since it was a contradiction in terms: the possibility of a democratic administration. The Revolution had come to an end because France had rediscovered its history, or rather had reconciled its two histories.

To understand this, one has only to agree to consider the Revolution in its conceptual centre, and not to dilute it in a vague evolutionism designed to dignify even more the virtues of the actors. The originality of contemporary France is not that it passed from an absolute monarchy to a representative regime or from the world of the nobility to bourgeois society: Europe took the same path without revolution and without Jacobins – even though events in France were able here and there to accelerate the evolution and to provide the model for its imitators. But the French Revolution was not a transition – it was a beginning and an original vision. This is what is unique in the French Revolution and gives it its historical interest; and it is this uniqueness which has become universal: the first experience of democracy.

Source Reprinted from *Government and Opposition*, 16:2 (Spring 1981): 200–18. Given as the first *Government and Opposition* public lecture at the London School of Economics and Political Science on 4 December 1980.

4

CONSTITUTION

Keith M. Baker

"Which is to say that, in the long run, it was opting for the Terror." With this now-classic line, Keith Baker dramatically ends this brilliant article on the making of the French Constitution of 1791. What does it mean to say that by September 1789, the members of the Constituent Assembly were "opting for the Terror?" It seems to suggest, in line with many revisionists, that the Terror was not an aberrant phase of the Revolution, brought about by war and other domestic problems, but rather, the Terror was the result of a logic set in place at the start of the Revolution – that the Terror was essential to the Revolution, rather than a moment in 1793 when the Revolution went off-track. Baker would insist that his claim is not deterministic – "opting" involved choice making, and there was nothing inevitable about the road to terror. At any point between 1789 and 1793, the deputies might have reversed themselves by choosing differently. Equally controversial to historians, Baker believes that the significance of what the deputies did lies not only in actual policy making, but equally in how the deputies chose to think about politics at all. In choosing among available discursive approaches to constitution making, the deputies were defining how they and their successors would think about politics and frame political issues, thus setting parameters that would affect policy making later in the Revolution. Baker's approach highlights the importance of the language used by political leaders in the debates surrounding important constitutional issues.

* * *

Between revolution and constitution there was, at the beginning, a fundamental link. Barely had it declared itself representative of the sovereign nation than the National Assembly, insisting that it was "called upon to fix the constitution of the realm, carry out regeneration of the public order, and maintain the true principles of monarchy," swore in the Tennis Court Oath to remain assembled "until the constitution of the realm is established and consolidated on a firm foundation." With this bold act of defiance against royal authority, a dramatic condensation of several decades' protests against arbitrary government and ministerial despotism, the Assembly defined the achievement of a settled constitutional order as the essential purpose of its revolutionary actions. Yet the task of "fixing" the French constitution was to prove an extraordinarily problematic one. Unlike the American Revolution, which effectively translated the assertion of revolutionary will into the establishment of a stable constitutional order, the French Revolution opened a widening gap between revolution and constitution, effectively resisting successive efforts to bring the revolutionary movement to its constitutional completion. It is impossible in these brief pages to follow the vicissitudes of that entire series of constitutions drafted, adopted, suspended, implemented, and subverted in France during the decade separating the Tennis Court Oath from the moment in 1799 when Napoleon Bonaparte, laying yet another constitution before the French people, once again declared the French Revolution ended. Instead, this article considers the uncertainty of the idea of constitution on the eve of the Revolution, the radical definition that the theorists of 1789 gave to the term, and the implications of this definition for the revolutionary dynamic.

* * *

What did it mean to "fix" the constitution of the realm? Despite the resolution with which it was taken, the Tennis Court Oath was not without its ambiguities. Certainly, it announced an end to despotic government, the substitution of a stable and predictable legal order for the disorder and uncertainty resulting from the tyrannical exercise of arbitrary will. But since a constitution was by definition something fixed and stable, the phrase *fixer la constitution* was a pleonasm, rather like talking of rounding a circle. If there was a constitution of the realm, it was fixed by definition; if it was not fixed, it was of necessity not a constitution. Thus to speak of "fixing" the constitution in this way left an essential problem: did it imply the existence of a constitution to be preserved and defended, or the absence of a constitution still to be created? On this question, the deputies to the Estates General remained divided, as did the *cahiers* they brought to Versailles. In referring to a constitution in the weeks preceding the Tennis Court Oath, deputies of the nobility, disagreeing among themselves, had used such verbs as *établir, rétablir, maintenir, se donner;* those of the Third Estate such verbs as *asseoir, donner poser* [*les bases*], *faire, faire entrer dans.* In relationship to these terms, however, the *fixer* of the Tennis Court Oath remained relatively unfixed: it could be understood equally well in the conservative sense of *rétablir* or *maintenir* (implying the existence of a constitution to be preserved and strengthened) or in the more radical sense of *établir, se donner,* or *faire* (implying the absence of a constitution that still remained to be created).

Thus the Tennis Court Oath left undecided, and for the National Assembly still to resolve, the central political question of the prerevolutionary decades: the existence, or nonexistence, of a traditional constitution of the monarchy. The issue had been clearly joined since the constitutional conflicts of the 1750s and 1760s, when parlementary theorists, following the lead of the redoubtable Le Paige in his *Lettres historiques,* had countered ministerial despotism by an appeal to the existence of a traditional monarchical constitution in which the arbitrary exercise of royal authority was prevented by fundamental laws and by the juridical responsibility of the magistrates for the registration and verification of royal edicts. In contesting this view, no voice was more powerful than that of Mably, whose historical refutation of parlementary theory exploded all claims to the existence of an enduring constitutional order, and revealed instead a domain of instability and revolutions alternating between anarchy and despotism. The lesson of this account of French history became explicit in the second volume of Mably's *Observations sur l'histoire de France*, completed in the context of the Maupeou coup and published at the height of the prerevolutionary debate over the convocation of the Estates General: the French lacked a constitution because they had yet to exercise the sustained political will necessary to fix the form of their political existence and preserve their liberty.

The political debate joined by Le Paige and Mably echoed throughout the prerevolutionary pamphlets, as the conflicts over the nature and limitations of royal power that forced the calling of the Estates General were intensified by new contestations over the mode of composition and the procedures of that body. In this new debate, political passions were fueled by yet another ambiguity still remaining in eighteenth-century uses of the term "constitution." For those who now insisted that France still lacked a constitution tended to emphasize the need for a settled order of government limiting the arbitrary exercise of power, while those who appealed to an established constitution used the term to include the necessary existence of a social order constituted by the division of orders and estates (and hence their separate and equal representation in the Estates General). Sieyès played on this ambiguity very effectively in *Qu'est-ce que le Tiers Etat?* "Six months ago . . . there was only one cry in France: we had no constitution, and we asked to create one. Today we not only have a constitution, but, if we believe the privileged, it contains two excellent and impregnable provisions. The first is the division of citizens by orders; the second is the equality of influence of each order in the formation of the national will."

What then was a constitution? Throughout the eighteenth century, the dictionaries hesitated between two general senses of the term. The first emphasized the activity of institution and establishment, as in the original use of the term in Roman and canon law to mean the laws and ordinances of emperors or popes, kings or ecclesiastical superiors, or an act like the constitution of a rente or dowry. The second emphasized the order of existence of an entity, its arrangement, mode of being, or disposition, as in the constitution of the world or the constitution of the human body. Apart from the usages deriving from Roman law, specifically political definitions of the term appeared relatively late in the laggard dictionaries. But this same ambiguity between institution and order also reappeared among the political writers upon whom the dictionaries were eventually to draw. Montesquieu, adopting English usage, gave the term "constitution" a new centrality in eighteenth-century political understanding, but he did so by emphasizing its reference to the order of existence of an entity – its arrangement, mode of being, or disposition – rather than to an act of establishment or institution that brought it into being. With *De l'esprit des lois*, "constitution" stood as the modern equivalent of the Aristotelian *politeia*, the indispensable term to describe the fundamental order of a state, the mode of political existence of a nation or people, the essential disposition of the elements or powers composing a form of government. With Montesquieu, too, England became the *locus classicus* of constitutional discussion, the test case for an ideal of a political order as a fixed, enduring structure (stable though not necessarily fixed in writing) in which the forms and functions of the constituent parts were clearly delimited and distributed for the preservation of liberty. In this respect, Montesquieu's analysis of English government – subsequently reworked by such authors as Delolme, Blackstone, and John Adams – was to provide a powerful model for the constitutional committee appointed by the National Assembly in 1789.

But could such a model be imitated? Could one nation indeed adopt a version of another's constitution? Such questions required a shift in the semantic register of the term "constitution" from its meaning as an existing order to its meaning as an act of institution or establishment. Their answers required further clarification of the relationship between the idea of the constitution of a state, the constitution of a people, society or nation, and the constitution of a government: notions that Montesquieu had continued to invoke quite indiscriminately. In both these respects, the essential arguments came from the theorists of the school of *droit naturel*, most notably Vattel and (in this respect) Rousseau.

In his *Droit des gens* (1758) Vattel offered a clear definition of a constitution as the form of government instituted by a society or nation to secure the advantages of political association, from which it followed that "the nation has every right to form its own constitution, to maintain it, to perfect it, and to regulate as it wishes everything that has to do with government, and no one may justly prevent it from doing so." This language soon appeared in other influential works, including the Swiss edition of the *Encyclopédie* edited by Barthélemy de Félice, and the section of the *Encyclopédie méthodique* devoted to political economy and diplomacy, edited by Jean-Nicolas Demeunier (later to play an active part in the constitutional debates of the National Assembly). But a far more radical elaboration upon Vattel's argument occurs in Rousseau's *Social Contract*, with its insistence on the theory of the general will and its fundamental distinction between sovereignty and government.

Rejecting the naturalistic implications of the traditional analogy between the constitution of the human body and the constitution of the state, the *Social Contract* emphasizes that if the former is the work of nature, the latter is the work of art. It is a political contrivance entirely contingent upon the will of the nation, an act of institution by which a sovereign people creates its particular form of government. Nor is this act of institution adequately accomplished once and for all. The constitution once fixed by the decision of "the people assembled," Rousseau argues, the sovereign body must nevertheless reassemble at regular intervals to manifest its force and presence. At such moments, in the immediate presence of the supreme political being, the effects of the constitution are suspended: "The moment the people is legitimately assembled in sovereign body, all jurisdiction of the government ceases: the executive power is suspended, and the person of the last citizen is as sacred and inviolable as that of the first magistrate, because the represented is found, there is no longer a representative." It followed from this argument that the constitution of the state depends not only on an original act of institution but on a perpetual reaffirmation of that act. Since "there is no fundamental law in the state that cannot be revoked, not even the social pact," the constitution remains in force only as the direct expression of the general will.

The implications of this radical voluntarism were made abundantly clear by Sieyès in *Qu'est-ce que le Tiers Etat?* Sieyès destroyed the traditional meaning of "constitution" in the sense of a necessarily existing social and political order inherent in the very nature of things, and gave powerful force to its meaning in the sense of the institution of a government. In repudiating the arguments of the privileged for a traditional constitution, Sieyès posited the existence of the nation as an ultimate political reality, immediately present, and prior to any constitutional form. "The nation exists before anything else. It is at the origin of everything else. Its will is always legal; it is the law itself." This political reality being the case, it was impossible to suppose the nation bound by existing social or political arrangements in the name of a prior constitution. "A nation is independent of any form. And however it may will, it is enough that its will appear for all positive law to end before it as before the source and the supreme master of all positive law." Powerful words against those who would defend a traditional constitution of the French monarchy, but no less dangerous for those who would establish a new constitution on secure foundations. The revolutionaries were to find that the implications of the conception of national sovereignty required to destroy an old order could not be contained in defense of the new. Sieyès inscribed a conceptual space between revolution and constitution, even before either had been achieved.

* * *

A constitution to be restored or a constitution to be created? The division over this matter, found in the mandates the deputies had brought to Versailles, was made clear to the Assembly by Clermont-Tonnerre, reporting on behalf of its constitutional committee, on July 27, 1789. "Our constituents want regeneration of the state. But some expected that it would come about through simple reform of abuses and reestablishment of a constitution that has existed for fourteen centuries. . . . Others have looked upon the existing social regime as so defective that they demanded a new constitution, and, with the exception of the monarchical government and forms, which every Frenchman cherishes and respects in his heart . . . they have given you all the powers necessary to create a constitution." Following a strategy proposed by Mounier, the committee sought to minimize these differences by emphasizing on the one hand the traditional devotion of the French to the monarchy as their historically chosen form of government, while on the other pointing to general recognition of the need to perfect the work of history through the institution of a fixed order of government in which the powers would be clearly separated and limited.

This same effort to find a middle ground between competing views also expressed itself in the committee's thinking on the question of a declaration of rights. Clermont-Tonnerre, reporting on the *cahiers*, stated that the demand for such a declaration was the only difference "between the *cahiers* that desire a new constitution and those that call only for reestablishment of what they regard as the existing constitution." Accordingly, the committee proposed a declaration that would precede the constitution in the form of a preamble but would not be published separately; it sought thereby to satisfy demands for a declaration of rights while placating those who feared the consequences of following the American example by enunciating abstract principles of liberty and equality. But when, in the restless early days of August, the Assembly finally came to discuss whether a declaration of rights should precede the constitution, the committee's effort at compromise began its slow but dramatic process of erosion. The debate over the necessity for a declaration of rights drew the line between those who would return to first principles and those who preferred to turn immediately to the "positive law appropriate to a great people, united for fifteen centuries." When, the very day of August 4, the Assembly decided almost unanimously that the constitution would indeed be preceded by a declaration of rights, it took a decisive first step away from the idea of a constitution to be preserved and towards that of a constitution to be created. Furthermore, after the deliberations set in train by the events of the night of August 4, the deputies moved rapidly to draw up a Declaration of the Rights of Man and of the Citizen before turning to the constitution itself. The Assembly would start its constitutional work from first principles.

But what principles? Three articles of the Declaration bore most directly on the task of "fixing" the French constitution. But none was without its ambiguities; nor were they necessarily compatible one with another. The sixteenth, "any society in which rights are not guaranteed and powers are not separated in a definite manner has no constitution," gave moderate expression to the funda-mental prerevolutionary concern to limit the arbitrary exercise of power through the legal protection of rights and the clear separation of powers. If it implied that France had hitherto lacked a constitution in the full sense of the term, it was also consistent with the constitutional committee's proposals to build the ramparts of liberty upon the historical foundations of the ancient monarchy, following the example of the English model. But since it left open the precise definition of the powers to be separated and of the nature of their separation, it was no less compatible with the Rousseauian notion of the division between the legislative and the executive power as a fundamental condition for the exercise of the general will. This latter interpretation, furthermore, was encouraged by the explicitly Rousseauian principle of the sixth article of the Declaration: "The law is the expression of the general will."

Nothing would seem clearer from this latter article than the need to create a constitution that would ensure the direct expression of the general will. But the article presented difficulties in this respect by adding that "all citizens have the right to participate personally or through their representatives in its formation."

How then was this statement of the idea of the general will to be understood, if it admitted the possibility of representation so emphatically denied by Rousseau? Nor was ambiguity on this point dispelled by the less than emphatic declaration of the principle of national sovereignty in article 3 of the Declaration: "The source [*principe*] of all sovereignty resides essentially in the nation. No corps and no individual man exercises authority that does not emanate expressly from it." To assert that the "source" of all sovereignty resided in the nation was not necessarily equivalent to saying that the exercise of sovereignty inhered directly in the nation as such, as Adrien Duquesnoy remarked in his journal: "Article 3 provides that the source of all sovereignty resides in the nation. That is not correct. It should have said: 'All sovereignty resides in the nation.' Indeed, it is clear that if the nation possesses only the source of sovereignty, then there is a sovereignty that is not the nation's and that only emanates from its sovereignty, which is both dangerous and false." The formulation accepted by the Assembly glossed over the considerable difference between the strong, Rousseauian version of the principle of national sovereignty embraced by its more radical members and the weaker one espoused by the moderates led by Mounier (whose language article 3 adopted).

Thus when, in late August and early September 1789, the deputies finally turned to debate the preliminary constitutional articles proposed by its committee, fundamental issues remained unresolved. The Assembly had endorsed the principles of national sovereignty and the general will, but the understanding of these principles remained far from clear; it had defined a constitution as an instrument for the separation of powers, while leaving the precise nature of that separation still undetermined. Furthermore, it had not yet resolved the ambiguity of whether it was "fixing" the French constitution by tempering an existing monarchy or creating a new one on the basis of first principles. Discussing the first constitutional article proposed by the committee – "The French government is a monarchical government" – the deputies found themselves passionately divided not only over the nature of the government that was to be called monarchical in France, but over the nature of their action in making such a statement. For some, it remained true that "when they were sent to the Estates General, they were not told: you will make a new constitution, but you will regenerate the old one. You will not say that you are erecting our government into a monarchical state, but you will confirm our old monarchy." Others insisted that they had been sent, as representatives of a sovereign nation, to exercise the full extent of its constituent power, "to make the constitution." In the famous debates over the royal veto, these issues were finally resolved. Pressed by the protagonists of national sovereignty in the Rousseauian mode, the spokesmen for the constitutional committee lost the middle ground they had sought to maintain since the Assembly's earliest debates on this question. The idea that France possessed a traditional form of government providing at least the elements of a constitution – whose principles could now be reaffirmed, perfected, and fixed in a written document – was finally rejected in favor of a conception of the constitution as created anew by an act of sovereign national will and instituted in accordance with abstract principles of political right. In the process, the ideological dynamic that was to drive subsequent revolutionary events – the insoluble problem of instituting and maintaining a form of government in direct, immediate, and constant relationship to the general will – was given its force.

During these debates, the principal spokesmen for the constitutional committee, Lally-Tollendal and Mounier, sought to hold a middle ground between history and philosophy. To their minds, the revolution meant the regeneration of an existing political order through the destruction of abuses, not the construction of a radically new order of things. They saw the idea that the Assembly had been charged, as a national convention, to exercise the right of the French people to decide its constitution *de novo* as the purest metaphysical nonsense. Such a notion required the absurd conception of the nation as a society existing prior to government, prior to laws, prior to magistrates. Nothing was more alien to their thinking than the idea of the revolution as a new founding moment in which all existing institutions were suspended before the general will; nor could they imagine it as a zero point in time at which society existed prior to, and independent of, its form of government. The National Assembly, they insisted, had been convoked by a king whose authority preceded its own; its members had been enjoined by their mandates to act, in concert with the crown, to preserve the monarchy from degeneration into despotism. Thus the monarch existed and possessed a power anterior to the constitution, and must necessarily remain a party to its establishment: "Being an interested party to the provisions of the constitution, responsible for making certain that they are respected, and possessing a prior power that it must regulate and not destroy, it is necessary that he sign and ratify it." Furthermore, Mounier argued, while the king could not refuse any constitution whatsoever, he could demand changes before giving his consent to the document proposed by the Assembly, thus giving him a historical title to a kind of suspensive royal veto over its establishment as a constitution.

If the committee spokesmen defended their proposals as grounded in the nature of the monarchical government the nation had chosen historically and now charged its deputies to affirm, however, they also justified those proposals as perfecting this inherited form of government in the light of historical experience and practical reason. In their eyes, experience was represented above all by the example of England, clarified by a side glance at recent constitutional choices in America; reason was represented by the arguments of Montesquieu, Blackstone, and Delolme on the one hand, Adams and Livingstone on the other. Taken together, these prototypes suggested that power must necessarily be divided to avoid arbitrariness and abuse; passions must be limited one by another; interests counterbalanced. And they suggested that no power was more dangerous than that of a unitary legislative assembly, which would be constantly subject to passion and caprice, and never bound to respect its own deliberations from one moment to the next. Hence the necessity of a distribution and balance of powers achieved by the existence of a strong executive authority, united in the person of the monarch, and a divided legislative power, shared among the monarch and two houses of representatives. The key to this system was the preservation of an absolute royal veto in matters of legislation. Without it, there would be no guaranteee of a balance between the executive and the legislative power, and no means of resolving disputes between the senate and the house of representatives. Without it, as Mounier maintained, the king would be not an integral part of the legislative body but merely "a magistrate under its orders. . . . The government would be no longer monarchical but republican."

Revealing words. For at the heart of the committee's proposals there lay a profound concern to limit the implications of the principle of national sovereignty announced in the Declaration of the Rights of Man. "I know that the source of sovereignty resides in the nation," Mounier acknowledged. "But to be the source of sovereignty and to exercise sovereignty are very different things." For the committee spokesmen, sovereign power found its source and justification in the nation, and must necessarily be exercised for the benefit of the nation; but it could not be exercised by the nation directly, or in a unitary manner. They saw the balance of powers guaranteed by an absolute royal veto as ensuring government in the interests of the people while preventing the arbitrariness inherent in the tyranny of the multitude. In the last analysis, while they appealed occasionally to the language of the general will, they could only imagine the general will as the end result of a balancing of particular wills. They lacked the fundamental assumption underlying that idea in its Rousseauian formulation, the postulate of a unitary will inhering in the nation by definition, prior to all government.

Nothing seemed more misguided to the principal opponents of the committee's proposals – men like Salle and Pétion, Grégoire, Rabaut Saint-Etienne and Sieyès – than this retreat from the principle of national sovereignty to the language of passions and interests, and of the balance and counterbalance of powers. To call them Rousseauians is not to claim that they invoked Rousseau at every point; explicit references to the citizen of Geneva were rare in these debates. Nor is it to assert that they followed the specific arguments of the *Social Contract* in every particular; according to such a criterion, Rousseau himself could hardly be counted a Rousseauian, since when faced with immediate political problems (as in the *Considérations sur le gouvernement de Pologne*) he himself modified particular arguments – most notably in the matter of representation. But Mounier was not entirely wrong in claiming that opposition to the proposals of the constitutional committee derived from the fact that "we are blindly invoking the maxims of a philosopher who believed that the English were free only when they appointed their representatives, who believed representation to be a kind of servitude." The most telling opponents of the model of the English constitution were Rousseauian in the sense (and to the extent) that they cast the constitutional problems facing the National Assembly in terms of a strong version of the language of the general will. They were Rousseauian in the sense that they demanded the institution of a constitution *de novo*, as a direct expression of the sovereignty of the general will. They were Rousseauian in the sense that they saw the purpose of such a constitution to be ensuring the continuing exercise of national sovereignty on the basis of the general will. And, with the important exception of Sieyès who in this respect drew upon a very different language, they were Rousseauian too in the sense that they saw the relationship between the general will and the practice of representation (unavoidable in a large state) as an essentially problematic one – to which the suspensive royal veto could provide a solution.

Opposition to the proposals of the constitutional committee rested, above all, on giving article 3 of the Declaration of the Rights of Man and Citizen its full Rousseauian meaning. "While granting the principle that sovereignty resides in the nation," Salle insisted, the defenders of the absolute royal veto "take refuge behind the idea that public utility, more imperious than the principle, requires that it be changed; what is more, that it is useful to act on behalf of the French people, because it is not a new people; that it is accustomed to being ruled." For Salle, on the contrary, the French were no longer slaves grown old in their bonds, but a people regenerated through the very act of revolution; they required only good laws to make this regeneration permanent. "The French are today all that they can be." Others among the Rousseauians were convinced that good laws were still necessary to transform subjects into citizens. But whatever their view on this point, it followed from their conception of the revolutionary moment that the idea of requiring any form of royal consent to the constitution was palpably absurd. As a constituted power, the monarchy was to be created anew by the constitution and was not a historical party to its creation – which could only be the work of the National Assembly acting as a constitutional convention endowed by its electors with the constituent power to institute *de novo*. "Charged by our mandates to rejuvenate the constitution or to create a new one on the ruins of the old," Grégoire proclaimed, "we are now exercising the constituent power."

From the perspective of this revolutionary moment, then, little was to be learned from that historical compromise between particular interests that was the English constitution. Having belatedly recovered their liberty, the French now had an advantage denied to the English in their slow search for freedom: that of ordering all the parts of their constitution simultaneously. Philosophical principles, not historical experience, were to be the touchstone of this moment of political choice. 'The history that is all too often invoked is an arsenal where each person finds weapons of every kind," Grégoire insisted. "The multiplicity of facts frequently does not bolster a principle but only demonstrates its violation." And of all these principles, the sovereignty of the general will of the nation was the most fundamental.

For the Rousseauians, national sovereignty did not mean merely that the nation was the ultimate source of all power, but that this power resided directly and inalienably in the general will. Rabaut spoke for many in identifying the two consequences of this strong version of the principle of national sovereignty. The first was the substitution of the Rousseauian dichotomy between sovereign legislative power and delegated executive authority for the balance of powers exemplified in the English model: "What [the sovereign] delegates is execution;

what it keeps is legislation." The second was the insistence on the need for a unitary legislature as the logical expression of a unitary sovereign will. 'The sovereign is a unitary and simple thing, since it is the collection of all without excepting a single one: hence the legislative power is unified and simple. And if the sovereign cannot be divided, legislative power cannot be divided." But this easy equation between a unitary legislature and a unitary national will concealed the fundamental problem posed for the Rousseauians by the necessity of representation in a populous nation: that of assuring (despite the argument of the *Social Contract*) that an elected legislature would indeed express the general will rather than its own corporate interests. Forced to acknowledge that "the decisions of the representatives of the nation may not always be those of the nation itself and that they may be mistaken," the principal Rousseauians in the Assembly opted for the idea of a suspensive royal veto. Understood not as the act of a co-legislator, but as a specific charge laid upon the king in his capacity as executive, the suspensive veto would function as an appeal to the people in cases where the king suspected that the will of the legislature was not identical to the general will. It therefore became the key to the revolutionary reconciliation of national sovereignty and representative government. Fully consistent with "the nature of a government in which sovereignty can only be exercised by proxies," Salle argued, "this right conserves the people's sovereignty without any disadvantage."

Understood in this sense, then, the suspensive veto was simply a mechanism to permit a direct appeal to the people in the primary assemblies – conceived as the ultimate expression of the general will – against the particular will of the representative body. It reflected at once the Rousseauians' acceptance of the necessity for representation in a large state and their continuing distrust of it. But was such a direct appeal to the people feasible? Powerful arguments against it came not only from Mounier, but from none other than Sieyès, the theorist who had perhaps done more than any other to interject Rousseauian notions of national sovereignty into the Assembly's debates. Sieyès was a passionate opponent of any kind of royal veto, be it absolute or suspensive. And he based his opposition to the suspensive veto precisely on the grounds of the incompatibilty of the idea of an appeal to the people with the principle of national sovereignty and the practice of representation.

Because the will of the electors in a *bailliage* is necessarily a particular will in relation to the will of the nation as a whole, Sieyès insisted, it follows that a deputy can never be bound by that particular will in his capacity as representative of the nation. This argument destroyed the case for the suspensive veto by insisting that the legislative decisions of the representatives of the nation could in no way be appealed to the sum of the *bailliages*, understood as constituting the body of the nation as a whole. "I know that by dint of distinctions on the one hand, confusion on the other, some have managed to consider the national wish as if it could be anything other than the wish of the nation's representatives," Sieyès maintained: "As if the nation could speak other than through its representatives. Here false principles become extremely dangerous." Given that direct democracy was impossible in a nation as populous in France, an appeal to the people would necessarily take the form of an appeal to an aggregate of particular communities, rather than to a common body of citizens. The effect would be "nothing less than cutting up, chopping up, tearing up France into an infinity of petty democracies, which would then be united only by the bonds of a general confederation." If France was to remain a single political body possessed of a unitary general will, that will could find expression only in the national assembly. "The people or nation can have only one voice, that of the national legislature. . . . The expression *appeal to the people* is therefore bad, for all that it is uttered in impolitic fashion. The people, I repeat, in a country that is not a democracy (and France cannot possibly be one), the people can speak and act only through its representatives."

In this respect, Sieyès – the only consistent theorist of representation in the assembly – went far beyond the more conventionally Rousseauian view of representative government as, in essence, a *pis aller* – an unavoidable alternative to democracy imposed by the imperious law of numbers in a populous state. In his conception, the unitary character of the general will necessarily implied not merely that the latter could only be expressed in a unitary national assembly, but that it could not even be considered to exist outside that assembly. At the same time, drawing upon a very different language, he also saw the practice of representation as a natural consequence of the division of labor in modern society, a device for the political application of the enlightenment that was one of the benefits of social progress. Since it was a necessary feature of modern society that the great majority of men could be no more than "laboring machines" occupied with their daily labor, it was in the interests of this majority to entrust the work of legislation to those with greater leisure, education and enlightenment, "far more capable than they themselves of knowing the general interest and interpreting their own will in this respect." For Sieyès, this emphasis on differential enlightenment as an essential feature of the theory of representation made the idea of an appeal to the people essentially incoherent. Representatives chosen to exercise a social function on the basis of their superior enlightenment could not make rational decisions if they were constrained to follow the wills of those who had elected them; nor should their enlightened formulation of the general will be appealed back to the sum of the ill-informed and particular wills in the primary assemblies.

Thus the constitutional debates of late August and early September 1789 presented the deputies with three principal choices. They could opt for the perfected historical constitution offered by the spokesmen for the constitutional committee, in which royal authority and national representation were to form mutually limiting principles in a complex system of the balance of powers. Or they could institute the radically new constitution offered by the Rousseauians on the basis of the principle of national sovereignty, with its radical division between a unitary legislative assembly and the subordinate executive authority placed in the crown, and its emphasis on the suspensive veto as the key to the reconciliation of the theory of the general will with the practice of representation.

Or they could implement the variant upon that new constitution proposed by Sieyès, a constitution also instituted *de novo* by an act of national sovereignty, but one that placed ultimate expression of the general will not in an appeal to the will of the people in the primary assemblies but in the rational deliberation of the unitary representative body. In the stormy votes of mid-September that concluded these fundamental and impassioned debates, Sieyès' arguments against the suspensive veto proved to be no more compelling than Mounier's for the absolute veto. The Assembly repudiated the constitutional committee's recommendations for a dispersion and balance of powers maintained by an absolute royal veto, in favor of a unitary legislative body, a subordinate executive authority exercised by the crown, and a suspensive royal veto. The consequences of these decisions for the nature and dynamics of the French Revolution were momentous.

* * *

A first implication of these constitutional choices of mid-September 1789 was that the Assembly opted for the radical, Rousseauian definition of the constitution as a formal organization of the organs and functions of government created *de novo* by an act of sovereign will. If, indeed, there was any remaining doubt on that matter, it was soon dispelled by the events of the October Days, which definitively resolved the issue of whether a form of royal consent was necessary for the constitution itself. Pressed by the Assembly on October 1 to accept the Declaration of Rights and the constitutional articles so far decided, Louis XVI replied on October 5 by according his "accession" – not his "acceptance" – only on the strict condition that the constitution, once completed, would preserve the full force of executive power in the hands of the monarch. This conditional response proved less than satisfactory – even "ambiguous and insidious" – to many deputies, who argued that in reserving the possibility that the king might subsequently modify or refuse – hence even destroy – the constitution, it threatened to subvert liberty, restore despotism, and annihilate the very principle of national sovereignty. "The king's response is destructive not only of the whole constitution but, even more, of the national right to have a constitution," insisted Robespierre; "He who can impose a condition on a constitution has the right to prevent that constitution. He is placing his will above the nation's right." Pétion in his turn reiterated the supremacy of the constituent over the constituted power by repudiating any lingering notion of the constitution as a reciprocal pact between king and nation: "They say that there is a social contract between the king and the nation. I deny the principle. The king cannot govern according to laws presented to him by the nation." Convinced by these arguments, the Assembly voted – immediately before a deputation of women marching from Paris appeared in its midst – to require the king to give the constitutional articles his "pure and simple assent." Carried to the château, with the women's demand for bread, by a combined deputation of representatives and marchers, the Assembly's demand was accepted by Louis XVI that very evening, under the threat of popular violence. Though it took almost two years for the Constituent Assembly to complete its work, the essence of the constitutional revolution was accomplished. Louis XVI, his new designation decided by the Assembly three days later, became not only "by the grace of God," but "by the constitutional law of the state, king of the French." From fixing the forms of a traditional monarchical constitution, the Constituent Assembly had moved to the decisive act of creating a constitutional monarchy instituted and organized on the basis of the principle of national sovereignty.

But if a constitution could be created anew in accordance with the principle of national sovereignty, could it not also be abolished and replaced on the same basis? And if popular action could force the acceptance of constitutional principles in the name of the nation, could it not also force their revision or repudiation once accepted? This possibility was a principal concern of a majority of the deputies almost two years later when, in the anti-popular mood that prevailed in the months following the king's flight to Varennes and the Champ de Mars Massacre, the Assembly decided upon the forms for subsequent constitutional change. While the Assembly declared in the Constitution of 1791 that 'the nation has the imprescriptible right to change its constitution," it also added a fateful "nevertheless" limiting this right to revision of particular constitutional articles "whose drawbacks had been revealed by experience" – and that only after three successive legislatures had agreed on the necessity for such action, and only by an assembly of revision composed of the fourth legislature augmented with additional members for this purpose. When it came to the need for constitutional change, the general will in such a matter was to be expressed, only under certain conditions, by the legislative body itself. Having unleashed the principle of national sovereignty, the National Assembly now faced the difficulties of containing it.

These difficulties were to be exacerbated by a second implication of the Assembly's decisions of mid-September 1789. For while accepting in effect the principle that they were instituting a constitution by an act of sovereign will, the deputies at the same time repudiated Sieyès' arguments for a constitution that would henceforth locate the expression of national sovereignty unambiguously in the representative body of the nation. They thereby opted, in effect, for the most unstable of the three choices with which they were presented – the the problematic combination of the Rousseauian principle of the inalienable sovereignty of the general will with the practice of representation. The suspensive royal veto was meant to close the gap between sovereignty and representation by allowing for an ultimate appeal to the people. In practice, by multiplying competing claims to express the general will, it simply exacerbated the problem it was meant to resolve.

Thus when the Constitution of 1791 was finally adopted, it embodied a fundamental contradiction, and a recipe for constitutional impasse. To safeguard national sovereignty from the dangers of representation, it permitted the monarch to veto legislative decrees – hence paralyze the Assembly – for the duration of two legislatures. But to protect the Constitution itself from the dangers of popular action in the name of national sovereignty, it required the assembly to delay constitutional revision for the duration of three legislatures. These provisions lay at the heart of the conflict between the principles of constitutionality and national sovereignty that occurred in the weeks preceding the revolution of August 10, 1792.

As a result of the veto, the Constitution of 1791, as Brissot remarked, could function only under "a revolutionary king." Thus, once it appeared in the spring of 1792 that Louis XVI's exercise of the veto was frustrating rather than upholding the sovereign will of the nation, not only the monarch but the Constitution itself was under siege. As growing popular demands for the king's suspension or deposition appealed to the principle of national sovereignty, so were they denounced in the Assembly as subversive of a constitution that made no explicit provision for such circumstances. The Constitution, the deputies insisted, could only be saved by constitutional means; but they were unable to agree on any such means. And as they dithered, so popular demands for action against the king were followed by demands for immediate action to change the Constitution – demands that also required repudiation of the restrictive provisions regarding constitutional revision established under the Constitution of 1791. Denouncing these provisions in the Assembly on July 25, 1792, as one more example of the truth that "no people on earth has ever been able to delegate its sovereignty for a moment without those to whom they delegated it trying to put them in chains," Isnard followed Chabot in maintaining that "the French people will always have the incontestable right to change its constitution when it deems it appropriate to do so." On August 4, a famous address of the Mauconseil section, declaring the impossibility of saving liberty by constitutional means, announced that the Constitution itself could no longer be considered an expression of the general will. Following the logic of such arguments, a petition opened for signatures on the Champ de Mars declared the nullity of all acts taken by the Constituent Assembly after the flight to Varennes, and appealed from the Constitution of 1791 to the principles of the Declaration of the Rights of Man. Presented to the Assembly on 6 July, this petition called for the deposition of the king, the election of a constitutional convention, and a program of revolutionary mobilization – all on the grounds that "the fatherland is in danger, the Revolution is starting again." The destruction of the Constitution of 1791 on August 10, 1792, was but the logical consequence of this call to renew the Revolution.

With the overthrow of the monarchy, French government became radically provisional – long before the Convention formally declared on October 10, 1793, that the government would remain "revolutionary until peace" returned. The revolutionary reassertion of national sovereignty on August 10, 1792, reopened the conceptual space between revolution and constitution – a space that the Constituent Assembly had been anxious to seal when, in concluding its deliberations less than a year earlier, it declared both the Revolution and the Constitution complete. Within this space the Terror would find its form, to be followed by the vicissitudes of the many efforts to bring the Revolution once again to its constitutional completion.

This consideration suggests a third and final implication of the constitutional decisions taken by the National Assembly in mid-September 1789. To the extent that the Assembly's acceptance of the suspensive veto implied a repudiation of Sieyès' arguments for a theory of representation based on the division of labor, the Assembly was in effect discarding a discourse of the social, grounded on the notion of the differential distribution of reason, functions, and interests in modern civil society, in favor of a discourse of the political grounded on the theory of a unitary general will. In the most general terms, it was opting for the language of political will rather than of social reason, of unity rather than of difference, of civic virtue rather than of commerce, of absolute sovereignty rather than of the rights of man. Which is to say that, in the long run, it was opting for the Terror.

NOTES

Source Reprinted by permission of the publisher from *A Critical Dictionary of the French Revolution*, ed. François Furet and Mona Ozouf, trans. Arthur Goldhammer (Cambridge, MA: Harvard University Press, 1989 by the President and Fellows of Harvard College), pp. 479–493.

Part III

RESPONSES TO REVISIONISM

The revolutions that have taken place in other European countries, have been excited by personal hatred. The rage was against the man, and he became the victim. But, in the instance of France, we see a revolution generated in the rational contemplation of the rights of man, and distinguishing from the beginning between persons and principles.

Tom Paine
Rights of Man

5

BOURGEOIS REVOLUTION
REVIVIFIED

1789 and social change

Colin Jones

One of the most interesting features of the new challenges to Revisionism is how much the challengers are indebted to the Revisionists themselves. Not only do they accept much of Revisionist work, but their closest colleagues, mentors, and teachers are often the same Revisionists whose work they are critiquing. Their debate, then, is more in the spirit of the Enlightenment philosophes than the fratricidal struggles between Jacobins and Girondins. Just as this was the case for William Sewell's critique of his colleagues Furet and Baker, so it is here with British historian Colin Jones, who combines sarcasm and humor with a perceptive analysis of the eighteenth-century French economy.

One of the hallmarks of Revisionism has been its rejection of an ascendant capitalist bourgeoisie hostile to privileged noblemen. On the eve of the Revolution, as Colin Lucas claimed earlier in this volume, the ruling élite was composed of both commoners and noblemen, and the most important social distinction did not concern birth, but rather, whether one performed manual labor. Colin Jones accepts parts of this analysis, but insists that it ignores the complexity of the late eighteenth-century economy, in which many parts of what we might call the privileged orders had become immersed in market capitalism. For example, Jones identifies the buying and selling of public offices as being a capitalist enterprise with its own national market. Such new forms of capitalism created sharp social antagonisms. The bourgeoisie may not have constituted a distinct class with its own sense of its potential, but that does not mean that large sections of the ruling élite were not influenced by bourgeois interests that stemmed from a nascent form of capitalism. In this sense, Jones agrees with Sewell that the French Revolution was truly a bourgeois revolution.

* * *

The decision on 16 July 1789 to demolish the Bastille presented a wonderful opportunity to Pierre-François Palloy.[1] The 34-year-old building contractor, who – so he said – had helped to storm the Bastille on 14 July, took on the job of demolition. The grim medieval fortress was soon a building site, offering

much-needed employment to about 1,000 hungry Parisian laborers and providing a diverting and edifying spectacle for the leisured élite. The famous
Latude, who had made his name by publishing an account of his imprisonment
in the state fortress, was on hand to act as tourist guide to the site. Latude's
publishers rushed out extra editions of his work, and Bastille commemorative
volumes were soon among the bestsellers. A further wave of popular interest
accompanied the discovery by Palloy's workmen in early 1790 of subterranean
cells filled with chains and skeletons. This was not the Man in the Iron Mask, but
it was something.

Palloy, however, was attracting some unwanted attention. When he presented
accounts to the National Assembly in October 1790, certain right-wing deputies
suggested that he had made a huge profit from the whole enterprise. Bertrand
Barère, the future colleague of Robespierre in the great Committee of Public
Safety, sprang to Palloy's defence. "It's not some deal that he made. . . . It's
political destruction; it's something truly revolutionary. . . . So the Bastille's
demolition turns a profit for the nation and provides honor for liberty."[2] Fine
words and flattery: but Palloy's books seem not to have balanced. Although he
managed to avoid investigation, he seems to have made a considerable profit
from merely selling off the stones of the Bastille; many went, for example, into
the construction of the Pont de la Concorde. He went further than this, moreover,
setting up a manufactory in his home in which huge numbers of the stones were
carved into little replicas of the Bastille. Chains and irons found on the site
were created into similar memorabilia: medals, dice-boxes, paperweights,
snuff-boxes, inkpots, and the like. Palloy enrolled a host of fellow *Vainqueurs de la
Bastille* to act as his travelling salesmen – he called them his apostles of liberty –
taking stocks around the departments to meet what was clearly a great demand.
Three parcels of Bastille memorabilia were presented gratis to each of France's
eighty-three departments – though the latter did pay the transport costs, which
allowed a profit to be made, and doubtless further stimulated local demand.

As he protests at his stone Bastille models being undercut by cheap plaster
imitations, we should perhaps tiptoe quietly away from this interesting entrepreneurial figure who clearly awaits his Samuel Smiles – or better still, his
Richard Cobb. From the vantage-point of the Bicentenary in 1989, with its
chocolate guillotines and Bastille boxer shorts, his story nevertheless neatly
demonstrates that the commercialization of the French Revolution is as old
as the Revolution itself. The character sketch does, moreover, illustrate some of
the themes I wish to develop here: namely, the Revolution and economic
opportunities; bourgeois entrepreneuralism; consumerism and fashion; civic
sensibilities; the interlocking of business and rhetoric.

To bring a bourgeois to the centre of the stage may, however, appear gloriously
dépassé. After all, 1989 marked not just the bicentenary of the Revolution, but
also the twenty-fifth anniversary of the publication, in 1964, of Alfred Cobban's
Social Interpretation of the French Revolution, the classic text of the Revolutionist
school which has come to dominate French Revolutionary historiography.[3] Over

the last quarter of a century, the Revisionist current has virtually swept from the board what is now identified as the Orthodox Marxist view. The idea, almost axiomatic to the historians whom Cobban attacked – Mathiez, Lefebvre, Soboul – that the Revolution marked a key episode in the passage from feudalism to capitalism is now either widely discounted or else viewed as a *question mal posée*. And the idea – regarded as a truism before the 1960s – that the Revolution was a bourgeois revolution is now held up to ridicule. Indeed, George V. Taylor, one of the Grand Old Men of Revisionism, recently warned off historians from using the term "bourgeois" which is, he contends, "freighted with too many ambiguities to serve in research as a general analytical tool or operational category."[4]

In the place of the old Marxist orthodoxy – the Revisionists always talk of the Marxist interpretation in the singular, as if Marxists never disagreed, or else robotically took their cue from the Politburo – a New Revisionist Orthodoxy has gradually sprung up, which by now has permeated into general interpretations and views, in much of French publishing as well as in English and American scholarship. The New Orthodoxy will have little truck with social interpretations in general, and the bourgeois revolution in particular. Far from being the heroic, world-historical, almost transcendental force which Karl Marx had seen him as, the bourgeois now cuts a shabby figure. Revisionist historians view him as pathetically insecure, anaemic, transitional – zombie-esque, in the view of Simon Schama.[5] The Old Regime bourgeoisie, so the New Orthodoxy goes, burnt its candle at both ends. At the top, merchants and manufacturers who built up sufficient wealth were swift to disinvest from productive activities and sink their capital in land, seigneuries, and venal office. Their propensity to ape their social betters was exemplified by their wish to achieve noble status, and indeed many former traders and manufacturers referred to themselves as *bourgeois vivant noblement*. The preference for status over profit which this behavior is alleged to exemplify can be dated back centuries, as Colin Lucas and William Doyle have reminded us, and may thus be dubbed, as George Taylor would have it, atavistic.[6] At its bottom end, the Revisionists tell us, the bourgeoisie was equally undynamic. Peasants who might have enriched themselves by production for the market preferred risk-avoidance and subsistence strategies, and coralled themselves away from their bourgeois betters in the ghetto of a "popular culture" they shared with guild-dominated, and equally "traditionalist" urban workers.[7]

This was a bourgeoisie more deeply riven by internal schisms than by class antagonisms – and indeed the Revisionists reserve some of their sharpest barbs for those starry-eyed "Marxist" idealists who retain some attachment to the concept of class struggle. Indeed, the New Orthodoxy has it that there was less unity shown by the bourgeoisie as a class than, for example, by the inter-class élite of upper bourgeois and nobles. One must admire the Revisionists' sleight of hand, for the Old Regime nobility, normally portrayed (they tell us) as monolithically parasitic and feudal in its outlook, are nowadays viewed as hyper-dynamic and entrepreneurial. The nobility dominated the key sectors of the economy, Guy

Chaussinand-Nogaret assures us, exercised overwhelming cultural hegemony, and generously held out a co-operative hand to those awestricken bourgeois wishing to enter France's social élite.[8] Once viewed as the agents of a "feudal reaction" which shut out talented commoners, the nobility is now seen as the leading partner in an enlightened élite, entry into which through venal office was still surprisingly easy.[9] The term "open élite" is now being used less in regard to eighteenth-century England, following the broadsides of Lawrence and Jeanne Stone, than to Old Regime France.[10] The Revolution's persecution of this enlightened noble-dominated group can only, in its injustice, its economic irrationality, and its lack of humanity, be compared to anti-Semitism (the comparison is Chaussinand-Nogaret's).[11] Yet the nobility would have the last laugh, for once the Revolution was over, they formed the backbone of the class of landowning and professional notables which dominated nineteenth-century France.[12]

The idea that France's late eighteenth- and nineteenth-century history essentially concerns the formation of an élite of notables (the latter, incidentally, every bit as much a portmanteau term as that of "bourgeois," against whose vagueness Cobban inveighed), with the Revolution as an unwelcome intrusion or even an irrelevant footnote, has become a keystone of the New Revisionist Orthodoxy.[13] It fits in very snugly with the systematic disparagement of the economic significance of the Revolution. Far from marking the passage from feudalism to capitalism, the Revolution could not even transform the economic structures and shortcomings of the economy: agrarian productivity only registered progress, Michel Morineau tells us, after 1840, and industrial capitalism had generally to await the railway age.[14] Late eighteenth-century France was in any case only just emerging from *l'histoire immobile*, Emmanuel Le Roy Ladurie's description of a kind of neo-Malthusian prison-camp in which French society had been interned since the fourteenth century.[15] The Revolution thus becomes little more than a minor fold in the flowing fabric of that *longue durée* so beloved of the *Annales* school.

This tendency within the Revisionist camp to minimize the social changes associated with the Revolution has led to most recent historiographical running being made by historians of politics and culture. Lynn Hunt has chided social historians for concentrating their interest on mere "origins and outcomes,"[16] and for failing to recognize that the revolutionary character of the 1790s resides in the fabrication of a new political culture. The outstanding work of Keith Baker, and the 1987 Chicago conference proceedings, *The Political Culture of the Old Régime*, which have been published under his direction, buttresses that view.[17] In the Brave New Revisionist World, discourse reigns supreme and social factors bulk exceedingly small. It often seems, for example, as if the new political culture had no long-term social roots, but emerged in a process of inspired and semi-spontaneous politico-cultural *bricolage* in 1788–9. François Furet, for example, the veritable pope of contemporary Revisionism, sees 1789 as ushering in a political logic and a proto-totalitarian discourse which lead in unilinear fashion to the Terror.[18] The idea that the Revolution's shift to the left in the early 1790s might have something to do with the counter-revolution is roundly dismissed: the revolutionaries are diagnosed as suffering from a plot psychosis predating any real threat to their work. The Revolution was on the track to Terror from the summer of 1789, socio-political circumstances notwithstanding.[19]

François Furet has been a devastating critic of the unreflective sociologism of the old Marxist approach as exemplified in some of the writings of Albert Soboul.[20] The pendulum has now swung to the other extreme, however, and many Revisionists seem to wish to reduce the history of the Revolution to political history with society left out. A typical recent example of the way in which discourse analysis and high politics over-ride the social angle is the treatment which a number of recent authors have given to the famous Night of 4 August 1789, when the National Assembly issued a decree formally abolishing feudalism. Overlooking or discounting evidence about the blatant fixing of this session, ignoring the ridiculously high rates of compensation for losses of feudal rights the deputies awarded, turning a blind eye to stories of violent peasant revolution which, magnified by rumor, were pouring into Paris and Versailles at the time, William Doyle, Norman Hampson, Michael Fitzsimmons, and Simon Schama all view the explanation of the behavior of the deputies as lying in the altruism of the old "enlightened" élite.[21] One of the key moments in the social transformation of France, the zenith of peasant influence on the course of events, thus merely becomes a vacuous chapter in group psychology, with the Assembly acting as if hermetically sealed from outside social influences. What Simon Schama characterizes as a "patriotic rhapsody" becomes for Michael Fitzsimmons a kind of beatific vision, a Close Encounter of the 4 August Kind, in which the deputies self-denyingly pledged themselves to "the sublimity of the Nation."[22] The Revolution as a whole thus becomes "the reaction of groups and individuals to the imposition by the National Assembly of its new vision of France," an approach congruent with George Taylor's famous characterization of the Revolution as a "political revolution with social consequences rather than a social revolution with political consequences."[23]

This denigration of the popular and collectivist aspects of the Revolution and the downplaying of social origins to the political crisis of 1789 keys in with some other recent accounts, moreover, which view French society as largely the opponent or the victim of the new political culture. From Donald Sutherland's account, for example, one gains the impression that nine-tenths of French society in the 1790s was objectively counter-revolutionary.[24] (This, incidentally, is a view which calls into question François Furet's diagnosis of plot psychosis.) If there was a popular revolution at all, Douglas Johnson tells us, it was the Counter-Revolution.[25] From evacuating the Revolution of all positive social content to viewing the repression of counter-revolution as "genocide" by a "totalitarian" power is only a short step – and one which certain historians have not been afraid to take.[26]

Perhaps we are wrong to judge the views of the New Revisionist Orthodoxy by the uses to which they are being put by the political Right; after all, the Old Marxist Orthodoxy was shamelessly exploited by the Left. What is, however, worrying for a social historian is the extent to which social change is disparaged in or omitted from the New Revisionist Orthodoxy. It is not my intention to pose as King Canute, vainly bidding the Revisionist wave to recede. On the contrary, I would contend that a great deal of Revisionist research being done in fact subverts the main, rather brittle assumptions around which the New Revisionist Orthodoxy has hardened.[27] In this essay, I would like to mine that seam in a way which suggests that we need to rethink our attitudes towards some of the key problems associated with the relationship of the Revolution to social change. While many may prefer cosily to relax in the platitudes of the New Revisionist Orthodoxy, we may in fact be moving towards a situation in which new research allows us to relate afresh to some of the problems of causation which concerned Marxist French Revolutionary historiography. This may come as a shock to many Revisionists, who tend to relate to that historiographical tradition by presenting a knockabout pastiche of the views of the alleged Old Marxist Orthodoxy, a kind of pantomime in which a succession of Revisionist Prince Charmings rescue Marianne from the clutches of a wicked, mean-spirited old Stalinist Baron – a part reserved in most scripts for the late Albert Soboul. Using the research of both Revisionist and Marxist scholars, I am going to be foolhardy enough to suggest that the Revolution did have long-term social origins. I will go on to suggest that these related directly to the development of capitalism and indeed that the much-disparaged term "bourgeois revolution" retains much of its force and utility.

One of the cardinal tenets of the New Revisionist Orthodoxy is that eighteenth-century France was – with the possible exception of the enlightened élite – "traditionalist," preferring a flight from capitalism rather than its warm embrace. Much of the force of this view has in the past resided in unfavorable comparisons made with the allegedly more mature capitalist economy of Great Britain, undergoing in the period from 1780 the classic Rostovian "take-off" into self-sustained economic growth. Against this, the argument runs, the French economy can only seem "backward" or "retarded."[28]

One has only to scratch the surface of this approach today to realize that it lies in tatters. The work of François Crouzet, Nicholas Crafts, Patrick O'Brien and others have pointed up the buoyancy of French economic performance over the eighteenth century, and shown that in many respects it even may have out-distanced Great Britain.[29] Annual averages of both agricultural and industrial growth were higher in France than in Great Britain.[30] If we are to believe Patrick O'Brien and Caglar Keyder, a broad comparability between the British and the French economies continued into the early twentieth century. France's per capita physical product tripled between the early nineteenth and early twentieth centuries, and the authors see this as part of a development which stretches back into the eighteenth century. Perhaps Britain's priority in emergence as First Industrial Nation owed less to her economic performance over the eighteenth century than to factors which predated 1700 – the stability of Britain's financial institutions grounded in the establishment of the Bank of England in 1694, and

Britain's early switch to mineral fuel, which stimulated the emergence of a coal-fuel technology which would contribute importantly to the industrialization process.[31] But rather than talk in terms of retardation or backwardness, perhaps we should just accept that there is more than one way towards industrialization, and that the British route, though first – or perhaps because it was first – was not necessarily the most appropriate for others. France did not have the sudden spurt in industrial performance which England enjoyed, but her more balanced and drawn-out pathway to industrialization was no less effective in the longer term, and may indeed be particularly deserving of attention in that it avoided many of the direst social costs which accompanied Britain's Industrial Revolution.[32]

I have thus far portrayed eighteenth-century France as a more and more commercial society, increasingly sensitive to the market, very different from the stagnating, traditionalist society encountered in the New Revisionist Orthodoxy. Seen from this viewpoint, it seems clear that the main intermediaries and beneficiaries of this growing commercialization were the allegedly "traditional" bourgeoisie. Merchants, artisans, shopkeepers, and the *paysannerie marchande* were in the fore, with only a sprinkling of the nobility. The size of the bourgeoisie grew over the century from 700,000 or 800,000 individuals in 1700 to perhaps 2.3 million in 1789 – getting on for 10 per cent of the global population.[33] The New Revisionist Orthodoxy that bourgeoisie and nobility were somehow identical in economic terms thus seems rather wide of the mark: even were we to take all of the 120,000 nobles Chaussinand-Nogaret claims to have been in existence in 1789 as engaged in entrepreneurial activity – a hypothesis very far from the mark, as Chaussinand-Nogaret would admit – they would still be sinking without trace in a bourgeois sea.[34] Entrepreneurial nobles were anyway more likely to be involved in monopoly capitalist ventures or financial dealing than in the more humdrum bread-and-butter mercantile and manufacturing activities which were the staple of French commercial capitalism.

In the New Revisionist Orthodoxy, the professions are usually patronizingly labeled the "traditional élites," the assumption being that they remained locked in the rigidities of the Society of Orders until 4 August 1789. In fact, they were in a state of institutional and intellectual ferment in the eighteenth century. Each seems to have undergone important institutional changes over the century, and developed in self-esteem, self-definition, and commitment. This was accompanied by a certain consumerism – one might say a bourgeoisification – in their lifestyles which reflects the extent to which they were adjusting to the inroads and the potentialities of commercial capitalism.

To look at any one of the professions in the late eighteenth century is to uncover a welter of ongoing debates – grounded, I would contend, in the changing size and nature of demand – on the nature of professionalism. In these debates, issues fundamental to the role of the service sector in a capitalist economy – the provision of services, rational organization, public accountability,

93

market forces, quality control, and so on – were addressed. These are matters which we can as yet glimpse only darkly, and on whose exact nature we can at this stage only hazard guesses. To make an outrageously bald generalization, however, it seems helpful to classify the arguments utilized into two broad camps. On the one hand there were arguments for professionalization which adopted a corporative framework, and which sought changes on a "vertical," internalist, and hierarchical basis. Expertise, internal discipline, and segregation from the wider society was the key. On the other hand, there were arguments which adopted a civic dimension, where the framework for professionalism was transcorporative, egalitarian, "horizontal." The profession should be opened up on to the wider society. Both sets of arguments utilized the same kinds of language, though if proponents of the corporative professionalism tended to think in terms of "subjects" of the "state" (sometimes even personalized still as "the king") the civic professionalizers referred to "citizen" and the "Nation" or, sometimes, "the public."[35] It is a language which in its most democratic and egalitarian formulations pre-figured the debates in the National Assembly in the summer of 1789.

Let us take the profession of arms as an example. David Bien, in a brilliant Revisionist article, has familiarized us with the notion of the professionalization of the army officer corps.[36] This took the form of measures aimed to produce an effective army, Spartan in its virtues (though Prussia was the real blueprint), operating within more bureaucratic and hierarchical structures, and enjoying more efficient training and a more articulated career structure. Even the infamous Ségur ordinance of 1781 which limited high command to officers enjoying four quarters of nobility can be regarded as a professionalizing measure.[37] The aim of the ordinance was to exclude not commoners so much as recently ennobled bourgeois who had bought their way into the corps through the system of venal office and were thought to lack the sense of inbred honor which only dynasties of military nobility could produce in young recruits. What has tended to be seen as a flagrant instance of feudal reaction thus takes on the more anodyne colors of military professionalization; privilege is legitimized by service, high birth by social utility. Unfortunately, this is only half of the story. Though Bien does not tell us so, in fact there was more than one way of construing professionalization. The corporative model of the old nobility was matched by a very different, civic model, reflected and furthered by the writings of Rousseau, but transcending any narrow lineages of literary influences.[38] Embraced by many younger officers, this model was grounded in the belief that professionalism could best be achieved through opening up the army on the wider society. The military man was a citizen before he was a soldier: this basic message comes through in a whole host of writings from the 1770s onwards, rising in a crescendo, as one might expect, with the American War of Independence. Guibert's *Essai de tactique* (dedicated *A ma patrie*) (1772) and Joseph Servan's *Le Soldat citoyen* (1780) may serve as instances of the genre.[39] Consider in this respect too the early career of Lazare Carnot, the "Organizer of Victory" in Year II, and a military engineer in the last years of the Old Regime.

Carnot's prize-winning "Eloge de Vauban" (1784) is a fine example of civic professionalism. Writing self-proclaimedly as a *militaire philosophe et citoyen*, Carnot praises the technical skills of Vauban as a servant, but he also sees him as a friend of the people, whose professional artistry was intended to defend *la Nation* from the sufferings of war. In this civic version, the professional ethic was combined with a critique of Ségur-style privilege, and the corporative professionalism which camouflaged it.[40]

Antagonistic strands of civic and corporative professionalism are to be found in the secular clergy prior to 1789 too, as Timothy Tackett has shown.[41] The corporative model owed much to the continuing post-Tridentine reforms of the Catholic hierarchy, which aimed to make of parish priests spiritual gendarmes working obediently under their bishops. Intensive training, through seminaries and apprenticeship as *vicaires*, bade fair to make the Catholic clergy a force quite as disciplined, quite as *pur et dur* as the professionalized army corps. The equation of professionalism with the wearing of the clerical cassock highlighted the congruity.[42] This conception of the parish priest had increasingly to compete, however, with a more civic view which stressed the duties the clergy owed to the Nation. The citizen-clergy, often fuelled by Richerist ideas, resented the overly hierarchical and disciplinarian character of the Church, as well as its social dominance by the high nobility; practised the virtues of charity and consolation to their fellow citizens; and invoked the rights of the Nation. Their lifestyle as well as their outlook became increasingly bourgeois: the watches, clocks, mirrors, books, and other decorative bric-à-brac found in their homes revealed them as very much part of the new consumer culture.[43] The large number of civic-minded lower clergy elected to the Estates-General were to play a crucial role in helping to win the political initiative for their bourgeois fellow deputies in the Third Estate.[44]

Schoolteachers – very largely within the aegis of the church – were a group amongst which this civic ideology made a particular mark.[45] The pedagogy of the last decades of the Old Regime was thoroughly infused with civic values. Schoolteachers included some of the most eloquent and persuasive members of the revolutionary assemblies: Lanjuinais, Fouché Billaud-Varenne, Daunou, François de Neufchâteau, Manuel, and Lakanal are a representative crop.

There was to be a good admixture of medical men among the deputies of the revolutionary assemblies too, the good doctor Guillotin not least.[46] Debates over professionalism in the world of medicine were complicated by the traditional split between university-trained physicians and the more artisanal surgeons. Medicine was a jungle: the physicians cordially despised the surgeons, and the major medical faculties were perennially at daggers drawn. Over the course of the century, however, important changes took place. Surgeons hoisted up their prestige, wealth, and status: a liberal education came to be required for a surgical career.[47] A growing professionalization on their part, grounded in their highly centralized organization – the King's First Surgeon was effectively "King of Surgery" throughout France – was helped by their proven utility in their service of the royal armies.[48] As the century wore on, many physicians also tried to transcend the corporative petty-mindedness for which they were famous, and to stress the public benefits of medical professionalism.[49] The foundation of the Royal Society of Medicine in 1776 was viewed as an attempt to give some corporative structure to the straggling bands of physicians throughout France; but it also made a great play of its mission as recorder and diagnostician of epidemics and as information network on disease and the environment.[50] Above all, it stood as the scourge of medical "charlatanism," and argued that social utility and public health required the enforcement of a monopoly of medical services by trained physicians.[51] Even before 1789, medical eulogists were portraying the dedicated physician as a bastion of citizenship, a cross between an altruistic notable and a secular saint devoted to his ailing flock.[52]

The legal profession seems in many respects to have been the least professionalized of the traditional professions prior to 1789. Though riddled with corruption and the object of tremendous popular hostility, as the *cahiers* were to make clear in 1789, legal practitioners still maintained a high estimation of their constitutional importance. They sometimes claimed to comprise a kind of Fourth Estate, for example, a position which clearly chimed in with the constitutional pretensions of the parlements.[53] As Sarah Maza and Keith Baker have shown, many legal practitioners came to exploit civil and criminal cases so as to develop significant civic and political arguments, which were widely followed by the literate public – as well as by others not so literate.[54] The Calas affair is only one example – there are many – in which a contentious lawsuit led to an outpouring of pamphlets and polemical writings, normally the work of lawyers or attorneys, which invoked *l'opinion publique* as a kind of supreme arbiter.[55] The sociological supports of this powerful concept clearly lay in the growing market for cultural products and services over the eighteenth century which I have already described.[56] Be that as it may, "public concern" in the mouths of pre-revolutionary lawyers and polemicists predicated a feel for natural justice soon to receive more famous embodiment in the Rights of Man and the Nation, promulgated by a National Assembly in which were to sit some 151 lawyers.[57] The "heap of blabbers, lawyers, prosecutors, notaries, bailiffs and other such vermin" who, in the charmingly unlovely language of the *Père Duchesne*,[58] dominated every subsequent revolutionary assembly owed much to their exposure before 1789 to the problems inherent in exercising their profession in a fast-changing commercial society whose service sector was being transformed.

The debate over professionalism, civic and corporative, is particularly interesting to follow in the state bureaucracy, where it is complicated by the system of venal office. Classic Weberian reforms were increasingly introduced over the last decades of the Old Regime, to limit the rampant patrimonialism which characterized the service generally. The most hated branch of the service, the General Farm, was most advanced in its corporative professionalism, having introduced a wide range of rational bureaucratic procedures, and also having installed a career structure for employees which included a contributory pensions fund.[59] Elsewhere, there was a reaction against the prevalence of venal office. The latter was widely blamed for, as one critic put it, "this insulting separation that sits between the administration and the Nation."[60] Venality was in fact reduced or abolished in a number of services in the last decades of the Old Regime, including the *maréchaussée*, the postal system, and the saltpetre service.[61] Necker attempted to centralize the multiple treasuries of the financial bureaucracy.[62] There were some valiantly civic-minded administrators who endeavored to move the popular imagination into believing them citizens as well as Crown servants. But bureaucrats continued to be seen essentially as peddlars of hope and protection, little despots, insolent petty kings, the very embodiment of privilege, without any social utility or public benefit.[63] One can understand why the revolutionary assemblies would desire to debureaucratize French society – familiar phantasm.[64]

Showing an awareness of the interpenetration of political and economic factors which is in itself an object-lesson to historians, many critics of venal office in the late Old Regime attacked the way in which such posts could entail what might be seen as unfair market advantage. This whole question of venal office has been reopened in recent years by a number of important Revisionist articles. In an article in the *Historical Journal* in 1984, for example, William Doyle demonstrated that the market for venal office was more buoyant than Marxists and indeed many Revisionists had held. The price of some offices falls, but far more rise, and Doyle concludes in general that overall the price of office was rising; he ascribes this to the traditionalism of the Old Regime bourgeoisie, who were failing to give up their secular preference for status over profit.[65]

Before this view finds its niche within the canon of the New Revisionist Orthodoxy, however, let us consider how this rise in the value of venal office might relate to the growth of the market for services. The post of court physician (*médecin du roi*), on which I have done some research, is an interesting starting-point. In 1720, only seventeen physicians could claim this title, while in 1789, eighty-eight, to whom might be added quite as many court surgeons and apothecaries.[66] The price of these posts seems to have been pretty buoyant. As only a handful of the individuals who could style themselves *médecin du roi* came near the person of the monarch, or even resided at Versailles, it might be concluded that here was a title that meant prestige and little else. In fact, this was far from the case. The purchase of a post was a means of circumventing the monopoly which the Paris Medical Faculty had on medical services within the capital. One has only to remember the wild enthusiasm of Parisians for every medical fad and fancy in the eighteenth century to see how valuable that access could be: Paris rocked to, and *médecins du roi* made money out of, the crazes for vapours, male midwives, smallpox inoculation, Mesmerism, and a good many forms of treatment for venereal disease – the most exotic of which must surely have been Lefebvre de Saint-Ildephont's anti-venereal chocolate drops. This particular court physician claimed that one could medicate one's wife against venereal infection by providing her with an unending supply of boxes of chocolates.[67]

Crudely put, purchase of a post within the royal medical Household was a means of cashing in on medical consumerism. It represented a headlong rush towards a market – even an entrepreneurial interest in stimulating it – rather than a flight from it. One wonders whether there are similar stories to tell about many of the other venal offices. Indeed, if we turn again to William Doyle's list of venal offices for which prices were rising, we find that a good number of them – attorneys, notaries, legal clerks, auctioneers, and wigmakers – do indeed relate to expanding markets for professional services or fashionable lifestyle.[68] Venal office (and perhaps a similar case might be mounted for land purchase) begins to look less like an option for status than a shrewd investment aimed to give the purchaser access to a market or edge within it.[69] Money bought privilege within this market as well as within the polity and within the social hierarchy.

Attacked by their co-professionals as the embodiment of privilege and social inutility, many venal officers themselves grew progressively disenchanted by their posts. The advantages of market edge plus the returns on the initial investment palled as the monarchy, increasingly beset by financial problems, came to interfere with the venal office market in a number of ways. The value of the investment was reduced by a series of injudicious decisions by the monarch to levy forced loans, for example (on the *corps* of financial officials in particular), to increase the number of offices in a particular *corps*, or to reduce wages.[70] The downturn in the economy from the 1770s may also have diminished the buoyancy of many markets for services. Economies in the state bureaucracy – pursued by all controllers-general in the last years of the Old Regime, but with no greater vigour than by Loménie de Brienne in 1787–8 – must have helped venal officers to see the writing on the wall.[71] In any event, with state bankruptcy on the horizon, it was a pretty shrewd move, on the Night of 4 August 1789, to agree to the abolition of all venal offices. For the abolition was agreed on the basis of compensation which, it was hoped, would be financially more advantageous than forcible expropriation or sale in depressed market conditions.[72] So much for the "patriotic rhapsodies" of altruism!

In the question of venal office were encapsulated many of the problems of the absolute monarchy. The state operated the most extraordinarily ornate system whereby it sold offices which thereby became the private property of their owners. The holders could not be bought out altogether – the expense was too colossal; so kings turned disadvantage to advantage by levying forced loans on the main bodies of venal office-holders to help it in its financial difficulties. The king was thereby to a certain extent digging his own grave, in that these loans ran up the National Debt to colossal proportions. In addition, the royal demands amplified the corporate awareness of the bodies of venal officeholders. This was particularly marked in the case of the towns, as Gail Bossenga has recently shown.[73] Venal municipal offices, constantly chopped and changed over the course of the century, bred discontent both within the charmed circle of municipal officials, and outside in sectional groups wanting to get in. This provided a seed-plot in which – over all sorts of issues, from street lighting to local taxes – could grow a civic awareness quite as cogent as that developing within the professions.

A growing sensitivity to civic issues is found elsewhere in Old Regime society too. Even at village level, Hilton Root finds Burgundian peasants deciding on local matters utilizing, in pretty sophisticated fashion, the concept of the General Will long before the latter term was dreamed up by Jean-Jacques Rousseau.[74] Urban guilds were often too the micro-sites for similar exercises in political education and the exercise of political democracy. They too, like Hilton Root's peasants, utilized the courts as means of redress, with lawyers playing the part of cultural intermediary between legal form and social issues.[75] If we suspend the New Revisionist Orthodoxy's certainty that modern political culture was born in 1789, we can glimpse within Old Regime society, even at these lowly levels supposedly locked away into the bromides of a "popular culture," a vibrant and developing political sensibility which cries out to be inventoried, classified, and understood.

Although what came to be at issue often had far wider ramifications, these burgeoning debates within the professions and other corporative cells of the Society of Orders were at first often localized and sectional. The courts and, by way of the press, the notion of "public opinion" provided a conduit along which civic sensibilities could penetrate the body social, as we have seen. A number of other institutions came to act as a crucible in which these fragmented disputes were fused into a supra-corporative consciousness. The Enlightenment Academies were a case in point.[76] Their internally democratic practices favored such fusion, for the niceties of the social hierarchy were normally not observed within them, and bourgeois rubbed shoulders with noble, as well as doctor with lawyer. To be frank, the Academies were often dominated by local nobles and dignitaries, and consequently stuffy, if worthy, in their procedures. The egalitarian, meritocratic sharing of experience which they embodied was doubtless important for some. Even more important, however, were the Masonic lodges.[77] The cult of Masonry had its adepts throughout the social pyramid; yet the numerical predominance among the body of 50,000 French Masons was clearly with the professional classes and with their social equivalents. Businessmen – often excluded from Academies for being lacking in tone and breeding – were here in massive numbers: they represented 36 per cent of members in major cities, and the proportion was often well over 50 per cent in numerous localities. Soldiers were the main professional category, although lawyers, administrators, and doctors – if few priests – were also there in bulk.[78] The same elements – in a slightly different mix – were found in reading clubs, small lending libraries and their like.[79]

These new forums for egalitarian mixing and discussion were as much organs of sociability as anything else. In his recent work on Masonry, Ran Halévi has dubbed this a "democratic sociability."[80] Halévi, like his close collaborator François Furet, is in fact particularly interested in the lodges as lineal ancestors of the Jacobin Clubs, and so chooses a narrowly political term. I prefer the term "civic sociability," which I think expresses rather better the urban and wider cultural implications of this form of social mixing, and has the additional merit of making explicit the clear affinities it has with the civic ideologies and practices exuded by the professional and corporative institutions of the Old Regime.

In the light of the previous discussion, we can now revisit the debate on the social origins of the Revolution of 1789. Given the development of commercial capitalism in eighteenth-century France, the spread of a consumer society, the development of professionalization within the service sector of the economy which this helped to spawn, and the appearance of associated forms of civic sociability, it no longer looks realistic to disparage the vitality nor indeed the ideological autonomy of the Old Regime bourgeoisie. Far from the social structure of Old Regime France being locked remorselessly into "traditional," "pre-capitalist," "archaic" forms, the progress of commercialization and the spread of a consumer society suggests a relative "bourgeoisification" of Old Regime society. Far from an élite of "notables" melding harmoniously and cosily together in the last years of the Old Regime, moreover, conflict over the role of privilege and the implications of citizenship was endemic and established an explosive agenda beneath the surface calm of the Society of Orders. Yet though civic sociability had achieved much, it had signally failed to capture control of the state apparatus. This was to be the achievement of the men of 1789.

Who, then, were the "revolutionary bourgeoisie" (if we can now assume there was one)?[81] Alfred Cobban characterized it as a mixture of landowners, venal officers, and professional men. To a certain degree he was correct. Yet he saw both the professions and the venal office-holders as declining, inferiority-complexed classes, so many shrinking violets easily written off as "traditional élites." What I have argued here is that the professions and indeed a great many venal office-holders, far from being sectional and "traditionalist" in their orientation and outlook, were in fact responding to and very much part of the development of capitalism in the Old Regime. These groups were more genuinely bourgeois than ever before, and exuded a new civic professionalism which had its roots in a developing "market-consciousness" and which clashed with the corporative values espoused by many of their fellows. They shared the vision and the reflexes of the commercial bourgeoisie of the Old Regime in a far more direct way than has hitherto been recognized. Moreover, although they thought through these problems at first perhaps largely through the corporative framework, the ongoing debts on professionalization nurtured widening perspectives. Masonic lodges, *sociétés de pensée*, and the like further elaborated and refined the debate and also opened it up so that it included sections of the economic bourgeoisie in the years leading up to 1789. Professionalization was thus not simply a part of the noble reaction, as David Bien might have us believe. In its civic form, professionalism legitimated the attack on privilege, even when the latter was defended by corporative values. It stimulated a conception of the state as something which was not so much embodied in the dynast as present in the "Nation," an ideological construct which developed *pari passu* with the growth and elaboration of the market. The organs of civic sociability, finally, provided forums in which new ideas of equality, democracy, and civic concern could take material form among an increasingly homogeneous bourgeoisie and their allies among the liberal aristocracy.

In his notorious *Qu'est-ce que le Tiers Etat?*, Sieyes showed himself very much the apologist for this new civic consciousness. He argued that the "Nation" was composed of useful classes and groups which with great lucidity he itemized as including agriculture, industry, the mercantile interest, services "pleasant to the person," and the public services of the army, the law, the Church, and the bureaucracy.[82] His thinking was not as much the early appearance of a revolutionary ideology which sprang out fully developed from the political context, as the Revisionists are prone to argue. Rather, as the list of groups suggests, the new ideology of the Third Estate was in essence the ideology of pre-revolutionary civic professionalism. Its presence in one of the cardinal texts of the Revolution of 1789 indicates something of the contribution this new and increasingly aggressive civic ideology made to the downfall of the Old Regime. The civic sociability which had developed among this fraction of the bourgeoisie in the last decades of the Old Regime was corrosive of the deferentialism and hierarchical structures of the Society of Orders.

The ability of the Old Regime state to provide social and political conditions free from privilege and corporatism was in question long before its financial shipwreck in 1787–8. In the decades which preceded 1789, successive ministers had found themselves trying to float public loans by appeals to a general public increasingly impregnated with civic consciousness. The mercantile and professional bourgeoisie – together with the liberal fraction of the noble class – were, however, loath to go on extending moral or financial credit to a state which continued to conjugate public interest with the entrenched privileges of the aristocracy. As a social force, public opinion stretched out and reached every corner of this increasingly commercialized society. As an intellectual construct, moreover, "public opinion" was too closely tied into the cultural hegemony established by the professions and the new organs of civic sociability to be plausibly invoked by a monarch who seemed to be indissolubly wedded to the maintenance of the institutions of privilege.[83] The Nation, credit, public opinion, professionalism, and civic sociability had become woven into a spider's web in which privilege became helplessly stuck – and was then devoured. Far from the financial crisis of 1789 being, as the Revisionists contend, somehow extrinsic to earlier social developments,[84] it was in many ways the apotheosis of the social, political, and cultural developments I have been outlining.

The influence of the professional classes upon the Revolution was not only at the level of cultural hegemony. When one looks at political participation in 1789 and in the following revolutionary decade, what strikes one at once is the importance of the professional classes at every level and their interpenetration with other branches of the bourgeoisie. Cobban's original perception that declining venal officers and liberal professions dominated the Constituent Assembly is at least a starting-point,[85] though his analysis is misguided: venal office-holders were not necessarily a declining group; and anyway further research has shown that their representation in later revolutionary assemblies fell drastically, while that of professional men (including, increasingly, what one might call career or professional politicians) stayed consistently high. Moreover, as Lynn Hunt has brilliantly shown, local administration was very much in the hands of lawyers, physicians, notaries, and local bureaucrats, often with a good admixture of the merchants and manufacturers found only rather rarely at national level. In 1793 and 1794, a bigger input of petty bourgeois elements – shopkeepers, artisans, and minor clerks – is often visible, and in the countryside wealthier peasants got a look in.[86] But this really only underlines the bourgeois and professional orientation. Recent work on Parisian local politics confirms the general picture: the districts of 1789–90, as R.B. Rose has shown, were a fairly representative bourgeois cross-section; while incisive work on the Parisian sans-culottes of Year II, conducted by Richard Cobb and others in his wake, has revealed the more solidly bourgeois backgrounds of many militants who, for reasons of political expediency, deflated their social rank in the democratic atmosphere of the Terror.[87]

The analysis of Edmund Burke, cited Lynn Hunt, that the Revolution was the work of "moneyed men, merchants, principal tradesmen and men of letters" thus seems pretty accurate, as a description of both the key participants in the political process after 1789 and many of the major proponents of "civic sociability" before that date.[88] It is important, in the light of my earlier arguments, however, to view Burke's "men of letters" not as an autonomous, free-standing group, but rather as the vocal representatives of the professions. This interpretation clashes, I am aware, with Robert Darnton's fine studies of men of letters as a significant influence on the revolutionary process.[89] However, to classify men of letters as an autonomous group seems to distort and to underplay the professional and corporative framework within which such men had done – and maybe continued to do – their thinking. Clearly the concept had an important role in revolutionary ideology and myth-making. In particular, there is a brand of counter-revolutionary interpretation which rejoices at seeing the Revolution allegedly in the hands of an anomic pack of Grub Street low-life, seedy intellectuals cut off from any experience of real-life political problems, and consequently wild and utopian in their aims. The professional prism puts quite a different, more solid, more pragmatic, more market-orientated view on the revolutionary bourgeoisie. The latter is no more synonymous with Darnton's riff-raff intelligentsia than Old Regime professionals are with David Bien's reactionary army officers.

I have suggested that there was a far closer, organic link between the development of capitalism in the eighteenth century and the emergence of more "market-conscious," and public-spirited intellectual élites than historians have normally allowed. The attractiveness of this hypothesis is amplified when we look at much of the social and economic legislation carried out by successive revolutionary assemblies which would do so much to shape nineteenth-century France. If one assumes that the liberal professionals who made up such an important constitutive part of the assemblies are socially autonomous from the economic bourgeoisie, then reforms as classically capitalistic in their character as the formation of a national market, the abolition of guilds, the introduction of uniform weights and measures, the removal of seigneurial excrescences, the redefinition of property rights come to be seen as the product of conspiracy, accident, or a hidden hand. The impregnation of the bourgeoisie with market values, the "bourgeoisification" of the professions, and the organic links developing between the professions and mercantile groups prior to 1789, on the other hand, help to provide a more viable political and cultural framework for understanding why such reforms were introduced. These phenomena constitute a "silent bourgeois revolution" which was the essential precursor of the noisier, messier, and better-known events of 1789.[90] They also help to explain why one of the most durable and toughest legislative legacies of the revolutionary years should be the so-called "career open to talents," a principle which was indeed tailored to the career interests and civic sense of the liberal professions by, precisely, the members of the liberal professions who dominated the assemblies.

A great deal more work still needs to be done on relations between the different branches of the bourgeoisie – the different types of professionals, the landed and commercial bourgeoisie, and so on – as well as what Colin Lucas has called the "stress zones" between them. These relationships, moreover, shifted, sometimes radically as a result of the revolutionary experience. The quotation by Barère with which I began [see above, p. 87] is symptomatic of the problem: Barère attacks commerce and speculation from a political viewpoint; yet, on the other hand, his rhetoric connives in a good commercial operation. We need to know more about how the Revolution affected the professions, and the arguments about professional standards, quality control, educational requirements, and public interest which had percolated within them throughout the late Enlightenment. The events of 1789 moved these debates which had gripped the professions under the Old Regime on to a new level, and their subsequent history highlighted the mixed and sometimes contradictory legacy of the revolutionary experience.

There was to be, it seems, no single trajectory for the professions in the 1790s, nor any common destiny for their members. The abolition of venal office on 4 August and the enunciation of the principle of the career open to talent in the Declaration of the Rights of Man on 26 August 1789 left a great deal of room for debate and disagreement of how professionalism should be conjugated with the exigencies of citizenship. The response of each of the professions differed, and new fault-lines emerged out of the process. The furore within the army is relatively well-known.[91] How far did the rights of soldiers as citizens entitle them to political activities which, in the opinion of many of their supporters, nullified professional *esprit de corps*? The path towards the patriotic citizen-soldier of Year II passed by way of the Nancy mutiny and its repression and the emigration of 60 per cent of the putatively "professional" noble officer corps. The late 1790s and the Napoleonic period were to see the reassertion of a more corporative version of professionalism, with the sacrifice of many of the more democratic procedures of Year II, such as election of officers.

The experience of the clergy was rather different.[92] The Civil Constitution of the Clergy may in many respects be viewed as the charter of a professionalized secular clergy, establishing as it did democratic procedures, rational hierarchies, and a well-founded career structure. Yet civic professionalism fell foul of corporative professionalism: many priests found it difficult to accept the loss of their monopoly of spiritual services consequent on the enunciation of the principle of freedom of conscience, and jibbed at National Assembly's failure to consult either the Church as a corporate entity or its hierarchical head, the Pope. The 1790s was to prove an often tragic backcloth against which the clergy rethought their attitudes towards ecclesiastical hierarchy, conscience, and civic responsibility.

A similar reassessment was necessary for the medical and legal professions and for the state bureaucracy.[93] The career open to talents and the attack on privilege within corporate hierarchies justified the attack on the Old Regime bureaucracy, the abolition of many of its services (such as the General Farm, probably the most corporatively professionalized of all state services,) the closure of legal and medical faculties, and the dissolution of first attorneys, then barristers. By the late 1790s, however, a barrage of complaints emerged from all quarters which highlighted how the opening up of a free field for medical and legal practice had damaged public interest and (so it was said) standards of professional competence. The public was, it was argued, prey to medical charlatans, legal sharks, and corrupt and ill-trained clerks. The reassertion of a corporative hierarchy and the reintroduction of better training methods under the Thermidorian Convention, the Directory, and the Consulate attested to a reworking of the relationship between profession, state, and public.

There is much about the civic-inspired deregulation of many of the professions in the 1790s and their corporative reprofessionalization later in the decade which remains obscure. Certainly the professions were transformed in the Revolution-ary decade – a fact palpable in the disappearance of many pre-revolutionary titles such as *procureur*, *avocat*, *chirurgien*, and so on. After the perils of the "free field" had been exposed, it looked as though for most the best guarantee of professional success after 1789 was state utility. Hence the unrivalled prestige of the armed forces from the late 1790s; hence the formidable strengthening of the state bureaucracy; hence the emergence of a prestigious scientific profession, very much under the wing of the state; hence too the arguments of state utility advanced by doctors and lawyers in their attempts to win government support.[94] The civic and corporative models of professionalization which had emerged in the Ancien Régime were transformed by the experience of the 1790s; but in broad terms, it was something akin to the corporative model which often pre-vailed, while maintaining the career open to talent which the civic model had required. The Revolution had changed both the context of and the protagonists in the debate over professionalism. And the transformed professions were to make a massive and well-documented contribution to the character of nineteenth-century France.

The professions remained after 1800, finally, still very much tributary to the market for their services. Though the state was often a valued client, most depended very considerably on the overall situation of the economy. As the Revisionists have pointed out with an often wearisome frequency, the Revolution did not mark a transition to industrialism in the French economy (Actually, Georges Lefebvre and Albert Soboul seem to have been pretty much aware of that fact too, as their balanced assessments of the sometimes contradictory social and economic legacy of the Revolution should make clear.)[95] France's economy was still in the commercial mould, and the professions inevitably reflected that fact.[96] *Pace* many Revisionists, however, the French economy was not irredeemably traditionalist nor stagnatingly precapitalist. France continued its measured and balanced way towards industrialization. Indeed, growth in the early nineteenth century, even before the creation of a national rail network, is now being recognized as having been far stronger than has often been thought. In that progress, the Revolution had been perhaps a less heroic and dramatic episode than the Old Marxist Orthodoxy would maintain; though it certainly had far more importance, and positive influence, than the New Revolutionist Orthodoxy would allow. The legislative achievement of successive Revolutionary assemblies and the eradication of Old Regime privilege provided a more appropriate environment for commercial capitalism in general to develop, and the bourgeoisie in particular to prosper. France moved slowly towards its industrializing goal at the end of a bourgeois nineteenth century for which the stage had been set by a bourgeois revolution, Revisionist reports of whose sad demise I persist in finding greatly exaggerated.

NOTES

Source Reprinted in an abridged format from *The French Revolution and Social Change*, ed. Colin Lucas (Oxford: Oxford University Press, 1990), pp. 69–118.

Acknowledgment Alfred Cobban, launching his famous broadside against the so-called "Marxist interpretation" of the French Revolution in 1964, regretted that "one cannot criticise an historical interpretation without appearing to criticise the historians who have held it." As I am sure was the case with Cobban, it is not my intention to launch *ad hominem* (or *ad feminam*) attacks – all the more in that numbers of the historians whose arguments I here criticize offered helpful and constructive comments following earlier versions of this paper read in Oxford, London, and Washington, DC. Particular thanks are due to Jonathan Barry, Bill Doyle, Colin Lucas, and Michael Sonenscher.

1 For a brilliantly written account of some of Palloy's activities, see S. Schama, *Citizens: A Chronology of the French Revolution* (London, 1989), pp. 408–16. Cf. Romi [pseud. Robert Miquel] *Le Livre de raison du patriote Palloy* (Paris, 1962); and H. Lemoine, "Les Comptes de démolition de la Bastille," *Bulletin de la Société de l'histoire de Paris et de l'Ile de France*, 1929.
2 *Archives parlementaires de 1787 à 1860*, 1st ser., 19 (1884), 433 (session 4 October 1790).
3 A. Cobban, *The Social Interpretation of the French Revolution* (London, 1964). Cobban's line of argument can be traced back to his Inaugural Lecture in 1954, "The Myth of the French Revolution," reprinted along with other of his polemical and scholarly pieces in *Aspects of the French Revolution* (London, 1968).

4 G.V. Taylor, "Bourgeoisie,", in B. Rothaus and S.F. Scott, *Historical Dictionary of the French Revolution*, 2 vols (Westport, Conn., 1985), i. p. 122.

5 Schama, *Citizens*, p. xiv for the zombies. This is little improvement on Colin Lucas's reference to 'indeterminate social mutants': C. Lucas, "Nobles, Bourgeois and the Origins of the French Revolution," *Past and Present* (henceforth *P&P*), 60 (1973), 90. [Reprinted as Chapter 2 in this volume.]

6 G.V. Taylor, "Noncapitalist Wealth and the Origins of the French Revolution," *American Historical Review* (henceforth *AmHR*), 72 (1967), 482; Lucas, "Nobles, Bourgeois and Origins," 89–92 and *passim*; W. Doyle, "The Price of Offices in pre-Revolutionary France," *Historical Journal*, 27 (1984), 844. These are major articles within a relatively small range of classic texts which together form the much remasticated pabulum of Revisionist argument. Other key works in the litany include G.V. Taylor, "Types of Capitalism in Eighteenth-Century France," *English Historical Review*, 79 (1964); *id.* Revolutionary and Non-Revolutionary Content in the *Cahiers* of 1789; An Interim Report," *French Historical Studies* (henceforth *FHS*), 7 (1972–3); E. Eisenstein, "Who Intervened in 1788?," *AmHR*, 71 (1965); C.B.A. Behrens, *The Ancien Régime* (London, 1967); *id.*, "Nobles, Privileges and Taxes in France at the End of the Ancien Régime," *Economic History Review* (henceforth *EcHR*), 15 (1962–3); W. Doyle, *Origins of the French Revolution* (Oxford, 1980); F. Furet and D. Richet, *The French Revolution* (London, 1970); F. Furet, *Interpreting the French Revolution* (London, 1981). T.C.W. Blanning, *The French Revolution: Aristocrats versus Bourgeois?* (London, 1987) is a brilliant summation of the debate and itself stands as a major contribution to Revisionism.

7 A good example of a "traditionalist" reading of Old Regime society from an authoritative Revisionist source in W. Doyle, *The Oxford History of the French Revolution* (Oxford, 1989), esp. ch. 1. Cf. *id.*, *The Ancien Régime* (London, 1986), 20 ff. For popular culture, see the classic R. Mandrou, *De la culture populaire aux XVIIe et XVIIIe siècles* (Paris, 1964); and, as a recent example, T. Brennan, *Public Drinking and Popular Culture in Eighteenth-Century Paris* (Princeton, NJ, 1988). For spirited onslaughts on the conceptual framework of much research on "traditional society" and "popular culture," see M. Sonenscher, *Work and Wages: Natural Law, Politics and the Eighteenth-Century French Trades* (Cambridge, 1989), pp. 44–6; and R. Chartier, "Culture as Appropriation: Popular Cultural Uses in Early Modern France," in S.L. Kaplan (ed.), *Understanding Popular Culture* (Paris, 1984).

8 G. Chaussinand-Nogaret, *The French Nobility in the Eighteenth Century: From Feudalism to Enlightenment* (Cambridge, 1985). Much of Chaussinand-Nogaret's evidence on entrepreneurship is culled from the (refreshingly unrevisionist) scholarship of Guy Richard, notably the latter's *La Noblesse d'affaires au XVIIIe siècle* (Paris, 1975). See too Chaussinand-Nogaret, *Une Histoire des élites, 1770–1848* (Paris, 1975); R. Forster, "The Provincial Noble: A Reappraisal," *AmHR*, 78 (1968); and D. Sutherland's trenchant views on the social élite in his *France 1789–1815: Revolution and Counter-Revolution* (London, 1985), pp. 19–21. A good counter-argument to Chaussinand-Nogaret is mounted by P. Goujard, "Féodalité et lumières au XVIIIe siècle: L'Exemple de la noblesse," *Annales historiques de la Révolution française* (henceforth *AhRf*), 227 (1977).

9 See W. Doyle, "Was There an Aristocratic Reaction in pre-Revolutionary France?" *P&P*, 57 (1972); D. Bien. "La Réaction aristocratique avant 1789: L'Exemple de l'armée," *Annales: Economies, sociétés, civilisations* (henceforth *AnnESC*), 29 (1974).

10 L. and J. Stone, *An Open Elite? England, 1540–1880* (Oxford, 1984). Cf. A. Milward and S.B. Saul, *The Economic Development of Continental Europe, 1780–1870* (London, 1973), esp. pp. 30–1. On the French side, note the important calculations on social mobility in Bien, "Réaction aristocratique," pp. 505–14.

11 Chaussinand-Nogaret, *French Nobility*, p. 1.

12 An authoritative overview of this widely held perspective in Doyle, *Ancien Régime*, pp. 25–6.

13 W.G. Runciman, "Unnecessary Revolution: The Case of France," *Archives européennes de sociologie*, 23 (1983).

14 M. Morineau, "Was There an Agricultural Revolution in Eighteenth-Century France?," in R. Cameron (ed.), *Essays in French Economic History* (London, 1970); and *id., Les Faux-semblants d'un démarrage économique: Agriculture et démographie en France au dix-huitième siècle* (Paris, 1970) – both key texts for the Revisionists' case which is also buttressed on this point by socio-economic historians who view structural economic change in France as a post-railway phenomenon. See, for example, R. Price, *The Economic Modernization of France, 1730–1914* (London, 1981); and E. Weber, *Peasants into Frenchmen: The Modernisation of Rural France, 1870–1914* (London, 1979). The gloomy diagnosis is confirmed in the non-scholarly but well-argued R. Sedillot, *Le Coût de la Révolution française* (Paris, 1987).

15 E. Le Roy Ladurie, "L'Histoire immobile," *AnnESC*, 29 (1974). This influential article, highly symptomatic of much contemporary writing on rural history, is available in English translation as "History that Stands Still," in *id., The Mind and Method of the Historian* (London, 1981).

16 L. Hunt, *Politics, Culture and Class in the French Revolution* (London, 1986), p. 9.

17 K.M. Baker (ed.), *The French Revolution and the Creation of Modern Political Culture*, i. *The Political Culture of the Old Regime* (Oxford, 1987). Reviews of this important work by J. Censer, "The Coming of a New Interpretation of the French Revolution?," *Journal of Social History*, 21 (1987); and P.R. Campbell, "Old Régime Politics and the New Interpretation of the French Revolution," *Renaissance and Modern Studies*, 32 (1989). The second volume of the series, ed. Colin Lucas, was *The Political Culture of the French Revolution* (Oxford, 1988).

18 Furet, *Interpreting the French Revolution*, esp. p. 47 ff., p. 61 ff.

19 *Ibid.* p. 53 ff. Cf. F. Furet and R. Halévi, "L'Année 1789," *AnnESC*, 44 (1989), esp. p. 21. This view by Furet contrasts with his own views as expressed in Furet and Richet, *The French Revolution* – where the Terror is seen as taking place as a result of the Revolution "skidding" unpredictably to the Left. Cf. the forceful statement of much of the Furet case (Mark II) in Schama, *Citizens*, esp. pp. 446–7, 623, 792, etc.

20 Notably Furet's essay "The Revolutionary Catechism" in *Interpreting the French Revolution*, Ch. 2.1.

21 M. Fitzsimmons, "Privilege and Polity in France, 1786–9," *AmHR*, 92 (1987); and *id., The Parisian Order of Barristers and the French Revolution* (Cambridge, Mass., 1987), pp. 41–2, 193–4; N. Hampson, *Prelude to Terror: The Constituent Assembly and the Failure of Consensus, 1789–1791* (Oxford, 1989), p. 56; Doyle, 'Price of Offices,' pp. 859–60; Schama, *Citizens*, p. 439.

22 Schama, *Citizens*, p. 439 Fitzsimmons, *Parisian Order of Barristers*, pp. 41–2.

23 Fitzsimmons, *Parisian Order of Barristers*, p. 197; Taylor, "Noncapitalist Wealth," p. 491.

24 Sutherland, *France, 1789–1815*: see esp. pp. 333–5, 438–42.

25 D. Johnson, "Fire in the Mind," *Times Educational Supplement*, 14 October 1988, p. 24.

26 See in particular the recent work of R. Sécher, *Le Génocide franco-français: La Vendée-Vengé* (Paris, 1986) and *La Chapelle-Basse-Mer: Révolution et contre-révolution* (Paris, 1986), dealing in highly contentious fashion with the repression of revolt in western France in the 1790s. For a sober assessment of some of the statistics involved, cf. F. Lebrun, "Reynald Sécher et les morts de la guerre de Vendée," *Annales de Bretagne* (henceforth *AB*), 93 (1986).

27 There are clear signs that historians are becoming increasingly dissatisfied with many Revisionist arguments. See, as a sampler, B. Edmonds, "Successes and Excesses of Revisionist Writing about the French Revolution," *European History Quarterly*, 17 (1987); P.M. Jones, *The Peasantry in the French Revolution* (Cambridge, 1988), esp. ch. 2; and P. McPhee, "The French Revolution, Peasants and Capitalism," *AmHR*, 94 (1989). Cf. too M.D. Sibalis, "Corporatism and the Corporation: The Debate on Restoring the Guilds under Napoleon I and the Restoration," *FHS* 15 (1987–8), esp. p. 720. It is

noticeable that even Schama, who espouses most of Furet's arguments on the Revolution, is still often critical of Revisionist stances: *Citizens*, e.g. p. 188 ff.

28 Cf. Doyle, *Origins*, p. 32; *id.*, *Ancien Régime*, 26–8; W.W. Rostow, *The Stages of Economic Growth: A Non-Communist Manifesto* (Cambridge, 1960). The "backwardness" thesis is stated with great force in the influential D. Landes, *The Unbound Prometheus: Technological Change and Industrial Development in Western Europe from 1750 to the Present* (Cambridge, 1972).

29 F. Crouzet's numerous articles around this point are conveniently collected in his *De la supériorité de l'Angleterre sur la France: L'Economique et l'imaginaire (XVIIᵉ–XXᵉ siècle)* (Paris, 1985). See too P. O'Brien and C. Keyder, *Economic Growth in Britain and France, 1780–1914: Two Paths to the Twentieth Century* (London, 1978); *id.*, "Les Voies de passage vers la société industrielle en Grande-Bretagne et en France (1780–1914)," *AnnESC*, 34 (1979); N. Crafts, "England and France: Some Thoughts on the Question 'Why was England first?'," *EcHR*, 30 (1977); *id.*, "British and French Economic Growth, 1700–1831: A Review of the Evidence," *EcHR*, 36 (1983); *id.*, "British Industrialisation in an International Context," *Journal of Interdisciplinary History*, 19 (1989); R. Roehl, "French Industrialization: A Reconsideration," *Explorations in Economic History*, 15 (1976); J.L. Goldsmith, "The Agrarian History of Pre-Industrial France: Where do We Go from here?," *Journal of European Economic History* (henceforth *JEEH*), 13 (1984); R. Aldrich, "Late-Comer or Early Starter? New Views on French Economic History," *JEEH*, 16 (1987). These are only a sampler from a list which could be considerably extended. The chorus does not sing in unison, there being a number of major differences of opinion between them. However, all are critical of the classic account, as is the wide-ranging C. Sabel and J. Zeitlin, "Historical Alternatives to Mass Production: Political Markets and Technology in Nineteenth-Century Industrialisation," *P&P*, 108 (1985). Overall it seems a fascinating historiographical paradox that Anglo-Saxon scholarship on Old Regime French society settled into a "traditionalist," "backward-orientated" mold just as economic historians of Britain, working comparatively, called into question the economic dynamism of the "First Industrial Nation." The edifice of French "backwardness" is thus a lot shakier than the confident tone of the Revisionists would suggest.

30 O'Brien and Keyder, *Economic Growth in Britain and France*, p. 57.

31 C.P. Kindleberger, "Financial Institutions and Economic Development: A Comparison of Great Britain and France in the Eighteenth and Nineteenth Centuries," *Explorations in Economic History*, 23 (1984); J.R. Harris, "Skills, Coal and British Industry in the Eighteenth Century," *History*, 61 (1976).

32 O'Brien and Keyder, *Economic Growth in Britain and France*, esp. pp. 186–8, 191–3. Cf. C. Heywood, "The Role of the Peasantry in French Industrialisation, 1815–80," *EcHR*, 34 (1981).

33 These figures are from Pierre Léon's contribution to Braudel and Labrousse, *Histoire économique et sociale* and are accepted by Doyle, who suggests they might even be revised upwards: *Origins*, pp. 129, 231.

34 Chaussinand-Nogaret, *French Nobility*, pp. 28–30, 87–8.

35 J. Merrick, "Conscience and Citizenship in Eighteenth-Century France," *Eighteenth-Century Studies*, 4 (1987); R. Robin, *La Société française en 1789: Semuren-Auxois* (Paris, 1970); and cf. J. Revel, "Les Corps et communautés," in Baker, *Political Culture of the Old Régime*, pp. 539–41. Those who have read W. Sewell, *Work and Revolution in France* will know how much I owe on some of what follows to this marvellous book (for a helpful, if critical review of which, see L. Hunt and G. Sheridan, "Corporatism, Association and the Language of Labor in France, 1750–1850," *JMH*, 58 (1986)). There remains a whole area of socio-cultural linguistic study to be done on the shifting meanings of key terms in these debates.

36 Bien, "Réaction aristocratique" (see above, n. 9). Cf. *id.*, "The Army in the French Enlightenment: Reform, Reaction and Revolution," *P&P*, 85 (1979). Incidentally, as

Bien admits, the artillery was both one of the most highly professional of all sectors of the armed forces in the late eighteenth century and one sector in which noble dominance was least marked. See too S.F. Scott, "The French Revolution and the Professionalisation of the French Officer Corps," in M. Janowitz and J. van Doorn, *On Military Ideology* (London, 1971).

37 Bien, "Réaction aristocratique," pp. 519–22; E.C. Léonard, *L'Armée et ses problèmes au XVIIIᵉ siècle* (Paris, 1958), pp. 286 ff.

38 See Léonard, *Armée*, Chs 12–14. There is relevant material too in J. Chagniot, *Paris et l'armée au XVIIIᵉ siècle: Etude politique et sociale* (Paris, 1985), particularly useful for not being orientated around the rural nobility. Chagniot also emphasizes the importance of lower non-noble officers in entrepreneurial activity (moneylending, petty trading, etc.).

39 J.A.H. de Guibert, *Essai général de tactique*; J. Servan de Gerbay, *Le Soldat citoyen*; and others discussed in Léonard, *Armée*, pp. 251 ff.

40 L. Carnot, "Eloge de Vauban," discussed in M. Reinhard, *Le Grand Carnot*, 2 vols (Paris, 1950–2), i. pp. 76–86. See too Ch.16, entitled "Le civisme du militaire."

41 T. Tackett, "The Citizen-Priest: Politics and Ideology among the Parish Clergy of Eighteenth-Century Dauphiné," *Studies in Eighteenth-Century Culture*, 7 (1978); B. Plongeron, *La Vie quotidienne du clergé français au XVIIIᵉ siècle* (Paris, 1974). See also Tackett's *Priest and Parish in Eighteenth-Century France: A Social and Political Study of the Curé in a Diocese of Dauphiné, 1750–97* (Princeton, NJ, 1977) and his *Religion, Revolution and Regional Culture in Eighteenth-Century France: The Ecclesiastical Oath of 1791* (Princeton, NJ, 1986); D. Julia, "Les Deux Puissances: Chronique d'une séparation de corps," in Baker, *Political Culture of the Old Régime*.

42 Plongeron, *Vie quotidienne du clergé*, p. 75.

43 Supporting older, anecdotal scholarship on this point, are recent studies based on post-mortem inventories: e.g. A. Pardailhé-Galabrun, "L'Habitat et le cadre de vie des prêtres à Paris au XVIIIᵉ siècle" and R. Plessix, "Les Inventaires après décès: Une piste d'approche de la culture matérielle des curés du Haut-Maine au XVIIIᵉ siècle," both *AB*, 95 (1988).

44 R.F. Necheles, "The Curés in the Estates General of 1789," *JMH*, 46 (1974); M.G. Hutt, "The Role of the Curés in the Estates General," *Journal of Ecclesiastical History*, 6 (1955).

45 A great deal on schoolteachers and civic values in this classic work of D. Mornet, *Les Origines intellectuelles de la Révolution française* (Paris, 1933), esp. pp. 319 ff. and 419 ff.

46 G. Saucerotte, *Les Médecins pendant la Révolution* (Paris, 1887).

47 T. Gelfand, *Professionalizing Modern Medicine: Paris Surgeons and Medical Science and Institutions in the Eighteenth Century* (Westport, Conn., 1980).

48 *Ibid.* pp. 43–4; and J. Guillermaud (ed.), *Histoire de la médecine aux armées; De l'Antiquité à Révolution* (Paris, 1982).

49 The history of medical practice is marvellously illuminated in M. Ramsey, *Professional and Popular Medicine in France, 1770–1830: The Social World of Medical Practice* (Cambridge, 1988). See too "La Médicalisation en France du XVIIIᵉ au début du XXᵉ siècle," *AB*, 86 (1979); J.P. Goubert (ed.), *La Médicalisation de la société française, 1770–1830* (Waterloo, Ontario, 1982); and C. Jones, "The Medicalisation of Eighteenth-Century France," in R. Porter and A. Weare (eds), *Problems and Methods in the History of Medicine* (London, 1987). For medical training, see L.W.B. Brockliss, *French Higher Education in the Seventeenth and Eighteenth Centuries: A Cultural Study* (Oxford, 1987).

50 C. Hannaway, *Medicine, Public Welfare and the State of Eighteenth-Century France: The Société Royale de Médecine (1776–93)*, University Microfilms edn (1975) of Johns Hopkins Ph.D. thesis (1974). See *id.*, "The Société Royale de Médecine and Epidemics in Ancien Régime France," *Bulletin of the History of Medicine*, 40 (1972); and J. Meyer, "L'Enquête de l'Académie de médecine sur les epidémies, 1774–94," *Etudes rurales*, 9 (1969).

51 Ramsey, *Professional and Popular Medicine; id.,* "Traditional Medicine and Medical Enlightenment: The Regulation of Secret Remedies in the Ancien Régime," in Goubert, *Médicalisation;* and T. Gelfand, "Medical Professionals and Charlatans: The *Comité de salubrité enquête,* 1790–1," *Histoire sociale/Social History,* 8 (1978).

52 D. Roche, "Talents, raison et sacrifice: L'Image du médecin des Lumières d'après les Eloges de la Société Royale de Médecine (1776–89)," *AnnESC,* 32 (1977); J.P. Goubert and D. Lorillot, 1789, *Le Corps médical et le changement: Cahiers de doléances (médecins, chirurgiens et apothicaires)* (Toulouse, 1984), pp. 25–6.

53 Berlanstein, "Lawyers," p. 164 ff.

54 S. Maza, "Le Tribunal de la Nation: Les Mémoires judiciaries et l'opinion publique à la fin de l'Ancien Régime," and K. Baker, "Politique et opinion publique sous l'Ancien Régime," both *AnnESC,* 42 (1987). Cf. M. Ozouf, "L'Opinion publique," in Baker, *Political Culture of the Old Régime;* and W. Doyle, "Dupaty (1746–88): A Career in the Late Enlightenment," *Studies in Voltaire and the Eighteenth Century,* 230 (1985), esp. p. 82 ff.

55 For Calas, see D. Bien, *The Calas Affair: Persecution, Toleration and Heresy in Eighteenth-Century Toulouse* (Princeton, NJ, 1961).

56 Maza, Baker, and Ozouf (see references at note 54) draw heavily on J. Habermas, *L'Espace public: Archéologie de la publicité comme dimension constitutive de la société bourgeoise* (Paris, 1978). It is symptomatic of the Revisionist approach that they neglect the aspects of Habermas's work which deal with the infrastructural aspects of the growth of a public, and also its bourgeois dimension, both of which are directly related to the present essay.

57 E.H. Lemay, "La Composition de l'Assemblée nationale constituante: Les Hommes de la continuité," *RHMC,* 24 (1977). The assembly also contained 315 office-holders, a great many of whom had legal training too.

58 Cited in F. Brunot, *Histoire de la langue française des origines à nos jours* (Paris, 1930), ix (1967), pp. 944–5.

59 G. Matthews, *The Royal General Farms in the Eighteenth Century* (New York, 1958); and V. Azimi, *Un modèle administratif de l'Ancien Régime: Les Commis de la ferme générale et de la régie des aides* (Paris, 1987). On the bureaucracy in general, see too C. Church, *Revolution and Red Tape: The French Ministerial Bureaucracy, 1770–1850* (Oxford, 1981); Doyle, "Price of Offices"; M. Antoine, "La Monarchie absolue," in Baker, *Political Culture of the Old Régime;* J.F. Bosher, *French Finances, 1770–1795: From Business to Bureaucracy* (Cambridge, 1970); and G. Bossenga, "From *Corps* to Citizenship: The *Bureau des Finances* before the French Revolution," *JMH,* 58 (1986).

60 V. Azimi, "1789: L'Echo des employés ou le nouveau discours administratif," *XVIIIe Siècle,* 21 (1989), p. 34.

61 Church, *Revolution and Red Tape,* p. 28.

62 Bosher, *French Finances,* pp. 142–65; R.D. Harris, *Necker, Reform Statesman of the Ancien Régime* (Berkeley, Calif., 1979); Bossenga, "From *Corps* to Citizenship," *passim.*

63 Azimi, "1789," p. 134.

64 Church, *Revolution and Red Tape,* p. 46.

65 Doyle, "Price of Offices," p. 844.

66 C. Jones, "The *Médecins du Roi* at the End of the Ancien Régime and in the French Revolution," in V. Nutton (ed.), *Medicine at Court, 1500–1800* (London, 1989).

67 *ibid.,* plus P. Delaunay, *Le Monde médical parisien au XVIIIe siècle (1906)* (p. 100 for Lefebvre), and R. Darnton's classic *Mesmerism and the End of the Enlightenment in France* (Cambridge, Mass., 1968), for insights into the general atmosphere.

68 Doyle, "Price of Offices," pp. 852–4, 856–7. See R. Giesey, "State-Building in Early Modern France: The Role of Royal Officialdom," *JMH,* 55 (1983) for some interesting ideas on office and markets.

69 Cf. in this respect the arguments of R.C. Allen on the economic rationality behind land purchase, allegedly for status reasons, in eighteenth-century England: "The Price of

Freehold Land and the Interest Rate in the Seventeenth and Eighteenth Centuries", *EcHR*, 41 (1988).

70 Bossenga, "From *Corps* to Citizenship"; and D. Bien, "Office, Corps and a System of State Credit: The Uses of Privilege under the Old Régime," in Baker, *Political Culture of Old Régime*.

71 Bosher, *French Finances*; J. Egret, *The French Pre-Revolution, 1787–8* (Chicago, 1977), pp. 43–61, 95–9; Harris, *Necker*, pp. 107–15.

72 Carey, *Judicial Reform*, p. 105.

73 G. Bossenga, "City and State: An Urban Perspective on the Origins of the French Revolution," in Baker, *Political Culture of the Old Régime*.

74 Root, *Peasants and King*, esp. Ch. 3. Cf. K. Tonnesson, "La Démocratie directe sous la Révolution française: Le Cas des districts et sections de Paris," in Lucas, *Political Culture of the Revolution*, pp. 295–6.

75 The outstanding work of Michael Sonenscher is especially illuminating of this theme: besides his *Work and Wages*, see too his article "Journeymen, the Courts and the French Trades, 1781–91," *P&P*, 114 (1987). Cf. Revel, "Corps et comunautés," pp. 239–41.

76 D. Roche, *Le Siècle des Lumières en province: Académies et académiciens provinciaux, 1680–1789*, 2 vols (Paris, 1978); id., "Académies et politique au siècle des Lumières: Les Enjeux pratiques de l'immortalité," in Baker, *Political Culture of the Old Régime*.

77 Roche, *Siècle des Lumières en province*, i. p. 257 ff.; R. Halévi, *Les Loges maçonniques dans la France d'Ancien Régime: Aux origines de la sociabilité démocratique* (Paris, 1984); D. Roche, "Négoce et culture dans la France du XVIIIe siècle," *RHMC*, 25 (1978); Hunt, *Politics, Class and Culture*, pp. 198–200; and the classic M. Agulhon, *Pénitent et franc-maçons dans l'ancienne Provence* (Paris, 1965). Cf. too the general overview of E. François and R. Reichhardt, "Les Formes de sociabilité en France du milieu du XVIIIe siècle au milieu du XIXe siècle," *RHMC*, 34 (1987).

78 Roche, *Le Siècle des Lumières en province*, ii. pp. 419–24; and cf. François and Reichhardt, "Formes de sociabilité," pp. 465 ff.

79 For a general overview, see M. Agulhon, "Les Sociétés de pensée," in M. Vovelle (ed.), *Etat de la France pendant la Révolution, 1789–99* (Paris, 1988), pp. 44–8.

80 Halévi, *Les Loges maçonniques*. Cf. Furet, *Interpreting the French Revolution*, pp. 37 ff.

81 Cf. W. Reddy, *Money and Liberty in Western Europe: A Critique of Historical Understanding* (Cambridge, 1987), p. 5: "There was no revolutionary bourgeoisie."

82 E.J. Sieyes, *Qu'est-ce que le Tiers Etat?*, ed. S.E. Finer (Chicago, 1963), pp. 63–4. Cf. Sewel, *Work and Revolution*, 79.

83 See e.g. the highly illuminating recent study of D.R. Weir "Tontines, Public Finance and Revolution in France and England, 1688–1789," *Journal of Economic History*, 49 (1989). On a different tack, see too the interesting perspective on the problem opened up in J. de Viguerie, "Le Roi, le 'public' et l'exemple de Louis XV," *Revue historique*, 278 (1987).

84 Reddy, *Money and Liberty*, pp. 128–9, for arguments along the same lines as here.

85 Cobban, *Aspects*, pp. 109–11.

86 Hunt, *Politics, Class and Culture*, Ch. 5; and L. Hunt, P. Hansen and D. Lansky, "The Failure of the Liberal Republic in France, 1795–9: The Road to Brumaire," *JMH*, 51 (1979).

87 R.B. Rose, *The Making of the Sans-Culottes* (Manchester, 1983); R. Cobb, *The Police and the People: French Popular Protest, 1789–1820* (Oxford, 1970), pp. 178–9; R. Andrews, "Social Structures, Political Elites and Ideology in Revolutionary Paris," *Journal of Social History*, 19 (1985); M. Sonenscher, "The Sans-Culottes of the Year II: Rethinking the Language of Labour in Revolutionary France," *Social History*, 9 (1984).

88 Hunt, *Politics, Culture and Class*, p. 161, citing E. Burke, "Thoughts on French Affairs," in R.A. Smith (ed.), *Burke on Revolution* (New York, 1968) p. 190.

89 Most famously in R. Darnton, "The High Enlightenment and the Low Life of Literature in pre-Revolutionary France," *P&P*, 51 (1971); and more recently in "The Facts of

Literary Life in Eighteenth-Century France," in Baker, *Political Culture of the Old Régime*. Cf. too Furet, *Interpreting the French Revolution*, pp. 36–7.

90 The phrase "silent bourgeois revolution" comes from D. Blackbourn and G. Eley, *The Peculiarities of German History: Bourgeois Society and Politics in Nineteenth-Century Germany* (Oxford, 1982), a work which has a number of similarities of approach to those outlined here, but which I unfortunately encountered only when writing the final draft of this essay.

91 S. Scott, *The Response of the Royal Army to the French Revolution: The Role and Development of the Line Army, 1787–1793* (Oxford, 1978); J.P. Bertaud, *The Army of the French Revolution: From Citizen Soldiers to Instrument of Power* (Princeton, NJ, 1989). Cf. too J. Godechot, *Les Institutions de la France sous la Révolution et l'Empire* (Paris, 1968), pp. 113–38, 353–74, 494–5.

92 Tackett, *Religion, Revolution and Regional Culture*; and J. McManners, *The French Revolution and the Church* (London, 1969) for introductions to this massive topic.

93 D.M. Vess, *Medical Revolution in France, 1789–96* (Gainesville, Fla., 1975) and D.B. Weiner, "French Doctors Face the War, 1792–1815" in C.K. Warner (ed.), *From the Ancien Régime to the Popular Front: Essays in the History of Modern France in Honor of S. B. Clough* (New York, 1969); Fitzsimmons, *Parisian Order of Barristers*, esp. p. 116 ff.; I. Woloch, "The Fall and Resurrection of the Civil Bar, 1789–1820s," *FHS*, 15 (1987–8). See too Godechot, *Institutions*, pp. 154–5, 449–53, 704–5 and *passim*.

94 C.C. Gillispie, "Politics and Science, with Special Reference to Revolutionary and Napoleonic France," *History and Technology*, 4 (1987); Bosher, *French Finances*; Church, *Revolution and Red Tape*; M. Brugière, *Gestionnaires et profiteurs de la Révolution* (Paris, 1986); *id.*, "Les Finances et l'Etat," in Lucas, *Political Culture of the French Revolution*.

95 See, for example, G. Lefebvre, *The French Revolution*, 2 vols (New York, 1962, 1964), ii. p. 303 ff.; and A. Soboul, *The French Revolution, 1787–1799* (London, 1974), p. 553 ff. Cf. Edmonds, "Successes and Excesses," pp. 198–200.

96 See generally the works cited above, n. 29, by O'Brien and Keyder, Crafts, Roehl, Goldsmith, and Aldrich, plus Heywood, "Role of the peasantry" and Lemarchand, "Du féodalisme au capitalisme." See too M. Lévy-Leboyer, "La Croissance économique en France au XIXe siècle," *AnnESC*, 28 (1973); W. H. Newell, "The Agrarian Revolution in Nineteenth-Century France," *Journal of Economic History*, 33 (1973); and J. Marczewski, "Economic Fluctuations in France, 1815–1938," *JEEH*, 17 (1988).

6

LUXURY, MORALITY, AND SOCIAL CHANGE

Why there was no middle-class consciousness in prerevolutionary France

Sarah Maza

Sarah Maza's essay picks up directly where Colin Jones leaves off, and so can be read as virtually a direct response to his intriguing argument. When Jones refers to the French Revolution as a "bourgeois revolution," he means essentially two things: first, that the Revolution was caused by a dynamic proto-capitalist economy that thrust the members of the middle class – the bourgeoisie – into the center of society; and second, that it was this middle class that made the French Revolution. Until now, however, all sides of the debate over the Revolution's causes agreed that both these conditions went hand-in-hand: discovering one implied the existence of the other.

Among Sarah Maza's original contributions to this debate is to distinguish between Jones's characterization of the French economy and his insistence upon the role played by the middle class or bourgeoisie. On the one hand, Maza accepts that the eighteenth-century French economy was far from static, and showed signs of dynamism, growth, and commercial capitalism. Yet Maza disputes the existence of a middle class that brought this about. Using a variety of sources, Maza is unable to find Frenchmen discussing a rising middle class; indeed, her argument is that Frenchmen rarely thought in terms of class at all, and tended to think about society in more universalistic terms. For Maza, if the French Revolution was a "bourgeois revolution," it was one in which the middle classes had not yet been discovered. Such a conclusion throws water on Jones's arguments, and forces us to return to questions about individual action and motivation raised thirty years earlier by Colin Lucas.

* * *

Was there a rising middle class in eighteenth-century France, and did it contribute decisively to the upheaval that began in 1789? Right now that question is murkier than ever for having been mostly abandoned in recent years. In the past two decades in the historiography of prerevolutionary France the spotlight has moved away from social issues; while excellent monographs dealing with society continue to appear each year, the central debate on the causes and nature of the French Revolution has focused lately on political life.[1] Amid the flurry of pathbreaking recent publications on political culture, print culture, and political ideologies, of debates on gender, sexuality, and the public and private spheres, we seem to have lost sight of the old question of the middle class.

How important, dynamic, and central to society and to historical change were the urban professional and commercial middle classes in eighteenth-century France? "Very," argued the now defunct orthodox interpretation, which in the Marxist tradition viewed the Revolution as the result of early capitalist development; "Not at all," answered the revisionists in the 1970s and 1980s, pointing to the lack of significant social and economic change in France prior to 1789. In recent years assessments of France's prerevolutionary development have become, if anything, more confusing. There are in fact two revisionist positions. One anti-Marxist argument sees the eighteenth-century French economy as, on balance, stagnant and traditionalist.[2] Other revisionists acknowledge expansion, modernization, and social mobility but maintain that these changes happened in the absence of significant social antagonism: with a booming economy in the hands of liberal nobles and their non-noble associates, France had no need for social or economic upheaval.[3] Further complicating the picture is an important recent article by the neo-Marxist Colin Jones in which he aptly points out that a whole array of recent work in the field has produced evidence of considerable socioeconomic dynamism and change before the Revolution: the figures lined up by economic historians and the evidence unearthed by historians of consumption all point to steady economic growth, commercial expansion, and what can only be called a consumer revolution. Is it not time, Jones asks, to return to some version of the idea of a "bourgeois revolution"?[4]

None of this work has brought about any real consensus on the matter of social change in general and the status of the middle class(es) in particular. The reason for this is, I would argue, that historians continue to address this question in conventional economic-determinist terms: questions about social values and social change are still considered subordinate to the "hard evidence" about prices, trade, or industrial concentration. That evidence is, however, particularly ambiguous. By all accounts, in the century before the Revolution all sectors of the French economy showed a pattern of slow, steady, cumulative growth (with the exception of overseas trade, which grew much faster). At the same time the country's deep structures remained unchanged – there was no rapid urbanization, no dramatic concentration of the industrial sector. As a result, historians have been able to see the glass as either half-empty or half-full. Some have pointed to all the signs of growing wealth and commerce in order to assert the presence of a dynamic middle class, while others have highlighted the equally solid evidence of socioeconomic traditionalism in order to argue the reverse.

The solution I will propose for this deadlock is to bring current developments in historical method to bear on the question of the middle class. In recent years, postmodern theory and practice have led us to question many of the categories we take for granted in organizing our identities and experiences – gender, sexuality, race, ethnicity, and nationhood – and to explore the ways in which these are socially constructed. It has taken longer for historians (or anyone else) to attack social class with the solvent of postmodernism, however – no doubt because it was easier, in coming to terms with the "social" construction of gender or nationhood, to continue to take that "social" for granted.

Most societies have harbored groups we would call "middle class," although the boundaries of such groupings are usually subject to dispute. The importance of "middle class-ness" is certainly related to such objective factors as industrialization, urbanization, and overall wealth; but I want to argue here that a decisive factor in determining the presence and role of a middle class is the discourse about it – whether and how it is named and invested with social, political, moral, or historical importance.

To ask whether the idea of a "rising middle class" existed in the discourse of the prerevolutionary educated elites amounts to asking several distinct but related questions: Did contemporaries discern a unified social "middle" in their society, as opposed to a constellation of different groups we might call middling? Or did they entertain the notion of a distinct upper-middle-class non-noble elite, similar to the English gentry or the postrevolutionary *notables*? If they did discern one or the other group, did they consider it to be central to society as it then existed, or to the nation's future? This article answers these questions mostly in the negative and offers an analysis of the ways in which the educated elites did perceive both society and social change. For the sake of clarity, I will use the term "middle class(es)" rather than "bourgeoisie" to refer to the group I discuss: in Old Regime France the term "bourgeoisie" had a precise set of meanings . . .

I hope it is already clear that my focus on linguistic and cultural categories should not be read as dismissive of the abundant evidence we possess on social experience in eighteenth-century France. Like many historians today, I believe that social experience and consciousness are mutually constitutive, that the concrete aspects of experience both shape and are shaped by the language through which they are apprehended; I choose to concentrate here on discourse because, unlike the facts of social and economic life, it has so far been neglected in the controversy about the existence and importance of the prerevolutionary middle class(es).

I will argue here that French writers of the later eighteenth century, in describing their society and its problems did not single out a middle class either as a problem or as a solution – indeed, they almost never identified such a class at all. My sources are the published works of French writers of all persuasions, ranging from the very well known (Diderot, d'Holbach, Turgot) to the utterly obscure. These writings cover three sorts of issues: descriptions and analyses of society in general; commentaries on perceived economic and social change; and discussions of positive social norms and values, such as marital and family life. I have read as many texts as possible in order to discover the commonplaces and banalities, the ideas and themes that recurred insistently in eighteenth-century discussions of society. I am not claiming that the idiom of educated writers represents the only possible discourse on social class at the time: the poor and barely literate no doubt had different views of the social world than did the writers featured here. Nonetheless, what follows represents, I believe, a description of the views common among educated and articulate French people in the second half of the eighteenth century.

* * *

In most contexts descriptions of the social order are a matter of dispute, and this was especially true of eighteenth-century France, where it would have been hard to find two people who agreed on what their society looked like, either in theory or in practice. Any number of people, however, would have agreed on what it did not look like – namely, the official three orders of clergy, nobility, and Third Estate, a tripartite division that was blithely dismissed or ignored in most discussions of what society was really about. When a meeting of the Estates-General was announced in 1788 for the first time in nearly two centuries, the division of deputies into those three orders provoked such a rush of definition, redefinition, and general outrage that it is hardly an exaggeration to say that the irrelevance of those categories was an immediate cause of the French Revolution.

There is no surer symptom of the bankruptcy of the official ordering of society than the mounting criticism in the eighteenth century directed at the nobility's traditional functions and prerogatives. Such criticism was not new, of course; in the sixteenth and seventeenth centuries there were plenty of non-noble writers like the jurist Charles Loyseau ready to denounce the old nobility as fatuous *traisneurs d'épée* (sword draggers).[5] The cultural climate of the eighteenth century was, however, increasingly and irrevocably hostile to a group identity based on bloodlines, martial prowess, court culture, and legal privilege. The clearest language of class in eighteenth-century France was anti-noble: philosophes, including those of noble descent, denigrated the nobility's uselessness and vanity; historians and legal scholars chronicled the origins of what they called "feudalism" in medieval land grants that became breeding grounds for violence and tyranny; lawyers portrayed aristocrats as bullies, cheats, and sexual predators in printed trial briefs that reached many thousands of readers.[6] The most telling sign of how well this sort of criticism hit its mark is that nobles themselves, or at least some of the most prominent and articulate among them, rushed to redefine the nature and functions of their order. In the second half of the century especially, propagandists for the nobility insisted that the raison d'être of their class was not race and honor but "capacity," "merit," and "virtue" – even if these were sometimes inherited.[7]

Since the nineteenth century, the strong antinoble bias that appeared everywhere from legal scholarship to street doggerel in prerevolutionary France has been interpreted as evidence of middle-class consciousness – as if the only possible obverse of nobility were middlingness. It has been considerably harder, however, to locate the other side of the coin, to find in prerevolutionary culture explicit endorsements or even mere acknowledgments of a middle class (or classes) as a central feature of society.

In the middle of the eighteenth century two main idioms for describing society prevailed among intellectuals, each in a different way building a bridge between ancient and newer sets of beliefs. Many writers still clung to the traditional division of the social world into a hierarchy of multiple "estates." By the 1750s, however, few commentators professed to believe in the intrinsic, hereditary superiority of the higher orders; the argument that was inevitably made, following Montesquieu, had to do with the connection between a society of orders and France's "moderate" monarchical constitution. The gentle slope of multiple social "degrees" guaranteed sociopolitical stability, it was maintained, by connecting the monarch to the full range of his subjects.[8] Alongside this updating of the language of orders, the burgeoning science of political economy was already producing different sorts of classifications based not on history and social dignity but on productivity. These, however, usually wound up glorifying the most traditional groups in society, landowners and agricultural workers.

The conflict between these two visions was played out in the course of the famous debate initiated in 1756 by the Abbé Gabriel Coyer with the publication of his pamphlet *La noblesse commerçante*.[9] Coyer's provocatively utilitarian argument for allowing French nobles to engage in commerce like their English counterparts (the law of *dérogeance* forbade them most forms of trade) prompted a number of heated responses, the most famous of which was penned by an aristocratic officer, the chevalier d'Arcq. In *La noblesse militaire*, d'Arcq seized upon the political implications of Coyer's suggestion, reminding his readers of the demonstrable link between commerce and republicanism – were Holland and England not proof of this?[10]

The debate prompted d'Arcq to restate the official tripartite ordering of society, although he subdivided each order in two so as to bring the ancient divisions more up to date: upper and lower clergy, upper and lower nobility, bourgeoisie and populace. Each of these orders pursued its designated function, and he insisted that any proposal to shift functions between classes would threaten the whole carefully balanced edifice.[11] Since a monarchical state was dependent on the existence of a long chain of mediated connections between the monarch and each of his subjects, any confusion of ranks could bring down the whole card-castle of society, causing the monarchy to dissolve into either "despotism" or "republicanism."

D'Arcq's polemic and the publicity around the debate pushed Coyer into a more aggressive stance. In his response, he drew upon history to point out that the hallowed three orders had not always been there: the Franks knew only a single class, the Gauls were their serfs, and it took centuries for the orders to emerge. If things had changed in the past, they certainly could do so in the present and future.[12] Coyer argued vigorously against social inequality and bluntly described the nation as divided into two classes, producers and parasites: the first was made up of all the working and commercial classes, the second of "the regular and secular clergy, the military, men of law and finance, rentiers, lackeys, beggars, wastrels, and *grands seigneurs*."[13]

Each of the two most prominent participants in the debate laid claim to one of the social idioms, d'Arcq waving the banner of a "monarchical" ordered society, Coyer proudly wearing the colors of political economy and productivity. But other participants in the controversy could invoke both languages within the same text. This happens in one of the most interesting contributions to the Coyer debate, a piece by a woman named Octavie Guichard, dame Belot, entitled *Observations sur la noblesse et le tiers-état*.[14]

Belot follows d'Arcq in arguing against noble commerce on the grounds that this will create too wide a gulf in society, leaving "no middling estate [*état mitoyen*] between the artisan and the nobleman, an interval hitherto filled by commerce."[15] Belot also echoes d'Arcq's political concerns, explaining in a striking passage that Coyer's proposal would make "the throne too steep" and the ruler appear as "a colossus" by removing the nobility that "step by step levels, in the eyes of the weak, the steep incline which exists between the sovereign and his subjects."[16] In many respects, then, Belot's view of society is quite traditional: she sees middling estates as necessary not because they are inherently better than the upper or lower estates but because mediation and gradualism are indispensable to the stability of an ordered monarchical society.

At the same time, the author declares her opposition to hereditary nobility and offers the model she would adopt if she were planning a state "as metaphysically as did Plato." At the top of society would be agriculturalists, its strongest and most useful members; second would come warriors, who deserve support on account of their sacrifices for the nation; and in last place would be those who engage in commerce and craft – they are the least deserving, as they face neither hard labor nor danger and give their fellow men neither sweat nor blood.[17] Belot thus moved back and forth between a defense of the traditional sociopolitical order and a model of a pastoral and warlike utopia.

Even when eighteenth-century writers based their social analyses on concepts of labor and productivity, they rarely came up with orderings of society that prefigured the advent of a recognizably modern class system. The best examples of this can be found in the writings of the physiocrats and their followers. Physiocracy was the school of economic thought that developed in France around the middle of the eighteenth century, defining itself in opposition to traditional mercantilist economic theories. Where mercantilism encouraged the production and foreign sale of luxury goods, the physiocrats built their systems around the primacy of agriculture and population as the source of all riches and campaigned for the freedom of domestic markets from internal tariffs and guild regulations.

In the work that is sometimes considered the founding text of physiocracy, *L'ami des hommes* (1756), the Marquis de Mirabeau sketched out a mostly traditional hierarchy of occupations in the state. The monarch is aided by the three *orders consultans:* the clergy, the military, and the magistrates. These are "the absolute essence of the constitution of the political edifice" and are followed by all those occupations whose function is to assist and adorn them: sciences, the fine arts, and the liberal and mechanical arts.[18] Agriculture, however, occupies a special, preeminent, almost suprasocial place: "Agriculture is in a word the universal art, the art of innocence and virtue, the art of all men and all ranks." And commerce is but its complement, "not a separate estate but only the brother of agriculture."[19] As Elizabeth Fox-Genovese points out, the founders of physiocracy faced a dilemma: their faith in the laws of economics led them to repudiate an ordering of society based on transcendent principles, yet they feared the void thus created and the dangerously dissolvent effects of the very freedom of trade they advocated. Singing the praises of agriculture was a way of trying to recreate community by valorizing a pursuit that in their eyes was closest to nature and transcended social divisions – especially since this had the practical result of leaving the traditional upper classes (landed proprietors) safely at the helm.[20]

There was virtually no room for an urban middle class in the social schemes, whether analytical or prescriptive, drawn up by the physiocrats and their many followers. Theirs was an ideology obsessed with "production," by which they meant agrarian and demographic fertility. The closer one stood, by work or ownership, to the bountiful earth, the higher one's spiritual and social ranking. The social class that was idealized in the eighteenth century was the peasantry – never any of the urban middling groups. In his *Réflexions sur la formation et la distribution des richesses* of 1766, for instance, the economist and statesman Turgot described the principal fault line in society as that dividing "salaried" workers, who earn only enough to live on and create neither employment nor surplus wealth, from "productive" workers – that is, rural *laboureurs* – who produce as much as the earth will yield, thereby generating excess wealth for their society. Historical evolution results in the most deserving rural "producers" increasing the size of their property, with the result that society is now divided into three classes: productive (rural) workers, salaried artisans (also called the "sterile" class), and a class of (rural) proprietors whose wealth frees them to engage in other occupations useful to society such as warfare or the administration of justice.[21] Some fifteen years later an author inspired by the physiocrats, Charles de Butré, came up with a very similar classification. Society, he wrote, falls "naturally" into three classes: a productive class of agricultural entrepreneurs, a class of rural property owners whose position allows them to "improve" the land, and a "sterile" class of salaried workers. Butré calls these the "natural laws" of the social order.[22]

Eighteenth-century writers came up with a variety of schemes for describing the society they lived in or the one they wished to inhabit. But one classification they never proposed was the one that seems commonsensical to the average inhabitant of the twentieth century: a division into upper, middle, and lower classes determined mostly on the basis of wealth and income.[23] This was unlikely to occur to a denizen of eighteenth-century France because wealth alone could not be imagined as a basis for explaining society, let alone running it; everyone knew that the effects of money were disjunctive rather than conjunctive, and a community would need some other principle to give it meaning.

Visions of society in the later eighteenth century coalesced around two competing principles: there were those who began to understand "society" as an autonomous concept, on the one hand, and those who clung to the belief that the (ordered) form of French society was inseparable from the political principle of a tempered monarchy, on the other. The latter continued to produce updated visions of France as a constellation of vertically ordered estates binding each subject to the sovereign and through him to God: in such a scheme the important social groups were at the top of the ladder, not in the middle.

As Daniel Gordon has shown, the idea that "society" rather than the afterlife was the framework for human existence, and hence that social life could be independent from the polity, was one that grew steadily in importance and influence in the writings of the philosophes and their followers. But Gordon also demonstrates how closely linked the idea of *société* remained to aristocratic, or at least elitist, ideals of *sociabilité*. The French Enlightenment's nascent concept of society was equally indebted to universalistic natural law theories and to the aristocratic culture of *politesse*.[24] Intellectuals influenced by physiocracy were among those who first understood and discussed "society" as an autonomous entity; but because they wanted to root society in "nature" they most often looked to the rural world of the landed gentry and the peasantry as a source of meaning and community. Neither in the older language of monarchy and orders nor in the newer one of nature and productivity did middling urban groups take on any special meaning or importance.

The reason why all attempts to locate and describe a middle class or (in the modern sense) bourgeoisie in eighteenth-century France have failed is that such efforts always amount to forcing nineteenth- and twentieth-century categories onto a society that would not have recognized them.[25] It is high time for us to stop trying to squeeze eighteenth-century French society into the procrustean bed of modern sociology.

*   *   *

I have argued that social observers and commentators in the later eighteenth century, while acknowledging the existence of what we would call the urban middle classes, did not view such groups as unified, important, or especially praiseworthy. To those who clung to updated versions of a social "chain of being," commercial, industrial, and professional groups were just some of the many rungs in the long ladder between king and pauper. As for those who held more "modern" views, physiocrats and others interested in political economy, they invariably sang the praises of agriculture. Writers who called for change in society typically believed that the nobility, the traditional elite, should take on new roles. Coyer and his partisans thought that nobles should be allowed to make commercial fortunes, while the physiocrats wanted them to take the lead in improving the land. Commoners still wanted to become nobles, and nobles now wanted to become useful; nobody thought, or at least nobody wrote, that the torch of leadership should be passed to a new social class.

This is all the more surprising in light of the fact that the society and economy of France changed significantly in the eighteenth century and that those changes were especially conspicuous in the decades after 1750. The consensus among economic historians nowadays is that French economic growth in the eighteenth century was remarkable. The country's foreign trade quintupled during that period, and its share of European (but not American) markets grew faster than England's. Economists Don Leet and John Shaw have calculated that France saw a sevenfold increase in its industrial output over the course of the century.[26] Historians still quarrel over whether or not there was an "agrarian revolution" in eighteenth-century France, but unquestionably some striking improvement occurred: famines abated in the century before the Revolution, and the population grew from 20 to 27 million.[27] Recent work by social historians also shows us that eighteenth-century France was a society on the move. To begin with, many more people lived in towns. Although the urban population only grew between 16 and 19 percent in the sixty years before the Revolution, given the overall demographic surge this meant an increase of 1.5 million. Most large towns saw their populations swell – on average by close to 48 percent – chiefly as a result of immigration.[28] And a succession of distinguished studies have demonstrated that France became, in the age of Enlightenment, a much more commercial society. Jean-Claude Perrot's classic study of Caen, for instance, shows the Norman town transformed from a local textile center to a hub for national and international commerce, its population growing with an influx of immigrants after 1740, increasing numbers of whom found jobs in the expanding service sector.[29]

Even areas of rural France were affected, we now know, by increased commercialism. Jonathan Dewald's remarkable study of the seigneury of Pont-Saint-Pierre over four centuries allows us to follow in one rural area the concentration of property, the monetarization of village economies, the expansion of rural markets, and the rise, by the eighteenth century, of what the author calls "rural capitalism."[30] Nobody would deny that many areas of France remained isolated and tradition bound; but there is on balance increasing reason to accept Colin Jones's description of France at the end of the Old Regime as "a society characterized as much by circulation, mobility, and innovation as by . . . traditionalism, subsistence farming and cultural stagnation."[31]

If this was the case, how did contemporaries perceive and react to these changes? How did large-scale, abstract developments like "urbanization" and "commercialization" translate into lived experience for, say, the inhabitants of eighteenth-century French towns? One answer to that question is becoming increasingly clear: at least for town dwellers living above subsistence level, the century brought profound changes in the material world and in people's relationships to objects, the result of what can only be called a consumer revolution. Thanks to the pioneering work of Daniel Roche, Cissie Fairchilds, and Annick Pardailhé-Galabrun on after-death inventories, and of Colin Jones on local advertising, we are beginning to understand how the eighteenth-century surge in commercial activity and overall wealth made a difference to the daily lives of people of all stations.[32]

In Paris the interior of even modest dwellings began to change in the early decades of the century. Apartments were larger, and because smaller and more numerous fireplaces were built into them families occupied different rooms instead of crowding around one enormous hearth in the common *salle*.[33] Brightly colored or patterned wallpapers and fabrics began to replace heavy drab tapestries on the walls. Mirrors, clocks, paintings, and statuettes, once a mark of significant wealth, became widespread, as did a range of utilitarian objects such as umbrellas, fans, snuffboxes, watches, and books. More and more families ate from matching sets of decorated earthenware instead of tin or pewter plates.[34]

The most conspicuous changes occurred in the volatile and symbolically charged area of clothing. The value of wardrobes in the Parisian working population multiplied over the course of the century: for women of the upper working classes it increased sixfold, for domestics fourfold, for professionals and their wives three- or fourfold.[35] As with furnishings, garments became more varied and cheerful: cotton and silk supplemented wool and broadcloth; bright colors and pastels gained ground; stripes, checks, and patterns proliferated.[36] Everyone above the poorest level of society owned more clothes, women especially (it was in the eighteenth century that fashion became decisively associated with femininity). The function of clothing evolved over the course of the century: where garments had once primarily marked a person's status, they became increasingly (for women especially) a sign of taste and fashion.[37] All of these changes provoked criticism of lower-class sartorial hubris and complaints plaints that it was becoming difficult to tell a person's rank from her or his clothing.

For all but the very poor, then, the material world changed dramatically in French towns from the 1730s to the eve of the Revolution, as more and more people in the middling and lower ranks of society had access to garments and furnishings once available only to the elites. As Colin Jones has pointed out, the evidence unearthed by recent studies of commercialism and consumerism seems to be bringing us back to the discarded paradigm of the "rise of the middle class." If commerce was on the rise, towns were growing, and the country's increasing wealth allowed middling and poorer groups access to consumer goods, does this not necessarily mean that France was becoming more middle class? The major problem with such a conclusion lies in the realm of consciousness: while the occasional text in praise of roturiers can be dug up, nowhere in the culture of prerevolutionary France can one find a substantial, conspicuous body of literature arguing for the separate merits, rights, or historical identity of a middle class or bourgeoisie.[38] Social observers certainly noted the country's marked increase in wealth and the effect it was having on behavior and identities, in towns especially. There does exist a large corpus of works commenting on, and mostly bemoaning, the drastic changes rocking this society, but in these works neither the problem nor the proposed solutions to it had anything to do with the middle classes.

* * *

The idealization of family relations (as opposed to family lineage) in the culture of the later eighteenth century has usually been interpreted as a glorification of a "bourgeois" or middle-class ethos, and indeed one can find in this culture plenty of portrayals of domestic bliss among people of "mediocre" condition. The association of middlingness and domestic happiness is, however, purely accidental (why should the middle of society care more about family life than either end?) yet so common both then and now that it has come to seem inevitable. A final look at the literary genre most commonly associated with the middle class in eighteenth-century France, the so-called *drame bourgeois*, will offer an illustration of the proposition that representations of family in this culture were not a vehicle of class consciousness but a substitute for it.

The *drame* has a precise birthdate, 1757, when Diderot published a dialogue that was a critical commentary on his new play, *Le fils naturel* (The illegitimate son). The themes of the *Entretiens sur le fils naturel* are well known to students of eighteenth-century literature: Diderot announced the need for a new genre situated between existing tragedy and comedy, one that would put onstage the experiences of ordinary people rather than kings and heroes and would show them in everyday settings, wearing ordinary clothes and speaking prose instead of spewing alexandrine verse. In style these new plays were to be expressive, even histrionic: Diderot stressed the importance of gestures such as weeping or falling to one's knees, which he called "pantomime" and which he valued more highly than vocal utterances. The subjects of these dramas would reverse the traditional primacy of character on the French stage. Instead of Molièresque plots revolving around an embodiment of pride, greed, or misanthropy, Diderot wanted a drama propelled by the tensions between different "conditions," by which he meant both social conditions (involving persons of different status and occupation) and family relations.[39]

Diderot's prescriptions for the contemporary stage included a call to "create domestic and bourgeois tragedy,"[40] and since the nineteenth century the genre he helped popularize has often been called *drame bourgeois* (although contemporaries most often referred to it as *genre sérieux* or simply *drame*). In this light it may seem odd that Diderot's two major plays in this genre, *Le fils naturel* (1757) and *Le père de famille* (1758), are set in what seems to be a very upper-class milieu and that the protagonists, who do not appear to work for a living, bear "aristocratic" stage names like Dorval, Clairville, Saint-Albin, and Germeuil. And this was not the case only for Diderot. Social characterizations in what was perhaps the most successful play in this genre, Sedaine's *Le philosophe sans le savoir* (1765), further illustrate the ambiguity of the *drame*'s social allegiances.

The hero of the play is a wealthy merchant, Monsieur Vanderck, who apparently embodies the dignity and usefulness of his occupation. It turns out,

123

however, that he was born a nobleman but took on, out of gratitude, the name and business of his late adoptive father, a Dutchman. In the course of a scene in which Vanderck lectures his son about the merits of trade, he mentions that he knows only two occupations he values more highly: that of the magistrate and that of the warrior – the traditional noble callings.[41] The play ends, after the requisite crises, with the marriage of Vanderck's daughter to a young noble of the robe in the presence of the Vandercks' new friends, a baron and his son. This is not to say that the *drame* was pro-noble; in good middle-of-the-road enlightened fashion these plays engaged in plenty of debunking of aristocratic vanities and abuses. And a later, more radical practitioner of the genre, Sébastien Mercier, featured a wide spectrum of social types among his protagonists, including the very poor. Questions of wealth and status do loom large in many plots, and quite a few feature celebratory portrayals of merchants and professionals. But on the whole their story lines and characters hardly support the traditional claim that these plays were written primarily for and about the "middle class."

What all of them do share is the cult of family: just about all of their plots include the portrayal of a highly emotional, expressive love between parents and children, brothers and sisters. (Such is the power of the association between family love and the social middle that this is no doubt the main reason why these dramas were tagged "bourgeois.") This celebration of family bonds often reaches a climax in the very last scene of the play, with the disclosure of previously unknown kinship between some of the characters. Obviously, the resolution of a crisis by the revelation of a foundling or lost child's true identity is not unique to this genre or even to this century. What is notable is how often this device is used in the *drame* to resolve tensions created by social differences.

The crisis in Diderot's *Le père de famille* is triggered by the infatuation of young Saint-Albin with a poor woman named Sophie – a love his good father tries gently to talk him out of, and his authoritarian uncle, the Commandeur (the bad father figure) attempts to forbid by force. All is resolved with the discovery that Sophie is the Commandeur's niece and Saint-Albin's cousin, and the play ends with the double betrothal of Saint-Albin to Sophie and of his sister Cécile to Germeuil, a young man raised in the household as their "brother"; in the last scene the good father blesses the merging of the four quasi-siblings into a family.

Mercier's most famous *drames* offer variations on this sort of plot. *Le juge* is about the dilemma of a highly moral judge whose conscience tells him to rule in a dispute over land in favor of a poor peasant family and against the local count who has been his protector and surrogate father. Although the furious count at first threatens to ruin the judge, he is ultimately moved, at the sight of the pathetic peasant family and of the judge with his delightful wife and daughter, to reveal that the magistrate is in fact his son from an early and clandestine marriage. The dispute over land involving three social strata thus vanishes when the count acknowledges and joins his real family.

As a final example we can take Mercier's *L'indigent*, in which a family of destitute spinners, old Rémi and his children, Charlotte and Joseph, inhabit a basement in the house of a callous young nobleman named De Lys. A crisis is provoked by De Lys's attempt to seduce Charlotte, first with money and then by proposing marriage. It turns out that Charlotte is not Rémi's daughter after all, but De Lys's lost sister whom he had been trying to disinherit. Charlotte is now a wealthy noblewoman, but she chooses to marry her ex-brother, Joseph, whom she has always loved. De Lys is promptly sucked into the family love between Charlotte, Joseph, and Rémi and has time before the curtain falls to realize that familial embraces are better than any other kind. Typically, what strikes the modern reader as an alarmingly incestuous triangle (Charlotte's eroticized relationships with both of her "brothers") is presented by Mercier as an ideal, moving instance of the deepest human connections.

What distinguishes the *drame* from, say, classical tragedy is that the crises at the heart of these plays are brought on by disparities of status, wealth, power, and prejudice. This was probably what Diderot had in mind when he argued that "conditions" should form "the basis of the plots and morals of our plays."[42] As Julie Hayes has suggested, what these plays illustrate above all is the proposition that human beings are social creatures, involved for better or worse in a network of human connections. "The good man lives in society; only the evil live alone," says a character in *Le fils naturel*, and many of these plays illustrate the point.[43] The Commandeur, De Lys, the count in *Le juge* – all are wealthy, isolated, and unhappy, saved (in most cases) by the news that they have an authentic human connection in their new families.

These dramas are almost never performed today, because modern spectators would find their hyperbolic sentimentalism – the weeping, collapsing, exclaiming, and pontificating – at best comic, and more likely, tedious and embarrassing. But critics have recently been drawing attention to the *sensible* style as a collection of signs that, like the plots of these plays, served to convey the message that "virtuous" feelings of compassion can and should transcend and negate differences of social status. If, as most educated people believed, identity was built on a succession of individual sensations and experiences, how could this serve as a basis for building a human community? The language of sensibility, David Denby argues, was a system of signs aimed at connecting individual sensation and collective existence by making inner experience visible and insisting on its universal character.[44]

This is why gesture (in its theatrical guise, pantomime) was even more important to Diderot and his successors than verbal language: the deepest emotions were ineffable and could only be "spoken" by the body.[45] A famous passage in Diderot's *Entretiens* illustrates the way in which the verbal and bodily languages of sensibility act as a solvent for class differences. It concerns a peasant woman whom the narrator happens upon just as she has discovered the body of her husband, murdered by a kinsman. The haggard woman has dropped to the ground by the corpse; she is clutching her husband's feet and sobbing that she never thought those feet would lead him to his death. Diderot comments that the same situation would have drawn the same words and "pathetic" gestures from a woman of any social rank: "What the artist must find is what anyone would say in a situation like this, what no one will hear without recognizing it in himself."[46]

The *drame* is emblematic of social attitudes among the educated public of prerevolutionary France. These plays promoted the ideal of a community that transcended social divisions, for which the metaphor of choice was the family. The *drame*'s dual, almost paradoxical, outlook is very much that of its time. Playwrights like Diderot and Mercier broke with classical theater through their assertion that the drama of human existence is not governed by transcendent forces but by day-to-day confrontations in the social world, the world of "conditions." But that social world was alarmingly devoid of coherence and a prey to the raw forces of money and power: the *drame* dealt with this potential threat by offering the family as the solution to dangerous social tensions.

*   *   *

The argument proposed in this article highlights, I believe, some of the particular features of French sociopolitical culture, features that have been obscured in the past by the imposition of Anglo-American or Marxian categories upon a cultural landscape they do not really fit. I have sought to describe the ways in which the educated elite of eighteenth-century France understood, and came to terms with, the effects of commercialization and increased social mobility. While the language of *moeurs* and the promotion of the sentimental family cannot be equated with class-consciousness, they are nonetheless socially *located* discourses, reflecting anxiety in the upper levels of society. The *drame*'s preoccupation with "conditions" as the motor of dramatic action undoubtedly points, as does the discourse on *le luxe*, to deep misgivings in the face of a rapidly changing social and material world. In response to such concerns, the educated classes of prerevolutionary France sought answers not in the leadership of a middle class or gentry but in the moralistic universalism conveyed by concepts such as family, *moeurs*, or *patrie*.

Why did the French adopt moralistic and universalistic discourses rather than, for instance, placing their hopes in an explicit redefinition of the nation's elite? At this stage the reasons can only be suggested; many of them probably involve long-term cultural trends particular to France. To explain why no new class was singled out to lead the nation, one can invoke the long-standing contempt of trade and "bourgeois" status, the growing critique of corporate society, and the collapse of traditional aristocratic preeminence – the fear of recreating any sort of "privilege" no doubt contributed greatly to the rhetoric of classlessness described above. To understand why the answer to the age's problems was couched in a language of moralistic holism, one can point to the enduring influence of both absolutist and Catholic universalism.

Various "enlightened" discourses, building upon a leveling tradition within monarchical absolutism, came increasingly to define the pursuit of particular or private interests as pernicious to the community. The formation of a new language of class was thus precluded, I would argue, even as legal privilege and the corporate idiom were cast aside. While the new idea of a "society" distinct from the polity did emerge in eighteenth-century France, it retained features strongly reminiscent of the absolutist synthesis.[47] The French persisted in their suspicion – and most often condemnation – of "English"-style definitions of society as an arena in which opposing groups played out their conflicts, balanced interests, and reached compromises. In contrast, French views of society remained highly functional, emphasizing the harmonious integration of various social groups into a transcendent whole. This was as true of the physiocratic or the sentimental-familial models as it had been of corporate and "ordered" ones.[48]

Dror Wahrman has recently argued that political language is the most common source of discourses about society – that competing interests within the polity will invoke the support of social groups that they themselves define to legitimate their claims.[49] I would like to suggest, in conclusion, that discursive influences can work both ways – that ideas about society can define the polity as well. The conception of the *patrie* as an expression of unmediated social bonds, rather than an arena in which social antagonisms are resolved, shaped a definition of the state reflected in a recent statement by a French politician: "The Republic does not recognize groups; it recognizes only individuals."[50] This, in turn, explains a great deal about the precarious status of the French bourgeoisie even when it did emerge, seemingly triumphant, in the nineteenth century.

NOTES

Source Reprinted in an abridged format from the Journal of Modern History 69 (June 1997), pp. 199–229.

* I am grateful for reactions to earlier versions of this article from audiences at the Woodrow Wilson Center in Washington, D.C.; the University of Virginia at Charlottesville; the University of Pennsylvania; Northwestern University; and Boston University; and from French history groups in the Washington, D.C., and New York City areas. For especially helpful comments and suggestions I thank in particular Christine Adams, Ken Alder, David Bell, Lenard Berlanstein, Jack Censer, Elizabeth Eisenstein, Jan Goldstein, Dena Goodman, Lynn Hunt, Margaret Jacob, Ted Koditschek, Joel Mokyr, Jerrold Seigel, Sean Shesgreen, and Dror Wahrman.

1 Some of the landmark contributions to these trends include Mona Ozouf, *La fête révolutionnaire, 1789–1799* (Paris, 1976); François Furet, *Penser la Révolution française* (Paris, 1978); Lynn Hunt, *Politics, Culture and Class in the French Revolution* (Berkeley and Los Angeles, 1984), and *The Family Romance of the French Revolution* (Berkeley and Los Angeles, 1992); Joan Landes, *Women and the Public Sphere in the Age of the French Revolution* (Ithaca, N.Y., 1988); Keith Baker, *Inventing the French Revolution* (Cambridge, 1990); and Keith Baker, ed., *The French Revolution and the Creation of Modern Political Culture*, 3 vols. (Oxford, 1987–94).

2 See William Doyle's influential syntheses, *Origins of the French Revolution* (Oxford, 1980), esp. pp. 30–34, and *The Oxford History of the French Revolution* (Oxford, 1989), esp. chaps. 1 and 17; or see the well-documented synthesis by T. C. W. Blanning, *The French Revolution: Aristocrats versus Bourgeois* (Atlantic Highlands, N.J., 1987).

3 Simon Schama, e.g., forcefully argues the revisionist thesis that the Revolution was the unfortunate result of a series of political contingencies, while stressing the

dynamism of the Old Regime, particularly in the area of "capitalist" enterprise; see *Citizens: A Chronicle of the French Revolution* (New York, 1989), pp. 183–99.

4 Colin Jones, "Bourgeois Revolution Revivified: 1789 and Social Change," in *Rewriting the French Revolution*, ed. Colin Lucas (Oxford, 1991), pp. 69–118.

5 George Huppert, *Les Bourgeois Gentilhommes: An Essay on the Definition of Elites in Renaissance France* (Chicago, 1977), p. 11 and passim.

6 Henri Carré, *La noblesse de France et l'opinion publique au XVIIIe siècle* (Paris, 1920); J. Q. C. Mackrell, *The Attack on "Feudalism" in Eighteenth-Century France* (London, 1973); Sarah Maza, *Private Lives and Public Affairs: The Causes Célèbres of Pre-revolutionary France* (Berkeley and Los Angeles, 1993); Patrice Higonnet, *Class, Ideology and the Rights of Nobles during the French Revolution* (Oxford, 1981).

7 Guy Chaussinand-Nogaret, *La noblesse au XVIIIe siècle: De la féodalité aux lumières* (Paris, 1976), chaps. 1, 2.

8 Elie Carcassonne, *Montesquieu et le problème de la constitution française au XVIIIe siècle* (Paris, 1927; Geneva, 1970), chap. 5.

9 Abbé Gabriel Coyer, *La noblesse commerçante* (Paris, 1756). For an overview of the debate between Coyer and his adversaries, see Chaussinand-Nogaret, chap. 5.

10 Philippe Auguste de Sainte-Foy, chevalier d'Arcq, *La noblesse militaire ou le patriote françois* (Amsterdam, 1756), pp. 7–13.

11 Ibid., pp. 16–19.

12 Abbé Gabriel Coyer, *Développement et défense du système de la noblesse commerçante* (Paris, 1758), pp. 47–48.

13 Ibid., p. 20.

14 Octavie Guichard, dame Belot, *Observations sur la noblesse et le tiers-état* (Amsterdam, 1758).

15 Ibid., p. 13.

16 Ibid., pp. 104–5.

17 Ibid., pp. 30–40.

18 Victor de Riquetti, marquis de Mirabeau, *L'ami des hommes ou traité de la population*, 4 vols. (Avignon, 1756; reprint, Aalen, 1970), 1:141.

19 Ibid., 1:142.

20 Elizabeth Fox-Genovese, *The Origins of Physiocracy: Economic Revolution and Social Order in Eighteenth-Century France* (Ithaca, N.Y., 1976), pp. 210–20.

21 Anne-Robert Turgot, *Oeuvres de Turgot et documents le concernant*, ed. Gustave Schelle, 5 vols. (Paris, 1913–23), 2:536–42.

22 Charles de Butré, *Loix naturelles de l'agriculture et de l'ordre social* (Neuchâtel, 1781), pp. 89–97.

23 A conspicuous exception among well-known social commentaries of the period is the description of the city of Montpellier in 1768 by an anonymous observer, the subject of a widely read essay by Robert Darnton ("Etat et description de la ville de Montpellier, fait en 1768," in *Montpellier en 1768 et 1836 d'après deux manuscrits inédits*, ed. Joseph Berthelé [Montpellier, 1909], pp. 9–174), and his *The Great Cat-Massacre and Other Episodes in French Cultural History* (New York, 1984), pp. 107–43. The manuscript's author certainly extols the "second" or "bourgeois" estate, made up of businessmen, merchants, professionals, and rentiers as "the most useful, the most important, and the wealthiest" (p. 67). But Montpellier, as the chronicler himself indicates, was unusual in its strong commercial vocation and in the small number of noble families it harbored – the "bourgeoisie" celebrated in this text is the oligarchy of an ancient trading center. Furthermore, Darnton's analysis of the "Description" does not suggest an unproblematic "bourgeois" point of view but stresses in the end the confusion of sociological idioms running through this complex account (pp. 139–40).

24 Daniel Gordon, *Citizens without Sovereignty: Equality and Sociability in French Thought, 1670–1789* (Princeton, N.J., 1994), introduction and chap. 2.

25 For a typical example of this, see Elinor Barber, *The Bourgeoisie in Eighteenth-Century*

France (Princeton, N.J., 1973), which explicitly relies on twentieth-century sociology to define an eighteenth-century group. Barber arbitrarily draws the lower line of the bourgeoisie just above those who worked with their hands (which excludes master artisans, whom their workers called *le bourgeois*) and the upper limit just short of the robe nobility. She acknowledges but then ignores the association of *bourgeoisie* with idleness, and the class she defines, principally "business and the professions," reflects a nineteenth- or twentieth-century view of which occupational groups were/are central to the "middle class": see esp. pp. 15–20.

26 Early and important contributions to this argument were Jan Marczewski, "The Take-Off and French Experience," in *The Economics of Take-Off into Sustained Growth*, ed. Walt Rostow (New York, 1963); and François Crouzet, "Angleterre et France au XVIIIe Siècle: Essai d'Analyse Comparée de deux croissances économiques," *Annales: Économies, sociétés, civilisations* 21 (1966): 254–91, translated in *The Causes of the Industrial Revolution*, ed. R. M. Hartwell (London, 1967). In the 1970s and 1980s a new generation of economic historians of France built the evidence of eighteenth-century growth into a revisionist argument: France's pace and pattern of industrial growth in the eighteenth and nineteenth centuries should not be seen as a failure to follow the English model but as an entirely different, and perhaps less socially traumatic, form of transition to a modern economy. Salient works in this vein include Richard Roehl, "French Industrialization: A Reconsideration," *Explorations in Economic History* 13 (1978): 233–81; Patrick O'Brien and Caglar Keyder, *Economic Growth in Britain and France, 1780–1914: Two Paths to the Twentieth Century* (London, 1978); Don Leet and John Shaw, "French Economic Stagnation, 1700–1960: Old Economic History Revisited," *Journal of Interdisciplinary History* 8 (Winter 1978): 531–44; Rondo Cameron and Charles E. Freedman, "French Economic Growth: A Radical Revision," *Social Science History* 7 (Winter 1983): 3–30; Nicholas Crafts, "Economic Growth in France and Britain, 1830–1910: A Review of the Evidence," *Journal of Economic History* 44 (March 1984): 49–67; and Robert Aldrich, "Late Comer or Early Starter? New Views on French Economic History," *Journal of European Economic History* 16 (1987): 89–100.

27 Leet and Shaw, pp. 536–37; Cameron and Freedman, pp. 16–17; François Crouzet, *De la supériorité de l'Angleterre sur la France: L'économique et l'imaginaire, XVIIe–XVIIIe siècles* (Paris, 1985).

28 Georges Duby et al., *Histoire de la France urbaine*, 4 vols. (Paris, 1981), 3:295–98.

29 Jean-Claude Perrot, *Genèse d'une ville moderne: Caen au XVIIIe siècle*, 2 vols. (Paris, 1975).

30 Jonathan Dewald, *Pont-Saint-Pierre, 1398–1789: Lordship, Community, and Capitalism in Early Modern France* (Berkeley and Los Angeles, 1987).

31 Colin Jones, "Bourgeois Revolution Revivified" (n. 4 above), p. 87.

32 Daniel Roche, *The People of Paris: An Essay on Popular Culture in the Eighteenth Century*, trans. Marie Evans and Gwynne Lewis (Berkeley and Los Angeles, 1987), and *The Culture of Clothing: Dress and Fashion in the Ancien Régime*, trans. Jean Birrell (Cambridge, 1994); Cissie Fairchilds, "The Production and Marketing of Populuxe Goods in Eighteenth-Century Paris," in *Consumption and the World of Goods*, ed. John Brewer and Roy Porter (London, 1993), pp. 228–48; Annick Pardailhé-Galabrun, *La naissance de l'intime: 3000 foyers parisiens, XVIIe–XVIIIe siècles* (Paris, 1988); Colin Jones, "The Great Chain of Buying: Medical Advertisement, the Bourgeois Public Sphere, and the Origins of the French Revolution," *American Historical Review* 101 (February 1996): 13–40. Colin Jones's article makes another case for putting the bourgeoisie back into the center of prerevolutionary history on the basis of abundant evidence of commercialism in the local advertising newspapers known as *affiches*; this piece appeared too late for me to integrate it centrally into my argument here. Jones's image of an inclusive, horizontal "chain of buying," which he sees as a concrete instance of Jürgen Habermas's bourgeois public sphere, is richly suggestive, as is the abundant empirical evidence he presents. But I remain unconvinced that the *affiches* tell us anything

decisive about the existence of a middle class. Jones's argument about the consumers of the *affiches* is circular: those who engaged in this form of buying and selling are presumed bourgeois (see pp. 18–19, 24); therefore, these newspapers document the existence of a bourgeois public sphere.

33 Pardailhé-Galabrun, chap. 6; Roche, *The People of Paris*, chap. 4.

34 Pardailhé-Galabrun, pp. 306–14, 368–429; Roche, *The People of Paris*, pp. 141–53; Fairchilds, pp. 228–48.

35 Roche, *The People of Paris*, chap. 6, and *The Culture of Clothing*, pp. 108–16.

36 Roche, *The Culture of Clothing*, pp. 134–45, and *The People of Paris*, pp. 167–75.

37 Jennifer Jones, "The Taste for Fashion and Frivolity: Gender, Clothing, and the Commercial Culture of the Old Regime" (Ph.D. diss., Princeton University, 1991), and "Repackaging Rousseau: Femininity and Fashion in Old Regime France," *French Historical Studies* 18 (Fall 1994): 939–67.

38 The few texts that appear to do so, such as [Abbé] Jaubert, *Éloge de la roture dédié aux roturiers* (London, 1766), are remarkable precisely because they are unusual; and Jaubert defines *roture* in the traditional sense of Third Estate – all commoners, regardless of status or income.

39 Denis Diderot, *Paradoxe sur le comédien précédé des entretiens sur le fils naturel* (Paris, 1967), see the discussion of "conditions," pp. 96–97 (hereafter cited as *Paradoxe*).

40 Ibid., p. 109.

41 Michel-Jean Sedaine, "Le philosophe sans le savoir," in *Four French Comedies of the Eighteenth Century*, ed. Casimir Zdanowicz (New York, 1933), p. 279.

42 Diderot, *Paradoxe*, p. 96.

43 Julie Hayes, "A Theater of Situations: Representation of the Self in the Bourgeois Drama of La Chaussée and Diderot," in *The Many Forms of Drama*, ed. Karelisa Hartigan (Lanham, Md., 1985), pp. 69–77; Denis Diderot, *Le fils naturel ou les épreuves de la vertu* (Amsterdam, 1757; reprint, Bordeaux, 1965), p. 97. In *La religieuse*, Denis Diderot makes similar statements to the effect that isolation from society of the sort practiced in convents and monasteries leads to evil and misery ([Paris, 1968], pp. 153–54).

44 David Denby, *Sentimental Narrative and the Social Order in France, 1760–1820* (Cambridge, 1994), esp. pp. 21–47.

45 Ibid., pp. 83–84.

46 Diderot, *Paradoxe*, p. 47.

47 On the emergence of "society," see Gordon (n. 26 above).

48 I wish to thank David Bell for stressing and clarifying this idea in response to an earlier draft of this article.

49 See Wahrman, *Imaging the Middle Class* (n. 6 above), pp. 9–10 and passim. I have also argued this in *Private Lives and Public Affairs* (n. 8 above), chap. 1.

50 Cited by Stanley Hoffman at a meeting of the French Historical Studies Association, Boston, March 22, 1996.

7

NOBLES AND THIRD ESTATE IN THE REVOLUTIONARY DYNAMIC OF THE NATIONAL ASSEMBLY, 1789–90

Timothy Tackett

In this richly detailed analysis of factional struggle within the Constituent Assembly, Timothy Tackett addresses many of the assumptions that the Revisionists have had regarding this early stage of the Revolution. In his view, the period 1789–90 was not some radical precursor to the Terror, but dominated by moderates who did what was required to avoid counter-revolution and make the country safe for constitutional government. Based in part on an unusually comprehensive grasp of correspondence between deputies and their constituents, Tackett argues that factions within the assembly broke out not simply over modes of thought or discourses (as Furet and Baker emphasize), but over fundamental cleavages. Deputies moved to the Left, not so much because they became more influenced by Rousseau's ideas, but rather because they became convinced that a group of powerful deputies on the Right were scheming to halt the Revolution and bring back absolute monarchy. Nor does Tackett think these were the images of some paranoic delusion: he provides evidence that for many months in 1789 and 1790, the danger of counter-revolution was a viable threat that patriotic deputies needed to take seriously. Moreover, Tackett argues that this political division reflected a genuine social hostility between commoners (who championed the Left) and former noblemen (who supported Right-wing efforts to roll back the clock). Like Sewell and Jones, Tackett challenges the Revisionist consensus by claiming that even in its first months, the French Revolution reflected not merely semiotic or ideological differences but more fundamentally, deep-rooted social conflicts.

* * *

For over two decades now, debate has raged between "Marxists" and "revisionists" over the question of the French Revolution.[1] The outlines of this debate have become familiar even to historians with no particular expertise in eighteenth-century French studies. In place of the Marxist or Marxist-inspired vision of a revolution arising out of class conflict between nobility and bourgeoisie, most revisionists would stipulate a revolution, "caused" ultimately by the internal collapse of the monarchy. In this view, the nobles and the upper-class commoners were converging in the late eighteenth century into a single "élite" group, bound by common economic interests and cultural experiences and by the substantial possibilities of social mobility into the nobility. When the two groups fell into conflict in 1789, it was either a kind of accidental aberration arising from misunderstandings, a difference in "style," or a failure of imagination and leadership.

Although most of the controversy to date has hinged on the question of revolutionary origins, François Furet, the leading French representative of revisionism, has also pushed a reconsideration of the revolutionary dynamic after the opening of the Estates-General in May 1789. In his widely read and influential book, *Penser la Révolution*, Furet argued that, once the Revolution had begun, it was impelled forward through the workings not of a class struggle but of a power struggle.[2] By June of 1789 and the creation of the National Assembly, the privileged orders, like the monarchy itself, had essentially "capitulated," and, by October, as Furet and Denis Richet wrote elsewhere, "the battlefield had essentially been conquered, the fight was over: the revolution had been won."[3] Thereafter, conflict within the National Assembly pitted various elements of the Third Estate against one other. The Revolution was progressively democratized and radicalized as successive factions of Patriots each claimed to be the authentic voice of popular sovereignty, the true mouthpiece of the general will. Political struggle thus became a battle of rhetoric and of ideology – but with no class content. It also became a battle of denunciations, as each faction tried to outdo its opponents in its condemnations of "aristocratic plots" and counter-revolutionary conspiracies. But, in Furet's view, these denunciations were largely contrived and the plots "imaginary," "the figment of a frenzied pre-occupation with power," and the indication also of an incipient terrorist mentality in evidence among the Patriots as early as 1789.[4]

But did the "aristocrats" really capitulate and abandon the political struggle so soon? And were early revolutionary developments so totally devoid of social dimensions? I have no intention of considering Furet's complex and suggestive thesis in all its ramifications, or of attempting to treat every aspect of the Revolution. Here, I would only present some of the results of recent research into factional organization and the revolutionary dynamic at the vital core of political life during the early Revolution, the Constituent Assembly. In fact, despite the revisionist call for a return to politics – and despite the awesome number of studies devoted to this period in French history – the internal political life of France's first National Assembly is still rather poorly understood. This is true in part for historiographical reasons. Interest in the process and functioning of the Constituent Assembly has frequently been overshadowed by historians' tenacious fascination with the problem of the origins of the Republic and the Terror. But research has also been hampered by difficulties with sources. The official accounts of events within the assembly halls are often incomplete and tendentious. No minutes at all were maintained by the Third Estate through the second week in June,[5] and, even after the appearance of official record-keeping, minutes were commonly sanitized and abridged by the secretaries in power to promote a desired public impression of assembly activities.[6] Moreover, the near absence of nominal roll-call votes – the principal meat of what once was called the "new" history of parliamentary behavior – renders the careful quantitative assessment of deputy alignments all but impossible.[7] Nevertheless, if it is not feasible to reconstitute voting records or follow the manifold, day-to-day fluctuations of every deputy, one can at least take note of such glimpses of collective behavior as revealed by the lists of adhesions to political clubs and the signatures on petitions.[8] One can also make use of the incomplete records of the periodic elections of National Assembly officers – presidents, secretaries, and committee members. And, perhaps most important, one can examine the considerable number of accounts – many of them still only in manuscript – written by the deputies themselves in letters and memoirs to their families and home constituencies.[9]

The earliest formation of political groupings within the Estates-General will probably always remain somewhat uncertain.[10] Yet the most important and influential of these could clearly trace their genealogies to the pre-revolutionary period. Within days of their arrival in Versailles, groups of liberal deputies of the second estate were regularly congregating at the residences of the Duc de La Rochefoucauld or the Marquis de Montesquiou or in the "Viro-flay Society" on the estates of the Duc de Piennes.[11] A substantial number of the participants, perhaps the majority, were veterans of the Paris-based association of Patriots, the so-called Society of Thirty – from whose membership no fewer than twenty-six had successfully sought election to the Estates-General.[12] Most of these men were Parisians who had long known each other and who were linked through a dense network of association in Masonic lodges, mesmerist groups, and a variety of Enlightenment and philanthropic societies. Many Nobles of the Sword in the group were also bound together as outsiders to the clique of courtiers then in favor in Versailles.[13] With considerable previous experience in political organization, young noblemen such as Adrien Duport, Charles and Alexandre de Lameth, the Marquis de Lafayette and the Comte de Clermont-Tonnerre mapped the strategy that ultimately led to the secession of the liberal nobles from their order and their union with the Third Estate.[14]

Several members of the "Commoners" – Antoine Barnave, Jean-Paul Rabaut-Saint-Etienne, abbé Emmanuel-Joseph Sieyes, for example – seem also to have attended meetings of the liberal noblemen.[15] But the most celebrated and influential of the early Versailles clubs was in fact indigenous to the Third Estate. There is no need to repeat here the well-known history of the Breton Club.[16] It should be emphasized, however, that many and perhaps most of the Breton deputies had previously participated in provincial estates or in the local committees that had co-ordinated opposition against the privileged orders and their attempts to dominate Breton affairs.[17] Even before arriving in Versailles, the newly elected Third Estate delegations had met in Rennes to discuss strategy, and many of the deputies then traveled to the capital together. After the opening of the Estates-General, they followed a procedure apparently already practiced during the last Estates of Brittany, debating important issues in a café each evening, arriving at a majority decision, deciding who would speak the next day in favor of that decision, and urging all participants to vote as a bloc. It was also the specific provincial context – coupled with the absence of all Nobles and bishops from the delegation – that rendered the Breton representatives so exceptionally radical.[18] From the earliest days of the Estates-General, they advocated a unilateral transformation of the Third Estate into a "salle nationale" or "assemblée nationale" – anticipating by some six weeks the famous motions by abbé Sieyes to this effect.[19] Indeed, for many in the Breton group, such a strategy was conceived not as a ploy for forcing joint deliberation with the Nobles and Clergy but as the first step in creating a constitution *without* the participation of the privileged orders.[20] They soon came to be identified with an unrestrained hatred of all nobles: "an extreme violence," "an implacable hatred of the nobility," as two of the more moderate deputies described it.[21]

Yet the Bretons' rapid rise to prominence in early June was by no means inevitable and was rarely anticipated by contemporaries. Although the Breton delegation began inviting representatives from other provinces to participate in its meetings early on, many deputies expressed their aversion and mistrust of the very idea of factions or "cabals" or an "esprit de parti," widely viewed as warping the representative process. The Lorraine landholder and sometime scholar Adrien Duquesnoy spoke harshly of the Breton delegation as "hotheads without measure and without moderation." For the Bordeaux merchant Pierre-Paul Nairac, they were "always moving toward extreme positions," while the Alsatian Etienne-François Schwendt sharply criticized them for attempting to "exercise a kind of domination over all opinions."[22] Others were clearly disconcerted by the Bretons' abrasive attitude toward the nobility. In this, they reflected the fears and ambiguities of men who were often socially and juridically at the very frontier between noblemen and commoners. The majority had probably spent many years of their lives imitating aristocratic values and patiently working within the aristocratic system. Whatever their views – and perhaps rage – against the injustice or irrationality of such a society, few had even dreamed that the system and its values could themselves be changed.[23] In any case, on 18 May, the motion by the Breton Isaac-René-Guy Le Chapelier, declaring that the deputies of the "National Assembly" did not represent specific orders but the whole nation, seems to have won the support of only sixty-six deputies – of whom forty-three were from Le Chapelier's own provincial delegation.[24]

The spectacular success of the Bretons in early June was probably the result of a number of factors. But, to believe the letters and diaries of the deputies themselves, no single factor was more important than the growing intransigence of the majority of the privileged deputies and their ultimate refusal to consider compromise or reconciliation in any form over the crucial question of voting procedure. For, in point of fact, the defenders of privilege and tradition among the deputies, no less than the deputy-Patriots, had also begun organizing in support of their positions. By the end of May – and probably a good deal earlier – bishops in the first estate were meeting with some regularity in the church of Notre-Dame in Versailles. Many of the prelates had known one another for years and were linked by ties of family as well as by a common educational experience at the seminary of Saint-Sulpice.[25] They readily reactivated a miniature version of the General Assembly of the Clergy – on which most of them had long collaborated – and they were notably effective in countering the activities of the more liberal curé-deputies, frustrating their efforts to unite with the Third Estate until after the unilateral decision of that estate to verify credentials in common.[26]

Unlike the Clergy, the conservative and reactionary Nobles – the great majority within the order – had no real institutional base on which to build an effective organization. Nevertheless, a substantial number of the nobles undoubtedly knew one another prior to the convocation of the Estates-General. Historians have not previously noted that almost 40 per cent of the Nobles were actually residents of Paris who had scattered into the provinces to seek election in districts where their families owned land and seigneuries.[27] At least 78 per cent of the Nobles had been educated for the military and were or had previously been commissioned officers in the army or navy. Close to two-thirds, moreover, could trace their families back to at least the sixteenth century, while over half could apparently prove lineage dating to the fourteenth century or earlier.[28] They represented most of the great families of France, and many were closely related to one another – and to the equally aristocratic episcopal families – and had long associated with one another at court and in Parisian societies. In short, the Nobles of 1789 were an extraordinarily "aristocratic" body in the full sense of the word – considerably more so than their counterparts in the Estates-General of 1614. As a corps, they occupied a dramatically different sphere of status and prestige – and probably of wealth – from that occupied by the Third Estate.[29] Although we know relatively few details about the political workings of the Nobles during this period, the substantial blocs of votes given to the winning candidates in the secret ballots for officers of the order in June 1789 strongly suggest some measure of organization.[30] Indeed, the Marquis de Ferrières spoke of the "club" of conservative noblemen, led by Jean-Jacques Duval d'Eprémesnil – judge in Parlement and renegade ex-associate of the Committee of Thirty – the Marquis de Bouthillier, and the Vicomte de La Queuille.[31] With the strong support and patronage of the Comte d'Artois and the reactionary court faction, this group proved remarkably successful through the end of June in maintaining the disciplined intransigence of the great majority of noble deputies. Indeed, several of the originally "liberal-leaning" noblemen, including some with statements of grievances (cahiers de doléances) mandating a vote by head in the Estates-General, are known to have been won over to the hard-line position.[32]

In any case, many of the Third Estate deputies became increasingly convinced of the threat of such organization to the reforming desires of the nation. The Breton deputy Jean-Pierre Boullé warned his constituents on 9 June that the "aristocratic committee" led by Eprémesnil was meeting daily to plot its strategy and that organized action by the Patriots was necessary if the "desires of the nation" were ever to triumph.[33] Even many of the normally moderate and prudent deputies – "les hommes sages," as they liked to call themselves – began commenting on the hopeless resistance to compromise on the part of the bishops and Nobles. With the "aristocrats" of the first and second estates rejecting any form of conciliation, the Third ultimately had no choice, it was argued, but to pull together and go it alone. The self-consciously moderate Antoine Durand, a lawyer from Cahors, was outraged by the Nobles' statement of 28 May, which accepted royal mediation but rejected in advance any discussion of a vote by head: the Nobles "refuse to yield an inch of ground." "Those who have led the Nobles," wrote the usually cautious judge Jean-Baptiste Grellet de Beauregard, "have blocked all roads to compromise"; while his colleague from Toul, the *lieutenant général* Claude-Pierre Maillot, concluded that "the violence of the Nobles' decisions have increased rather than weakened the determined reso- lution of the Third." The wealthy landholder and mayor of Laon, Laurent de Visme, noted in his diary that under normal circumstances he would never have accepted Sieyes's motion of 10 June, but now he was inclined to do so: "The Nobles' actions have justified it."[34]

The Breton Club probably reached the pinnacle of its ascendancy toward the middle and end of June. Boullé wrote on 9 June that "during the last few days our salon has become the rallying point for all good citizens. . . . All the best citizens from all of the provinces are assembling there." On that evening, the Breton group seems to have sent out delegates to argue its case within the individual *bureaux* – the small discussion groups into which the Assembly had recently divided itself – thus measurably contributing to the development of opinion in favor of the motion to be voted on the next day.[35] To be sure, one should not underestimate the role played by the abbé Sieyes himself, whose prestige and eloquent articulation of revolutionary objectives had an enormous impact on many of the deputies.[36] But, in fact, each of Sieyes's motions seems to have been discussed and debated in the Breton Club before being brought to the full assembly of the Third Estate, and the principles in question had been con- tinuously advocated by the Breton delegation for well over a month.[37] Once viewed with considerable mistrust by the majority of deputies, the Breton "committee" now became the center of all political activity in the Third Estate. Impelled by the absolute intransigence of the Nobles and the apparent deadlock of the Clergy, buoyed and invigorated by the support of the Versailles crowds, the Third Estate achieved a remarkable consensus around the Tennis Court Oath and the revolutionary declarations of 10, 17, and 23 June: a new definition of sovereignty and political legitimacy in open defiance of the monarchy that would probably have seemed impossible or unthinkable to most of the deputies just a few weeks earlier.[38]

By all accounts, the period from late June to early August witnessed a substantial transformation of the political chemistry of the Assembly, a restructuring of many of the positions and alliances of the middle of June. Two developments in particular seem to have contributed to cracking the solidarity and apparent consensus of the nascent National Assembly. The first was the popular violence that exploded in the capital in mid-July but that continued in both Paris and the provinces well into August. In short order, the image of the "people" held by many of the deputies – as revealed in their letters and diaries – was dramatically altered. The Rousseauist conception of the Common Man as repository of goodness and truth was frequently replaced, or at least strongly modified, by the image of the violent, unpredictable, and dangerous classes of July and August.[39] To judge by the deputies' own writings, the most shocking event was usually not the storming of the Bastille on 14 July but the popular executions about a week later of the royal officials Joseph Foulon de Doué and Louis Berthier de Sauvigny, the details of which were luridly recounted in the Assembly by deputies who had witnessed them.[40] Although several of the radicals revealed obvious sympathy for the past suffering of the people, and others were pushed by events toward a new, more expansive definition of the electorate they represented,[41] the overall reaction was one of outrage and horror: "barbarous and atrocious violence" (Visme), "scenes of cruelty and horror" (the Third Estate deputies from Marseille), "arbitrary executions that arouse horror" (Joseph Delaville Le Roulx from Brittany).[42] In any case, the July violence is known to have been a key factor in the movement of many deputies away from the more democratic vision of the new regime that had garnered increasing favor in June. It was certainly a major element in the changing position of the "Monarchien" Jean-Joseph Mounier and his liberal noble ally, the Comte de Clermont-Tonnerre. Looking back on this event, Clermont-Tonnerre wrote in 1791: "I feared that we were inciting atrocities; I remembered the St. Bartholomew's Day Massacre . . . and I sadly asked myself, 'Are we even worthy of being free?' "[43]

The second development that contributed to breaking down the earlier consensus within the Third Estate was the entry of the privileged orders into the National Assembly. In point of fact, the process of integrating the first two estates into the Assembly was long and difficult. Even though a majority of the Clergy and a small minority of the Nobles came over to the Third of their own accord between 22 and 26 June, the forced union of the remainder was nothing short of traumatic. Many of the recalcitrants were even ready to refuse the king's request for union on 27 June, and it was only after receiving a warning from the Comte d'Artois that the king's life was in danger that they sullenly marched into the National Assembly, "tears in their eyes, and rage and despair in their hearts."[44] For the next three weeks, a significant minority of both the Nobles and the Clergy continued to boycott all votes and discussions and returned daily to their own meeting halls, frequently voting formal protests of decrees made in the Assembly.[45] It was only after the Parisian insurrections of mid-July that the "parti protestant" agreed to take part in the proceedings.[46] "Severed heads," as one caustic deputy remarked, "were frightfully instructive."[47] But, even at that, it was early August before Jacques-Antoine-Marie de Cazalès and the abbé Jean-Siffrein Maury and several other of the most conservative deputies who had fled – and, in many cases, been chased back by their own constituencies –

formally announced their intention of participating in the National Assembly.[48] Yet prolonged opposition of this kind was almost certainly not the norm. After the initial shock of 27 June, the majority of the newly arrived clergy and noblemen seemed to adapt themselves to the situation with surprising grace. After a two-day break in late June, according to the Comte de La Gallissonnière, "the deputies had calmed down a bit and were less frightened, and a new order of things seemed to appear."[49] The Baron de Pinteville described the sharp reversal in sentiment of many of his colleagues who had long held back because of fear and pride and pressure from the reactionary "party" but who were now swept by sentiments of patriotism and duty to the Nation: "all was forgotten as they came forward with this act of self-sacrifice."[50] For the Marquis de Ferrières, the experience was a revelation: nervous at first, he soon discovered that he was far more at ease with the commoners of the Third Estate than with the great court nobles, whom he had always detested. The Marquis de Guilhem-Clermont-Lodève, the Chevalier de Boufflers, Bishop Talleyrand, the bishop of Nancy, the archbishop of Aix, and numerous others made the transition with relative ease and were soon participating in the debates, some simply "bending to the circumstances," as Boufflers described it, others with a real measure of idealism and enthusiasm, convinced that "the nobles . . . could be equally useful within the common hall of the Assembly."[51]

It was not only these new recruits to the National Assembly who were affected. The entry of the privileged orders into their midst also had a profound effect on the deputies of the Third Estate. Numerous letters give expression to the explosion of joy and the feelings of fraternity with which the Third progressively welcomed the new arrivals. Whatever their rhetoric in late May and early June against the "aristocrats," the majority of the commoners were still awed by the great nobles and flattered that they might sit with them in the same assembly. Adrien Duquesnoy was effusive with praise for "the finest names in the kingdom," "the most virtuous men in the kingdom," who now gave the Assembly "an aura of seriousness . . . that was previously lacking." François-René-Pierre Ménard de la Groye, who had felt almost ashamed of his growing anger with the aristocrats in early June, again felt at ease when he dined with them and was delighted to observe "a great deal of unity and cordiality among all the members of the Assembly."[52]

Members of the Third Estate clearly went out of their way to encourage the participation of their new colleagues. The Vicomte de Malartic noted with evident satisfaction the deferential efforts of the commoners in his *bureau* to elicit his opinions on Saint-Domingue, where he had once lived.[53] Félix Faulcon waxed poetic as he described the camaraderie of nobles and commoners spending the night together in the assembly hall during the mid-July crisis: "These proud nobles, who once so greatly profited from their alleged privileges and the chance occurrence of their birth, now sleep or walk side by side with the commoners."[54] The astute Ferrières rapidly sized up the new situation. "The Upper Third will be flattered," he wrote his sister, "by the consideration shown them by the Nobles. . . . Let the Nobles take a single step and the Third will take ten."[55]

138

Despite their suspicions of the "aristocrats" and the latter's pretensions of social superiority and political dominance, the Commoners' ultimate desire at this stage in events was not to destroy the Nobles but to be treated by that body as equals. Indeed, this surge of fraternal sentiments among the orders should not be underestimated in evaluating the night of 4 August, the dramatic session during which substantial portions of Old Regime institutions were swept away in the space of a few hours. Even though most interpretations of the event emphasize the behind-the-scenes manipulations of the Breton Club, it is doubtful that such tactics would have been effective without the short-lived atmosphere of brotherhood that permeated much of the Assembly in early August.[56]

Only a few of the Third Estate deputies, several of them future Jacobins, seem to have viewed the situation with a more cynical eye. The Breton deputy Delaville Le Roulx despaired that the Assembly would be "captivated by the seductive manners" of the Nobles and bishops and wondered how the Patriots might "bring fresh energy to the Assembly and prevent it from slipping into error." Maillot noted that the "flattery and familiarity" of the privileged were more dangerous than their previous "arrogance and pride." And Jacques-Antoine Creuzé-Latouche, who had never wanted a union of the three orders in the first place, and who would have preferred that the Third Estate act on its own to write a constitution, saw only divisions ahead in the Assembly. "Feeble individuals," he wrote, previously brought into conformity with correct principles by the "vigorous and virile" in the Assembly would now be won over by the nobles, and "aristocratic and antipatriotic maxims" would become the order of the day.[57]

Creuzé's fears were probably not unfounded. After the heroic days of the early Revolution, there is considerable evidence that the Breton Club's influence went into decline. Whether or not the number of adherents actually diminished, the entry of 600 new deputies into the National Assembly – most of whom were clearly conservatives or moderates[58] – invariably decreased the proportionate size of the radical contingent and reduced their hold on the large bloc of moderate Patriots within the Third Estate. In fact, by September, the "comité breton" seems to have reverted to an exclusively provincial organization, no longer attended by deputies from other provinces. It was apparently badly divided over the issue of the royal veto and was meeting less frequently than before.[59] Undoubtedly, the Patriots continued to meet to plan strategy in one way or another, but the meetings probably took place outside any formal organization. The Provençal deputy, Jacques-Athanase de Lombard-Taradeau, who openly aligned himself with the most advanced faction of the Patriots, never referred to the "Breton Club" after July but only to "what we call the 'Palais royal' of the Assembly" or simply "our party." And his descriptions of the group's operations portray an extremely loose factional organization improvised on the spot, "in the morning, before the beginning of the session, after much discussion among groups in the hall." Indeed, if Lombard's accounts are at all typical, it seems likely that the lengthy hours passed in the National Assembly and in the various discussion groups and committees throughout the months of August and September, the sheer fatigue from the work involved, made nightly club meetings substantially more difficult.[60]

One indication of the decline in the Breton group's fortunes and the general movement of deputy opinion during this period comes – in the absence of roll-call records – from the various elections of officers to the National Assembly. The organizational regulations of the Assembly specified that every two weeks the deputies would meet in their *bureaux* – the thirty discussion groups, to which all members were assigned – to vote for a president and three secretaries. The president would serve for a two-week period and would be chosen in multiple ballots if necessary – in an effort to obtain a winner by absolute majority; the secretaries would be chosen by simple plurality on a single vote and would hold office for a month (so that there were always six secretaries in service at a given moment).[61] Although a great deal depended on the personalities of the individuals holding the posts, all the officers had considerable potential power: the president to set the order of debate and designate – or reject – speakers, the secretaries to control the minutes of the meetings and to sort correspondence and decide which letters and petitions went to which committees. Since the votes were organized through the thirty individual *bureaux* – in isolation from the pressures of the galleries – and were apparently taken by secret ballot, they can be interpreted as a useful index of the evolution of deputy sentiment and perhaps also of the degree of organization of the various political factions.[62]

The earliest elections seem generally to confirm the atmosphere of a united front previously identified for this period. To be sure, with the possible exception of the abbé de Montesquiou, Agent-General of the Clergy, all fourteen of the individuals elected as officers between 3 July and 3 August had earlier reputations as Patriots.[63] But while four of these – Le Chapelier, Sieyes, the abbé Henri Grégoire, and Jérôme Pétion de Villeneuve – were probably considered radicals and later became members of the Jacobin Club, six others would undoubtedly have been classed as moderates, and four – Clermont-Tonnerre, Mounier, the Comte de Lally-Tollendal, and the abbé de Montesquiou – soon embraced the more conservative "Monarchiens" position.[64] Perhaps equally significant, no less than ten of the fourteen were members of the privileged orders – though not all had actually been elected by their "natural" estates. This marked preference for nobles and clergymen as assembly officers continued throughout the entire first year of the Constituent Assembly with nineteen of twenty-seven presidents and fifty-one of eighty-eight secretaries being drawn from members of the first two estates.[65] The first three presidential contests were scarcely contests at all, with votes going overwhelmingly to the Duc d'Orléans (who declined), the archbishop of Vienne, and the Duc de Liancourt. The first and only Breton Club president, the Rennes lawyer Le Chapelier, obtained the post almost by accident in early August. In fact, he had come in third in the initial contest and was chosen in a second election only after the victor, the moderate Jacques-Guillaume Thouret, had resigned.[66] And it was to be the last time a member of the Left would control the rostrum for almost seven months. Through the end of the year, the future Jacobins were largely an insignificant force in the presidential tallies, their candidates unable to muster more than 183 votes (out of over a thousand) in any of the elections for which voting totals are preserved.[67] Indeed, to judge by the deputies elected to office from mid-August to mid-October, the best organized and most influential faction within the Assembly was not on the Left at all but on the Right.[68]

Throughout the month of July, the organization of the recalcitrant privileged action seems never entirely to have dissolved, despite the popular upheavals and the temporary flight of many of its adherents. Even after the meeting halls of the Nobles and the Clergy had been closed and converted into offices by Jacques Necker, director-general of finance, a core of the most conservative noblemen and bishops continued to meet in the homes of individuals. They were clearly acting as a corps on 16 July when they announced to the Assembly that they would henceforth join in the votes and the debates.[69] It was most likely this same coalition that then co-ordinated the considerable deputy discipline involved in placing several of its numbers on the new Committee on Research at the end of July and in the election of Thouret to the presidency at the beginning of August.[70] Significantly, it was toward the beginning of August that several Patriots first took note of the "cabal" of Nobles and Clergy that was opposing them and voting as a bloc.[71]

An initial turning point in the new evolution was undoubtedly the night of 4 August. While in some respects this sweeping attack on privilege marked the ultimate fruition of the earlier flowering of fraternal generosity, it also carried with it the seeds of renewed factional strife. To judge by the reflections of the deputy letter-writers, the suppression of seigneurial rights was accepted with resignation and sometimes with enthusiasm. "If it leads to advantages for the public good," wrote Ferrières to his wife, "I will easily be able to console myself for my losses as a noble and as a seigneurial lord." The chevalier Garron de la Bévière was more morose about the economic prospects of his order, but he, too, in a letter to his wife, accepted the inevitable: "In the end, if it will promote general happiness, I have no regrets. . . . One must yield to necessity."[72] Yet large numbers of the clerical deputies were clearly upset by the suppression of the tithes without reimbursement and by the first proposals for the nationalization of church property. According to numerous witnesses, however, the key issue that united many of the nobles and clergymen as a solid and cohesive group was the debate two weeks later over including religious toleration in the Declaration of the Rights of Man and the Citizen and the counter-proposal that Catholicism be made the state religion. In what were widely described as the most tumultuous debates to date, a number of deputies in all three estates seem to have dramatically crystallized their opposition to the Revolution.[73] Thus curé Emmanuel Barbotin, previously a strong supporter of the Third Estate, now became convinced that many Third Estate deputies were "philosophers who have neither faith nor discipline"; while Guilluame Gontier de Biran, a chief *bailliage* magistrate from Bergerac, first came to perceive a dual menace to religion and the throne. For the Baron de Gauville – who had been irritated by the loss of his hunting rights on 4 August but who had generally accepted the abolition of seigneurial dues – it was precisely during these debates of late August that "we began to recognize one another" and that he and his colleagues began sitting together consistently on the right side of the president's table.[74]

Nevertheless, the critical achievement in the organization of the Right was to be the work of a new coalition of more moderate conservatives, a number of them recruited from the Third Estate. The formation and general character of the "Monarchiens" have been described in some detail by Jean Egret and, more recently, by Robert Griffiths.[75] Unlike the extreme right of the recalcitrant Nobles and Clergy, who sought either a return to the Old Regime or a system of reforms based on the king's declaration of 23 June, the Monarchiens sought to affirm the transformations of that summer but to ensure that ultimate sovereignty remained in the hands of the king as a buttress against the dangers of popular violence. Centered on the delegation from Dauphiné – the only provincial delegation that could match the Bretons in its cohesiveness and its tradition of group action – but also including important contingents from Auvergne and Normandy and a bevy of moderate nobles, the group resolved sometime in late July or early August to beat the Breton Club at its own game.[76] In relatively short order, the Monarchiens had surpassed the Patriots in their level of factional organization. While the Breton Club had operated in an essentially democratic fashion, with relatively loose discipline and public debates in a café to which all were invited, the Monarchiens followed their more authoritarian and hierarchical penchant by establishing a small decision-making "central committee," which convened in private at one of the member's homes – and sometimes in the château of Versailles itself – and which then sent out directives through a system of subcommittees to all its potential adherents. Before votes in the *bureaux* for committee members or National Assembly officers, someone passed out notes listing the names that deputies were to inscribe on their ballots.[77] On the floor of the National Assembly, Mounier's friend and colleague from Dauphiné, the Comte de Virieu, assumed the role of a veritable party whip: "he can be seen in every corner of the hall, speaking, entreating, shouting, peering to see who will vote for or against."[78] By early September, the progressively tighter coalition between moderate and extreme right was clearly in place, with Cazalès, Eprémesnil, and the abbé Maury participating in the Monarchien central committee and speaking frequently in the Assembly in defense of Monarchien positions.[79] On 17 September, the radical printer-deputy from Lyon, Jean-André Périsse-Duluc, wrote that "the coalition of nearly all of the Clergy and the Nobles, along with a lesser number of Commoners, has become so strong that the deputies involved never differ on their votes: without exception, all of them rise together or remain seated [in order to vote]."[80] Clearly, many of the "aristocrats" were increasingly prepared to follow the rules of the game and work within the newly evolved parliamentary system, convinced of the real possibility of halting and perhaps reversing the revolution through political organization and majority votes.

The growing power of this new coalition was apparent in the choice of

Assembly officers. After the middle of August, the Monarchiens not only won four successive presidential elections but also largely dominated the secretariat's table as well. In the election of 31 August, they even obtained a clean sweep of the president – the bishop of Langres – and all three secretaries. Indeed, there is good evidence that the Monarchien coalition was the only group systematically organizing for elections during this period. The scraps of voting records remaining reveal that, in September, the Monarchien candidates alone received significant blocs of votes in every *bureau*, the remainder of the votes being spread out over an enormous range of individual deputies.[81] "For three weeks now," wrote Virieu after the election of the bishop of Langres, "the reasonable and upright deputies have quietly reclaimed the majority. The *enragés* have been beaten back on all fronts. In spite of their efforts, we have chosen the president and all three secretaries."[82] The election in mid-September of the Monarchien Comte de Clermont-Tonnerre was perhaps even more galling to the Left in that, by the rotation procedure tacitly agreed on since July, the post should normally have gone to a member of the Third Estate.[83]

To be sure, the coalition was frequently more successful in the electoral *bureaux* than on the floor of the Assembly itself, and it came up short on several of the key constitutional votes for which it militated with particular fervor – above all, the effort in early September to obtain a two-house legislature and an absolute royal veto on all legislation. Indeed, the alliance would seem to have broken down entirely on the issue of the number of chambers, with the extreme right apparently following a *politique du pire* and voting with the Patriots. But most of the deputies perceived the veto decision as a compromise vote between the Right's desire for an absolute veto and the Left's desire for no veto at all. And the Monarchiens and their allies won a considerable victory later in the month when it was decided that three successive legislatures would have to pass the same law in order to override a royal veto – a complication considered by some as tantamount to an absolute veto.[84]

In any event, the deputies of the Left clearly believed themselves under siege from late August to early October. Lombard wrote home that "our party is absolutely in the minority." Louis-Prosper Lofficiel was convinced that, without the support of about forty clergymen and a hundred or so liberal nobles, "we would certainly be defeated" on every vote. Périsse estimated that as many as two-thirds of all the deputies were influenced by the "cabal" – although fortunately half of these were open-minded and could sometimes be won over.[85] For the celebrated writer, Constantin-François Chassebeuf de Volney, deputy from Anjou, the Assembly was now so divided and in danger of being won over by the aristocrats that it was necessary to elect a whole new assembly and a new set of deputies, chosen this time to represent the true social composition of the French population – notably, by eliminating most of the noble and clerical deputies. And after losing the vote on the manner of overriding a royal veto, the delegation from Brittany seriously discussed abandoning the Assembly altogether, an Assembly now deemed to be entirely dominated by the "aristocrats."[86]

*

The political history of the Constituent Assembly after the dramatic events of 5–6 October – the march on Versailles that led to the transfer of both monarchy and Assembly to Paris – is generally less well known than the earlier period of the Revolution. Many series of correspondence ended in the later half of 1789 or toward the beginning of the following year, as deputies found themselves burdened with ever-increasing demands on their time and as a growing national distribution of newspapers removed one of the principal *raisons d'être* for the letters home.

Nevertheless, it seems clear that the October Days did not mark the demise of the Right as a meaningful force in the National Assembly. The mass desertion of the conservative deputies – 300 are sometimes said to have taken out passports[87] – is apparently a myth, altogether unsubstantiated by the evidence available.[88] Although four of the Monarchien leaders did indeed leave the Assembly,[89] Pierre-Victor Malouet, Clermont-Tonnerre, Virieu, and their associates continued their efforts on behalf of the Monarchien platform to the very end of the Constituent Assembly. Together, they formed first a "Club des Impartiaux" and later a "Club Monarchique."[90] Despite his initial despondency over the October events, Virieu ultimately repudiated the desertion of his friend Mounier and vowed to fight on: "the sacred flame that burns within me is not yet extinguished, and is reviving . . ." "I will stay with the Assembly," wrote Archbishop Boisgelin, "and I will go with it [to Paris]." Gontier de Biran also affirmed his determination to stay on despite his anguish and disappointment over the events: "I think that if it were not for the honor and desire of doing our duty, few of us would remain here."[91]

For the next few months, the focus of power seemed to shift back toward the center of the political spectrum, with the unaligned "Center" Patriots – Emmanuel-Marie Fréteau de Saint-Just, Armand-Gaston Camus, Thouret, and Jean-Nicolas Démeunier – picking up five of the six presidencies to the end of the year.[92] Yet the factional organization, the very considerable coordinating capabilities created by the Monarchiens, seem to have been maintained. On occasion, the group was still able to elect its candidates as president: Boisgelin in November and the abbé de Montesquiou in early January.[93] Basking in his recent victory, the prelate congratulated himself for having rejected all the predictions of doom by Mounier and Lally-Tollendal and for having stayed on to fight. Where would he be now, he mused, "if I had listened to the advice everyone was giving me?"[94] Like many other deputies, he was convinced that the decree of 2 November placing ecclesiastical lands "at the disposal of the Nation" was actually a victory for his side. Everyone knew that some church lands would have to be sold, he wrote, but they had succeeded in simply admitting the principle without in any way turning all lands over to the state: "They will perhaps be satisfied to sell off monastic property."[95] The Monarchiens and their allies also continued to obtain election of their adherents to various committees, culminating in a dramatic vote in late November that gave them effective control of the powerful organ of investigation and repression, the Committee on Research.[96]

Yet the October Days may well have marked the beginning of a certain shift within the Right coalition in favor of the more reactionary elements. This evolution is particularly evident if one examines the breakdown of those deputies actually participating in Assembly debates – as suggested by entries in the index to the proceedings and debates of the Constituent Assembly. (See Figure 7.1.[97]) The frequency of participation of the Monarchiens dropped precipitously from September to March, continuing downward even after the departure of the four Monarchien leaders in October. During the same period, the most notable speakers of the extreme Right were participating ever more

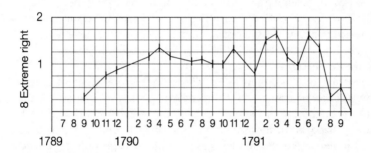

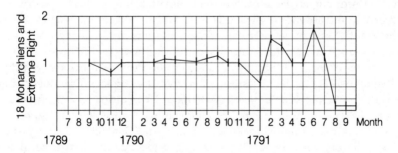

Figure 7.1 Index of participation of Monarchiens and Extreme Right speakers in the proceedings and debates of the Constituent Assembly

145

frequently, so that from early 1790 to the end of the Constituent Assembly they had become the principal spokesmen for the Right. Unfortunately, much less is known of the factional organization of the extreme Right during this period. But the religious issue, and particularly the question of church property seems increasingly to have become the central rallying point in binding together the most conservative elements of the Nobles, the Clergy, and the Commoners – or such, at least, was the opinion of the conservative Baron de Gauville.[98]

Significantly – in the midst of the debates over ecclesiastical land and monastic vows – the group began holding its meetings in the Grands Augustins, in the same hall where the bishops had been accustomed to holding their *Assemblées générales* for generations. Here, according to the elderly Patriot lawyer René-Antoine-Hyacinthe Thibaudeau, "They begin by preparing in their committees the insidious measures that they then try to push through the Assembly.[99] When the faction was forced to leave under the pressures of the Parisian crowds, they took refuge in the Capuchin monastery, which was directly attached to the assembly hall and which allowed the deputies to enter through a private passageway unseen by the crowds outside.[100] It was here that the "Capuchin Society" as they came to be known, drew up their declaration of 19 April 1790, adhering to Dom Christophe-Antoine Gerle's motion six days earlier that Roman Catholicism be declared the state religion.[101] Chased away once again by the Parisian crowds, the group seems to have continued its coordination in more secretive fashion through a series of small "committees" that met in the homes of individuals, each committee delegating one of its members as liaison with a central steering committee. On occasion, they seem also to have met jointly with the Club des Impartiaux – confirming a continued loose alliance between the two alignments on the Right.[102]

By the spring of 1790, there were already numerous signs of a shift of the Assembly's center of gravity in the direction of the Left. To believe the analysis of Visme, at the beginning of December the deputies were divided almost exactly into two equal parts. In the important vote of 7 December, when the radicals attempted to revise the election laws to promote broader political participation, "the Assembly divided into two almost equal parts sitting at opposite ends of the hall."[103] And Périsse-Duluc noted the hesitancy of the Left to have any of its adherents sent out as *commissaires du roi* to organize the new local governments, for fear that the absence of even a few Patriots would tip the balance in favor of the Right.[104] But, by late December and early January, a number of deputies from various points on the political spectrum were becoming aware of an evident erosion of the Right. By the year's end, the Protestant banker from Lyon, Guillaume-Benoît Couderc, was convinced that "the aristocratic influence in the hall is declining appreciably from day to day." The Patriot curé Thomas Lindet concurred: "The opposition party is diminishing. . . . It is winning some small victories, but it is losing the major questions." And Delaville, so pessimistic for the Left the previous September, now suggested, for the first time, that his "party" was clearly in control of the situation: "les hommes forts," as he described them. "Those who know anything of the Assembly," wrote

Duquesnoy, "cannot help but notice the progressive desertion and depopulation of that part of the hall where the abbé Maury sits, and that there is no longer a sufficient number of seats at the other side of the hall." By mid-January, the Assembly staff was having to install more benches on the Left to accommodate all the new arrivals.[105] To be sure, the Right retained a considerable residual strength through at least the middle of 1790 and was able to attract enough votes from the still rather volatile uncommitted deputies to win several presidential elections and a certain number of constitutional votes. Indeed, from late February through the middle of July, the elections suggest an Assembly more polarized than ever before. One might be tempted to speak of a veritable two-party system during this period, with nine of the eleven presidential victories going to either the Jacobin or the Capuchin candidates.[106] But, by and large, the momentum and the initiative within the Assembly were increasingly passing to the left of hall.[107]

The reasons for this evolution at this particular moment in the Assembly's history are not entirely clear. It was related in part, no doubt, to the increasing dominance within the Right of the most reactionary strand of conservatism, the strand associated in the minds of most deputies with the trio of Maury, Cazalès, and Eprémesnil. Many of the Monarchiens had built earlier reputations as patriots and reformist leaders. But the leaders of the opposition most in evidence by the end of 1789 had been identified from the beginning with a complete return to the Old Regime. As Duquesnoy suggested, far fewer people wanted to sit on the Right when the abbé Maury became the central figure on his side of the hall.[108] The situation was compounded in that the geography of the new meeting hall in Paris no longer provided any intermediate places in which to sit. The hall in Versailles had been essentially oval in its layout, while the long, narrow "Manège," divided in the middle by the speaker's platform and the president's table, forced every deputy to make a daily symbolic affirmation as to which side he was on.[109]

Yet perhaps the single most important development in the resurgence of the Left was the formation in late November or early December of the Jacobin Club and the rapid emergence of this association as a highly organized political force. In fact, the new *société* was not – as is often suggested – the simple continuation of the Breton Club, transferred from Versailles to Paris. By the end of the summer, the Breton group had already lost its character as the central rallying point for all Patriots. Once in Paris, the Bretons apparently continued their separate meetings for a time even after the creation of the Friends of the Constitution.[110] Although a great many of the members of the new association had probably also been members of the earlier Breton Club, the Jacobins created a new kind of Patriot structure, more highly centralized and organized, patterned in many respects after the organization of the Right. Indeed, according to Louis-Marie de La Revellière-Lépeaux, the initial formation of the Jacobin Club in late November was in direct response to the organizational offensive of the Right. Everyone knew, wrote La Revellière, that "the aristocratic party normally chose the Assembly officers because it held meetings in which it was decided in advance who was to be elected." For this reason, the Left "decided to hold meetings of their own so that they could ensure the Patriots' control of the bureau."[111]

The details of this organization are still poorly known. It seems certain, how-ever, that in addition to their general public meetings in the Dominican convent, the Jacobins created a central committee with prime responsibilities for guiding the general direction of the club and set up a far more efficient means of dis-ciplining voting. But if, in many respects, they simply emulated the organization of the Monarchiens, the Jacobins also went beyond the Right in their efforts to systematically mobilize public opinion in favor of their initiatives through the creation of a correspondence committee as liaison with affiliated clubs in the provinces.[112] It was almost certainly this new organization that allowed the Jacobins to increase their influence in the election of Assembly officers – first, from November onward, the secretaries and, by March 1790, the presidents as well. The same organization enabled the Left to begin systematically taking con-trol of most of the committees. Thus, in the December election of the Committee on Research, the club engineered a dramatic turnabout, with the elimination of all the deputies on the Right and their replacement by twelve known Patriots, eight of whom were Jacobins.[113] While in 1789 they obtained only a fourth of the committee assignments, in 1790 the Jacobin group was able to gain half of all new positions. Over the same period, the deputies on the Right saw their share of committee posts decline from one-fifth to less than one-tenth of all assignments.[114]

By the early weeks of 1790, both outside observers and the deputies themselves were aware of the growing polarization of the National Assembly and of the extent to which developments in that assembly were increasingly dominated by two politicized and well-organized "parties." As L'Observateur remarked, "For the last month, two associations have existed in Paris. Each is composed of members of the National Assembly. The first ... meets in the Jacobins of the rue Saint-Honoré; the second ... meets in the Grands-Augustins. Both have a numerous membership; both are a source of uneasiness for Parisians from the influence they may have over the National Assembly."[115] Lindet, in a letter to his brother, expressed it even more simply, "A singular division reigns in the Assembly: the hall has become a battlefield where two enemy armies face one another."[116]

But who were these two armies? What differences can one find in the character and composition of their respective contingents? Unfortunately, the participants in the Breton Club and the Monarchien group will probably never be known for certain. Membership in the Jacobin group can be generally reconstructed, however, through the research of Alphonse Aulard.[117] Based on this source, 205 Constituent Assembly deputies would seem to have adhered to the "Amis de la Constitution" in the months following December 1790. Although membership had undoubtedly varied somewhat since the club first formed in late 1789, this number is surprisingly close to the round figure of 200 who were supporting

Jacobin candidates for committee assignments in April 1790.[118] As for the "Capuchins Society," a substantial portion of its participation can be ascertained from the petition signed during the faction's meeting on 19 April.[119] Even though the specific object of the petition, the maintenance of Catholicism as the sole state religion, may have prevented the association of a few anticlerical conservatives – like the Marquis de Ferrières – the petition remains the best single record of factional adhesion to the Capuchins for the first half of 1790. In all, 292 deputies signed this document – suggesting an alignment on the Right significantly larger than the Jacobin group.[120]

A preliminary analysis of the two groups of deputies suggests that the collective biographies of the Capuchins, on the one hand, and the Jacobins, on the other, were in certain respects dramatically different.[121] Without a doubt, the most salient distinction was the remarkable alignment by Old Regime estate. More than eight out of ten Jacobins were deputies of the Third Estate, while more than nine out of ten Capuchins represented the two privileged orders.[122] Indeed, among the handful of twenty-three Third Estate deputies belonging to the Capuchins, a third were actually nobles or clergymen who had been elected by the commoners.[123] To be sure, the single largest contingent of Capuchins – slightly over half – were clergymen. They included almost all of the bishops, as well as some 40 per cent of the parish priests in the Assembly.[124] We have already noted the importance of opposition to the Constituent Assembly's religious policies in the general cohesion of the group. It is not surprising that the coalition soon came generally to be known as "les noirs." Yet if one includes the deputies from all three estates, some 54 per cent of the Capuchins are found to have come from noble families. And of these, two-thirds were true "aristocrats" who could trace back their lineage to the sixteenth century or earlier.[125] Much can be made of the relatively modest family backgrounds of the three most visible leaders of the Right: Maury, Cazalès, and Eprémesnil – the first a commoner, the second two of first-generation nobility. Yet one should also not overlook the strong "aristocratic" imprint on the Capuchins as a whole – aristocratic not only in the revolutionary meaning of "conservative ideology" but with the older implication of ancient social or caste origins. Beyond Maury, Cazalès, and Eprémesnil, seven of the ten most common Capuchin speakers originated in families of this kind.[126]

As for the Jacobins in the Assembly, the commoners among them – the vast majority – differed very little in their social contours from the Third Estate deputies as a whole.[127] There was, however, a distinct over-representation of those calling themselves "avocats" and a corresponding under-representation of the various categories of royal officeholders.[128] Unfortunately, the socio-economic position of the "lawyers" in question is difficult to define and was almost certainly very diverse – from practicing court lawyers to wealthy land-owners who had never set foot in a court and whose law degrees were essen-tially symbols of status.[129] The paucity of officeholders among the Jacobins is not insignificant, however, in that many of them – particularly the royal magis-trates – occupied what was perhaps the highest status level of the entire Third

Estate. They were also among those Commoners deputies with the greatest vested interests in the Old Regime. In all, only eleven clergymen and forty-two noblemen – representing any of the three estates – had thrown in their lots with the Jacobins. A few of the nobles – the Duc d'Aiguillon, the Vicomte de Noailles, the brothers Lameth, for example – were from among the greatest families of the kingdom. Of the central club leadership, both Alexandre Lameth and the parlementary magistrate Adrien Duport had been members of the second estate. It is significant, nevertheless, that this small group of Jacobin nobles was distinctly less "aristocratic" than the large contingent of Capuchin nobles, with only a little over one-third holding titles dating before the seventeenth century.[130] Indeed, almost half of all the newly ennobled Third Estate deputies – eighteen of thirty-eight – joined the Jacobins. Among the twelve most important leaders of the Constituent Assembly from the Jacobin deputies, those participating most frequently in National Assembly debates, only one – the Comte de Mirabeau – was an "aristocrat" by birth.[131]

Beyond the question of social differences, a preliminary prosopography would suggest two other ways in which the two political factions can be distinguished. In the first place, Capuchins and Jacobins would seem to have had somewhat differing residences. A full 26 per cent of the Capuchins, compared to only 11 per cent of the Jacobins, are known to have lived in Paris. Most of the Parisian Capuchins in question were in fact from great noble families who had won election in provincial *bailliages* by virtue of their names and status. Half of the Jacobins, by contrast – compared to only 30 per cent of the Capuchins – came from small to medium-size provincial towns, with populations of from 2,000 to 50,000 inhabitants. Among those Capuchins who did come from the provinces, however, a significantly larger proportion came from southern France – south of a line between La Rochelle and Geneva – and notably from the Massif Central and other interior provinces of the Midi, regions that were among the most isolated and economically backward in the kingdom.[132]

In the second place, the Capuchins were distinctly older, on the average, than their opponents. Among those deputies for whom dates of birth are known, the Jacobins averaged 43.2 years old in 1790, three years younger than the average for all deputies, while the Capuchins averaged 49.5.[133] Indeed, among totality of the youngest deputies, those under thirty at the beginning of the revolution, no less than 40 per cent adhered to the Jacobins – compared to 11 per cent who associated with the Capuchins. Among those deputies over sixty-five at the opening of the Estates-General, 28 per cent became Capuchins and only 5 per cent became Jacobins. Moreover, such differences cut across all three orders: the average ages of Jacobin clergymen, Jacobin noblemen, and Jacobin commoners were all lower than their respective counterparts within the rival faction. The differences were particularly dramatic among the small group of radical nobles, whose mean age was nearly ten years younger than that of their noble colleagues on the right side of the hall.[134] A generational effect was clearly operational in the radicalism and conservatism of many of the deputies.

*

Factional confrontations between Left and Right continued as a characteristic feature of the Constituent Assembly to the very end of that body's existence in September 1791. Indeed, to judge by the participation index (see Figure 7.1) the principal speakers on the Right were never more active than during the spring of 1791.[135] Yet the political influence of the conservative coalition within the Assembly was ebbing sharply by the middle of 1790. Two extraordinary successes by the Patriots at the beginning of the summer undoubtedly contributed to breaking the momentum and the energy of the Capuchin–Impartial alliance: the formal suppression of the nobility on 20 June and the passage of the Civil Constitution of the Clergy three weeks later. Taken together, the two measures fostered a deep sense of fatalism and demoralization on the part of many of the deputies of the Clergy and the Nobles.[136] The last president elected by the Right retired from office in the middle of July. From September of that year – after a succession of moderate Patriots – the Jacobins effectively came to dominate the presidency, as they already controlled the secretariat, through the end of the Constituent Assembly. By November, the Jacobin curé Lindet could write to his brother, "The aristocracy no longer has an influence, it seems to me, on the choice of Assembly officers."[137]

Yet the rise of the Jacobins to pre-eminence within the National Assembly had been neither rapid nor inevitable. Their triumph, if triumph it was, came not in 1789, as is usually suggested, but only in the second half of 1790.[138] And the chronology is significant. Events during that first formative year of the Revolution helped set the tone of the parliamentary process and establish many of the basic political presuppositions for years to come. Far from capitulating, the representatives of privilege and conservatism had asserted a dynamic presence within the Estates-General and the National Assembly from the very beginning. Many of the reactionary deputies of the Clergy and the Nobles, whose initial intransigence had greatly contributed in crystallizing the revolutionary sentiment of June 1789, had eventually been won over by the successful organizational achievements of the Monarchiens and, rapidly adapting to circumstances, had set out in an alliance with the more moderate conservatives to exploit to their advantage the new system and its rules. Learning from the methods of the Breton Club, this coalition had soon taken the initiative, pioneering many of the electoral tactics usually attributed to the Jacobins, and playing a key role in the transformation of the more archaic Old Regime faction into a first sketch of the modern political party. In their heyday, their numbers closely matched – actually were somewhat superior to – those of the Jacobins, and they could feel justified in their ambition to win over a sufficient number of the non-aligned moderate majority to seize control of the Assembly. The Monarchien Malouet certainly believed this was possible, and he speculated, many years later, on what might have happened if a relatively small number of deputies on the Right had not decided to abandon the battle so early in the Revolution. The Jacobin leader Alexandre Lameth made much the same argument, musing that the presence in the Estates-General of deputies from the Breton nobility and upper clergy – groups that had boycotted the elections in the spring of 1789 – might have entirely transformed the situation.[139]

Inevitably, the Patriots were intensely aware of the offensive of the Right and often, understandably, felt harried and besieged. They were also clearly conscious of the social composition of the group that opposed them at the other end of the hall. It was not a question of mere rhetoric, of the Jacobins concocting imaginary machinations by the aristocrats. In fact they faced genuine, genealogically certified aristocrats, swords at their sides, day after day in the Assembly itself: aristocrats who, for a time, were prominent elements in a highly organized political faction or alliance of factions, and who, for a time, could harbor the plausible hope of a "legal" counter-revolution engineered through the Constituent Assembly itself.[140] Little wonder that the Patriots on the Left soon felt compelled to match the organization of the Right with their own, highly centralized party organization. Little wonder that many deputies on the Left came to view all opposition parties as dangerous and illegal, and that the very concept of a "loyal opposition" failed to develop in the early revolution. Obviously, a close "internal" analysis of this kind does not answer all the questions about the dynamics of the Revolution, or even about the dynamics of the National Assembly. A more general synthesis will have to take into account those exogenous factors – economic trends, crowd activities, international relations, and the pressures of newspapers, clubs, home constituencies, and Parisian assemblies – all those forces that exerted an overwhelming impact on revolutionary developments as a whole. A broader account will also have to confront the seemingly intractable problem of the influence of pre-revolutionary ideologies on the men of 1789.

But the approach taken here does reveal the extent to which the political behavior of a significant and highly influential – if minority – segment of the National Assembly was associated with social divisions among the deputies. To be sure, the social divisions operative were not those of class. Most of the Nobles and most of the wealthy commoners who represented the Third Estate – as revisionist historians never tire of demonstrating – had basically similar relationships to the means of production.[141] A Marxian analysis, whatever its utility for explaining other aspects of the Revolution, is ultimately not very useful for the problems of the National Assembly. It seems likely that, for understanding social interaction within the Constituent Assembly, an analysis based on a complex of categories – such as wealth, status, education, and previous political experience – will prove far more helpful. In terms of the subjective element of status within the traditional value system – a value system with which the deputies, as revealed in their letters, long maintained an ambiguous relationship – there was clearly a world of difference between the majority of those individuals participating in the two major factional divisions of the Assembly.[142] And it seems evident that the political-social dialectic between Left and Right, a dialectic whose origins can be traced to the earliest days of the Estates-General and the National Assembly, would exert a major influence on the development of the new political culture of the French Revolution and of modern France.

NOTES

Source Reprinted from the *American Historical Review* 94 (April 1989): 271–301.

Acknowledgment Much of the research on which this article is based was supported by a fellowship from the John Simon Guggenheim Memorial Foundation. Earlier versions were presented at the Washington/Baltimore French history study group and at the 1988 meeting of the Society for French Historical Studies. May I express my particular appreciation to Jack Censer and Donald Sutherland for their careful readings and criticisms.

1 Perhaps the best general summaries of the debate are in William Doyle, *Origins of the French Revolution* (Oxford, 1980), pp. 7–40; Lynn Hunt, *Politics, Culture, and Class in the French Revolution* (Berkeley, Calif., 1984), pp. 3–10; and D.M.G. Sutherland, *France, 1789–1815: Revolution and Counterrevolution* (Oxford, 1985), pp. 15–18. See also the recent articles by Michael P. Fitzsimmons, "Privilege and the Polity in France, 1786–1791," *AHR*, 92 (April 1987): 269–95; and Michel Vovelle, "L'historiographie de la Révolution française à la veille du bicentenaire," *Annales historiques de la Révolution française*, 272 (1988): 113–26. Vovelle would substitute "Jacobins" for "Marxists," since not all historians embracing the synthesis of Jean Jaurès and Georges Lefebvre were themselves Marxists. There is also, of course, a wide variety of nuances and approaches among the various scholars in the "revisionist" line.

2 François Furet, *Penser la Révolution* (Paris, 1978). In citations, I will use the English version, *Interpreting the Revolution*, trans. Elborg Forster (Cambridge, 1981). Translated into several languages, Furet's work has become standard reading in university courses on the Revolution and provided a central theme for discussion in a recent international conference. See also Keith Michael Baker (ed.), *The French Revolution and the Creation of Modern Political Culture*, vol. 1, *The Political Culture of the Old Regime* (Oxford, 1987), esp. the introduction by Baker; and Jack R. Censer, "The Coming of a New Interpretation of the French Revolution," *Journal of Social History*, 21 (1987): 295–309. Among the few other revisionist or quasi-revisionist works treating the revolutionary period itself, see esp. Patrice Higonnet, *Class, Ideology, and the Rights of the Nobles during the French Revolution* (Oxford, 1981); and Norman Hampson, *Prelude to Terror: The Constituent Assembly and the Failure of Consensus* (Oxford, 1988).

3 Furet, *Interpreting the Revolution*, p. 46; François Furet and Denis Richet, *La Révolution française* (Paris, 1973), p. 99.

4 Furet, *Interpreting the Revolution*, p. 54.

5 The first official minutes of the Third Estate seem to have been taken on 12 June; Jérôme Mavidal, *et al.*, (eds.), *Archives parlementaires, Première série*, 82 vols (Paris, 1867–1913), 8:94. (Hereafter, *AP*.) The early minutes were partially reconstructed several weeks later.

6 See, for example, the Assembly's decision on 29 April 1790, to expunge the Comte de Virieu's speech resigning the presidency because it was deemed "injurieuse" to the Assembly; *Réimpression de l'ancien Moniteur (mai 1789–novembre 1799)*, 31 vols (Paris, 1858–63), 4:241.

7 Motions to create such lists were rejected on 9 July, 29 August, and again on 8 December 1789; *AP*, 8:510 and 10:776–77; Philip Dawson, *Provincial Magistrates and Revolutionary Politics in France, 1789–1795* (Cambridge, Mass., 1972), p. 194; and Jean-François Gaultier de Biauzat, *Gaultier de Biauzat, député du Tiers-Etat aux Etats-Généraux de 1789: Sa vie et sa correspondance*, ed. Francisque Mège, 2 vols (Clermont-Ferrand, 1890), 2:168.

8 The present study is based on a new computerized prosopography of the 1,315 deputies who sat at any time during the Constituent Assembly. See also the works of Harriet B. Applewhite: "Political Legitimacy in Revolutionary France, 1788–1791," *Journal of Interdisciplinary History*, 9 (1978): 245–73; and "Political Alignment in the

French National Assembly, 1789 to 1791," *Proceedings of the Annual Meeting of the Western Society for French History*, 8 (1980): 265–75. For a complementary study based on a linguistic analysis of newspaper accounts, see Pierre Rétat, "Partis et factions en 1789: Emergence des désignants politiques." *Mots*, 16 (1988): 69–89.

9 To date, I have located memoirs, letters, or diaries describing the events of the Constituent Assembly, written by a total of 114 deputies. About half of these are in manuscript. Edna Hindie Lemay has consulted some of these materials in her *La vie quotidienne des députés aux Etats généraux, 1789* (Paris, 1987).

10 Among the few general studies, see Rudolf Von Albertini, "Parteiorganisation und Parteibegriff in Frankreich, 1789–1940," *Historische Zeitschrift*, 193 (1961): esp. 529–46.

11 See Alexandre Lameth, *Histoire de l'Assemblée constituante*, 2 vols (Paris, 1828–29), 1:34–6; G. Michon, *Essai sur l'histoire du part Feuillant: Adrien Duport* (Paris, 1924), p. 48; Augustin Challamel, *Les clubs contre-révolutionnaires, cercles, comités, sociétés, salons, réunions, cafés, restaurants, et librairies* (Paris, 1895), pp. 129, 133; Charles Du Bus, *Stanislas de Clermont-Tonnerre et l'échec de la Révolution monarchique 1757–92* (Paris, 1931), p. 84.

12 Daniel L. Wick, *A Conspiracy of Well-Intentioned Men: The Society of Thirty and the French Revolution* (New York, 1987). pp. 342–7, 354–5. The list given by Wick on pp. 354–5 includes one *suppléant* deputy and overlooks the Duc de Luxembourg. The "thirty" seem actually to have consisted of about fifty-five individuals.

13 See Ran Yadid-Halévi, "La sociabilité maçonique et les origines de la pratique démocratique" (thèse de 3ᵉ cycle, Paris, Ecole des Hautes Etudes en Sciences Sociales, 1981). Among the known Mesmer enthusiasts were Nicolas Bergasse, Jean-Jacques Duval d'Eprémesnil, Pierre-Victor Maclouet, François-Dominique de Reynaud de Montlosier, Adrien Duport, Jérôme Pétion de Villeneuve, Jean-André Périsse-Duluc, the Marquis de Lafayette, the Duc de Coigny, and perhaps the Comte de Virieu. See Robert Darnton, *Mesmerism and the End of the Enlightenment in France* (New York, 1970), pp. 68, 74, 78–9; Etienne Lamy, *Un défenseur des principes traditionnels sous la Révolution: N. Bergasse* (Paris, 1910), p. 46; François-Dominique de Reynaud de Montlosier, *Mémoires*, 2 vols (Paris, 1830), 1: pp. 133, 324–7; Pierre-Victor Malouet, *Mémoires*, 2 vols (Paris, 1874), 1: p. 195. The Viroflay Society was said to have had a distinctly Masonic character. See also Wick, *Conspiracy of Well-Intentioned Men*, pp. 49, 90–9; and Daniel L. Wick, "The Court Nobility and the French Revolution: The Example of the Society of Thirty," *Eighteenth-Century Studies*, 13 (1979–80): 263–84.

14 Lameth, *Histoire de l'Assemblée constituante*, 1: pp. 420–1; Michon, *Essai sur l'histoire du parti Feuillant*, pp. 48–52.

15 Michon, *Essai sur l'histoire du parti Feuillant*, p. 48.

16 See, for example. F.-A. Aulard, *La Société des Jacobins*, 6 vols (Paris, 1889–97), 1: "Introduction"; Gérard Walter, *Histoire des Jacobins* (Paris, 1946), pp. 1–55; A. Bouchard, *Le club breton: Origine, composition, rôle à l'Assemblée constituante* (Paris, 1920); and Lemay, *La vie quotidienne*, Part 2, Chap. 4.

17 Bouchard, *Le club breton*, pp. 21–3.

18 Walter, *Histoire des Jacobins* pp. 12–15; Bouchard, *Le club breton*, pp. 21–2; Lemay, *La vie quotidienne*, pp. 212–13; Jean-Pierre Boullé, "Ouverture des Etats généraux de 1789," ed. Albert Macé, *Revue de la Révolution: Documents inédits*, 10 (1887): 162–65; Léon Dubreuil, "Le clergé de Bretagne aux Etats généraux," *La Révolution française*, 70 (1917): 483–84. Joseph Delaville Le Roulx to Municipality of Lorient, 15 May 1789, BB 12, Archives Communales de Lorient (hereafter, AC, Lorient), describes the voting procedures followed. The Breton nobles and upper clergy had boycotted the elections in the spring of 1789 and had consequently sent no deputies to Versailles.

19 Delaville Le Roulx, 3 and 8 May 1789, BB 12, AC, Lorient; Boullé, *Revue de la Révolution*, 10 (1887), p. 169. Sieyes had proposed an "Assemblée nationale" the previous January. See his *Qu'est-ce que le Tiers Etat?*, ed. Edme Champion (Paris, 1889). p. 79.

20 Reported by Antoine Durand to Delcamp-Boytré in Gourdan, 6 May 1789, carton 5–56, Archives diocésaines de Cahors; François-René-Pierre Ménard de la Groye to his wife, 19 May 1789, 10 J 122, Archives Départementales de la Sarthe (hereafter, AD, Sarthe); and Jacques-Antoine Creuzé-Latouche, *Journal des Etats généraux et du début de l'Assemblée nationale, 18 mai–29 juillet 1789*, ed. Jean Marchand (Paris, 1946), p. 130.

21 Adrien Duquesnoy, *Journal d'Adrien Duquesnoy*, ed. R. de Crèvecoeur, 2 vols (Paris, 1894), 1: p. 13; Laurent de Visme, 14 May 1789, ms. "Journal des Etats généraux," Nouv. acq. fr. 12938, Bibliothèque Nationale.

22 Duquesnoy, *Journal*, 1: p. 2; Pierre-Paul Nairac, 19 May 1789, ms. "Journal," 5 F 63, Archives Départementales de l'Eure; Etienne-François Schwendt in Rodolphe Reuss, (ed.), *L'Alsace pendant la Révolution française*, 2 vols (Paris, 1880–94), 1: p. 108. See also Gaultier de Biauzat, *Correspondance*, 2: p. 118; and Jean-Baptiste Poncet-Delpech, *La première année de la Révolution vue par un témoin*, ed. Daniel Ligou (Paris, 1961) pp. 11–12.

23 Many remained wary of the nobles' power and fearful of jeopardizing even minimal gains by overly bold action. Thus the Poitevin deputy René-Antoine-Hyacinthe Thibaudeau had warned his son earlier against "un acte de hardiesse qui n'aurait eu d'autre effet que de nous attirer à dos le clergé et la noblesse." And Durand would recall to a friend how cautious and prudent they had to be in drawing up their *cahiers*: "Il fallait encore se garder de trop alarmer le despotisme"; Durand, 4 September 1789, carton 5–56, Archives diocésaines de Cahors; Antoine-Claude Thibaudeau, *Biographie, Mémoires, 1765–92* (Paris, 1875), p. 64. Research on the social origins of the Third Estate deputies will be published subsequently. See also Edna Hindie Lemay, "La composition de l'Assemblée nationale constituante: Les hommes de la continuité," *Revue d'histoire moderne et contemporaine*, 24 (1977): 340–63; and Colin Lucas, "Nobles, Bourgeois, and the Origins of the French Revolution," *Past and Present*, 60 (August 1973): 90. [Published as Chapter 2 in this volume.]

24 Michel-René Maupetit, "Lettres de Michel-René Maupetit," ed. E. Quéruau-Lamerie, in *Bulletin de la Commission historique et archéologique de la Mayenne*, 2e serie, 18 (1902): 136. Le Chapelier's motion was made on 13 May; *AP*, 8:36–7. See also the Vicomte de Mirabeau's interpretation of this motion; *AP*, 8:42.

25 Michel Peronnet, *Les évêques de l'ancienne France* (Lille, 1977), esp. pp. 1337–43.

26 The first curés came over to the Third Estate on 13 June. Many had originally hoped to join much earlier. See my article, "Les députés du premier ordre: Le Clergé aux Etats généraux et à l'Assemblée constituante, 1789–1791," in *Croyances, pouvoirs et sociétés: Des Limousins aux Français: Etudes offertes à Louis Pérouas* (Treignac, 1988), pp. 85–99.

27 Based on *Almanach de Paris, Première partie, contenant les noms et qualités des personnes de condition pour l'année 1789* (Paris, 1789). Only about 20 per cent of the Nobles were country gentlemen known to have resided in their chateaus. See also James Murphy and Patrice Higonnet, "Les députés de la noblesse aux Etats généraux de 1789," *Revue d'histoire moderne et contemporaine*, 20 (1973): 230–47.

28 For military experience, I have used Armand Brette, *Recueil de documents relatifs à la convocation des Etats généraux de 1789*, 4 vols (1894–1915), vol. 2; and Adolphe Robert, *et al.*, *Dictionnaire des parlementaires français*, 5 vols (Paris, 1891). For the approximate dates of ennoblement, I have used Henri Jougla de Morenas, *Grand armorial de France*, 6 vols (Paris, 1934–49); and François Bluche, *Les honneurs de la cours* (Paris, 1957). More precise conclusions must await the biographical dictionary of the Constituent Assembly to be edited by Edna Lemay. Such proportions would, of course, have been largely similar for the liberal nobility. Within this group, as we shall see below, age was probably the critical factor.

29 J. Michael Hayden, *France and the Estates General of 1614* (Cambridge, 1974), esp. pp. 82–5. See also Sutherland, *France, 1789–1815*, pp. 19–21.

30 The Duc de Luxembourg won on the first ballot for president, with 145 out of 251. The Duc du Croy won the vice-presidency with 160 out of 239; the Marquis de Bouthillier was elected secretary with 139 out of 184. See Ambroise-Eulalie de Maurès de Malartic, 12, 15, and 16 June 1789, "Journal de ma députation aux Etats généraux," MS. 21, Bibliothèque Municipale de la Rochelle (hereafter, BM, La Rochelle).

31 Marquis de Ferrières, *Mémoires*, 3 vols (Paris, 1825), 1: pp. 37, 60.

32 Among those won over to a position of intransigence were the Marquis de Guilhem-Clermont-Lodève and the Duc de Châtelet: Guilhem to the Municipality of Arles, 21 May 1789, AA 23, Archives Communales d'Arles. Note also the interpretation of the Marquis de Ferrières, *Mémoires, passim*. Malartic claimed that, on 25 June, six noble deputies with mandates for votes by head were refusing to join the Third Estate and were writing home for new mandates supporting their intransigence: see Malartic's entry for that date, "Journal," MS. 21, BM, La Rochelle. Of the twenty-seven Noble deputies from *bailliages* indicated by Guy Chaussinand-Nogaret to have had imperative mandates for a vote by head, only fifteen actually joined the Third Estate before 27 June; *La noblesse au XVIIIe siècle* (Paris, 1976), pp. 184–5 and Murphy and Higonnet, "Les députés de la noblesse," pp. 244–6.

33 Boullé, *Revue de la Révolution*, 12 (1888), p. 50.

34 Durand, 30 May 1789, carton 5–56. Archives diocésaines de Cahors; Jean-Baptiste Grellet de Beauregard, "Lettres de M. Grellet de Beauregard," ed. Abbé Dardy, *Mémoires de la Société des sciences naturelles et archéologiques de la Creuse*, 2e sér., 7 (1899): 10 July 1789; Claude-Pierre Maillot to an unnamed municipal official of de Toul, 3 June 1789, JJ 7. Archives Communales de Toul (hereafter, AC, Toul); and Visme, "Journal des Etats généraux," 26 May and 10 June 1789. All four men were moderates who never joined the Jacobin Club. See also Pierre-Joseph Meifrund, 10 June 1789, ms. journal; copy in Institut de la Révolution française (Paris).

35 Nairac, "Journal," 9 June 1789, 5 F 63, Archives Départementales de l'Eure; Boullé, *Revue de la Révolution*, 12 (1888), pp. 40, 49. Visme also described "une grande conférence tenue par les Bretons et leurs partisans"; "Journal des Etats généraux," 10 June 1789.

36 See Maupetit, "Lettres," 18 (1902), pp. 157–8.

37 Walter, *Histoire des Jacobins*, p. 22; Henri Grégoire, *Mémoires*, ed. H. Carnot, 2 vols (Paris, 1837–40), 1: p. 380. According to Gaultier de Biauzat, the motion had already been decided by the Breton group when it was voted to have Sieyes present it: "pour donner plus de poids à la motion"; Gaultier de Biauzat, *Correspondance*, p. 102.

38 There was a near-perfect consensus in the Tennis Court Oath of 20 June. While eighty-nine Third Estate deputies voted against Sieyes's motion on 17 June, this was primarily a disagreement over the specific name to be given to the new assembly. On the very next vote that day, the National Assembly unanimously decided that all taxes would be subject to reorganization; see, for example, Jean-Sylvain Bailly, *Mémoires*, 3 vols (Paris, 1821–2), 1: pp. 179–80; Maupetit, "Lettres," 19 (1903), p. 215; Nairac, "Journal," 17 June 1789, 5 F 63, Archives Départementales de l'Eure; and Meifrund, ms. journal, 17 June, 1789, Institut de la Révolution française. The evidence does not seem to sustain Georges Lefebvre's assertion that the eighty-nine deputies "disavowed the juridical Revolution"; *The Coming of the French Revolution* (Princeton, N.J., 1947) p. 82.

39 In general, the Constituent deputies' attitudes toward the people were very complex. But, through the end of June, the Third Estate deputies' views of the crowds in Versailles were almost universally favorable; see, for example, Jean-Baptiste Poncet-Delpech, "Documents sur les premiers mois de la Révolution;" Daniel Ligou (ed.), *Annales historiques de la Révolution française*, 38 (1966): pp. 430; Duquesnoy, *Journal*, 1: pp. 133–4; Creuzé-Latouche, *Journal*. pp. 25–6: Boullé; *Revue de la Révolution*, 11 (1888), p. 18. Afterward, many of the deputies, not only of the Clergy and the Nobles but of the Commoners as well, seem to have felt directly threatened. See, for

example, Félix Faulcon, *Correspondance*, vol. 2, *1789–91* ed. G. Debien (Poitiers, 1953), journal entry of 13 July 1789; Grellet, "Lettres," pp. 76–7.

40 *AP*, 8:263–67.

41 For examples, see Creuzé-Latouche, *Journal des Etats généraux*, pp. 270–1; Ménard de la Grove, 24 July 1789, 10 J 122, AD, Sarthe; Maximillien Robespierre, *Correspondance*, (ed.) Georges Michon, 2 vols (Paris, 1926–41), p. 50; François-Joseph Bouchette, *Lettres*, (ed.) C. Looten (Lille, 1909), p. 234.

42 Visme "Journal des Etats généraux," 22 July 1789; letter of the deputies of Marseille, 27 July 1789, BB 361, Archives Communales de Marseille; Delaville Le Roulx, 24 July 1789, BB 12, AC, Lorient. Numerous other examples could be given.

43 Du Bus, *Stanislas de Clermont-Tonnerre*, p. 123. See also Jean Egret, *La révolution des notables: Mounier et les monarchiens* (Paris, 1950), pp. 92–103; and Montlosier, *Mémoires*, 1: p. 251.

44 August-Félix-Elizabeth Barin de La Gallissonnière, 27 June 1789, ms. journal, A4 LVI, Archives de la Guerre, also Louis-Henri-Charles de Gauville, *Journal*, (ed.) Edouard de Barthélémy (Paris, 1864), p. 8. On the Nobles' initial refusal to obey the king, see Malartic, "Journal," 27 June 1789, MS. 21, BM, La Rochelle; and Jean-Baptiste de Cernon de Pinteville to his brother, undated letter of *ca.* 27 June, J 2286, Archives Départementales de la Marne.

45 La Gallissonnière, ms. journal, A4 LVI, folio 155, Archives de la Guerre; Durand, 30 June 1789, carton 5–56, Archives diocésaines de Cahors; Malartic, "Journal," 9 and 11 July 1789, MS. 21, BM, La Rochelle; Delaville Le Roulx, 11 July 1789, BB 12, AC, Lorient.

46 The term was used by Maupetit on 11 July; "Lettres," 18 (1902): p. 461.

47 Maillot, 18 July 1789, JJ 7, AC, Toul. For a nobleman's interpretation, see Malartic, "Journal," 16 July 1789, MS. 21, BM, La Rochelle.

48 Visme, "Journal des Etats généraux," 10 August 1789; see also Dominique-Georges-Frédéric du Four de Pradt, "Quelques lettres de l'Abbé de Pradt, 1789–92," (ed.) Michel Leymarie, *Revue de la Haute-Auvergne*, 56ᵉ année, 34 (1954): introduction, pp. 89–91; and Charles-Elie de Ferrières, *Correspondance inédite*, (ed.) Henri Carré (Paris, 1932), pp. 82, 87, 108.

49 La Gallissonnière, ms. journal, A4 LVI, folio 154, Archives de la Guerre.

50 Pinteville, 27 June 1789, J 2286, Archives Départementales de la Marne.

51 La Gallissonnière, ms. journal, 27 June 1789, A4 LVI, Archives de la Guerre; also Ferrières, *Correspondance*, 3 July 1789; Guilhem-Clermont-Lodève, 2 August 1789, AA 23, Archives Communales d'Arles. Also Bernard de Brye, *Un évêque d'ancien régime à l'épreuve de la Révolution: Le cardinal A. L. H. de La Fare (1752–1829)* (Paris, 1985), pp. 249–59; Charles-Maurice de Talleyrand, *Mémoires*, (ed.) Duc de Broglie, 5 vols (Paris, 1891–2), 1: pp. 123–4; Eugène Lavaquery, *Le Cardinal de Boisgelin. 1732–1804*, 2 vols (Paris, 1920), 2: pp. 13–15.

52 Duquesnoy, *Journal*, 26 June 1789; Ménard de la Groye, 7 July 1789, 10 J 122, AD, Sarthe.

53 Malartic, "Journal," 7 July 1789, MS. 21, BM, La Rochelle. Note also Visme's entry of 6 July "j'ai vu avec plaisir . . . que les idées d'un membre de la noblesse n'aient point été négligées"; "Journal des Etats généraux."

54 Faulcon, *Correspondance*, journal entry of 3 a.m., 15 July 1789, p. 69.

55 Ferrières, *Correspondance*, 10 August 1789. Compare the analysis of Talleyrand, *Mémoires*, 1: p. 124.

56 Numerous deputies commented on the unity and concord in the Assembly in the days before the event; see Maillot, 1 August 1789, JJ 7, AC, Toul; Charles-François Bouche to the Commissaires de communautés de Provence, 2 August, 1789, C 1046, Archives Départementales des Bouches-du-Rhône; Charles Francoville to the Municipality of Ardres, 3 August 1789, in François de Saint-Just, *Chronique intime des Garnier d'Ardres* (Paris, 1973), p. 118. Newspaper accounts of the period also placed enormous

emphasis on the intense "désir d'union, . . . de la 'fraternité' retrouvée dans l'élan du coeur" just prior to 4 August; Rétat, "Partis et factions en 1789," p. 76. This is in no way to underestimate the influence of the Great Fear and the general anarchy of late July 1789 in the psychology of the deputies. See also Fitzsimmons, "Privilege and the Polity in France," pp. 286–91.

57 Delaville Le Roulx, 29 July 1789, BB 12, AC, Lorient; Maillot, 1 August 1789, JJ 7, AC, Toul; Creuzé-Latouche, *Journal des Etats généraux*, pp. 165–66. See also Durand, 29 June 1789, carton 5–56, Archives diocésaines de Cahors.

58 See the discussion of "party" composition below.

59 Bouchard, *Le club breton*, pp. 90–2. On approximately September 2, Boullé, deputy from Pontivy, mentioned a special request by the Rennes representatives that the provincial delegation meet again to discuss a petition from the town of Rennes. The other Breton deputies apparently rejected the request; Boullé, *Revue de la Révolution*, 15 (1889), p. 117 (the letter is incorrectly dated 28 September by the editor). Delaville Le Roulx, 18 September 1789, BB 13, AC, Lorient, wrote that the Breton delegation had "de nouveau" opened its doors to deputies of other delegations as "avant et après le 17 juin," clearly suggesting that the doors had previously been closed. But there is no indication in Delaville's later letters that anything came of this initiative. Neither Walter, *Histoire des Jacobins*, nor Aulard, *Le Société des Jacobins*, mention the Breton Club between 4 August and late November or early December.

60 Jacques-Athanase de Lombard-Taradeau, "Lettres (1789–91)," (ed.) L. Honoré, *Le Var historique et géographique*, 2 (1925–27): pp. 245, 247, 261, 274–5, 324.

61 See the *règlement* of 29 July 1789; AP, 8:300–3.

62 *AP*, 33:88–91, lists the winners, but it is not entirely complete. To complete the list and to locate information about votes cast and opposition candidates, one must consult a wide range of sources, notably the minutes of the meetings in the *AP*, the *Moniteur*, and the official *Procès-verbaux*, as well as various newspaper accounts and deputy memoirs and letters. There were apparently sixty-three presidential elections, if one counts those replacing presidents who refused their elections or who resigned immediately. The generally perceptive deputy Duquesnoy was convinced that the votes for president mirrored his colleagues' political affiliations at a given point in time; Duquesnoy, *Journal*, 2: p. 127.

63 Note that several of the fourteen were chosen more than once. Lafayette is included for his election as vice-president on 13 July – the only time such an office was filled.

64 On Monarchien and Jacobin membership, see below.

65 This deference shown toward the privileged classes was equally in evidence in the choice of presidents for the thirty *bureaux* elected at intervals during the summer: at least twenty-seven of the thirty in early July and fifteen of sixteen for which data exist in mid-September were either Nobles or bishops; *AP*, 8: 185; and C 83, dossier 818 (14), Archives Nationales (hereafter, AN). Note that the family of Le Chapelier was newly ennobled. Sieyes was, of course, a clergyman.

66 On the election of 1–3 August, see Boullé, *Revue de la Révolution*, 15 (1889), p. 101; Gaultier de Biauzat, *Correspondance*, 2: p. 221; Ernest Lebègue, *La vie et l'oeuvre d'un constituant: Thouret* (Paris, 1910), pp. 142–3; Paul Bastid, *Sieyes et sa pensée* (Paris, 1939), p. 78.

67 Pétion received 183 votes on 12 September and 143 on 28 September – although some of the votes of the Left may have gone to Jacques-Guillaume Target, who received thirty-seven and fifty-two votes, respectively. On 23 November, the Duc d'Aiguillon received 166; AN, C 83, dossier 818 (1–3); Comte de Virieu to the Marquis de Viennois, 29 September 1789, Archives of the Château de Viennois, from a copy kindly loaned to me by Jean-Louis Flandrin: and Daniel Ligou, *La première année de la Révolution vue par un témoin* (Paris, 1961), p. 169.

68 On the general problem of the Right in the early revolution, see Paul Beik, *The French Revolution Seen from the Right* in *Transactions of the American Philosophical Society*, 46

(1956), part 1; Philip Kolody, "The Right in the French National Assembly, 1789–91" (Ph.D. dissertation, Princeton University, 1967); Jean-Paul Bertaud, *Les Amis du roi: Journaux et journalistes royalistes en France de 1789 à 1792* (Paris, 1984); William James Murray, *The Right-Wing Press in the French Revolution, 1789–1792* (London, 1986).

69 La Gallissonnière, undated entry, ms. journal, A4 LVI, folio 155, Archives de la Guerre. Several deputies noted the presence of Eprémesnil – one of the key leaders of the reactionary group – among the nobles making the announcement that day; see Delaville Le Roulx, 17 July 1789, BB 12, AC, Lorient.

70 Jacques Jallet, *Journal inédit*, (ed.) J.-J. Brethé (Fontenay-le-Comte, 1871), 28 July 1789, was impressed by the unusually large number of "aristocrats" who appeared on 28 July for the committee elections. See also Maillot, 1 August 1789, JJ 7, AC, Toul.

71 Maillot, 1 August 1789, JJ 7, AC, Toul; Delaville Le Roulx, 4 August 1789, BB 12, AC, Lorient; Lombard-Taradeau, "Lettres (1789–91)," 5 August 1789, Boullé, *Revue de la Révolution*, 14 August 1789.

72 Ferrières, *Correspondance*, 6 August 1789; Claude-Jean-Baptiste Garron de la Bévière to his wife, 5 August 1789, 1 Mi 1, Archives Départementales de l'Ain.

73 On the violence and intensity of the debates in mid-August, see Boullé, *Revue de la Révolution*, 14 (1889), p. 104; and Maupetit, "Lettres," 19 (1903): p. 226. The original motion of 4 August had called for suppression of the tithes with some form of reimbursement, but this was changed in the days that followed. The earliest motions for the expropriation of church lands had been made on 8 August by the Marquis de Lacoste and Alexandre Lameth.

74 Guillaume Gontier de Biran to the Municipality of Bergerac, retrospective letter of 22 May 1790, carton 1, Archives Communales de Bergerac, Fonds Faugère; Emmanuel Barbotin; *Lettres de l'abbé Barbotin*, (ed.) A. Aulard (Paris, 1910), 23 and 29 August 1789; Gauville, *Journal*, 16–20. A similar picture is confirmed by the patriots Lombard-Taradeau; "Lettres (1789–91)," p. 263; Gaultier de Biauzat, *Correspondance*, 2: pp. 269–70; and François-Antoine Boissy d'Anglas, "Lettres inédites sur la Révolution française," (ed.) René Puaux, *Bulletin de la Société de l'histoire du Protestantisme français*, 75 (1926): 433. It was also in August that the newspapers first began mentioning "cabals" and "coalitions" in the Assembly; Rétat, "Partis et factions en 1789," p. 77.

75 Egret, *La révolution des notables*; Robert Griffiths, *Le centre perdu: Malouet et les "monarchiens" dans la Révolution française* (Grenoble, 1988). Griffiths placed the Monarchiens in the "center." However, the group is known to have allied itself with the extreme right and, on most issues, to have voted to the "right" of the large group of unaligned deputies. I would prefer to use the term "center" for the latter group.

76 Jean-André Périsse-Duluc to J. B. Willermoz, 17 September 1789, MS. 5430, Bibliothèque Municipale de Lyon (hereafter, BM, Lyon), claimed the Normans led by Thouret were initially part of the coalition. There were at least seven deputies from Auvergne, led by Malouet; Egret, *La révolution des notables*, pp. 126–8; Griffiths, *Le centre perdu*, pp. 109–10.

77 Montlosier, *Mémoires*, 1: p. 277; Malouet, *Mémoires*, 1: 301–2. Gaultier de Biauzat also observed this; *Correspondance*, 2: pp. 269–70.

78 Périsse-Duluc, 17 September 1789, MS. 5430, BM, Lyon. Virieu himself described his role in similar terms: "je me suis promis de faire toutes les avant gardes dangereuses et difficiles dont d'autres ne se seront pas chargés"; Virieu to the Marquis de Viennois, 25 August 1789, Archives of the Château de Viennois.

79 Montlosier, *Mémoires*, 1: p. 277; Périsse-Duluc, 17 September 1789, MS. 5430, BM, Lyon; Albert Mathiez, "Etudes critiques sur les journées des 5 et 6 octobre 1789," *Revue historique*, 67 (1898): 266, 273. On the general question of an alliance between the extreme right and the Monarchiens, see especially Kolody, "The Right in the French National Assembly," pp. 122–34.

80 Périsse-Duluc, 17 September 1789, MS. 5430, BM, Lyon.

81 Thus, in the secretarial election of 29 August 1789, only the three Monarchien candidates, Claude Redon, Pierre-Suzanne Deschamps, and Jean-Louis Henry de Longuève, obtained large blocs of votes; the remainder of the votes apparently represented individual, uninstructed choices; AN, C 83, dossier 818 (6–7).

82 Virieu, 1 September 1789, Archives of the Château de Viennois. See also the analysis of Théodore Vernier to the Municipality of Lons-le-Saunier, 30 August 1789, "Lettres de Vernier," Archives Communales de Bletterans (non-classé).

83 The rotation system arranged by verbal agreement was described by Bouche, 31 August 1789, C 1046, Archives Départementales des Bouches-du-Rhône. He also noted his anticipation that the mid-September election would go to a commoner. See also La Gallissonnière, undated entry, ms. journal, A4 LVI, folio 153, Archives de la Guerre. It is clear that most of the deputies were still voting by the rotation system in the previous election: 802 out of 834 votes were cast for clergymen; AN, C 83 (1–3).

84 Delaville Le Roulx, 22 September 1789, BB 13, AC, Lorient; and Jean-François-Marie Goupilleau to his cousin, senechal in Rocheferviève, undated letter of late September, Collection Dugast-Matifeux, no. 98, Bibliothèque Municipale de Nantes.

85 Lombard-Taradeau, "Lettres (1789–91)," p. 271; Louis-Prosper Lofficiel, "Lettres de Lofficiel," (ed.) M. Leroux-Cesbron, La nouvelle revue rétrospective, 7 (1897): 111; Périsse-Duluc, 2 September 1789, MS 5430, BM, Lyon. Note also Durand: "il y a dans l'Assemblée une telle division … qu'il est encore bien problématique lequel aura le dessus"; 5 September 1789, carton 5–56, Archives diocésaines de Cahors. Maillot spoke of the patriots as "le parti de la minorité"; 30 August 1789, JJ 7, AC, Toul. See also the letter of Robespierre, Correspondance, p. 51; and of Goupilleau, undated, ca. late September, Collection Dugast-Matifuex, no. 98, BM, Nantes.

86 On the Volney motion, see Lofficiel, "Letters," 14 and 18 September 1789, pp. 111–13; and Visme, "Journal des Etats généraux," 18 September 1789. On the Breton discussion, Delaville Le Roulx, 22 September 1789, BB 13, AC, Lorient; and Barbotin, Lettres, p. 61.

87 Apparently first reported by Hippolyte Taine and followed by numerous other historians. See Eric Thompson, Popular Sovereignty and the French Constituent Assembly, 1789–91 (Manchester, 1952), p. 24.

88 Malouet wrote that the Monarchien leadership hoped for 300 resignations; perhaps this is the origin of the myth. But he admitted that only twenty-six deputies actually requested passports; Mémoires, 2: pp. 4–5. This is approximately confirmed by the records of the National Assembly itself; AN, C 32, dossier 266. Mirabeau spoke of 300 requests on 9 October, but this was probably an exaggeration; AP, 9:389.

89 Mounier and Lally-Tollendal resigned almost immediately; Bishop La Luzerne resigned within a month; Bergasse abandoned the Assembly without ever formally resigning.

90 In early January 1790, the group met with Lafayette, La Rochefoucauld, and a faction of the moderate patriots – and perhaps secretly with Mirabeau – and almost succeeded in engineering a new "coalition" on the center right. See Malouet, Mémoires, 2: pp. 45–8; Montlosier, Mémoires, 2: p. 35; Mercure de France, January 1790, p. 164.

91 Virieu, 12 and 16 October 1789, Archives of the Château de Viennois; Jean-de-Dieu Boisgelin de Cucé to Comtesse de Gramont, 6 October 1789, AN, M 788; Gontier de Biran, 12 October 1789, carton 1, Archives Communales de Bergerac, Fond Faugère.

92 None of the four would be members of the Jacobin Club during the period of the Constituent Assembly or sign the petition of the "Capuchin" group; see below.

93 Note also that, in the election of 13 November, Boisgelin came within seven votes of a victory on the second round; Boisgelin de Cucé, undated, c. 13 November 1789, pièce 136, AN, M 788.

94 Boisgelin de Cucé, undated, c. mid-November 1789, pièce 141, AN, M 788.

95 Boisgelin de Cucé, 3 November 1789; also 7 and 23 November, AN, M 788. Similar views were also expressed by the moderates; Maupetit, "Lettres," 19 (1903): p. 371; Visme, "Journal des Etats généraux," 2 November 1789; André-Marie Merle to the Municipality of Mâcon, 4 November 1789, D2 no. 13 (carton 21 bis), Archives Communales de Mâcon; Jean-François Begouen-Demeaux to municipal officers of Le Harvre, 31 October 1789, D (3) 38–39, Archives Communales du Harvre; and by the future Jacobin, Vernier, Archives Communales de Bletterans, 3 November 1789. Not all deputies agreed, however; see, for example, Robespierre. Correspondance, p. 57; and Goupilleau, 2 November 1789, Collection Dugast-Matifeux, no. 98, BM, Nantes.

96 Visme, "Journal des Etats généraux," 21 November 1789. Seven of the twelve members elected were future "Capuchins" (see below); AN, C 32, dossier 274.

97 I have used vol. 33 of the AP, which is the index to vols 8–32, dealing with the Constituent Assembly. Represented are the leading speakers of the Monarchiens and the extreme right as determined by the length of the entries for each deputy in the index: for the Monarchiens: Jean-Joseph Mounier, Comte de Lally-Tollendal, Nicolas Bergasse, Bishop La Luzerne, Comte de Virieu, Clermont-Tonnerre, Malouet, Pierre-Joseph de Lachèse, Amable-Gilbert Dufraisse-Duchey, and Noël-Joseph Madier de Montjau; for the extreme right: Abbé Maury, Cazalès, Eprémesnil, Marquis de Foucauld Lardimalie, Marquis de Bonnay, Marquis de Folleville, Reynaud de Montlosier, and Vicomte de Mirabeau. Displayed on the graph [Figure 7.1] is the average weekly frequency of participation plotted as an index around the overall mean for the entire period of the Constituent Assembly, where the mean is set at 1.0. Although the index does not give precise dates, these can be extrapolated from the volume numbers – which are given. The Archives parlementaires is undoubtedly the best single source for debates in the National Assembly, but unfortunately it does not include all speeches given in the Constituent Assembly, and approximately 5 to 10 per cent of those that it does mention seem to be missing in the index – probably through the carelessness of the editors.

98 Gauville, Journal, p. 59.

99 Thibaudeau to Faulcon, undated but probably early January 1791; printed in Faulcon, Correspondance, p. 141.

100 Lavaquery, Le Cardinal de Boisgelin, 2: pp. 74–6. Du Bus, Stanislas de Clermont-Tonnerre, p. 224, equated the Grands Augustins meetings with the Club des Impartiaux. This is probably not correct, although there was a substantial overlap between the two groups.

101 Thomas Lindet, Correspondance de Thomas Lindet pendant la Constituante et la Législative (1789–92), (ed.) A. Montier, (Paris, 1889), pp. 115–16; Lameth, Histoire de l'Assemblée constituante, 2: pp. 148–9; Gaultier de Biauzat, Correspondance, 2: pp. 307–12. Also, Louis-Jean-Baptiste Leclerc de Lassigny de Juigné to his wife, 14 April 1790, Archives of the Château de Saint-Martin (Taradeau, Var).

102 Lavaquery, Le Cardinal de Boisgelin, 2: pp. 74–6. The home of Eprémesnil seems to have been one of the central meeting places; Montlosier, Mémoires, 2: pp. 328, 334.

103 Visme, 7 December 1789, "Journal des Etats généraux." The vote was 453 for the Right and 443 for the Left. See AP, 10: 414–15.

104 Périsse-Duluc, 27 December 1789, MS. 5340, BM, Lyon.

105 Guillaume-Benoît Couderc, "Lettres de Guillaume-Benoît Couderc (1781–92)," ed. M.O. Monod, Revue d'histoire de Lyon, p. 420; Lindet, Correspondance, p. 38; Delaville Le Roulx, 18 January 1790, BB 13, AC, Lorient; Duquesnoy, Journal, 2: pp. 196–7, 269. See also Faulcon, Correspondance, 2: pp. 140–1; Ménard de la Grove, 1 January 1790, 10 J 122, AD, Sarthe; and Goupilleau, 11 January 1790, Collection Dugast-Matifeux, no. 98, BM, Nantes.

106 The presidents on the Right: Abbé de Montesquiou, the Marquis de Bonnay (twice), and the Comte de Virieu; on the Left: Rabaut-Saint-Etienne, Baron de Menou,

Bon-Albert Briois de Beaumez, Abbé Sieyes, and Louis-Michel Le Pelletier de Saint-Fargeau.

107 This was particularly the case in the series of major decrees concerning the reorganization of the church, culminating in the Civil Constitution of the Clergy. But the Left also won major victories in votes on the judicial system and the right to declare war.

108 Duquesnoy, *Journal*, 2: p. 269. See also Jean-François Campmas to his brother, vicaire in Carmaux, 24 December 1789, MS. 177, Bibliothèque Municipale d'Albi.

109 Armand Brette, *Histoire des édifices où ont siégé les assemblées parlementaires de la Révolution* (Paris, 1902).

110 Bouchard, *Le club breton*, p. 94; and Lemay, *La vie quotidienne*, p. 216. Delaville Le Roulx, 30 November 1789, BB 12, AC, Lorient, and others, mentions Breton Committee meetings in Paris discussing general subjects.

111 Louis-Marie de La Revellière-Lépeaux, *Mémoires*, 3 vols (Paris, 1895), 1: p. 85.

112 Walter, *Histoire des Jacobins*, p. 55. Grégoire describes the importance of mobilizing petitions from Jacobins throughout France in order to pressure the decisions of the National Assembly; *Mémoires*, 1: p. 387. See also Michael L. Kennedy, *The Jacobin Clubs in the French Revolution: The First Years* (Princeton, N.J., 1982). esp. Chap. 1.

113 *AP*, 32:564. At the last and final election of the Comité, in April 1790, nine of the twelve men elected – all Jacobins or known Patriots – received almost **exactly** the same number of votes – between 196 and 206, a sure sign of the collusion **involved;** AN, C 38, dossier 334.

114 In 1789, future Jacobins obtained 160 (25 per cent) and future Capuchins obtained 118 (19 per cent) of a total of 636 committee assignments; in the first six months of 1790, Jacobins obtained eighty-six (48 per cent) and Capuchins twenty-one (12 per cent) of a total of 180 new assignments. Faulcon thought that it was impossible to be named to a committee in 1790 unless one belonged to a club; *Correspondance*, 29 May 1789, p. 236.

115 Quoted in Walter, *Histoire des Jacobins*, pp. 93–4.

116 Lindet, *Correspondance*, p. 38.

117 The most complete list of the Jacobins – as Aulard himself indicates – is to be culled from the index at the end of his *La Société des Jacobins*, vol. 6. This must be used to complement the list of December 1790, published in the introduction of his vol. 1.

118 See above, note 112.

119 *Déclaration d'une partie de l'Assemblée nationale sur le décret rendu le 13 avril concernant la religion* (Paris, 1790).

120 The petition was signed by 293, but one deputy later retracted his signature. A part of the group around Malouet and Clermont-Tonnerre seems also to have remained aloof from the Capuchins for tactical reasons; Malouet, *Mémoires*, 2: pp. 41–3. Of the core group of Monarchiens listed by Egret who were still active as deputies in April 1790, eleven of seventeen signed the petition.

121 More detailed analysis must await the completion of Edna Lemay's biographical dictionary.

122 One hundred sixty-eight (82 per cent) of 205 Jacobins. Two hundred sixty-nine (92 per cent) of 292 Capuchins. The importance of the deputies' estate in Left/Right alignments has been noted by Applewhite, "Political Alignment," pp. 267–8.

123 Seven nobles and one *chanoine* (canon).

124 One hundred sixty-two (55 per cent) of the signers were clergymen. This included 102 (49 per cent) of all 207 curés sitting at this time, and thirty-four (87 per cent) of the thirty-nine bishops.

125 One hundred sixty-seven (57 per cent) of the 292 are known to have been nobles. One hundred and seven (64 per cent) of the 167 could trace their lineage before 1600. Of course, the non-aligned nobles in the Assembly would have had much the same lineage breakdowns. I am not arguing that aristocratic origins determined political options but that they may have been a factor in such options, and that the social

origins of the Capuchins were strongly weighted by a large bloc of aristocratic deputies, a bloc that was clearly in evidence to contemporaries.

126 Marquis de Folleville, Vicomte de Mirabeau, Comte de Virieu, Marquis de Foucauld-Lardimalie, Chevalier de Murinais, Marquis d'Ambly, and Bishop de Bonal. Among the Capuchin group, by my count, Maury spoke the most, Folleville was second, and Cazalès was third, while Eprémesnil was eighth.

127 For instance, the proportion of all Third Estate deputies with agriculturally related professions was 12 per cent; it was the same for Jacobin deputies from the Third. For all deputies from commercial professions: 12 per cent; for Jacobin deputies: 14 per cent.

128 Thirty-two per cent of all deputies called themselves "avocats," while 42 per cent of Third Estate deputies in the Jacobins described themselves in this way. Thirty-five per cent of all deputies were officeholders – including 17 per cent who were judges; while 26 per cent of the Jacobins were officeholders – including 12 per cent who were judges.

129 See Lenard R. Berlanstein, *The Barristers of Toulouse in the Eighteenth Century, 1740–1793* (Baltimore, 1975), pp. 11, 16.

130 Sixteen (38 per cent) of 42.

131 The others, in order, were Charles-François Bouche, Le Chapelier, Jean-Denis Lanjuinais, Gaultier de Biauzat, Barnave, Jacques Defermon, Guillaume-François-Charles Goupil de Prefelne, Jean-François Reubell, Duport, Philippe-Antoine Merlin, Pierre-Louis Prieur, and Robespierre.

132 By my count, 48 per cent of the Capuchins and 30 per cent of the Jacobins represented districts south of this line. Approximately 30 per cent of all deputies seem to have come from southern France; Edna Lemay, "La composition de l'Assemblée constituante: Les hommes de la continuité?" *Revue d'histoire moderne et contemporaine*, 24 (1977): 349.

133 Ages are taken primarily from Robert, *Dictionnaire*.

134 Among the Clergy the Jacobins averaged 45.4 years, the Capuchins averaged 50.7; among the Nobles, the Jacobins were 37.0, the Capuchins 46.5; among the Third Estate, the Jacobins were 42.3, the Capuchins 43.7. Murphy and Higonnet, "Les députés de la noblesse," p. 240, noted the relative youth of the "liberal" nobles.

135 After Louis XVI's attempted flight from the kingdom in June 1791 and the majority's decision to suspend the king's powers, however, much of the Right boycotted the debates.

136 There are many comments on the demoralization of the bishops; Bouchette on the archbishop of Aix, *Lettres*, p. 484; and Boisgelin, speaking for himself in his letter of late June, Boisgelin de Cucé, *pièce* 114, AN, M 788; Ménard de la Graye on the bishop of Le Mans, 28 May 1790, 10 J 122, AD, Sarthe; also Brye, *Un évêque d'ancien regime*, pp. 269–70, on the bishop of Nancy. Among the Capuchins in general, eight are known to have left the Assembly in the first half of 1790, thirteen in the second half of 1790, and twenty-eight in the first half of 1791.

137 Lindet, *Correspondance*, 22 November 1790, p. 247.

138 It is not possible here to follow the political developments of the Assembly through its completion in September 1791. Significantly, it was only *after* the Right had effectively collapsed as a power within the Assembly that major splits began to appear within the Left coalition – splits that were clearly in evidence before the king's attempted flight. See, especially, Michon, *Essai sur l'histoire du parti Feuillant*, pp. 182–5.

139 Malouet, *Mémoires*, 2: p. 36; Lameth, *Histoire de l'Assemblée constituante*, 1: p. 421. Lindet said much the same thing in a letter of 8 May 1790; *Correspondance*, p. 155.

140 Compare the thesis of Sutherland in his *France, 1789–1815*. As I have argued here, I would push back the inception of the revolutionary–counter-revolutionary dialectic to the very beginning of the Estates-General and the National Assembly.

141 See the classic study of Alfred Cobban in *Aspects of the French Revolution* (New York, 1968), pp. 100–2, 109–11. See also George V. Taylor, "Noncapitalist Wealth and the Origins of the French Revolution," *AHR*, 72 (January 1967): 469–96; and Lemay, "La composition de l'Assemblée constituante."

142 We have seen above that Capuchins and Jacobins also represented, in part, different generations. Although it would be impossible to demonstrate here, they probably also differed significantly in education and overall wealth.

8

VIOLENCE, EMANCIPATION, AND DEMOCRACY

The countryside and the French Revolution

John Markoff

With the ascendancy of intellectual history, recent Revisionists have minimized the role peasants played in the Revolution. For the most part, they have seen the peasants as bystanders during much of the Revolutionary struggle. After the summer of 1789, having won the abolition of feudalism and the right to own private property, they pretty much sat out the rest of the ordeal. When they became involved, it was usually trying to resist revolutionary programs (such as military conscription) and keeping the new government at bay. The peasants, recent historians tell us, were at best lukewarm supporters of a Revolution that never was especially popular in the countryside.

John Markoff argues against such an interpretation. "There was a peasant revolution that was emancipatory and egalitarian in its consequences," he writes. Such liberation, he emphasizes, "was not achievable in the 1790s without this violence." Away with the Neo-Conservative dismissal of revolution as an inherently oppressive process. Markoff's perspective returns us to a Liberal perspective that sees revolutions as doing much good, especially for the poor and rural folk. Peasant violence was not irrational; it was a way to overcome the oppression of aristocratic landlords whose privileges yielded despotic power over their peasants. However disparate their subjects, Markoff's article nicely dovetails with Tackett's in seeing a class of privileged noblemen standing in the way of a new political culture based upon the values expressed in the Declaration of the Rights of Man.

* * *

As heads of state gathered in Paris in the summer of 1989 for the celebration of the French Revolution's bicentennial, Prime Minister Margaret Thatcher faced a question in Parliament about her own imminent crossing of the English Channel. Comparing the changes brought about in her administration to those of France in the 1790s, she commented that "our revolution in the past ten years ... has been managed more quietly and very well." A Tory MP then advised her to consider the historical dimensions of British superiority: while visiting Paris, she ought to bear in mind the "virtually bloodless" character of the Glorious

Revolution, whose tricentennial had been celebrated the previous year. An unnecessary admonition: Thatcher had already explained to interviewers for *Le monde* that the British had considerably preceded the French in institutionalizing a respect for human rights and had done so "calmly, without a bloodbath." Even the way the British commemorated their historical turning points was calmer.[1]

Although her remarks earned her a public history lesson from Christopher Hill,[2] it could hardly be said that the prime minister was out of touch with the current wisdom of students of French history. Two hundred years after the Revolution, it was not only a political personality of the Right who doubted that plebeian violence had contributed to human advance. Many a historian was thinking the same thing. The Revolution's effects are now widely seen as perverse (as in the claim that the Revolution so damaged the French economy that it assured British economic dominance)[3] or non-existent (as in the claim that the advances often attributed to the Revolution were already being carried out by the reforming élites of the Old Regime).[4] Recent writing is particularly critical of the claim that revolutionary violence made much of a contribution to the history of democracy. In line with the debunking just described, either the contribution to democracy is taken to be negative or, alternately, that contribution is attributed primarily to mutations in élite political culture rather than to mass action.[5]

Not that popular insurrection has been shunted aside as an arena for historical research; rather, the connection between plebeian actions and revolutionary outcomes has come to be seen as extremely complex in the recent literature. Where George Rudé's work had suggested that plebeian violence was a conceivably rational means to a morally defensible end, much recent writing has focused on violence as having its own logic: we are alerted by Brian Singer to the ritual characteristics of violent confrontations or led by Roger Chartier to see popular violence as a symptom of the incompleteness of what Norbert Elias called "the civilizing process."[6] And, where popular action is seen as purposive, an important theme in the recent literature has been "resistances to the Revolution," to use a now common phrase that denotes the many ways in which people in villages and urban neighborhoods evaded revolutionary tax collectors and recruiting sergeants, rejected the symbols and personnel of the Revolution's Constitutional Church, deserted from the Revolution's armed forces, as well as engaged in armed and open counter-revolution.[7] So deeply has the recent literature been permeated by the notion of popular resistance, some writers are suggesting that historians should see overt counter-revolution as merely the most dramatic form taken by a profoundly widespread resistance to a visionary and brutal revolutionary élite.[8] It was an important advance to be able to see the disorderly actions of insurrectionary people as having a culture, as being part of, in Charles Tilly's fine phrase, a "repertoire of contention," just as it was an advance to rediscover the ways in which plebeians were injured by a revolution to which they sometimes responded with violence.[9]

In summary, much recent literature has focused on popular hostility to the Revolution, on the expressive and traditional aspects of popular violence, and on the dynamic role played by the Revolution's élites in creating a modern society. Nonspecialists of the 1990s, coming to much of this recent literature, will probably readily find the French Revolution to be another buttress for the current multi-continental disillusion with revolutionary projects of any sort. Yet the prevailing picture, itself in part a corrective to an earlier oversimplification, will be a seriously misleading one. There *was* a peasant revolution that was emancipatory and egalitarian in its consequences, that did more than accept the reforms of élite power-holders, that pushed those power-holders far beyond their initial positions, that was not merely a ritualized expression of violence but exhibited choices of targets and tactics guided by reason. I refer to the struggle waged in the countryside against the lords. It is hard to see how there could have been much in the way of democratic advance in France without the full emancipation of the French countryside from the "odious remains of the tyranny of the powerful," as the Third Estate of Etampes put it in the spring of 1789.[10]

There is little dispute that this emancipation was achieved with a great deal of insurrectionary violence;[11] but if a revolutionary élite, steeped in the enlightened ideas of the late Old Regime, was fully committed to the reform of rural social relations and capable of organizing it through legislative action, such violence would have to be regarded as a tragically unnecessary sideshow. In spite of an opposition to feudalism from that revolutionary élite, however, an emancipation in the countryside was not achievable in the 1790s without this violence. This is to restate a proposition central to Georges Lefebvre's analysis of the part played by the people of the countryside in the Revolution, elaborated in more detail by Anatoly Ado.[12] To demonstrate it, I shall be examining two bodies of evidence and glancing at a third: the grievances expressed at the onset of revolution, the targets and timing of insurrectionary events in the countryside, and then the legislative debates.

I have three main points. First, élite proposals for reorganizing the seigneurial rights, widely expressed in the spring of 1789, were real and significant but were also significantly limited. Second, the subsequent legislative action that alleviated peasant burdens was in large degree a response to rural violence. Third, a look at projects for reform of roughly comparable social relationships elsewhere on the European continent, at least into the middle of the nineteenth century, also suggests that popular violence or the fear of it was a major element of rural emancipation elsewhere.[13]

In the 1780s, a French lord could collect a variety of monetary and material payments from his peasants, could insist that nearby villagers grind their grain in the seigneurial mill, bake their bread in the seigneurial oven, press their grapes in the seigneurial wine press, could set the date of the grape harvest, could have local cases tried in his own court, could claim favored benches in church for his family and proudly point to the family tombs below the church floor, could take pleasures forbidden the peasants – hunting, raising rabbits or pigeons – in the pursuit of which pleasures the peasants' fields were sometimes devastated.[14]

How did the French respond to these privileges at the onset of revolution? To begin with the positions being staked out by the élites in the spring of 1789: the grievance lists that assemblies around France provided their deputies in the complex, multi-stage elections to the Estates-General yield national data of unparalleled richness. Let us focus particularly on what are known as the general *cahiers* of the Third Estate, those documents adopted by assemblies in county-sized electoral districts whose deputies were to convene in Versailles, where they were to meet with the separately chosen deputies of the clergy and nobility. Roughly speaking, the assemblies adopting these Third Estate *cahiers* were dominated by the urban notables. The electoral rules, as modified in practice by local conflict and central confusion, meant that these Third Estate assemblies chose rather more than half of what became the National Assembly.

Table 1 displays the broad lines of proposals on those seigneurial rights that were commonly discussed.[15] While there is almost no support in the *cahiers* for retaining the seigneurial rights as they were at the time, proposals for uncompensated abolition are distinctly in the minority, and a small minority at that, for one important class of rights, the periodic dues. Contrasting the views expressed on serfdom, tolls, or compulsory labor, we can see that the urban notables were capable of taking a much tougher position on other aspects of the seigneurial regime. Not only is some sort of indemnification the favored position on periodic dues but uncompensated abolition is not even the second choice: a significant minority of Third Estate assemblies favors reform proposals. This is particularly interesting, since seigneurial rights generally tended not to attract reform proposals at all.[16]

We may compare these figures with those the deputies of the nobility carried to Versailles on the one hand and those adopted by preliminary assemblies in the countryside on the other. While the most striking noble trait is an avoidance of discussing seigneurial rights, those *cahiers* with such discussions include a significant number that both demand the continuation of some seigneurial rights and lack any reform proposal. Twenty-one per cent of noble *cahiers* made no mention of the seigneurial regime. Of those that do so, some 13 per cent of the demands favor maintaining at least one seigneurial right substantially unaltered, as compared to 1 per cent for the Third Estate. In the same vein, noble demands to abolish a seigneurial right without indemnification amount to some 10 per cent of their grievances, which may be contrasted with 27 per cent for the Third Estate.[17] The noble presence in the soon-to-be-created National Assembly included a significant body of representatives who carried *cahiers* that, by silence or open advocacy, were notably less disposed to the abolition of seigneurial rights than those carried by the delegates of the Third Estate. The distinctiveness of the *cahiers* of the urban notables on seigneurial rights is their emphasis on the indemnification option where periodic payments were concerned.

Among the élite, then, some notion of a gradual buy-out rather than simple abolition of seigneurial rights was in the air. It was the course that had been advocated in Pierre-François Boncerf's notorious pamphlet on "feudal rights," condemned by the Paris Parlement in 1776.[18] And, perhaps even more important,

Table 8.1 Percentages of Third Estate *cahiers* with various positions on seigneurial rights

Right[a]	Maintain	Reform	Abolish without compensation	Abolish with indemnification	(Number of cahiers discussing right)
Periodic dues					
Cens (a cash payment)	7	32	4	57	(28)
Champart (a portion of the crop)	2	26	13	60	(61)
Cens et rentes (a cash payment)	3	35	0	59	(37)
Periodic dues in general	0	23	7	55	(30)
Miscellaneous periodic dues	0	36	7	9	(22)
Seigneurial monopolies					
Monopoly on ovens	2	8	56	29	(50)
Monopoly on milling	0	13	44	25	(70)
Monopoly on wine press	0	5	59	31	(44)
Monopolies in general	0	15	40	43	(103)
Assessments on economic activity					
Seigneurial tolls	0	9	53	27	(117)
Dues on fairs and markets	0	16	36	33	(45)
Property transfer rights					
Dues on property transfers	0	39	37	12	(49)
Retrait (substitution of lord for purchaser of property)	4	25	44	0	(48)

Table 8.1 cont.

Right[a]	Maintain	Reform	Abolish without compensation	Abolish without compensation	Abolish with indemnification	(Number of cahiers discussing right)
Justice						
Seigneurial courts in general	3	19	53		10	(90)
Seigneurial courts, miscellaneous	2	18	23		0	(56)
Recreational privileges						
Hunting rights	2	39	14		2	(107)
Right to raise pigeons	0	18	38		0	(96)
Right to raise rabbits	0	13	51		0	(39)
Fishing rights	0	21	21		0	(24)
Symbolic deference						
Right to bear arms	0	5	24		0	(41)
Serfdom						
Mainmorte (extreme restriction on property transfers)	0	17	56		30	(36)
Serfdom in general	0	4	69		15	(26)
Other						
Compulsory labor services	0	14	51		32	(109)
Miscellaneous rights	3	9	44		27	(79)
Regime in general	2	18	18		22	(91)

[a] Rights discussed in at least twenty documents

it was the course being followed in neighboring Savoy.[19] The *cahiers* show that the assemblies electing the Third Estate delegates were not prepared to stray far from Savoy's model. Those noble assemblies that cared or dared to express themselves at all sometimes did not want to go even that far. Delegates elected to the National Assembly by the assemblies that adopted these documents could not be expected easily to support the more radical option of abolition.

The indemnification option had many appealing aspects, and it may well have seemed more, rather than less, attractive, when those elected in the spring found themselves responsible for enacting legislation to deal with the financial crisis. To members of the Third Estate who were themselves seigneurs, a matter made much of by Alfred Cobban, indemnification was a way to eliminate seigneurialism and thereby march into the modern world at minimal personal cost (or even to gain if the indemnification terms were set high enough). Cobban sees the National Assembly as trying to limit change under an anti-feudal smoke screen.[20] But Cobban does not take note of a less personally interested motive: those concerned about the finances of the state were also likely to worry about the consequences of simply abolishing the king's own seigneurial dues at a time of crisis. This would be even more important for those who saw some sort of royal land sale as a step toward raising funds: abolition would plainly lower the value of royal properties whose purchasers would be counting on acquiring the associated seigneurial rights. It would also eliminate a minor source of state revenue.[21] For those advocating a state takeover of church landholdings to fill the empty fisc, the seigneurial rights of ecclesiastical institutions would also have to be taken into account.[22] For those interested in a compromise that might pacify the peasants without sparking the lords to rebel, the indemnification option could appear the moderate, reasonable, centrist position.[23] And, for those who simply wished to stall, the social impact of indemnification would depend on the rates – which could be set later.[24]

Far closer to the people of the countryside, the preliminary *cahiers* of the rural parishes are less enthusiastic than the Third Estate documents for indemnification, even for periodic dues, and correspondingly more prone to advocate an uncompensated abolition.[25] In contrast, for example, to the 60 per cent of Third Estate *cahiers* proposing to indemnify the *champart* (an annual payment of a portion of the crop), the 21 per cent of parish *cahiers* that do so appears meager.[26] It is in their support for indemnification that the Third Estate *cahiers* differ most sharply from the parish texts, a difference with great consequences for the subsequent relationship of revolutionary legislature and revolutionary village.[27] In the debates and discussion around the drafting of *cahiers* and the election of deputies, village France had many opportunities to discover both the strength and the limits of the anti-seigneurial program of the urban élites.[28]

On "the eternally memorable night of 4 August," as it was almost instantly known, and during the discussions of the following week, many dramas were taking place, but one of the most important was establishing the distinction between those rights to be abolished outright and those to be compensated. In the final decree of 11 August, which announced the abolition of "the feudal regime," and in the detailed legislation of March and May 1790, it was clear that the National Assembly was prepared to move within the conceptual framework of the Third Estate *cahiers*, devoting considerable energy to the question of precisely which rights were to be in which group, working out the rates of indemnification, and developing a complex set of historical and legal arguments to justify the structure. These actions of the Assembly help explain why the targets of peasant violence were even more likely to be aspects of the seigneurial regime after that initial legislation than they had been up to that point. And without that peasant violence, in part a response to the legislators' actions, the further legislative actions would be difficult to understand. Although the 11 August decree spoke of the destruction of the feudal regime "in its entirety," many peasant obligations continued, pending indemnification. Until well into 1792, indeed, revolutionary legislation combined conceptually radical statements of the termination of one historical epoch with detailed prescriptions for the indefinite continuation of much of what peasants had always paid. The fusion of the two was effected rhetorically by Merlin de Douai, who argued that precisely because "the feudal regime is abolished," peasants were now morally as well as legally obliged to pay whatever was not abolished.[29]

In the dialogue between legislators and peasants, the relevant evidence on the legislative side is relatively unproblematic. We have the laws enacted, the debates on the floor of the legislatures, and a good number of letters and memoirs of the legislators to ponder. On the peasant side, however, we do not have an enumeration of the time, place, and nature of rural actions on a national scale. There are excellent and invaluable monographic studies of particular regions, forms of conflict, and time periods but nothing that approximates what is needed here.[30] Even the Herculean triumph of Anatoly Ado, invaluable in its documentation of the spatiotemporal aspects of anti-feudal action as well as conflicts over food supply, needs supplementation.[31] The archival exploration of rural conflict from 1661 through the spring of 1789 being carried out by the team directed by Jean Nicolas and Guy Lemarchand is an inspiring but also daunting model.[32] Rather than attempt to follow these models of archival exploration, I opted for the more limited task of assembling as complete a set of data as possible from already published accounts.[33] Such a data set carries with it the limitations and selection biases of historians of France; yet it also has the considerable virtue of being a far more modest undertaking than the multi-year, transatlantic archival search to be carried out by a research team requiring training and supervision. It is essential to recognize the biases. The collective research of historians is likely to under-report smaller incidents, is likely to over-count events that took place in the much-studied summer of 1789 relative to events in 1790 or 1791, is likely to under-count taxation conflicts compared to the anti-feudal events central to important historical interpretations, and is likely to over-count events in the rural zones around the cities that are pleasant to live in while doing research. (I recall Richard Cobb observing something to the effect that the Muse of History was no closer in Paris than in the Massif Central but that everything else was a lot closer.) But, as justification for such an enterprise, even a rough tracing of the flow of insurrection as it unfolds in time and space permits a fuller appreciation of the richness of rural political action and helps fill in an important context for the behavior of other parties to revolutionary struggles.

I put together a file on events in which people from the countryside, acting publicly as a group, directly engaged in the seizing or damaging of the resources of another party (including an attack on persons) or in defending themselves against another party's claims on them. Such a definition includes many forms of anti-seigneurial, anti-tithe, or anti-tax actions, a variety of subsistence-oriented events, invasions of land, labor conflicts, and even many panics (such as the Great Fear) induced by the belief that one is under attack. I identified some 4,700 such events from June 1788 through June 1793 and recorded what I could learn of the geographic location, the date the event commenced, the target and nature of the action.

Among the incidents identified from the summer of 1788 to the summer of 1793, there was considerable variation in the level of detail reported. Sometimes, all that was clear was that there had been some sort of clash; at other times, one could say that a group of peasants entered the lord's château, but one had no idea of what they did there; in still other instances, there was a rich account. The date could often be discovered; but, sometimes, I could date an event only roughly (for example, an anxious report to the National Assembly on food riots over the preceding few months). In general, the published literature on which I relied is clearer about when a conflict commenced than when it ended, to the degree, indeed, that I abandoned the attempt to analyze the duration of actions altogether. Nor were these sources usable for the reconstruction of sequences of action within a single event: I was far more likely to get a catalog of the various things the invaders did in the château, monastery, or tax office than any clear sense of the order in which they did those things; still less often did I arrive at a clear picture of the process that brought them to the château. Did they assemble elsewhere? Did they come from church or parish assembly? Had they been working in the fields or chatting in the tavern? Did they converge individually before the lord's dwelling? And what happened next? Did they disperse to their homes? Did they plan another attack? I often had only the vaguest indication of which members of the rural community participated. Were they landless laborers, sharecroppers, rural textile-workers, smallholders? Only rarely was there any indication of gender. I recorded the level of detail I did have concerning the character of the event and, in the case of dates, the approximate level of precision. Indications of the number of participants in an action were vague, when they existed at all. While I was sure that a "very large" group was at least twenty, I was often less sure if two hundred or two thousand was closer to the mark. Far more successful, however, was the discovery of the targets of the action: that one gathering stormed a monastery while another looted a household's grain was usually clear enough. Given these limitations, my analyses must focus on places, dates, targets, and tactics.

An examination of the targets of these actions, aggregating together all events from June 1788 through June 1793 that meet the criteria, offers a sense of the multifarious nature of rural mobilizations during the revolutionary crisis. The antiseigneurial events formed a very large group – somewhat more than one third of all events found – and were quite widespread. Their diversity is depicted in Table 8.2, which shows the percentages of anti-seigneurial actions of various sorts. Note that the categories are not exclusive: a single event could involve a crowd that invades the lord's wine cellar and manhandles him prior to seizing his papers. Such an event would fall under several of the rubrics used in this table.[34] Some of the categories used are subcategories of others: to choose the first three figures as an example, more than half of all anti-seigneurial events involved some violence against persons or property, but a much smaller number involved personal violence, and a somewhat smaller number still, violence against the lord.

Peasants invaded the lord's fields, destroyed his crops, felled his trees, pastured communal animals on his property, destroyed his fences, and attempted to redraw the boundaries of communal and seigneurial property (often insisting that usurped land was being reclaimed). The lord's château could be broken into and, once entered, a variety of actions undertaken: furniture could be seized or damaged, the lord's archives could be ransacked in search of seigneurial titles or – particularly if the search was resisted – the documents could be set on fire. The invaders could demand food or drink, even, in a tense parody of some old norm of hospitality, compel the lord to have them served a feast right then and there.

There was also plenty of damage to be done outside the château. Lords were dragged outside and forced to make public renunciations of their rights, often recorded by a notary (himself sometimes under compulsion). The lord's amusements were the targets of some actions: his rabbits or pigeons killed (or sometimes seized for food) and their habitations destroyed, his fishpond emptied or fouled, his compulsory mill or oven destroyed. Sometimes, the focus was specifically the lord's collection of dues: he was forced to make restitution of dues, the scales used to measure his portion of the crops was smashed, or the community openly announced its solidarity in future non-payment, sometimes backed by coercive measures taken (or at least threatened) against any who chose to continue paying. At times, the agents of the lord were the target: his judge, his notary, his rent collector, or his guard who had often engaged in a battle of wits with would-be poachers and violators of hunting rights; sometimes, the lord himself was beaten, an action usually (but not always) halted short of his death.

An important group of actions was the attacks on the lord–church nexus: the lord's family bench in the local church was sometimes dramatically torn out and unceremoniously dumped outside – and on occasion smashed or set on fire; more rarely but even more dramatically, the family tombs in the church were desecrated. As the Revolution grew more radical, in one of the many inversions of the old order by which the Revolution continually demonstrated its reality,

Table 8.2 Types of anti-seigneurial insurrection

Targets and modes of action	Percentage of anti-seigneurial events
Violence	
Violence against persons or property	54.2
Violence against persons	4.7
Violence against lord	3.1
Château penetrated and interior invaded, with varying degrees of damage	27.3
Château a target; interior penetrated or exterior damaged	52.5
Destruction of food sources, rather than seizure (killing pigeons, fish, or rabbits; destruction of lord's crop; destruction of lord's trees)	5.2
Claims to rights	
Coerced renunciation of rights	7.7
Searches, seizures, and demands for documents (at château or at notary's office)	16.3
Subsistence	
Search for food stores, seizure of goods in wine cellar, compelling lord to feed the invaders	7.1
Recreational privileges	
Attacks on lord's right to hunt, raise pigeons or rabbits, or to maintain a fishpond (includes both acts or seizure and of destruction)	9.4
Hunting only	2.9
Lord–Church nexus	4.3
Dues	
Collective and public statement of refusal to pay	10.2
Public refusals to pay, demands for restitution, attacks on scales	18.4
Coerced restitution only	9.1
Land conflict	
All land conflicts	10.7
Conflicts over ownership or use rights in woods	4.9
Monopolies	0.5
Agents	3.9
King as Lord	0.7
Symbolics	
Honorific symbols of seigneurial status (weather vanes, coats of arms, gallows, turrets, battlements)	11.9

the lord's (or later on, ex-lord's) dwelling might be searched for firearms or hidden counter-revolutionaries, just as lords had once joined the state in searching peasant homes for forbidden weapons or concealed criminals.

In all these ways, the lord's prerogatives were challenged, his material accumulations reclaimed, damaged, or desecrated, the legal basis of his authority seized from his archives as a text or from his mouth as a sworn renunciation, his connection with the sacred grounding of the community severed just as the family tomb or family bench was torn from the local church. Assaults also took place on the symbols of seigneurialism that made the lord more than another man. The weather vane was one likely target, as were turrets and battlements. Although the advance of the central state had long since rendered the fortress aspect of the medieval castle out of date, many a lord maintained reminders of a warrior identity in the form of architectural motifs of a decorative sort in his elegant lodgings, only to have these pretty turrets and graceful battlements attract the rage of peasant communities. Any display of the family coat of arms was a tempting target as well. With its turrets knocked down and its coat of arms destroyed, the château was just a house.

One interesting cluster of actions involves the destruction of food sources. Some peasant communities obtained meat by defying the lord's exclusive rights and hunting on his preserves; others appear to have killed the game and left the carcasses.[35] Some forced the lord to feed them, and others destroyed the lord's crop.[36] Some made use of the products of the lord's forests, and others appear to have primarily damaged the trees.[37] Some seized the creatures the lord was privileged to raise (pigeons, rabbits, fish), and others seem to have been primarily concerned to destroy dovecotes, warrens, and ponds (and their feathered, furry, or finny inhabitants).[38] It is striking that these acts of destruction are scarcely less numerous in the data than are seizures of food from the lord.

Perhaps such actions arose from the blind anger of those for whom adequate diets were uncertain, while among them lived lords who made provisioning a form of play. Perhaps they were an assertion of a claim to a social order in which peasants, like lords, could defend their productive labors against pests.[39] Perhaps they were an assertion of peasant dignity, of the right to define their own activities as valuable and the lords' game – and games – as nuisances (which merely eating the rabbits would not do).[40]

It is also worth pausing over the relatively small number of incidents in which seigneurial agents are targets. It is commonly asserted that the lord's agents, in acting as intermediaries – whether as dues collectors, judges, estate managers, or legal advisers – became, for the peasants, the personification of the ills inflicted by the seigneurial regime. These agents thereby absorbed blows that might otherwise have been directed at the more distant lord.[41] The evidence of the actual insurrections (as well as the evidence of the parish *cahiers*)[42] suggests that, on a national scale, these intermediaries, these dwellers in the world between the lord and the peasant, were in fact of relatively minor concern to the country people. While the French peasants may not have loved the lord's agents, the agents did not constitute a major target of grievance or rebellion.[43] The peasants' target seems to have been a social institution and not, primarily, its human beneficiaries.[44] The country people were not, as some of the literature has it, sidetracked by the lord's agents, nor were they blinded by the search for revenge on the lord himself. The pattern of violent action, like the pattern of expressed grievances, suggests that peasants had an abstract conception of a social system. Their actions were violent, to be sure, and often inherently violent, not merely by-products of resistance to peaceable protests – although resistance might well augment the violence. But to be angry does not mean that one is blinded by anger, and to be violent does not mean that one's actions are unreasoned.

Finally, there was a striking bit of by-play around the meaning of a wooden pole. Lords who had proudly demonstrated their claims to possess the rights of "high justice" often decorated their lawns with gallows,[45] whose lack of utility did not spare them destruction in some parishes and replacement by a different pole, by which rural communities indicated their own power and their newly seized freedoms. In early 1790, anti-seigneurial events in Périgord and Quercy began to include the installation of the trimmed trunk of a very straight tree, often decorated with anti-seigneurial mockery and warnings, in place of the front-lawn gallows. Sometimes, indeed, the new pole was itself conceived as a gallows, but now it was the peasants' gibbet rather than the lord's.[46]

In considering the relative frequency of the different ways of challenging the seigneurial regime, it must be remembered that the nature of these sources makes it certain that many incidents are not fully described and that, therefore, many of the figures for the percentage of events with particular characteristics err on the low side. One would think that, with regard to the scale of violence in particular, the reverse would be the case. The more frightening aspects of these events would be the most likely to be reported in the first place, and historians searching for the dramatic anecdote would be more likely to recover from their archival locations accounts of severe damage to property and persons than respectful petitioning. (If we accept Simon Schama's indictment of the historical profession as squeamish, however, there might be a powerful countervailing tendency.) If one is willing to lend credence to the data (or to regard them as likely to overstate violence), the results are fascinating. While more than half the incidents involved overt violence (injuries to persons or property) in contrast to public declarations, demands, or threats, almost all of the violence was property damage. While lords may have been terrified by these events – some were hurt or killed and many threatened – revenge on the person of the lord played a fairly small role.[47]

The aggregated statistics, however, conceal at least as much as they reveal. What is most obscured is that revolution is not so much a state as a process involving an ebb and flow of events and alterations in the nature of those events. Figure 8.1 shows the number of incidents in each month from June 1788 through June 1793 as well as something of the changing character of the events at the moment of peak intensity. For example, in March 1789, about two-thirds of the incidents involved subsistence issues.[48]

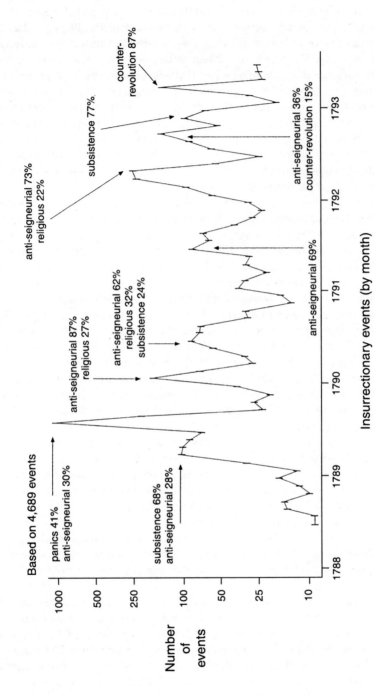

Figure 8.1 Number and character of insurrectionary events, June 1788 through June 1793 (based on 4,689 events)

The anti-seigneurial activity is far from being a constant from beginning to end. It is dominant in the waves of revolt that peaked in February 1790, June 1790, June 1791, and April 1792; but earlier and later, the story is different. In March and July 1789 and again in November 1792, anti-seigneurial events share the spotlight with other sorts of actions, and earlier and later still they are even less salient.

This is evident from a different angle when comparing the rhythms of anti-seigneurial actions with other kinds of actions. Figure 8.2 displays the trajectories of eight kinds of events. Each graph charts the changing proportions of events falling into various rough categories. The upper left graph shows the anti-seigneurial actions to have a clear rise and fall. Rather than an indiscriminate rural violence, attacks on varying targets have varying histories. In the summer of 1788, there are hardly any anti-seigneurial events. Subsistence events are the opening wedge of rural insurrection. In late 1788, anti-seigneurial events assume increasing significance and climb through 1789, remaining high – apart from a dip late in 1791 – until well into 1792, when they are eclipsed by other rural actions. It is worth pausing over this pattern. I suggest that in the course of the convocation of the Estates-General, and then in the patterns of debate and legislation, the anti-seigneurial character of the new revolutionary élites is becoming apparent to the peasants. Although the deputies of the Third Estate were more gradualist than the countryside wished – note their support for indemnifying the lords – peasants had come to believe that rural action against seigneurial rights had a good chance of paying off.

Peasant action against seigneurial rights continued until substantial gains were made. To the frustration of many deputies in the various legislatures, many villagers did not consider as a substantial gain the ringing declaration of 4 August 1789, that the feudal regime was destroyed but would accept only significant alterations in what had to be paid to whom and in how disputes over such claims were to be resolved. The outright abolition of many seigneurial rights was not enough, in village France, if payments to the lords were to continue, pending an indemnification. The country people were fighting the claims of the lords, not an esoteric conception of "feudalism" defined by the National Assembly.[49] The significant achievements as far as the dues were concerned awaited piecemeal enactments of the spring of 1792, which culminated in a new law in late August of that year – after which anti-seigneurial actions plummeted. The trajectory of anti-seigneurial actions shows that rural action was not merely a blind and angry reflex. There may have been anger, but the uprisings developed as the moment seemed opportune and faded as goals were achieved.

I will not recount here the story of how rural insurrection persuaded the deputies to whittle away at the initial detailed legislation of March 1790, except to pause at one crucial moment in early 1792.[50] The legislators, from the initial language of the night of 4 August onward, had spoken in self-congratulation of the radicalism of their abolition of the feudal regime, while French villagers, from late in 1789 on, were mounting wave after wave of insurrection. February

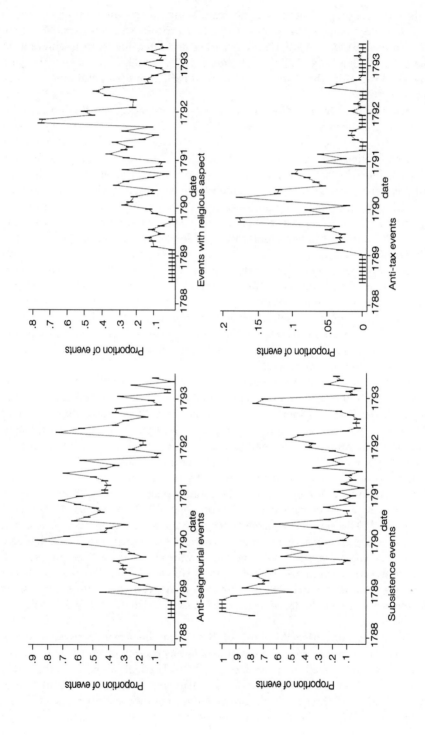

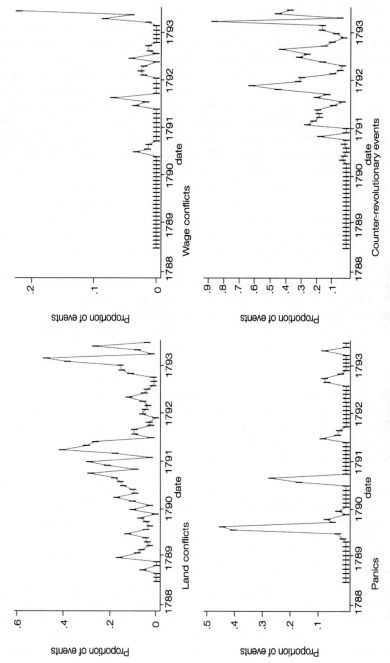

Figure 8.2 Proportions of eight kinds of rural insurrection, late 1788 through late 1793

through April of 1792 was the largest such wave after the summer of 1789; it was also the eve of war with Europe, and it was within this context that peasant action was especially efficacious.

Seigneurial rights had become a central element of interstate tension on the night of 4 August. German princes, whose seigneurial claims in Alsace were guaranteed in the Treaty of Westphalia in 1648, hoped to find a powerful backer in the Holy Roman Empire. The landgrave of Hesse-Darmstadt, the bishop of Spire, and the duke of Württemberg had already been at odds with the French government over the flurry of institutional innovation of the pre-revolutionary period. For these princes, the new local and regional assemblies set up in 1787 raised the specter of popular sovereignty. The tax reform proposals of 1787 and 1788, the judicial reorganization of 1788 that threatened seigneurial courts, and the anti-feudal discourse in which public affairs were already being discussed were issues in Alsace even before the Estates-General met.[51] On 4 August these tensions were raised, on the French side, from a problem to a national commitment. From a problem that pitted local privileges against monarchical reform and state centralization, this conflict was transmuted into a struggle of the new epoch being born against the lay and clerical lords who fought to keep humanity in chains.

What may have appeared at first as simply the conflicting claims of France and the empire appeared to some in the Assembly as a question of whether the sovereignty of the French people (which the legislators took themselves to embody) could be assigned limits under the treaties of past monarchs. Merlin de Douai, speaking for the Committee on Feudal Rights, found a legal principle to sustain the jurisdiction of the National Assembly: the social contract took precedence over all. Since the people of Alsace had never consented to the Treaty of Westphalia but had participated in the election of the deputies that enacted the 4–11 August decree, the "treaties of princes" were illegal.[52] By implication, all interstate treaties were illegitimate, and no European structure of authority, except France's, had the basis in popular consent that made it worthy of respect.[53] Here, as in other pronouncements on seigneurial rights, Merlin's sharp and absolute statement of principle was as radical as the totality of concrete measures was moderate. The Diplomatic Committee, appropriate to its mission, took a more diplomatic view and proposed compensating the princes, but the princes refused.[54] Because the empire was unwilling to back the princes, there was no immediate threat of military action, but the rhetorical linkage of anti-feudalism in France and hostility toward the European monarchies had been forged.[55]

As tensions between states increased, those in France who favored war convinced themselves that not only would the conscript armies of their enemies crumble when confronting a free people but that the subject peoples of Europe would rise in emulation of the liberated French. Maximin Isnard's inflammatory speech of late November 1791 linked French émigrés and German princes in a common concern with lost rights and warned that, "if foreign courts try to raise a war of kings against France, we will raise a war of peoples against kings." [56]

When a Prussian radical told the Legislative Assembly in December 1791 that interstate conflict would prompt peasants in Germany and Bohemia to rise against their lords, he was only reaffirming what many were already prepared to hear.[57] Jacques-Pierre Brissot and his political associates persistently defined the war they advocated as a war against feudalism.[58] There were, to be sure, some who proposed cooling the rhetorical temperature. As war neared in February 1792, the Diplomatic Committee of the Legislative Assembly reiterated the conciliatory proposal of indemnifying the German princes, a proposal dismissed by Jean-Baptiste Mailhe for its weakness.[59] (If it was wrong to indemnify lords across the Rhine, did some of the listeners wonder why was it proper to do so on their side?) And Robespierre's attempted deflation of the yoking of liberation and European war is well known.[60] Nonetheless, the sense of national mission prevailed.

Until the approach of actual war, most of the legislation on the seigneurial regime still amounted to tinkering with the basic structure embodied in the declarations of 4–11 August 1789, as given detailed elaboration by the enactments of March and May 1790. As interstate tensions become more ominous, peasant insurrection began to suggest a dangerous failure of the existing scheme. When rural incidents mounted in February 1792 – they were to reach the second largest insurrectionary peak of the Revolution in April – Georges Couthon urged a new course in the Legislative Assembly. He reminded his fellow deputies of the great size of the French army. But he urged them to recall that sheer size was far less significant than the moral unity of army and nation. The benefits of the Revolution, unfortunately, had not yet been fully received in the French countryside; village France had largely received fine words.

> Each of us has seen that ever-memorable night of August 4, 1789, when the Constituent Assembly ... pronounced in a holy enthusiasm the abolition of the feudal regime ... But these striking decisions were soon to present nothing more to the people than the idea of a beautiful dream, whose deceitful illusion left nothing but regrets. It was ... on August 4, 1789, that a decree was joyously received in all parts of the empire that abolished ... the feudal regime. Eight months later, a second decree preserved everything of value of this regime, so that far from having served the people, the Constituent Assembly could not even retain for them the consoling hope of being able to one day free themselves from the despotism of the former lords and the exaction of their agents.

Couthon alluded to the earlier work of abolishing the honorific aspects of the regime while insisting on indemnities for lucrative rights: "You will surely understand, gentlemen, that it was not exactly the honorific aspects of the feudal regime that weighed on the people." And he summed up: "We want [the people] to believe in the reign of liberty when they rest chained in dependence beneath their former lord."[61]

In the months that followed, a series of critical attacks occurred on the anti-seigneurial edifice as conceived by Merlin, and the war with Europe continued to be identified as a war about feudalism.[62] With the war came the overturning of the assumptions of the initial legislation, a process culminating in the August decrees of the Legislative Assembly.[63] By virtue of these new enactments, the burden of proof in disputes between peasant communities and lords was dramatically shifted. One of the most important aspects of the legislation that had initially spelled out what was to be abolished outright and what indemnified (and at what rates), starting with the spring of 1790, had been its allocation to the peasants of the burden of proof in the event of a dispute over the legitimacy of particular claims. A community had the right to challenge the lord's claim to payment pending indemnification, but that community was required to furnish evidence that the right in dispute had originated in an initial act of coercion, a formidable legal hurdle. The new enactments of August 1792 reversed this: it would now be up to the lords to demonstrate that a contested right had been initiated in an uncoerced contract. Even if a lord actually had some relevant documentation, how many would run the risk of attempting to make good such a claim in the threatening climate of the fall of 1792, a claim that would have to be pressed in a revolutionary court not likely to be very sympathetic?[64] Although the legislature had not yet declared the entire seigneurial regime illegitimate in principle, the August legislation made it nearly impossible for the lords to make claims on peasants in practice. It is striking that anti-seigneurial actions in the countryside declined sharply in the fall; with the lords no longer able to collect, peasant attention turned elsewhere.[65]

Even after the new anti-seigneurial legislation of August 1792, anti-feudal language surrounding the war continued to outrun the law in France. The Convention continued to expound the fusion of anti-feudalism and the struggle against foreign kings. In November 1792, the Convention discussed "the principles," as Brissot put it, "under which France must grant her protection to all the peoples who ask it," Mailhe interjected that, whatever else these principles might be, they must include instructing other peoples "in the natural rights on which the destruction of feudal rights in France was based." And he went on to speak of a national mission: "Citizens, it is in France that feudal rights and their consequences unhappily were born: it is from France that enlightenment must come; it is the French who must raise the thick veil which, among all our neighbors, still conceals the fundamental rights of nature."[66]

Pierre-Joseph Cambon, urging on behalf of the finance, war, and diplomatic committees, the policies to be pursued by French forces, advanced a famous slogan: "[The committees have asked first of all] what is the purpose of the war you have undertaken. It is surely the abolition of all privileges. War against the châteaux, peace to the cottages."[67] On 15 December 1792, the Convention decreed the abolition of seigneurial rights in French-controlled areas of Belgium and Germany with no mention of any provision for appeal.[68] Peasants outside of France were to be promised French support for insurrection: "show yourselves free men and we will guarantee you against their vengeance." Although the seigneurial regime was no longer a primary target of French peasant action, the wartime Convention could hardly ignore the turbulent countryside, particularly with the radical increase in the frequency and scale of rural mobilization in March 1793. One symptom of the gravity with which the rural situation was viewed is Bertrand Barère's speech of 18 March. Advocating a complex package of proposals that combined repression with benefits for both the rural poor and the well-off, he urged the creation of a (not yet "the") "committee of public safety."[69] Three months later, the Convention proclaimed the entire seigneurial regime illegitimate.[70]

The wartime discussions of seigneurial rights were rooted in the war-promoting rhetoric of the Girondins, in statements of war aims, in policy declarations by generals in Belgium, in inspirational pep talks to the troops. The rhetorical climate was changing. If the sons of French villagers were to die in order to free German or Piedmontese villagers from feudal oppression, could the legislators stick to a definition of feudal rights so narrow that it appeared an utter fraud in rural France? Couthon's bitter observation in February 1792 that much of the anti-seigneurial legislation was "like that which the former lords would have dictated themselves" did no more than echo the claims of sharecroppers in the countryside around Gourdon as early as the fall of 1790.[71] If the Convention encouraged anti-feudal insurrection in France's neighbors, could it manage to prosecute anti-feudal peasants at home? Mailhe went beyond supporting the wartime proclamation of liberation of occupied territories from feudal rights and protecting peasants against their lords; on 15 December, he proposed abolishing nobility itself where French arms triumphed. It seems but a matter of consistency for him to have advocated, ten days later, that legal proceedings against French peasants rebelling against seigneurialism be dropped.[72] (After the counter-revolutionary explosion in the western countryside of March 1793, in the name of what ideal were French peasants to be ordered into the vicious counter-insurgency campaign against other French peasants?)

The war made it impossible to maintain the disjunction between the sense of a radical rupture in history and a detailed specification that altered little of what peasants owed lords. In presenting the French armies as the agents of liberty in battle against the slave armies of the crowned tyrants, the legislators had to accept the victory of defiant French villagers who doggedly refused the co-existence of the narrow and the broad senses of the abolition of the feudal regime.[73] It took years of rural violence to push the revolutionary legislatures to make of the dismantling of feudalism a reality recognizable in the villages. And it is far from obvious that they would have done so without the wartime stresses.

Was a more peaceful termination of seigneurial rights, carefully controlled by a forward-looking élite, possible? The question demands speculation about the consequences of an élite-driven anti-seigneurial program pursued without the threat of effective peasant disruption. Such counter-factual speculation is fraught with hazards, but a failure to pose the question has its own hazard, namely, the ignoring of an important perspective on the rural revolts. Some parallel experiences are available to draw on in other European efforts to remove broadly similar rights.

Élite desires partially or wholly to dismantle anti-seigneurialism drew on many sources apart from fears of rebellion: the conviction that agricultural productivity could be advanced, that state revenues would increase, that an emancipated peasantry was more reliable in wartime, that a "civilized" country required a juridicial commitment to personal freedom, and that at least some seigneurial claims cost more to extract than they were worth even to the seigneurs. As discussed above, French élites did have an anti-seigneurial program at the onset of revolution, though one well short of what many French villagers would accept. Were there rural emancipations pushed by similar élite reformers in which fear of rural plebeians was minimal?

Jerome Blum's comparative survey of the formal emancipations of continental Europe's rural populations shows that almost everywhere emancipation was a protracted process.[74] Three states preceded France. Savoy's duke freed his own serfs in 1762 and went beyond the later similar act of Louis XVI by decreeing an indemnified redemption for other peasants. In 1772, the indemnification terms were altered in favor of the peasants, but the incapacity of the country people to buy their freedom caused the process to drag on until the French army entered two decades later and ordered an immediate and unindemnified abolition.[75] Baden's initial proclamation dates from 1783, but seigneurial claims did not definitively end until 1848.[76] After a series of false starts as early as 1702, Denmark proclaimed an effective abolition in 1788 but did not complete the process until 1861.[77]

Emancipations hardly proceeded any more rapidly in those many instances in which reform began in the wake of the revolution. Emancipation decrees were issued in Prussia, Württemberg, Mecklenberg, Bavaria, and Hesse between 1807 and 1820, but the processes were not completed until the revolutionary wave of 1848. Still other emancipatory processes did not even commence until the pressures of the agitated early 1830s (Hannover and Saxony), and others awaited the still more intense pressures of 1848 (Austria, Saxe-Weimar and Anhalt-Dessau-Köthen). Austrian officials were keenly affected by a Galician revolt in 1846.[78]

All of these emancipations outside France involved indemnifications. Many were limited to certain categories of peasants. Denmark's 1788 law, for example, did not free serfs between fourteen and thirty-six years old; its 1791 law denied landless farm workers the right to seek other employment.[79] Some of these indemnified emancipations required the consent of both lord and peasant, a measure that enabled those lords who wished to retain their rights to do so, at least until, as invariably happened, subsequent legislation removed the voluntary element.[80] The rapidity of the French transition from a process in large part indemnificatory to one thoroughly abolitionist stands out as unique among all European cases that commenced before 1848.

Apart from Savoy, Baden, and Denmark, moreover, the initial impulse for all the pre-1815 cases was French. French arms sometimes brought varying degrees of rural emancipation, as in Belgium at the start of the long war, the Helvetic Republic, and various western German states in 1798, the Grand Duchy of Warsaw in 1807, and various north German states in 1811; these actions in turn triggered pre-emptive emancipation by fearful neighbors, as in a number of German instances in 1807. Beyond the direct use of force, however, the knowledge of the dangers of revolution in which French peasants instructed the world certainly helped spur some reform even after Napoleon's armies went down to defeat.[81] And in 1848 itself, insurrectionary peasants may have more rapidly won concessions in German-speaking lands because many governments had learned from 1789–93 the futility of half-measures in the countryside: thus the termination of several decades-long emancipatory processes and the commencement and rapid completion of others in 1848–9. (In Hungary in 1848, the Diet appears to have been panicked into abolishing serfdom by a false report of 40,000 mobilized peasants.)[82] In other words, in Central and Western Europe through the mid-nineteenth century, there are many instances of élite-driven emancipations, but, if we credit Blum's survey, not a single one that came to completion without the presence of the French army, the specter of popular insurrection, or both.

This glance to the east strengthens the view that without the determined, violent, and frightening popular battle, French peasants would still have been responsible for seigneurial obligations at the midpoint of the nineteenth century – at the very least. The Third Estate's delegates did carry indemnificatory proposals to the Estates-General, where they joined with nobles, some of whom represented more conservative constituencies. Considering the role of popular uprising in promoting the initial decrees of 4–11 August 1789, one might well wonder if emancipation would have taken place at all without further pressure from the peasants.[83] Even the positions expressed in the general *cahiers* of the spring of 1789 were surely taken with an awareness of the riots rising in the French countryside; the assemblies, moreover, though dominated by urban notables, had a significant number of village delegates. The positions taken in the Third Estate *cahiers* already reflect rural pressures.

The years of disruptive insurrection of the French countryside in revolution are a part of the modern history of democracy, despite the view expressed in much of the recent literature that emancipation from the chains of the past was largely the work of highly educated élites, that plebeian violence only helped to emphasize the illiberal leanings of those élites, and that much rural mobilization was directed against the revolutionary regime rather than in tacit alliance with it. Democracy is a highly charged and profoundly contested notion,[84] but essential to virtually all conceptions is some sense of "self-rule," not a state of affairs one could readily imagine extending to those in relations of dependence on others. This has been a continuing and potent rationale for the exclusion from public life and full political rights of many – of the poor, servants, and women at various points during the Revolution, of a variety of groups at other times and in other places, of the continuing exclusion of children from active citizenship everywhere. A rural world of lords and peasants is a world of very limited democratic possibilities: the attack on seigneurial rights was therefore an important component of creating the possibility of a democratic future.

A case can be made that the essential ingredient in this attack was a revolution in thought, largely promoted by the revolutionary élite and enunciated as early as the summer of 1789. François Furet remarked, on the conceptual achievement of the National Assembly,

> the decrees of August 4 to August 11 number among the founding texts of modern France. They destroyed aristocratic society from top to bottom, along with its structure of dependencies and privileges. For this structure they substituted the modern, autonomous individual, free to do whatever was not prohibited by law. August 4 wiped the slate clean by eliminating whatever remained of intrasocial powers between the individual and the social body as a whole.[85]

We ought to question the real extent of these individual rights. Women were hardly emancipated from structures of dependence by 4–11 August, to take one very important example.[86] Conflict over the definition of who is seen as autonomous and free, in fact, has been a central but not always noticed feature of democracy for the past two centuries. Even if we may not wish to take the next step to equate a conception with the actual experience of social relationships, we may, nevertheless, agree on the radicalism of a conception of a society in which all dependence and privilege have given way before autonomous individuals. But is the National Assembly to be credited with the destruction of rural structures of dependence because it issued a text in which it credited itself? We may wonder, first of all, whether the National Assembly, which added a considerable dose of noble conservatism to the clear but clearly limited anti-feudal program of the Third Estate, would have even gone as far as it did in early August without the social explosion of July 1789. And we may ask whether this conceptual break would be easy to see as anything other than hypocrisy without the measures taken later, in 1792, to gain the support of peasants unwilling to settle for the removal of the symbols of deference without a far more dramatic change in material obligation. Even on the level of such symbolics, how quickly would the legislatures have acted, looking ahead from 4–11 August, without the vast destruction of church benches, weather vanes, and coats of arms carried out by the country people?

The rural popular violence and the élite conceptual radicalism, moreover, were hard to separate, for each sustained the other. Not only did violent peasants push the legislature forward, but conceptually radical legislators showed peasants that if they pushed, they could win.

Does any of this argument indicate that the élite's own anti-feudal program, which I have not treated in any detail here, was an insignificant matter? Not at all. The people of the countryside rose against different targets at various times and places, and those in a position to write laws or command armed force responded in various ways. Consider the two contrasting cases: overt rejection of the central institutions and symbols of the Revolution in the west was met by savage violence on the part of the authorities; rejection of the revolutionary freeing of the grain trade (in which rural people were joined by urban popular forces) led to the spectacular, but only temporary, reimposition of controls. If the anti-seigneurial campaign, though difficult, was such a success, was it not in considerable part because revolutionary legislators had their own anti-feudal agenda?

Furthermore, insurrectionary peasants were responding to the élites just as the legislators were responding to rural disruption. Consider again the trajectory of peasant insurrection (see Figure 8.1): it was not, at first, predominantly anti-seigneurial, but it became so. As the elections to the Estates-General approached, the struggle for the hearts and minds of the country people could not have failed to have made them aware of urban élite sympathies for significant alterations in the seigneurial regime; the night of 4 August was even more instructive. And, the data show, it is following 4 August that rural turbulence became predominantly focused on seigneurial rights. The debates in the spring over the contents of the *cahiers* and the legislative events of early August were demonstrations that an assault on the seigneurial regime might not quite be, as the French say, kicking in an open door, but it surely was not a stoutly defended oaken door, either. The dealings of villagers and legislators with each other over the rights of the lords radicalized both parties, but this is another story.

Let us speculate for a moment about a less violent revolution, in which a conceptually radical National Assembly abolishes feudalism but manages to obtain peasant compliance in paying what they have always paid, no doubt inspiring a host of programs by which all manner of states, following France, Savoy, Baden, and Denmark, discovered how to be modern without expropriating a landed upper class. We would have fewer documents that tell us of the terrors of the countryside in revolution. Yet it is hard to see how such a state of affairs would have advanced democracy. No doubt, for many, such an outcome would nevertheless be preferable to all the pain that occurred.

The structures that made one man more than another, grounded in force, were abolished in principle by the National Assembly, helped along by rural violence against the visible signs of honor for the lords and the counterpart humiliations for the villagers. But the initial legislative program, more or less following the intentions voiced by the urban notables in the spring of 1789, was not accepted in much of rural France; it took years of battle in the countryside and the pressure of war with Europe for the legislators to translate their own sense of a break with a feudal past into terms recognizable in the villages. While the idea of a world of contractual relations among juridically equal persons may be an essential component that underlies evolving democratic practice, in which no one governs by age-old right and governors are accountable for their performances to citizenries, many in the French countryside plainly did not accept the claim that they had in some sense consented to their material obligations to their now former lords. Without the genuine end to those payments, there might as well be lords in village France, regardless of what the lawyers wrote in Paris. Merlin held early on that the Treaty of Westphalia to which the people had not consented could not obligate them to continue to pay lords across the Rhine; but the revolutionary legislatures tried for three years to act as though the same country people had consented to pay French lords. It took considerable violence to go beyond a gradual phase-out. Such violence had many consequences: the counter-mobilizations of the terrorized (the nineteenth-century Right and ultra-right fed off French revolutionary terrors), the repressive measures of a revolutionary state eager to remove initiative from the village and the street, and the sufferings of the victims (whose complicity in the earlier sufferings of their own now-violent tormentors varied greatly). So the revolution, and its popular insurrections, opened the way for new forms of non-democratic and even anti-democratic politics. But they also made a more democratic social order possible. To the extent that over the past two centuries those in command in France had to take into consideration their accountability to the French people (rather than, like Louis XV, only their responsibilities before God),[87] the thousands of violent incidents of rural France in revolution made an essential contribution.

NOTES

Source Reprinted from the *American Historical Review* 100 (April 1995): 360–386.

Acknowledgement An earlier version of this article was presented at the conference "Violence and the Democratic Tradition in France," University of California, Irvine, February 1994. The essay benefited from the comments of participants in that event, particularly Colin Lucas, as well as from suggestions by Seymour Drescher, Jeremy Popkin, Donald Sutherland, and Isser Woloch.

1 *The London Times* (12 July 1989): 12; *Le monde* (12 July 1989): 1, 4.
2 "Mrs. Thatcher Set to Rights." *Guardian*, 15 July 1989.
3 See François Crouzet, *De la supériorité de l'Angleterre sur la France: L'économique et l'imaginaire, XVIIe–XXe siècles* (Paris, 1985), esp. pp. 248–98; Pierre Chaunu, *Le grand déclassement: A propos d'une commémoration* (Paris, 1989), pp. 265–84; and René Sédillot, *Le coût de la Révolution* (Paris, 1987).
4 From Simon Schama's preface to *Citizens*: "The drastic social changes imputed to the Revolution seem less clear-cut or actually not apparent at all . . . [T]he modernization of French society and institutions seem to have been anticipated by the reform of the 'old regime.' " Schama, *Citizens: A Chronicle of the French Revolution* (New York, 1989), p. xiv.
5 For John Mueller, the Revolution's contribution to the history of democracy was a "disastrous" bad example; and Jack A. Goldstone stresses the revolutionary violence "that systematically destroys the political space necessary for freedom and liberty to flourish." See Mueller, "Democracy and Ralph's Pretty Good Grocery: Elections, Equality and the Minimal Human Being," *American Journal of Political Science*, 36 (1992): 994; Goldstone, "Révolutions dans l'histoire et histoire des révolutions," in *Revue français de sociologie*, 30 (1989): 421. For surveys of the recent stress on élite political culture, see Sarah Maza, "Politics, Culture and the Origins of the French Revolution," *Journal of Modern History*, 61 (1989): 704–23; and Jack Censer, "The Coming of a New Interpretation of the French Revolution," *Journal of Social History*, 21 (1987): 295–309.

6 Brian Singer, "Violence in the French Revolution: Forms of Ingestion/Forms of Expulsion," in Ferenc Fehér, *The French Revolution and the Birth of Modernity* (Berkeley, Calif., 1990), pp. 150–73. To argue that violence is not fully explained as a means to an end outside itself, as Singer brilliantly does, is by no means the same as demonstrating that violence never has an instrumental aspect. The leap that identifies violence with the gratuitously anti-rational is an important element of Schama's rhetoric. If the revolution is violence and violence is senseless, a reader can easily draw the implied conclusion about all revolutionary action. See also Roger Chartier, *The Cultural Origins of the French Revolution* (Durham, N.C., 1991), pp. 193–4: Norbert Elias, "The Civilizing Process: Sociogenetic and Psychogenetic Investigations (New York, 1982).

7 The recent literature on resistance is voluminous beyond ready citation: there is a useful survey in Michel Vovelle, *La découverte de la politique: Géopolitique de la Révolution française* (Paris, 1993).

8 The most compelling portrait along these lines is Donald Sutherland, *France 1789–1815: Revolution and Counterrevolution* (New York, 1986). Sutherland's preview of his argument: "The history of the entire period can be understood as the struggle against a counterrevolution that was not so much aristocratic as massive, extensive, durable and popular" (p. 10).

9 Charles Tilly, *The Contentious French* (Cambridge, Mass., 1986), p. 2.

10 J. Mavidal and E. Laurent, *Archives parlementaires de 1787 à 1860 (première série)* (Paris, 1879), 3: 285. (This series will be abbreviated *AP* in subsequent references.)

11 Hilton Root has expressed some skepticism on this point. See Root, "The Case against Georges Lefebvre's Peasant Revolution," *History Workshop*, 28 (1989): 88–102; and the reply by Peter Jones in the same number.

12 Georges Lefebvre *The Coming of the French Revolution* (New York, 1947), pp. 127–45; Anatoly Ado, *Krest'ianskoe dvizhenie vo frantsii vo vremia velikoi burzhuaznoi revoliutsii kontsa XVIII veka* (Moscow, 1971).

13 There were many other targets of rural insurrection besides the seigneurial regime that are not treated in this essay; there are also important regional differences in the types and timing of anti-seigneurial actions. On these matters, as well as more on the legislative context, see John Markoff, *The Abolition of Feudalism: Peasants, Lords and Legislators in the French Revolution* (University Park, Pa., forthcoming).

14 The search for a precise evaluation of the weight of the seigneurial regime has generated a large and complex literature because there were many different sorts of seigneurial rights, much variation from region to region and even *seigneurie* to *seigneurie*, difficulty in adequately measuring the total revenues of peasants and lords against which the place of the seigneurial rights is to be weighed, and many problems in making judgments about the role of seigneurialism in conferring power and honor as well as income. It is clear from this literature, however, that there were many French peasants on whom the lord's claims were heavy and many lords for whom these rights were a significant component of income; it is also evident from the grievance lists of 1789 that many a lord took the honor attached to some of the rights with the greatest seriousness, while others in France took with equal seriousness the associated dishonor. For one example of an attempted monetary evaluation of seigneurial revenues, see M. Leymairie, "Les redevances foncières seigneuriales en Haute-Auvergne," *Annals historiques de la Révolution française*, 40 (1968): 299–380; the issue of honor and dishonor is treated in Markoff, *Abolition of Feudalism*.

15 The figures presented are drawn from a quantitative content analysis of the *cahiers* carried out with Gilbert Shapiro. Our code distinguishes more than one thousand institutions under discussion and hundreds of actions demanded. We coded virtually all the extant general *cahiers* of the Third Estate and nobility as well as a sample of 748 of the parish *cahiers*. Since we did not code the clerical *cahiers*, there is a missing part of this picture. The procedures for counting demands in the *cahiers* are spelled out in detail in Gilbert Shapiro and John Markoff, *Revolutionary Demands: A Content Analy-*

sis of the Cahiers de Doléances of 1789 (Stanford. Calif., forthcoming); a briefer account may be found in John Markoff, Gilbert Shapiro, and Sasha Weitman, "Towards the Integration of Content Analysis with General Methodology," David Heise (ed.), *Sociological Methodology* (San Francisco, 1974), pp. 1–58.

16 By contrast, taxation was an arena that attracted many reform proposals. By one measure, 16 per cent of Third Estate grievances about seigneurial rights called for reform, compared to 39 per cent when taxation was at issue. See John Markoff, "Peasants Protest: The Claims of Lord, Church and State in the *Cahiers de Doléances* of 1789," *Comparative Studies in Society and History*, 32 (1990): 428–9.

17 Markoff, "Peasants Protest." pp. 428–9: Markoff, *Abolition of Feudalism*, Chap. 2.

18 Pierre-François Boncerf, *Les inconvéniens des droits féodaux* (London, 1776).

19 Max Bruchet, *L'abolition des droits seigneuriaux en Savoie* (1761–1793) (Annecy, 1908).

20 Alfred Cobban, *The Social Interpretation of the French Revolution* (Cambridge, 1965), pp. 27, 39, 43–8.

21 George T. Matthews, *The Royal General Farms in Eighteenth-Century France* (New York, 1958), p. 175.

22 As the legislative reconstruction of France proceeded, concern among the deputies for the continued collection of seigneurial rights on former royal or church property was evident. When the departmental and district administrations, to whom the supervision of "national property" was originally entrusted, proved lax in the collection of seigneurial rights, the National Assembly assigned this responsibility elsewhere. See Jean Noël Luc, "Le rachat des droits féodaux dans le département de la Charente-Intérieure (1789–1793)," in Albert Soboul (ed.), *Contributions á l'histoire paysanne de la Révolution française* (Paris, 1977), pp. 314–15.

23 Merlin de Douai introduced his committee's report on the feudal rights to the National Assembly on 8 February 1790: "it is high time that we present the people a law whose justice will silence the selfish feudatory who has been screaming so indecently about spoliation for the past six months, a law whose wisdom may lead the peasant to return his duty, that peasant whom resentment over a long oppression could temporarily lead astray." *AP*, 11: 498–9.

24 The National Assembly voted on which rights to indemnify in March 1790 but did not settle on the rates until May. The rates of indemnification discussed varied and, over time, became more favorable to the peasants. Boncerf's pamphlet of 1776 proposed fifty or sixty times their annual value, the duke d'Aiguillon suggested thirty times on 4 August 1789, and the rate established in May 1790 was twenty to twenty-five, depending on the particular right. See Boncerf, *Les inconvéniens*, p. 11; *AP*, 8: 344, *AP*, 15: 365–6.

25 The extent to which rural France authentically speaks through the parish *cahiers* has been debated among historians for a long time. For a detailed treatment of this issue, see Gilbert Shapiro and John Markoff, "L'authenticité des cahiers de doléances," *Bulletin d'histoire de la Révolution française* (1990–1): 17–70.

26 Markoff, "Peasants Protest," p. 433.

27 The peasants rarely paid the indemnities. In some places, very few took advantage of the indemnificatory aspects of the new laws; in others, some people did, but these were largely not peasants. In Charente-Inférieure, merchants, legal professionals, administrators, and urban *seigneurs* were the main users of the elaborate indemnification procedures. Similarly in the *départements* studied in Brittany, Normandy, Franche-Comté, Champagne, and Limousin, indemnification seems hardly to have taken place at all. The *département* of Corrèze appears unusual in the extent of peasant utilization of the legal route (at least in the hill country – lowland Corrèze refused participation). See Luc, "Le rachat des droits féodaux," pp, 332–3, 345; and J.N. Luc, *Paysans et droits féodaux en Charente-Inférieure pendant la Révolution française* (Paris, 1984), pp. 125–59; André Ferradou, *Le rachat des droits féodaux en Haut-Vienne* (Limoges, 1939); Jean Millot, *L'abolition des droits seigneuriaux dans le département du*

Doubs et la région comtoise (Besançon, 1941), pp. 172–96; Georges Lefebvre, *Les paysans du Nord pendant la Révolution française* (Paris, 1972), pp. 387–90; Philippe Goujard, "L'abolition de la féodalité dans le district de Neuchâtel (Seine-Inférieure)," in Soboul, (ed.), *Contributions à l'histoire paysanne*, pp. 366–73; Donald Sutherland, *The Chouans: The Social Origins of Popular Counter-revolution in Upper Brittany, 1770–1796* (Oxford, 1982), pp. 139–41; Jean-Jacques Clère, *Les paysans de la Haute-Marne et la Révolution française: Recherches sur les structures foncières de la communauté villageoise (1780–1825)* (Paris, 1988), pp. 189–91; Jean Boutier, *Campagnes en émoi: Révoltes et Révolution en bas-Limousin, 1789–1800* (Treignac, 1987), pp. 146–51.

28 A country lawyer representing his parish at the electoral assembly in Ploërmel recalled in his memoirs how he first gained and then lost the support of other rural delegates in the course of debating the *cahier*. An initial denunciation of privilege brought him considerable notice and made him a front runner for election to the Estates General: a later, judicious speech on behalf of indemnification as a compromise could not even be finished in the face of shouts, threats, and clenched fists. See Roger Dupuy, "Les émeutes anti-féodales de Haute-Bretagne (janvier 1790 et janvier 1791): Meneurs improvisés ou agitateurs politisés?," in Jean Nicolas (ed.), *Mouvements populaires et conscience sociale, XVIᵉ–XIXᵉ siècles* (Paris, 1985), p. 452.

29 *AP*, 11: 500.

30 For a few instances among many, see Boutier, *Campagnes en émoi*; Clère, *Paysans de la Haute-Marne*; Hubert C. Johnson, *The Midi in Revolution: A Study of Regional Political Diversity, 1789–93* (Princeton. N. J., 1986); Michel Vovelle, "Les campagnes à l'assaut des villes sous la révolution," in Vovelle (ed.), *Ville et campagne au 18ᵉ siècle: Chartres et la Beauce* (Paris, 1980), pp. 227–76.

31 Ado, *Krest'ianskoe dvizhenie vo frantsii*.

32 Jean Nicolas, "Les émotions dans l'ordinateur: Premiers résultats d'une enquête collective" (paper presented at Université Paris VII, 1986); "Une jeunesse montée sur le plus grand ton d'insolence," in Robert Chagny (ed.), *Aux origines provinciales de la Révolution* (Grenoble, 1990); Guy Lemarchand, "Troubles populaires aux XVIIIᵉ siècle et conscience de classe: Une préface à la Révolution française," *Annales historiques de la Révolution française*, no. 279 (1990): 32–48.

33 The sources for the data file on insurrection included reports to the revolutionary legislatures found in *Archives parlementaires* as well as the monographic research of later historians, more than one hundred of which were used. The ultimate sources for nineteenth and twentieth-century publications are usually administrators' reports, police and judicial records, and the letters or memoirs of witnesses (who were often victims).

34 If a group of country people invades the lord's château and menacingly insist that he feed them, is this primarily an invocation of a rule of hospitality, mockingly parodied in order to demonstrate that the lord's former dependents are now the enforcers of the rules? Or are these essentially hungry people seeking food? Is it an "anti-seigneurial" or a "subsistence" action? We cannot reconstruct the state of mind of the participants, but there were no doubt diverse motives within a group insisting that the lord feed them. Some (or all) of the participants may have had a mixture of motives. It is, in any event, improbable that we can discover the precise mix in any particular crowd. Nor are the attributions of motive by participants and observers necessarily more credible than those of historians. One should not take a frightened lord's testimony or the hastily penned letter of a local official as authoritative on such a matter – even when the reporter comments on motive. Rather than attempt to decide whether to regard such an event as essentially anti-seigneurial or essentially subsistence in character, I regard it as both.

35 For instance, at the same time that neighboring villages in Cambrésis were breaking into local abbeys to seize grain, in early May 1789 a dozen communities around Oisy

exterminated a lord's game. Georges Lefebvre, *Les paysans du Nord pendant la Révolution française* (Paris, 1972), p. 356.

36 For example, on 26 March 1789, the holdings of the count de Gallifet near Draguignan were attacked by peasants who drove their livestock onto his sown fields, ruining them. Jules Viguier, *La convocation des Etats-Généraux en Provence* (Paris, 1896), pp. 269–70.

37 Local officials reported on 25 November 1790, that fruit trees of the abbey of Beaubec in Normandy were cut down, a rather late date for collecting fruit. See Philippe Goujard, *L'abolition de la "féodalité" dans le pays de Bray (1789–1793)* (Paris, 1979), p. 99.

38 To take one large group of instances: in the spring of 1791, peasant communities around Uzerche, Tulle, and Brive fought what Jean Boutier calls "the war against the ponds," in which large numbers of peasants seized the lords' fish and, in the process, destroyed them, a point seen favorably by local urban radicals who regarded the ponds as environmentally damaging. See Boutier, *Campagnes en émoi*, pp. 118–24.

39 Keeping rabbits and pigeons and hunting were often, in principle, activities constrained by customary legal codes, a set of codes often violated, however. A typical rule might be that all lords in the province could have "closed" warrens (surrounded by walls or water-filled moats), but "open" warrens were only permitted to those with enough land so that neighbors' crops were not ravaged. See Marcel Garaud, *La révolution et la propriété foncière* (Paris, 1958), p. 92.

40 In a similar vein, Jean-Pierre Hirsch distinguishes between those for whom hunting in the summer of 1789 was "a pleasure long forbidden," those who experienced "the sensation of at last achieving the dignity of bearing arms," and those "moved simply by hunger." See Hirsch, *La nuit du 4 août* (Paris, 1978), p. 234. Jean-Sylvain Bailly, first mayor of revolutionary Paris, believed that the "disastrous" outpouring of hunting that first summer spared the lands of "patriot princes" such as the duke of Orléans. If this claim could be confirmed, it also would assign hunger a reduced place as motive. See *Mémoires de Bailly* (Paris, 1821), 2: p. 244.

41 See, for example, Saint-Jacob, *Les paysans de la Bourgogne du Nord*, pp. 428–34: Cobban, *Social Interpretation of the French Revolution*, pp. 47–9.

42 See Markoff, *Abolition of Feudalism*.

43 Indeed, in some places, the agents may have turned into the local leadership once the lord was pushed aside, as Jean-Pierre Jessenne found in the most detailed study to date of the revolution's transformation of village politics. In Artois, those whose power had been conferred by the lords before 1789 did well in the municipal elections of 1790, unless the local community was at legal loggerheads with the lord – a situation that identified the agent too closely, Jessenne contends, with his master. The lord's appointed *lieutenant* became the revolution's elected mayor. The 1790 elections were no fluke, for the same groups did well in 1791. While the 1792 upheaval brought in mid-size landowners, urbanites, and artisans, these newcomers continued the same policies locally; and the post-Thermidor era saw the triumphant and long-lived return of the village élite. Perhaps future research may reveal whether the success of the former seigneurial agents of Artois was duplicated elsewhere – especially in the zones of staunch early anti-seigneurial activism such as around Mâçon, in Franche-Comté, Dauphiné, and coastal Provence or in later anti-seigneurial epicenters such as Quercy, Périgord, and upper Brittany. At present, the *cahiers* data show how rare verbal attacks on these agents were. See Jessenne, *Pouvoir au village et Révolution: Artois 1760–1848* (Lille, 1987).

44 For a similar judgment, see Jessenne, *Pouvoir au village*, p. 59.

45 Even Voltaire had the right to display an elaborate gallows when he climbed his way to the proper status. See Fernand Caussy, *Voltaire, seigneur de village* (Paris, 1912), p. 3.

46 Mona Ozouf, *La fête révolutionnaire 1789–1799* (Paris, 1976), pp. 280–316.

47 Schama recognizes how little violence there was in the countryside against the lord's person, as opposed to the emblems of his authority, but that does not lead him to a more complex analysis of violence. See Schama, *Citizens*, p. 434.

48 I remind the reader that these classifications are not exclusive ones. In early 1790, Figure 2 shows 87 per cent of incidents having an anti-seigneurial character, while 27 per cent have a religious aspect. This comes about because some of those anti-seigneurial events are attacks on ecclesiastical lords (usually monasteries).

49 Régine Robin, "Fief et seigneurie dans le droit et l'idéologie juridique à la fin du XVIIIᵉ siècle, *Annales historiques de la Révolution française*, 43 (1971): 554–602; Claude Mazauric, "Note sur l'emploi du 'régime féodal' et de 'féodalité' pendant la Révolution française," in his *Sur la Révolution française: Contributions à l'histoire de la révolution bourgeoise* (Paris, 1970), pp. 119–34; Alain Guerreau, "Fief, féodalité, féodalisme: Enjeux sociaux et réflexion historienne," *Annales: Economies, sociétés, civilisations*, 45 (1990): 134–66; Rolf Reichardt and Eberhard Schmitt, "La Révolution française – rupture ou continuité? Pour une conceptualisation plus nuancée," in Reichardt and Schmitt (eds.), *Ancien Regime: Aufklärung und Revolution* (Munich, 1983), pp. 4–71; Diego Veinturino. "La naissance de l'Ancien Régime," in Colin Lucas (ed.), *The French Revolution and the Creation of a Modern Political Culture* (New York, 1987), 2: pp. 11–40; John Markoff, "Burzÿ uazja rewolucyjna definiuje system feudalny," in Andrzej Zybertowicz and Adam Czarnota (eds.), *Interpretacje Wielkiej Transformacji: Geneza kapitalizmu jako geneza wspótczesności* (Warsaw, 1989), pp. 357–89.

50 The history of the revolutionary legislation is treated in Henri Doniol, *La Révolution française et la féodalité* (Paris, 1876); Emile Chénon, *Les démembrements de la propriété foncière avant et après la Révolution* (Paris, 1923); Philippe Sagnac, *La législation civile de la Révolution française* (Paris, 1898); Alphonse Aulard, *La Révolution française et le régime féodal* (Paris, 1919); Garaud, *La Révolution et la propriété foncière*; Peter M. Jones, *The Peasantry in the French Revolution* (Cambridge, 1988).

51 Pierre Muret, "L'affaire des princes possessionés d'Alsace et les origines du conflit entre la Révolution et l'Empire," *Revue d'histoire moderne et contemporaine*, 1 (1899–1900): 433–56, 566–92.

52 *AP*, 20: 81.

53 T.C.W. Blanning, *The Origins of the French Revolutionary Wars* (London, 1986), pp. 74–5.

54 *AP*, 20: 84.

55 Sydney Seymour Biro, *The German Policy of Revolutionary France* (Cambridge, Mass., 1957), 1: pp. 39–42. See also T.C.W. Blanning, *The French Revolution in Germany: Occupation and Resistance in the Rhineland, 1792–1802* (Oxford, 1983), pp. 59–69; Muret, "L'affaire des princes possessionés."

56 *AP*, 35: 441–3.

57 *AP*, 36: 79. The speaker, Anacharsis Cloots, might have been buoyed by thoughts of the recent peasant uprising, in August 1790, in Saxony. See Jerome Blum, *The End of the Old Order in Rural Europe* (Princeton, N.J., 1978), pp. 337–8.

58 For example, Louvet in December 1791 (*AP*, 36: 381).

59 *AP*, 39: 89–90, *AP*, 39: 97.

60 Maximilien Robespierre, *Oeuvres* (Paris, 1950), 8, p. 81.

61 Georges Couthon, *Discours sur le rachat des droits seigneuriaux prononcé à la séance du mercredi 29 février 1792* (Paris, 1792), pp. 2–3, 3, 7.

62 *AP*, 39: 595, 41: 470–74, 42: 21, 45: 17–18, 119–23, 53: 473, 55: 70, 75, 101.

63 *AP*, 45: pp. 119–23.

64 It seems a reasonable assumption that few peasant challengers availed themselves of the opportunity to mount a legal challenge under the earlier legislation and that fewer lords did so after August 1792. Withholding payments would seem to have been a more promising action for peasants in the earlier phase and despair the most likely response of the lords later on. But scholarly research into the utilization (or presumed

lack of it) of the judicial arena in peasant/lord conflict during the revolution is too inadequate to permit certainty.

65 This is in accord with the notion of a peasantry engaged in aggressive actions for instrumental ends; but note that just before this sharp decline, there is a short, sharp rise in anti-seigneurial acts. In this latter group of actions, which are among the most destructive of property in the entire data series, we are probably seeing acts of vengeance against the now politically vulnerable fomer lords.

66 *AP*, 53: 473.

67 *AP*, 55: 70.

68 *AP*, 55: 76.

69 *AP*, 60: 290–94.

70 *AP*, 66: 4, *AP*, 69: 98.

71 Couthon, *Discours*, p. 5. A puzzled National Assembly was told that the rural National Guards would not enforce decrees held to be fraudulent, that the new laws were not believed to be the work of the Assembly at all but of the former lords. *AP*, 21: 457.

72 *AP*, 55: 72–73, *AP*, 56: 65, 74.

73 The other European powers, when triumphant over French arms, sometimes showed an acceptance of the French definition of the international struggle as a war over feudalism by attempting to undo the emancipatory reforms, as in Hannover, Hesse-Cassel, or the Napoleonic Kingdom of Westphalia. Blum, *End of the Old Order*, pp. 362–70. The most interesting such restoration attempt was in the Austrian-occupied portion of northern France in 1793–94. With the half-hearted support of the Austrian army, lords and ecclesiastics attempted to collect but were largely stymied by peasant evasion of payment. Lefebvre, *Paysans du Nord*, pp. 551–5.

74 Given the variety of rights lords held over peasants, there is some ambiguity in defining just which measure should be taken as initiating effective emancipation. Does one date France's process from the decree of 4–11 August 1789, for example, or from the king's limited abolition of serfdom on his own holdings in 1779? The ambiguities of dating the end points of emancipation are even more hazardous: many emancipatory processes trailed off with monopoly rights or tolls or sometimes other claims still alive and well, for example. As a guide through these and other difficulties in comparative observation, I have largely relied on Blum.

75 Max Bruchet, *L'abolition des droits seigneuriaux en Savoie (1761–1793)* (Annecy, 1908).

76 Blum, *End of the Old Order*, p. 386.

77 Blum, *End of the Old Order*, pp. 219–20, 385–6. Unmarried male servants, for instance, could not leave their employer until 1840 and then only if they were over twenty-eight.

78 Blum, *End of the Old Order*, p. 364.

79 Blum, *End of the Old Order*, pp. 384–5.

80 Blum, *End of the Old Order*, p. 406.

81 This is not to deny that, at points, élites made fearful by the French example may well have delayed or aborted emancipation processes. In Austria, for example, the French Revolution further energized a conservative current that was already successfully combating the reforms of Joseph II. See Ernest Wangermann, *From Joseph II to the Jacobin Trials: Government Policy and Public Opinion in the Habsburg Dominions in the Period of the French Revolution* (Oxford, 1969).

82 G. Spira. "La dernière génération des serfs de Hongrie: L'exemple du comitat de Pest," *Annales: Economies, sociétes, civilisations*, 23 (1968): 366–2.

83 Readers might object, following Figure 8.2, that the great peak of rural unrest immediately preceding the August decrees was not primarily anti-seigneurial. True enough, but the crescendo of rural violence of the second half of July surely concentrated the legislators' minds on taking some action to pacify the countryside.

84 Robert R. Palmer, "Notes on the Use of the Word 'Democracy,' 1789–1799," *Political Science Quarterly*, 68 (1953): 203–26; Otto Brunner, Werner Conze, and Reinhart

Koselleck (eds.), *Geschichtlich Grundbegriffe: Historisches Lexikon zur politisch-sozialen Sprach in Deutschland* (Stuttgart, 1972–84), Vol. 1, pp. 821–99; John Dunn, *Western Political Theory in the Face of the Future* (Cambridge, 1993), pp. 1–28.

85 "Night of August 4," in François Furet and Mona Ozouf (eds.), *A Critical Dictionary of the French Revolution* (Cambridge, Mass., 1989), p. 131.

86 On this topic, see Carol Pateman, *The Disorder of Women: Democracy, Feminism and Political Theory* (Stanford, Calif., 1989).

87 Michel Antoine, *Le Conseil du Roi sous le règne de Louis XV* (Paris, 1970), pp. 7–9.

Part IV

GENDER AND
COLONIAL STUDIES

Women, wake up; the tocsin of reason sounds throughout the universe; recognize your rights. The powerful empire of nature is no longer surrounded by prejudice, fanaticism, superstition, and lies. The torch of truth has dispersed all the clouds of folly and usurpation. Enslaved man has multiplied his force and needs yours to break his chains.

Olympe de Gouges
The Declaration of the Rights of Women

9

THE MANY BODIES OF MARIE ANTOINETTE

Political pornography and the problem of the feminine in the French Revolution

Lynn Hunt

Lynn Hunt formulates a new question for historians to ponder, and the answers she develops take scholarship in an exciting direction. She does not ask whether Marie Antoinette was guilty or innocent of the crimes charged against her; nor is she interested per se in why the queen was so hated by the French people even before the Revolution began. Rather, she wonders why such a rich pornographic literature about the queen – reaching as many as 126 pamphlets – infiltrated the country both before and during the revolutionary epoch.

Armed with both feminist and literary criticism at her side, and echoing current debates over the ways in which obscene literature exploits women in our own society, Hunt uses the case of Queen Marie Antoinette to reveal Jacobin attitudes towards gender and sexuality. The queen became emblematic of any woman's attempt to play a public and political role. The revolutionaries tended to view republican politics as an ordinary man's game: not only were monarchs excluded, but all women as well. Here Hunt offers a sharp indictment of revolutionary political culture as being self-consciously masculinist.

* * *

It has long been known that Marie Antoinette was the subject of a substantial erotic and pornographic literature in the last decades of the Old Regime and during the Revolution itself. Royal figures at many times and in many places have been the subject of such writing, but not all royal figures at all times. When royal bodies become the focus of such interest, we can be sure that something is at issue in the larger body politic. As Robert Darnton has shown, for example, the sexual sensationalism of Old Regime *libelles* was a choice means of attacking the entire "establishment" – the court, the church, the aristocracy, the academies, the salons, and the monarchy itself.[1] Marie Antoinette occupies a curious place in this literature; she was not only lampooned and demeaned in an increasingly ferocious pornographic outpouring, but she was also tried and executed.

A few other women, such as Louis XV's notorious mistress Madame Du Barry, suffered a similar fate during the Revolution, but no other trial attracted the same attention or aired the same range of issues as that of the ill-fated queen. The king's trial, in contrast, remained entirely restricted to a consideration of his political crimes. As a consequence, the trial of the queen, especially in its strange refractions of the pornographic literature, offers a unique and fascinating perspective on the unselfconscious presumptions of the revolutionary political imagination. It makes manifest, more perhaps than any other single event of the Revolution, the underlying interconnections between pornography and politics.

When Marie Antoinette was finally brought to trial in October 1793, the notorious public prosecutor, Antoine-Quentin Fouquier-Tinville, delivered an accusation against her that began with extraordinary language, even for those inflamed times:

> In the manner of the Messalinas-Brunhildes, Fredegond and Médecis, whom one called in previous times queens of France, and whose names forever odious will not be effaced from the annals of history, Marie Antoinette, widow of Louis Capet, has been since her time in France, the scourge and the bloodsucker of the French.

The bill of indictment then went on to detail the charges: before the Revolution she had squandered the public monies of France on her "disorderly pleasures" and on secret contributions to the Austrian emperor (her brother); after the Revolution, she was the animating spirit of counter-revolutionary conspiracies at the court. Since the former queen was a woman, it was presumed that she could only achieve her perfidious aims through the agency of men such as the king's brothers and Lafayette. Most threatening, of course, was her influence on the king; she was charged not only with the crime of having had perverse ministers named to office but more significantly and generally with having taught the king how to dissimulate – that is, how to promise one thing in public and plan another in the shadows of the court. Finally, and to my mind most strangely, the bill of indictment specifically claimed that

> the widow Capet, immoral in every way, new Agrippina, is so perverse and so familiar with all crimes that, forgetting her quality of mother and the demarcation prescribed by the laws of nature, she has not stopped short of indulging herself with Louis-Charles Capet, her son, and on the confession of this last, in indecencies whose idea and name make us shudder with horror.[2]

Incest was the final crime, whose very suggestion was cause for horror.

The trial of a queen, especially in a country whose fundamental laws specifically excluded women from ruling, must necessarily be unusual. There was not much in the way of precedent for it – the English, after all, had only tried their king, not his wife – and the relatively long gap between the trial of Louis (in

December and January) and that of his queen ten months later seemed even to attenuate the necessary linkage between the two trials. Unlike her husband, Marie Antoinette was not tried by the Convention itself; she was brought before the Revolutionary Criminal Tribunal like all other suspects in Paris, and there her fate was decided by a male jury and nine male judges.[3]

Because queens could never rule in France, except indirectly as regents for under-age sons, they were not imagined as having the two bodies associated with kings. According to the "mystic fiction of the 'King's Two Bodies'" as analyzed by Ernst Kantorowicz, kings in England and France had both a visible, corporeal, mortal body and an invisible, ideal "body politic," which never died. As the French churchman Bossuet explained in a sermon he gave with Louis XIV present in 1662: "You are of the gods, even if you die, your authority never dies. . . . The man dies, it is true, but the king, we say, never dies."[4] It is questionable whether this doctrine still held for French kings by 1793, but it is certain that it never held for French queens. We might then ask why the destruction of the queen's mortal body could have had such interest for the French. What did her decidedly non-mystical body represent? In this chapter, I argue that it represented many things; Marie Antoinette had, in a manner of speaking, many bodies. These many bodies, hydralike, to use one of the favorite revolutionary metaphors for counter-revolution, were each in turn attacked and destroyed because they represented the threats, conscious and unconscious, that could be posed to the Republic. These were not threats of just the ordinary sort, for the queen represented, not only the ultimate in counter-revolutionary conspiracy, but also the menace of the feminine and the effeminizing to republican notions of manhood and virility.

Most striking is the way in which the obsessive focus on the queen's sexualized body was carried over from the pamphlets and caricatures to the trial itself. In the trial there were frequent references to the "orgies" held at Versailles, which were dated as beginning precisely in 1779 and continuing into 1789. In his closing statement Fouquier-Tinville collapsed sexual and political references in telling fashion when he denounced "the perverse conduct of the former court," Marie Antoinette's "criminal and culpable liaisons" with unfriendly foreign powers, and her "intimacies with a villainous faction."[5] Herman, president of the court, then took up the baton in his summary of the charges against her: he too referred to "her intimate liaisons with infamous ministers, perfidious generals, disloyal representatives of the people." He denounced again the "orgy" at the chateau of Versailles on October 1, 1789, when the queen had presumably encouraged the royal officers present to trample on the revolutionary tricolor cockade. In short, Marie Antoinette had used her sexual body to corrupt the body politic either through "liaisons" or "intimacies" with criminal politicians or through her ability to act sexually upon the king, his ministers, or his soldiers.

In Herman's long denunciation, the queen's body was also held up for scrutiny for signs of interior intentions and motives. On her return from the flight to Varennes, people could observe on her face and her movements "the most marked desire for vengeance." Even when she was incarcerated in the

Temple her jailers could "always detect in Antoinette a tone of revolt against the sovereignty of the people."[6] Capture, imprisonment, and the prospect of execution, it was hoped, were finally tearing the veil from the queen's threatening ability to hide her true feelings from the public. Note here, too, the way that Herman clearly juxtaposes the queen and the people as a public force; revelation of the queen's true motives and feelings came not from secrets uncovered in hidden correspondence but from the ability of the people or their representatives to "read" her body.

The attention to the queen's body continued right up to the moment of her execution. At the moment of the announcement of her condemnation to death, she was reported to have kept "a calm and assured countenance," just as she had during the interrogation. On the road to the scaffold, she appeared indifferent to the large gathering of armed forces. "One perceived neither despondency nor pride on her face."[7] More radical newspapers read a different message in her demeanor, but they showed the same attention to her every move. The *Révolutions de Paris* claimed that at the feet of the statue of Liberty (where the guillotine was erected), she demonstrated her usual "character of dissimulation and pride up to the last moment". On the way there she had expressed "surprise and indignation" when she realized that she would be taken to the guillotine in a simple cart rather than in a carriage.[8]

The queen's body, then, was of interest, not because of its connection to the sacred and divine, but because it represented the opposite principle – namely, the possible profanation of everything that the nation held sacred. But apparent too in all the concern with the queen's body was the fact that the queen could embody so much. The queen did not have a mystic body in the sense of the king's two bodies, but her body was mystical in the sense of mysteriously symbolic. It could mean so much; it could signify a wide range of threats. Dissimulation was an especially important motif in this regard. The ability to conceal one's true emotions, to act one way in public and another in private, was repeatedly denounced as the chief characteristic of court life and aristocratic manners in general. These relied above all on appearances – that is, on the disciplined and self-conscious use of the body as a mask. The republicans, consequently, valued transparency – the unmediated expression of the heart – above all other personal qualities. Transparency was the perfect fit between public and private; transparency was a body that told no lies and kept no secrets. It was the definition of virtue, and as such it was imagined to be critical to the future of the Republic.[9] Dissimulation, in contrast, threatened to undermine the Republic: it was the chief ingredient in every conspiracy; it lay at the heart of the counter-revolution. Thus, for example, to charge Marie Antoinette with teaching the king how to dissimulate was no minor accusation.

Dissimulation was also described in the eighteenth century as a characteristically feminine quality, not just an aristocratic one. According to both Montesquieu and Rousseau, it was women who taught men how to dissimulate, how to hide their true feelings in order to get what they wanted in the public arena.[10] The salon was the most important site of this teaching, and it was also the one place where society women could enter the public sphere. In a sense, then, women in public (like prostitutes) were synonymous with dissimulation, with the gap between public and private. Virtue could only be restored if women returned to the private sphere.[11] Rousseau had expressed this collection of attitudes best in his *Letter to M. d'Alembert on the Theatre* (1758):

> Meanly devoted to the wills of the sex which we ought to protect and not serve, we have learned to despise it in obeying it, to insult it by our derisive attentions; and every woman at Paris gathers in her apartment a harem of men more womanish than she, who know how to render all sorts of homage to beauty except that of the heart, which is her due.

And, as Rousseau warned ominously about women in the public sphere, "no longer wishing to tolerate separation, unable to make themselves into men, the women make us into women."[12] With her strategic position on the cusp between public and private, Marie Antoinette was emblematic of the much larger problem of the relations between women and the public sphere in the eighteenth century. The sexuality of women, when operating in the public sphere through dissimulation, threatened to effeminize men – that is, literally to transform men's bodies.

Central to the queen's profane and profaning body was the image of her as the bad mother. This might take many, even surprising forms, as in Fouquier-Tinville's charge that she was the calumniator of Paris – described in his closing statement as "this city, mother and conservator of liberty." The queen was the antonym of the nation, depicted by one witness in the trial as the "generous nation that nurtured her as well as her husband and her family."[13] The nation, Paris, and the Revolution were all good mothers; Marie Antoinette was the bad mother. It should be noted, however, that the nation, Paris, and the Revolution were motherly in a very abstract, even non-feminine fashion (in comparison to Marie Antoinette).

The abstractness and non-sexual nature of these political figures of the mother reinforces what Carole Pateman has tellingly described as the characteristic modern Western social contract:

> The story of the original contract is perhaps the greatest tale of men's creation of new political life. But this time women are already defeated and declared procreatively and politically irrelevant. Now the father comes under attack. The original contract shows how his monopoly of politically creative power is seized and shared equally among men. In civil society all men, not just fathers, can generate political life and political right. Political creativity belongs not to paternity but masculinity.[14]

Thus, *La Nation* had no real feminine qualities; she was not a threatening effeminizing force and hence not incompatible with republicanism. *La Nation* was, in effect, a masculine mother, or a father capable of giving birth. Marie Antoinette's body stood in the way, almost literally, of this version of the social contract, since under the Old Regime she had given birth to potential new sovereigns herself.[15]

Pateman is unusual among commentators on contract theory because she takes Freud seriously. As she notes,

> Freud's stories make explicit that power over women and not only freedom is at issue before the original agreement is made, and he also makes clear that two realms [the civil and the private, the political and the sexual] are created through the original pact.[16]

She is less successful, however, at explaining the preoccupation with incest in a case such as Marie Antoinette's.

The charge of incest in the trial was brought by the radical journalist Jacques-René Hébert, editor of the scabrous *Père Duchesne*, the most determinedly "popular" newspaper of the time. Hébert appeared at the trial in his capacity as assistant city attorney for Paris, but his paper had been notorious for its continuing attacks on the queen. Hébert testified that he had been called to the Temple prison by Simon, the shoemaker who was assigned to look after Louis's son. Simon had surprised the eight-year-old masturbating ("indecent pollutions"), and when he questioned the boy about where he had learned such practices, Louis-Charles replied that his mother and his aunt (the king's sister) had taught him. The king's son was asked to repeat his accusations in the presence of the mayor and city attorney, which he did, claiming that the two women often made him sleep between them. Hébert concluded that

> There is reason to believe that this criminal enjoyment [*jouissance* in French, which has several meanings including pleasure, and orgasm] was not at all dictated by pleasure, but rather by the political hope of enervating the physical health of this child, whom they continued to believe would occupy a throne, and on whom they wished, by this maneuver, to assure themselves of the right of ruling afterwards over his morals.

The body of the child showed the effects of this incestuousness; one of his testicles had been injured and had to be bandaged. Since being separated from his mother, Hébert reported, the child's health had become much more robust and vigorous.[17] What better emblem could there be of effeminization than the actual deterioration of the boy's genitals?

As sensational as the charge was, the court did not pursue it much further. When directly confronted with the accusation, the former queen refused to lower herself by responding "to such a charge made against a mother."[18] But there it was in the newspapers, and even the Jacobin Club briefly noted the "shameful scenes between the mother, the aunt, and the son," and denounced "the virus that now runs through [the boy's] veins and which perhaps carries the germ of all sorts of accidents."[19] Since it seems surprising that republican men should be so worried about the degeneration of the royal family, it is not farfetched to conclude that the incest charge had a wider, if largely unconscious, resonance. On the most explicit level, incest was simply another sign of the criminal nature of royalty. As Hébert complained rhetorically to the royalists: "You immolate your brothers, and for what? For an old whore, who has neither faith nor respect for the law, who has made more than a million men die; you are the champions of murder, brigandage, adultery, and incest."[20] Although incest can hardly be termed a major theme in revolutionary discourse, it did appear frequently in the political pornography of both the last decades of the Old Regime and the revolutionary decade itself.[21] Perhaps the most striking example is the pornography of the marquis de Sade, which makes much of incest between fathers and daughters and brothers and sisters.[22]

The official incest charge against the queen has to be set in the context provided by the longer history of pornographic and semi-pornographic pamphlets about the queen's private life. Although the charge itself was based on presumed activities that took place only after the incarceration of the royal family in the Temple prison, it was made more plausible by the scores of pamphlets that had appeared since the earliest days of the Revolution and that had, in fact, had their origins in the political pornography of the Old Regime itself. When the *Révolutions de Paris* exclaimed, "Who could forget the scandalous morals of her private life," or repeated the charges about "her secret orgies with d'Artois [one of the king's brothers], Fersen, Coigny, etc.," the newspaper was simply recalling to readers' minds what they had long imbibed in underground publications about the queen's promiscuity.

Attacks on the queen's morality had begun as early as 1774 (just four years after her arrival in France) with a satirical lampoon about her early morning promenades. Louis XV paid considerable sums in the same year to buy up existing copies in London and Amsterdam of a pamphlet that detailed the sexual impotence of his grandson, the future Louis XVI.[23] Before long, the songs and "little papers" had become frankly obscene, and the first of many long, detailed pamphlets had been published clandestinely. The foremost expert on the subject found 126 pamphlets he could classify in the genre of Marie Antoinette, libertine.[24] Even before the notorious Diamond Necklace Affair of 1785, and continuing long after it, the queen was the focus of an always-proliferating literature of derision preoccupied with her sexual body.[25]

Although fewer than 10 per cent of the anti-Marie Antoinette pamphlets were published before 1789, they often provided the models for later publications.[26] It is difficult to find out much about the publication (the precise dates or location) or authorship of the pre-revolutionary pamphlets, since they were necessarily produced clandestinely. As Robert Darnton has vividly demonstrated, those authors who can be traced were from the French version of Grub Street.[27] Men such as Théveneau de Morande and the count of Paradès worked sometimes for the French crown (as spies), sometimes for rival members of the court, sometimes for foreign printers, and always for themselves. The connection to members of the court is most significant, since it shows the intensity of the interlacing of social networks of communication under the Old Regime. The author of one of the best-known pamphlets, *Portefeuille d'un talon rouge*, made the connection explicit, tracing the circuit from courtiers to their valets, who passed the verses on in the market, where they were picked up by artisans and brought back to the courtiers, who then hypocritically professed surprise.[28] The "popular" images of the queen, then, had their origin in the court, not in the streets.

Politically pornographic pamphlets were often traced to London, Amsterdam, or Germany, where the most notorious of the French Grub Street types made their livings, and the French crown evidently spent large sums having such pamphlets bought up by its agents abroad and destroyed before they could reach France. Indeed, this new industry seems to have become a very lucrative one for those hack writers willing to live abroad, since large sums were paid to secret agents and printers, who were most likely in collusion with the writers themselves.[29] In 1782 the *Mémoires secrets* described the government's reaction to the recently published *Essais historiques*:

> The dreadful *libelle* against the queen, of which I've spoken [in a previous entry], and others of the same genre, have determined the government to make an effort on this subject and to sacrifice money, which is very distasteful; with this help they have gotten to the source and asked for the assistance of foreign governments. They undertook searches in all of the suspect printing shops of Holland and Germany; they took away everything that deserved to be, and they have even had the printer-booksellers arrested who have taken the chance of coming to France to introduce their merchandise; they have had them condemned to large fines.[30]

Needless to say, copies still made their way into France; in 1783, 534 copies of *Essais historiques sur la vie de Marie-Antoinette* were officially destroyed at the Bastille prison along with many other offensive productions.[31]

Many of the major accusations against Marie Antoinette were already present in the pre-revolutionary pamphlets. The *Portefeuille d'un talon rouge* (also condemned in 1783) begins in classic eighteenth-century fashion with a preface from the presumed publisher announcing that someone had found a portfolio while crossing the Palais-Royal (the notorious den of prostitution and gambling that was also the residence of the king's cousin, the duke of Orleans, who was assumed to have paid for many of the pamphlets). In it was found a manuscript addressed to Monsieur de la H— of the Académie française. It began, "You are then out of your mind, my dear la H—! You want, they tell me, to write the history of tribades at Versailles." In the text appeared the soon-to-be-standard allegation that Marie Antoinette was amorously involved with the duchesse de Polignac ("her Jules") and Madame Balbi. The comte d'Artois was supposedly the only man who interested her. These charges, as harshly delivered as they were, formed only part of the pamphlet's more general tirade against the court and ministers in general. Speaking of the courtiers, the author exclaimed, "You are an abominable race. You get everything at once from your character as monkeys and as vipers."[32]

The short and witty *Amours de Charlot et de Toinette* took up much the same themes, though in verse, but this time focused exclusively on the queen, the comte d'Artois, and the princesse de Lamballe (who would become the most famous victim of the September Massacres in 1792). Marie Antoinette was depicted as turning to lesbianism because of the impotence of the king. Then she discovers the delights of the king's brother.[33]

The long 1789 edition (146 pages in the augmented French edition) of the *Essai historique sur la vie de Marie-Antoinette* (there had been many variations on the title since its first publication in 1781)[34] already demonstrated the rising tone of personal hostility toward the queen that would characterize revolutionary pornographic pamphlets. In the most detailed of all the anti-Marie Antoinette exposés, it purported to give the queen's own view through the first person: "My death is the object of the desires of an entire people that I oppressed with the greatest barbarism." Marie Antoinette here describes herself as "barbarous queen, adulterous spouse, woman without morals, polluted with crimes and debaucheries," and she details all the charges that had accumulated against her in previous pamphlets. Now her lesbianism is traced back to the Austrian court, and all of the stories of amorous intrigues with princes and great nobles are given substance. Added to the charges is the new one that she herself had poisoned the young heir to the throne (who died in early 1789). Characteristic, too, of many of the later pamphlets will be the curious alternation between frankly pornographic staging – descriptions in the first person of her liaisons, complete with wildly beating hearts and barely stifled sighs of passion – and political moralizing and denunciation put into the mouth of the queen herself. The contrast with the king and his "pure, sincere love, which I so often and so cruelly abused" was striking.[35] The queen may have been representative of the degenerate tendencies of the aristocracy, but she was not yet emblematic of royalty altogether.

With the coming of the Revolution in 1789, the floodgates opened, and the number of pamphlets attacking the queen rapidly rose in number. These took various forms, ranging from songs and fables to presumed biographies (such as the *Essai historique*), confessions, and plays. Sometimes, the writings were pornographic with little explicit political content; the 16-page pamphlet in verse called *Le Godmiché royal* (the royal dildo), for example, told the story of Junon (the queen) and Hébée (presumably either the duchesse de Polignac or the princesse de Lamballe). Junon complained of her inability to obtain satisfaction at home, while pulling a dildo out of her bag ("Happy invention that we owe to the monastery"). Her companion promises her penises of almost unimaginably delicious size.[36] In the much more elaborately pornographic *Fureurs utérines de Marie-Antoinette, femme de Louis XVI* of two years later, colored engravings showed the king impotent and d'Artois and Polignac replacing him.[37]

The Marie Antoinette pamphlets reflect a general tendency in the production of political pornography: the number of titles in this genre rose steadily from 1774 to 1788 and then took off after 1789. The queen was not the only target of hostility; a long series of "private lives" attacked the conduct of courtiers before 1789 and revolutionary politicians from Lafayette to Robespierre afterwards. Aristocrats were shown as impotent, riddled with venereal disease, and given over to debauchery. Homosexuality functioned in a manner similar to impotence in this literature; it showed the decadence of the Old Regime in the person of its priests and aristocrats. Sexual degeneration went hand in hand with political corruption.[38] This proliferation of pornographic pamphlets after 1789 shows that political pornography cannot be viewed simply as a supplement to a political culture that lacked "real" political participation. Once participation increased dramatically, particularly with the explosion of uncensored newspapers and pamphlets, politics did not simply take the high road.[39]

Marie Antoinette was without question the favorite target of such attacks. There were not only more pamphlets about her than about any other single figure, but they were also the most sustained in their viciousness. Henri d'Almeras claimed that the *Essais historiques* alone sold between twenty and thirty thousand copies.[40] The year 1789 does appear to mark a turning-point not only in the number of pamphlets produced but also in their tone. The pre-1789 pamphlets tell dirty stories in secret; after 1789 the rhetoric of the pamphlets begins self-consciously to solicit a wider audience. The public no longer "hears" courtier rumors through the print medium; it now "sees" degeneracy in action. The first-person rendition of the 1789 French edition of *Essai historique* is a good example of this technique.

Obscene engravings with first-person captions worked to the same effect. The engravings that accompanied the long *Vie de Marie-Antoinette d'Autriche, femme de Louis XVI, roi des français; Depuis la perte de son pucelage jusqu'au premier mai 1791*, which was followed by volumes 2 and 3, entitled *Vie privée, libertine, et scandaleuse de Marie-Antoinette d'Autriche, ci-devant reine des français*, are an interesting case in point. They showed Marie Antoinette in amorous embrace with just about everyone imaginable: her first supposed lover, a German officer; the aged Louis XV; Louis XVI impotent; the comte d'Artois; various women; various ménages à trois with two women and a man; the cardinal de Rohan of the Diamond Necklace Affair; Lafayette; Barnave, and so on. The captions are sometimes in the first person (with the princesse de Guéménée: "Dieux! quels transports ah! mon âme s'envole, pour l'exprimer je n'ai plus de parole"), sometimes in the third (with the comte d'Artois: "gémis Louis, ta vigeur inactive, outrage ici ta femme trop lascive"). The effect is the same: a theatricalization of the action so that the reader is made into voyeur and moral judge at the same time. The political effect of the pornography is apparent even in this most obscene of works. In volumes 2 and 3, the pornographic engravings are interspersed with political engravings of aristocratic conspiracy, the assault on the Tuileries palace, and even a curious print showing Louis XVI putting on a red cap of liberty and drinking to the health of the nation in front of the queen and his remaining son and heir.[41]

That the pamphlets succeeded in attracting a public can be seen in the repetition of formulaic expressions in non-pornographic political pamphlets, "popular" newspapers, petitions from "popular societies," and the trial record itself. The *Essai historique* of 1789 already included the soon-to-be-standard comparisons of Marie Antoinette to Catherine de Médecis, Agrippina, and Messalina. These comparisons were expanded at great length in a curious political tract called *Les Crimes des reines de France*, which was written by a woman, Louise de Keralio (though it was published under the name of the publisher, Louis Prudhomme).[42] The "corrected and augmented" edition dated "an II" simply added material on the trial and execution to an already-long version of 1791.[43] The tract is not pornographic; it simply refers to the "turpitudes" committed by the queen as background for its more general political charges. Keralio reviews the history of the queens of France, emphasizing in particular the theme of dissimulation: "The dangerous art of seducing and betraying, perfidious and intoxicating caresses, feigned tears, affected despair, insinuating prayers" (p. 2). These were the weapons of the queens of France (which had been identified as the arms of all women by Rousseau). When the author comes to the wife of Louis Capet, she lists many of the queen's presumed lovers, male and female, but insists upon passing rapidly over the "private crimes" of the queen in favor of consideration of her public ones. Marie Antoinette "was the soul of all the plots, the center of all the intrigues, the foyer of all these horrors" (p. 440). As a "political tarantula," the queen resembled that "impure insect, which, in the darkness, weaves on the right and left fine threads where gnats without experience are caught and of whom she makes her prey" (pp. 445–6). On the next page, the queen is compared to a tigress who, once having tasted blood, can no longer be satisfied. All this to prove what the caption to the frontispiece asserts: "A people is without honor and merits its chains / When it lowers itself beneath the scepter of queens."

The shorter, more occasional political pamphlets picked up the themes of the pornographic literature and used them for straightforward political purposes. A series of pamphlets appeared in 1792, for example, offering lists of political enemies who deserved immediate punishment. They had as their appendices lists of all the people with whom the queen had had "relationships of debauchery." In these pamphlets, the queen was routinely referred to as "mauvaise fille, mauvaise épouse, mauvaise mère, mauvaise reine, monstre en tout" (bad daughter, bad wife, bad mother, bad queen, monster in everything).[44]

The movement from sexual misdemeanors to bestial metaphors was characteristic of much "popular" commentary on the queen, especially in her last months. In the *Père Duchesne* Hébert had incorporated the Fredegond and Médecis comparisons by 1791, but still in a relatively innocent context. One of his favorite devices was to portray himself as meeting in person with the queen and trying to talk sense to her.[45] By 1792 the queen had become "Madame Veto," and once the monarchy had been toppled, Hébert made frequent reference to the "ménagerie royale." In prison the former queen was depicted as a she-monkey ("la guenon d'Autriche"), the king as a pig. In one particularly fanciful scene, Père Duchesne presents himself in the queen's cell as the duchesse de Polignac ("cette tribade") thanks to the effect of a magic ring, whereupon the former queen throws herself into her friend's arms and reveals her fervent hopes for the success of the counter-revolution.[46] After her husband had been executed, the tone of hostility escalated, and Marie Antoinette became the she-wolf and the tigress of Austria. At the time of her trial, Hébert suggested that she be chopped up like meat for paté as recompense for all the bloodshed that she had caused.[47]

Local militants picked up the same rhetoric. In a letter to the Convention congratulating it on the execution of the queen, the popular society of Rozoy (Seine-et-Marne department) referred to "this tigress thirsty for the blood of the French ... this other Messalina whose corrupt heart held the fertile germ of all crimes; may her loathsome memory perish forever." The popular society of Garlin (Basses-Pyrénées department) denounced the "ferocious panther who devoured the French, the female monster whose pores sweated the purest blood of the sans-culottes."[48] Throughout these passages, it is possible to see the horrific transformations of the queen's body; the body that had once been denounced for its debauchery and disorderliness becomes in turn the dangerous beast, the cunning spider, the virtual vampire who sucks the blood of the French.

Explicit in some of the more extreme statements and implicit in many others was a pervasive anxiety about genealogy. For example, the post-1789 pamphlets demonstrated an obsession with determining the true fathers of the king's children (they were often attributed to his brother, the comte d'Artois). In a fascinating twist on this genealogical anxiety, *Père Duchesne* denounced a supposed plot by the queen to raise a young boy who resembled the heir to the throne to take the heir's place.[49] The culminating charge, of course, was incest; in the trial, this was limited to the queen's son, but in the pamphlet literature, the charges of incest included the king's brother, the king's grandfather Louis XV, and her own father, who had taught her "the passion of incest, the dirtiest of pleasures," from which followed "the hatred of the French, the aversion for the duties of spouse and mother, in short, all that reduces humanity to the level of ferocious beasts."[50] Disorderly sexuality was linked to bestialization in the most intimate way.

Promiscuity, incest, poisoning of the heir to the throne, plots to replace the heir with a pliable substitute – all of these charges reflect a fundamental anxiety about queenship as the most extreme form of women invading the public sphere. Where Rousseau had warned that the salon women would turn their "harem of men" into women "more womanish than she," the radical militant Louise de Keralio would warn her readers that "a woman who becomes queen changes sex."[51] The queen, then, was the emblem (and sacrificial victim) of the feared disintegration of gender boundaries that accompanied the Revolution. In his controversial study of ritual violence, René Girard argues that a sacrificial crisis (a crisis in the community that leads to the search for a scapegoat) entails the feared loss of sexual differentiation: "one of the effects of the sacrificial crisis is a certain feminization of the men, accompanied by a masculinization of the women."[52] A scapegoat is chosen in order to reinstitute the community's sense of boundaries. By invoking Girard, I do not mean to suggest that the French Revolution followed his script of sacrificial crisis, or that I subscribe to the nuances of his argument. In fact, the Revolution did not single out a particular scapegoat in the moment of crisis; it was marked instead by a constant search for new victims, as if the community did not have a distinct enough sense of itself to settle upon just one (the king or the queen, for example). Nevertheless, Girard's suggestion that an intense crisis within a community is marked by fears of de-differentiation is very fruitful, for it helps make sense of the peculiar gender charge of the events of the fall of 1793.

The evidence for a feared loss of sexual differentiation in the Revolution is in fact quite extensive. Just two weeks after the execution of the queen (which took place on October 16, 1793), the Convention discussed the participation of women in politics, in particular the women's club called the "Sociéte des républicaines révolutionnaires." The Jacobin deputy Fabre d'Eglantine insisted that "these clubs are not composed of mothers of families, daughters of families, sisters occupied with their younger brothers or sisters, but rather of adventuresses, knights-errant, emancipated women, amazons."[53] The deputy Amar, speaking for the Committee on General Security of the Convention, laid out the official rationale for a separation of women from the public sphere:

> The private functions for which women are destined by their very nature are related to the general order of society; this social order results from the differences between man and woman. Each sex is called to the kind of occupation which is fitting for it. . . . Man is strong, robust, born with great energy, audacity and courage. . . . In general, women are ill suited for elevated thoughts and serious meditations, and if, among ancient peoples, their natural timidity and modesty did not allow them to appear outside their families, then in the French Republic do you want them to be seen coming into the gallery to political assemblies as men do?

To re-establish the "natural order" and prevent the "emancipation" of women from their familial identity, the deputies solemnly outlawed all women's clubs.

In response to a deputation of women wearing red caps that appeared before the Paris city council two weeks later, the well-known radical spokesman (and city official) Chaumette exclaimed:

> It is contrary to all the laws of nature for a woman to want to make herself a man. The Council must recall that some time ago these denatured women, these *viragos*, wandered through the markets with the red cap to sully that badge of liberty. . . . Since when is it permitted to give up one's sex? Since when is it decent to see women abandoning

the pious cares of their households, the cribs of their children, to come to public places, to harangues in galleries, at the bar of the senate?

Chaumette then reminded his audience of the recent fate of the "impudent" Olympe de Gouges and the "haughty" Madame Roland, "who thought herself fit to govern the republic and who rushed to her downfall."[54]

Marie Antoinette was certainly not in alliance with the women of the "Société des républicaines révolutionnaires," with Madame Roland or Olympe de Gouges; they were political enemies. But even political enemies, as Louise de Keralio discovered, shared similar political restrictions if they were women. Keralio herself was accused of being dominated by those same "uterine furies" that beset the queen; by publishing, Keralio too was making herself public. Her detractors put this desire for notoriety down to her ugliness and inability to attract men.[55] As Dorinda Outram has argued, women who wished to participate actively in the French Revolution were caught in a discursive double bind; virtue was a two-edged sword that bisected the sovereign into two different destinies, one male and one female. Male virtue meant participation in the public world of politics; female virtue meant withdrawal into the private world of the family. Even the most prominent female figures of the time had to acquiesce in this division. As Madame Roland recognized, "I knew what role was suitable to my sex and I never abandoned it."[56] Of course, she paid with her life because others did not think that she had so effectively restrained herself from participating in the public sphere.

Read from this perspective on the difference between male and female virtue, the writings and speeches about the queen reveal the fundamental anxieties of republicans about the foundations of their rule. They were not simply concerned to punish a leading counter-revolutionary. They wanted to separate mothers from any public activity, as Carole Pateman argues, and yet give birth by themselves to a new political organism. In order to accomplish this, they had to destroy the Old Regime link between the ruling family and the body politic, between the literal bodies of the rulers and the mystic fiction of royalty. In short, they had to kill the patriarchal father and also the mother.

Strikingly, however, the killing of the father was accompanied by little personal vilification. Hébert's references to the pig, the ogre, or the drunk were relatively isolated; calling the former king a cuckold ("tête de cocu") hardly compared to the insistent denigration of Marie Antoinette.[57] Officials chose not to dwell on the king's execution itself. Newspaper accounts were formal and restrained. On the day of the event, one of the regicide deputies who spoke in the Jacobin Club captured the mood: "Louis Capet has paid his debt; let us speak of it no longer." Most of the visual representations of the execution (medals or engravings) came from outside of France and were meant to serve the cause of counter-revolution.[58] The relative silence about Louis among the revolutionaries reflects the conviction that he represented after all the masculinity of power and sovereignty. The aim was to kill the paternal source of power and yet retain its virility in the republican replacement.

The republican ideal of virtue was profoundly homosocial; it was based on a notion of fraternity between men in which women were relegated to the realm of domesticity. Public virtue required virility, which required in turn the violent rejection of aristocratic degeneracy and any intrusion of the feminine into the public. The many bodies of Marie Antoinette served a kind of triangulating function in this vision of the new world. Through their rejection of her and what she stood for, republican men could reinforce their bonds to one another; she was the negative version of the female icon of republican liberty but nonetheless iconic for the rejection. She was perhaps also an object lesson for other women who might wish to exercise through popular sovereignty the kind of rule that the queen had exercised through royal prerogative. The republican brothers who had overthrown the king and taken upon themselves his mantle did not want their sisters to follow their lead. In this implicit and often unconscious gender drama, the body of Marie Antoinette played a critical, if uncomfortable, role. The bodies of Marie Antoinette could never be sacred by French tradition, but they could certainly be powerful in their own fashion.

NOTES

Source Reprinted from *Eroticism and the Body Politic*, ed. Lynn Hunt (Baltimore: Johns Hopkins University Press, 1991), pp. 108–30.

1 Robert Darnton, "The High Enlightenment and the Low-Life of Literature," reprinted in *The Literary Underground of the Old Regime* (Cambridge: Harvard University Press, 1982), pp. 1–40, esp. p. 29.

2 I have used the report on the session of 14 October 1793, in the *Moniteur Universel*, 16 October 1793.

3 At least that is how many judges signed the arrest warrant on 14 October 1793 according to the *Moniteur*, 16 October 1793. For the workings of the Revolutionary Tribunal, see Luc Willette, *Le Tribunal révolutionnaire* (Paris: Denoël, 1981). Since it was not established until March 1793, the tribunal was not in existence at the time of the king's trial.

4 As quoted in Ernst H. Kantorowicz, *The King's Two Bodies: A Study in Mediaeval Political Theology* (Princeton: Princeton University Press, 1957), p. 409, n. 319.

5 *Moniteur*, 27 October 1793, reporting on the trial session of 14 October.

6 *Moniteur*, 27 October 1793.

7 *Ibid.*

8 *Révolutions de Paris*, no. 212 (3 August–28 October 1793).

9 I develop the notion of transparency in a somewhat different context in *Politics, Culture, and Class in the French Revolution* (Berkeley and Los Angeles: University of California Press, 1984), pp. 44–6, 72–4.

10 On the *philosophes'* attitudes toward women, see Paul Hoffmann, *La Femme dans la pensée des lumières* (Paris: Editions Ophrys, 1977), esp. pp. 324–446.

11 I am indebted to the analysis of Joan Landes, *Women and the Public Sphere in the Age of the French Revolution* (Ithaca: Cornell University Press, 1988). Dorinda Outram concludes that the Revolution was committed to anti-feminine rhetoric because it ascribed power in the Old Regime to women. I think that this exaggerates the identification of women with power in the Old Regime, but it nonetheless leads to fruitful reflections about the way in which male revolutionary politicians tried to escape feelings of guilt. See Outram, "*Le Langage mâle de la vertu*: Women and the Discourse of

the French Revolution," in *The Social History of Language*, Peter Burke and Roy Porter (eds.) (Cambridge: Cambridge University Press, 1987), pp. 120–35, esp. p. 125.

12 Jean-Jacques Rousseau, *Politics and the Arts: Letter to M. d'Alembert on the Theatre*, Allan Bloom (trans) (Ithaca: Cornell University Press, 1968), pp. 100–1.

13 Quotes from *Moniteur*, 27 October 1793, and 18 October 1793 (the latter the testimony of Roussillon, a barber-surgeon and cannoneer).

14 Carole Pateman, *The Sexual Contract* (Stanford: Stanford University Press, 1988), p. 36.

15 Chantal Thomas argues that the anti-Marie Antoinette pamphlets became especially virulent from the moment of her first pregnancy in 1777 (*La Reine scélérate: Marie-Antoinette dans les pamphlets* [Paris: Editions du Seuil, 1989], p. 40).

16 Pateman, *Sexual Contract*, p. 12.

17 *Moniteur*, 18 October 1793.

18 *Moniteur*, 19 October 1793.

19 *Moniteur*, 20 October 1793.

20 *Père Duchesne*, no. 298 (October 1793).

21 On the last half of the eighteenth century, see Hector Fleischmann, *Les Pamphlets libertins contre Marie-Antoinette* (Paris, 1908 rpt., Geneva: Slatkine, 1976), esp. the chapter, "La France galante et libertine à la fin du XVIIIe siècle," pp. 13–36.

22 See, for example, *La Philosophie dans le boudoir*, where Sade offers a defense of incest in the parodic tract "Français, encore un effort si vous voulez être républicains" (Paris: Gallimard, 1976), pp. 229–30.

23 Hector Fleischmann, *Les Pamphlets libertins*, pp. 103–9.

24 Hector Fleischmann, *Marie-Antoinette libertine: Bibliographie critique et analytique des pamphlets politiques, galants, et obscènes contre la reine. Précédé de la réimpression intégrale des quatre libelles rarissimes et d'une histoire des pamphlétaires du règne de Louis XVI* (Paris: Bibliothèque des Curieux, 1911).

25 This essay was written before I had a chance to read the interesting and lively book by Thomas, *La Reine scélérate*. Her account differs from mine in several respects. It is especially strong on the analysis of the anti-Marie-Antoinette pamphlet literature, but has virtually nothing to say about the trial records.

26 Fleischmann gives likely publication dates for the 126 pamphlets that he found in *Marie-Antoinette libertine*, pp. 277ff. These are not all separate pamphlets but include major revised editions. Fleischmann no doubt ignored some pamphlets in existence, but the basic balance of pamphlets is most likely correctly rendered in his bibliography.

27 Darnton, "High Enlightenment and the Low-Life of Literature."

28 *Portefeuille d'un talon rouge, contenant des anecdotes galantes et secrètes de la cour de France* (rpt., Paris: Bibliothèque de Curieux, 1911), p. 22. Based on the edition dated "l'an 178–, De l'Imprimerie du Comte de Paradès." The passage is translated in Robert Darnton, "Reading, Writing, and Publishing," in *Literary Underground*, p. 201. See also *ibid.* p. 248, n. 63.

29 Fleischmann, *Les Pamphlets libertins*, pp. 117–29. See also, Henri d'Almeras, *Marie-Antoinette et les pamphlets royalistes et révolutionnaires: les amoureux de la Reine* (Paris: Librairie Mondiale, 1907), pp. 299–328.

30 As quoted in d'Almeras, *Marie-Antoinette*, pp. 309–10.

31 Fleischmann, *Marie-Antoinette libertine*, p. 64.

32 Quotes from the edition cited in n. 28 above.

33 Sections of the pamphlet are reproduced in d'Almeras, *Marie-Antoinette*, pp. 56–60. According to Maurice Tourneux, this eight-page pamphlet was published in 1779 and it cost 17,400 livres for the crown to have it destroyed. It was reprinted several times after 1789 (*Marie-Antoinette devant l'histoire: Essai bibliographique* (Paris: Leclerc, 1895), p. 42).

34 See d'Almeras, *Marie-Antoinette*, pp. 399–403, for title variations.

35 Quotations from *Essai historique sur la vie de Marie-Antoinette, reine de France et de*

Navarre, née archiduchesse d'Autriche, le deux novembre 1755: Orné de son portrait, et rédigé sur plusieurs manuscrits de sa main ("A Versailles, Chez La Montensier [one of her supposed female lovers], Hôtel des Courtisannes," 1789), pp. 4, 8, 19–20. Some have attributed this pamphlet to Brissot, but d'Almeras and Fleischmann both dispute this (d'Almeras, *Marie-Antoinette*, p. 339; Fleischmann, *Marie-Antoinette libertine*, pp. 67–70). Fleischmann reports the view that the marquis de Sade wrote the second part of this 1789 edition (p. 68). Earlier in 1789 a shorter, 88-page work titled *Essais historiques sur la vie de Marie-Antoinette d'Autriche, reine de France; pour servir à l'histoire de cette princesse* (London, 1789) struck a much less violent tone. It was not written in the first person and though it discussed the queen's amorous intrigues in detail, it was not particularly pornographic in style. This version was written very much in the vein of attempts to convince the queen of her errors: "Fasse le ciel cependant que ces vérités, si elles sont présentées à cette princesse, puissent la corriger, et la faire briller d'autant de vertus qu'elle l'a fait par ses étourderies" (p. 78).

36 *Le Godmiché royal* (Paris, 1789).
37 The publication page after the title read: "La mère en proscrira la lecture à sa fille. Au Manège. Et dans tous les bordels de Paris, 1791." It is interesting to note that one of the early editions of Sade's *La Philosophie dans le boudoir* includes on its title page the obvious parody: "La mère en prescrira la lecture à sa fille." This was the 1795 London edition. See Pascal Pia, *Les Livres de l'Enfer, du XVIe siècle à nos jours* (Paris: C. Coulet and A. Favre, 1978), 2: 1044.
38 See, for example, *Les Enjans de Sodome à l'Assemblée Nationale* (Paris, 1790), Enfer no. 638, Bibliothèque Nationale. For a general overview emphasizing the contrast between aristocratic degeneracy and republican health, see Antoine de Baecque, "Pamphlets: Libel and Political Mythology," in *Revolution in Print: The Press in France, 1775–1800*, Robert Darnton and Daniel Roche (eds) (Berkeley and Los Angeles: University of California Press, 1989), pp. 165–76.
39 See the remarks by Darnton, esp. p. 33, in "High Enlightenment."
40 He provides no evidence for this assertion, however (d'Almeras, *Marie-Antoinette*, p. 403).
41 Enfer nos. 790–92, Bibliothèque Nationale.
42 The correct attribution was brought to my attention by Carla Hesse. While working on another project, I came across a denunciation that verified Keralio's authorship. The anonymous pamphlet *Les Crimes constitutionnels de France, ou la désolation française, décrétée par l'Assemblée dite Nationale Constituante, aux années 1789, 1790, et 1791. Accepté par l'esclave Louis XVI, le 14 septembre 1791* (Paris: Chez Le Petit et Guillemard, 1792) included the following:

> Mlle de Keralio. Laide, et déjà sur le retour; dès avant la révolution, elle se consolait de la disgrace de ses *cheveux gris* et de l'indifférence des hommes, par la culture paisible des lettres. Ses principes étoient purs alors, et sa conduite ne démentoit point la noble délicatesse de sa famille. Livrée, depuis la révolution aux désordres démagogiques, sans doute aussi dominée par les *fureurs utériées*, elle s'est mariée au nommé Robert, ci-devant avocat, sans talens, sans cause, sans pain, à Givet, et maintenant jacobincordelier. Abandonée de sa famille, méprisée des honnêtes gens, elle végète honteusement avec ce misérable, chargé de dettes et d'opprobres, en travaillant à la page, pour le compte de l'infâme *Prudhomme*, au journal dégoûtant de la révolution de Paris. Les *crimes des reines de France* ont mis le comble à sa honte, ainsi qu'à sa noire méchanceté.

43 The full title of the edition I used is *Les Crimes des reines de France depuis le commencement de la monarchie jusqu'à la mort de Marie-Antoinette; avec les pièces justificatives de son procès* ("Publié par L. Prudhomme, avec Cinq gravures. Nouvelle édition corrigée et augmentée. Paris: au Bureau des Révolutions de Paris, an II").

44 See, for example, *Têtes à prix, suivi de la liste de toutes les personnes avec lesquelles la reine a eu des liaisons de débauches*, 2nd ed. (Paris, 1792), 28 pp., and the nearly identical *Liste civile suivie des noms et qualités de ceux qui la composent, et la punition dûe à leurs crimes . . . et la liste des affidés de la ci-devant reine* (Paris, n.d., but Tourneux dates it 1792).

45 *Père Duchesne*, no. 36.

46 *Père Duchesne*, no. 194.

47 *Père Duchesne*, nos. 296 and 298.

48 As quoted by Fleischmann, *Marie-Antoinette libertine*, p. 76.

49 *Père Duchesne*, no. 36 (1791).

50 *Vie privée, libertine et scandaleuse*, as reprinted in Fleischmann, *Marie-Antoinette libertine*, pp. 173–4. This section concludes with the most extreme of all possible epitaphs: "Ci-gît l'impudique Manon, Qui, dans le ventre de sa mère, Savait si bien placer son c—, Qu'elle f— avec son père."

51 [Keralio] *Les Crimes*, p. vii.

52 Rena Girard, *Violence and the Sacred*, Patrick Gregory (trans.) (Baltimore: Johns Hopkins University Press, 1977), p. 141.

53 *Réimpression de l'Ancien Moniteur*, 18: 290 (session of 8 Brumaire, year II, 29 October 1793).

54 Quotes from Darline Gay Levy, Harriet Branson Applewhite, and Mary Durham Johnson, *Women in Revolutionary Paris, 1789–1795* (Urbana: University of Illinois Press, 1979), pp. 215–16, 219–20.

55 See quotation in n. 42 above.

56 Outram, *"Le Langage mâle de la vertu,"* p. 125, quotation from p. 126. See also the chapter on "Women and Revolution," in Landes, *Women and the Public Sphere*, pp. 93–151.

57 *Père Duchesne*, no. 180, for example.

58 Lynn Hunt, "The Sacred and the French Revolution," in *Durkheimian Sociology: Cultural Studies*, Jeffrey C. Alexander (ed.) (Cambridge: Cambridge University Press, 1988), pp. 25–43, quotation from p. 32.

10

WAR BETWEEN BROTHERS AND SISTERS

Inheritance law and gender politics in revolutionary France

Suzanne Desan

Lynn Hunt's article on Marie Antoinette exemplifies a trend among feminist historians demonstrating how Jacobin ideology, inspired by the writings of Jean Jacques Rousseau and others, introduced new forms of sexism that were meant to exclude women from the newly-found democratic republic. Politicians often questioned female political participation; they closed women's clubs and ridiculed prominent women such as Madame Roland. Perhaps more important, unlike emancipation for Black slaves or full civic rights for Jews and other religious minorities, the topic of women's suffrage was never even debated on the floor of the National Assembly – this despite the fact that among its deputies were those today regarded as heroic champions of women's rights, such as Condorcet. Not even he insisted on making a speech to his peers on the subject. Thus there is consensus among historians today that those who led the French Revolution did not even want to consider the possibility of extending to women their full civic rights.

However, the French Revolution was not simply the result of its leaders' intentions. Often events took their own course in contrast and often despite the ideological fervor of the leadership. In this case, the issue of how Jacobin men felt about female civic participation may be very different from asking how the changes wrought by the French Revolution actually affected women. No one has pursued this line of thinking better than Suzanne Desan. Less interested in examples of feminist activism per se, Desan's focus is on how ordinary women made use of the new legal landscape provided by the Revolution. After all, even though women were denied the right to vote, run for office, serve as judges and administrators, etc., they could still own property, earn wages, have the rights and benefits of legal marriage, and sue in a court of law. It turns out that this gave women in the revolutionary era considerable advantages over their counterparts in the Old Regime. In this article, Desan demonstrates through precious examples drawn from French provincial archives how the establishment of family law courts and inheritance law reforms allowed women to reclaim family property for themselves, often at the expense of their brothers and parents. Looked at from this angle, the first French republic was not some misogynist Rousseauian dystopia, but relative to eighteenth-century Europe, was a progressive and even humane society, empowering women in unprecedented ways.

* * *

In the spring of 1795 the *citoyenne* LeFranc of Caen penned an angry warning to the National Convention: "You have only passed one law beneficial to women, the law of 17 *nivôse* [which guarantees equal partitions of inheritance]. If you destroy this law of equality that has converted to the Republic an infinity of women and girls led astray by the fanaticism of priests, they will say with good reason that you are unjust and that you have taken advantage of the fact that we are not represented at the Convention. . . . They will say to you that men have made the laws and they have made them for themselves." LeFranc was not the only French citizen with strong opinions about the new inheritance laws designed to introduce equality into the family, nor was she the only one to view the reform of the family as, at least in part, a contest over gender dynamics within family and nation. In their petition to the deputies several months earlier, the male citizens Lenoir and Lammarré had argued from the opposite viewpoint, denouncing the new laws, which had torn apart the "tranquility of families" and "had depaternalized, defraternized, and desocialized [France]. . . . The social order is entirely overturned. . . . The sister is engaged in open warfare with her brother."[1]

In their ambitious attempt to rebuild society from the ground up, regenerate the family, and transform the very fabric of private life, the French revolutionaries had embarked on a far-ranging and controversial reform of family law: they weakened paternal authority, lowered the age of majority, legalized divorce, secularized marriage, overhauled inheritance practices, facilitated adoption, and offered illegitimate children new civil rights.[2] The legalization of divorce may be the most well known of these reforms, but no aspect of family restructuring generated more contention in court or more outbursts of popular anger or approval than the new inheritance laws. As the Revolution radicalized, successive legislatures passed increasingly egalitarian inheritance laws. After abolishing primogeniture in 1790, the National Assembly decreed in April 1791 that intestate legacies must be divided equally among all children – regardless of sex or birth order. By 1793–94 the convention extended this egalitarian principle to *all* forms of inheritance in both direct and collateral lines: the deputies pronounced that all offspring – including illegitimate ones – would divide family property evenly. Most controversially, this egalitarian partition was made retroactive to July 1789. Striking at the core of property relations, family structure, and agrarian customs, the reforms provoked intense and bitter controversy. While thousands of family tribunals across France sought to untangle the intricacies of Old Regime practices, revolutionary law, and family relations, men and women flooded the various national legislatures with petitions, pamphlets, and individual appeals. Indeed, during the 1790s the French wrote more petitions on inheritance reform than on any other aspect of civil law.[3]

Inevitably, the revision of inheritance law had a profound impact on gender relations within families, not only because many regions of France traditionally favored sons over daughters as heirs, but also because marriage arrangements were inextricably bound up with the eventual partitions of estates. Moreover, by offering equal inheritance rights to women as rights-bearing individuals, the reforms undermined family strategies and called into question traditional assumptions about the status and position of women. The revolutionary state was reaching its hand into the family and tampering with the complex web of mutual obligation, built along generational and gendered lines. Finally, although the legal reforms would affect individual women differently, the demand for inheritance reform became a basic arena of female politicization, particularly in Normandy, the Midi, and pockets of the north, east, and center, where daughters generally had no claim on parental legacies beyond their original dowry or their *légitime* portion. Keenly aware of their new relationship to the state, many women in these regions developed various political and legal means to make their demands known and implemented whenever possible. This article explores their legal contestation and political petitioning to gain insights into some women's activism and into the gender politics of the Revolution.

With the exception of a few works dealing mainly with divorce,[4] historians of family law in the 1790s have not analyzed in depth how the new legal structures complicated the relationship between the sexes and created new political and legal opportunities for women. Conversely, despite the crucial importance of civil law reforms, feminist historians interested in the impact of the Revolution on gender roles have left the question of women's new legal status within the family virtually unexamined, in part because of a wariness of subsuming women's actions and identity to "family history."[5] Anxious to recapture women as active political agents, some historians have analyzed Parisian *sans-jupons'* activism and, to a lesser extent, the engagement of counterrevolutionary women.[6] Others have scrutinized revolutionary discourse about women and asked why they were increasingly excluded from the public sphere of politics.[7] We have learned much from these approaches, but some women's historians have been too quick to equate politics solely with public participation and to speak of the "private" as an entirely separate and undefined arena to which women were relegated.[8] While other historians, most notably Lynn Hunt, have theorized changing attitudes toward the family and politics during the Revolution, their explorations have focused primarily on cultural representation and have not delved into popular practices and negotiations of these new attitudes.[9] Yet, in order to understand the ambiguous impact of revolutionary politics on women, we need to ask how the Revolution fundamentally transformed women's legal, as well as cultural, relationship to the state and to the family. We need to examine the family as a terrain of political contestation rather than as a separate private sphere and to analyze women's political and legal choices as a renegotiation of family relationships, as well as an attempt to influence public policy. In practice, how did provincial women negotiate the new legal structures governing domestic matters and how did they envision the cultural redefinition of the family? What expectations did they have for the new state?

This article will explore contestation over inheritance as one window into the complex interplay of law, gender, politics, and the state. I will argue that despite local resistance to carrying out the new legislation, the egalitarian inheritance laws and the innovative court structure of "family tribunals" fused with the revolutionary political context to open up new legal opportunities for women in certain regions of France. Women in certain positions within the family were especially likely to embrace these reforms. Legal reform and politicization became fundamentally intertwined: the women who challenged traditional family unity and strategy in the courts sometimes also proposed new visions for the family in petitions, briefs, or pamphlets. In reimagining the family and its gender dynamics, these female political activists did not simply embrace republican motherhood and domesticity; rather, they wove together Old Regime and revolutionary moral codes to promote an egalitarian family based on mutual affection and reciprocity. They fused the languages of law, equal rights, and morality to make an incisive critique of traditional family structures and to demand their reform as the crucial underpinning of the new republic. In order to examine these issues, I will analyze litigation over inheritance law in Normandy through a case study of the family courts in the district of Caen between 1790 and 1796, with some consideration of the ongoing contestation until 1799 under the Civil Tribunal's jurisdiction. I will then set this examination within the broader context of popular petitioning and agitation from across France over the controversial legislation, paying particular attention to petitioning by women.

New laws and old geography

"We will attack aristocracy even in the tomb and take away its surest means of destroying our liberty," proclaimed the Jacobin deputy Pénières in March 1793 as he demanded that the National Convention affirm every citizen's right to an equal share of inheritance.[10] Such antiaristocratic and egalitarian sentiments, along with the desire to unify France's "feudal and privilege-ridden" legal system, spurred progressively more radical inheritance laws, which incidentally granted greater inheritance rights to daughters, as well as younger sons. The fight against paternal "despotism," so ardently voiced by Mirabeau, influenced reformers throughout the early 1790s and led in March 1790 to the abolition of primogeniture along with *lettres de cachet*. On 8 April 1791 the deputies not only mandated equal partition of intestate estates, but also suppressed customary exclusions of daughters or younger sons without their consent.[11] By 1793, as the mood of the revolutionary leadership turned more antihierarchical, they decreed that in principle citizens must leave their property equally to all offspring. A few months later, illegitimate children were granted an equal share in family legacies, provided that they were recognized by their fathers and were not the product of adultery.[12]

Finally, inspired by the desire to spread wealth widely, favor youth, and prevent parental favoritism, the convention passed its most controversial inheritance laws. The laws of 5 *brumaire an* II (26 October 1793) and 17 *nivôse an* II (6 January 1794), retroactive to July 1789, outlined detailed rules for egalitarian partition among direct descendants and in their absence, among collateral relatives. Testators now had very little freedom to choose heirs: they could dispose of only small portions of their property: one-tenth if they had direct descendants and one-sixth if they had no children.[13] The attempt to implement these laws unleashed a torrent of popular petitioning on both sides of the issue: that outburst in turn provoked extensive debate and explanatory decrees. Although the retroactive prescriptions of these laws would be overturned in the fall of 1795, their stringent egalitarianism persisted throughout the Revolution. Ultimately, the Civil Code tempered that stance: it reiterated the principle of equal partition among offspring, but increased the disposable portion to one-quarter, one-third, or one-half, depending on the number of children; the testator could privilege one child or more with this additional share.[14]

Like so many other revolutionary reforms, revisions in inheritance law affected different parts of France unevenly because of regional variations in family structure, landholding systems, and law. While various forms of "written" or Roman law governed family practice in the Midi, civil law in the north was regulated by sixty primary "customs" and some three hundred local variations. As Voltaire commented ironically, "A man travelling in this country changes laws almost as often as he changes horses."[15] In much of the west and across north-central France from the Loire valley up through the Paris region to Champagne, customs favored more or less egalitarian successions. The revolutionary laws provoked litigation but did not strike at the core of family structures; little formal reaction for or against the new laws surfaced. In contrast, demands for change arose early in the Revolution across the Midi where fathers generally chose one son as primary heir according to Roman law, in Normandy where daughters were customarily excluded from inheritance, and in regions operating by primogeniture, such as the Boulonnais, Béarn, Navarre, and the Pays de Caux (within Normandy). In some cases, popular cries for reform also echoed in areas slightly north of the written-law boundary, such as the Auvergne, Burgundy, and Berry, where customs influenced by Roman law tended to favor preferential legacy (*préciput*).[16] As new laws sought to equalize inheritance shares later in the Revolution, all of these same regions, especially the Midi and Normandy, witnessed bitterly fought court contests and widespread petition campaigns regarding the laws of 5 *brumaire* and 17 *nivôse*.[17]

The varying geography of Old Regime inheritance law and marital practices played a large role in influencing the specific impact of these reforms on individual women. Each woman's particular position within the family was a second crucial factor in determining her reaction to the new laws. Some favored daughters without brothers and also the wives of favored sons lost out in property redivisions. Widows in certain marital property regimes could be hurt by the limitations on gifts between spouses and the suppression of customary dowers, and some courts interpreted the 17 *nivôse* law as having suppressed existing dowers.[18] But the new laws enabled numerous daughters to demand a larger share of legacies, and the abolition of the male prerogative to the lion's share of inheritance implicitly gave women higher status within the family. Many women who petitioned for egalitarian inheritance seemed to share the opinion of an anonymous journalist who wrote in 1789: "One of the most harmful effects of primogeniture is that it regularly exposes the mother of a family to the contempt and vexations of her husband and the sons preferred by him."[19] In the regions of contestation noted above, while traditional resistance to the legal changes was deeply rooted, daughters, wives, and widows wrote petitions asserting their succession rights; widows and sisters – often allied with younger brothers – used the courts to demand equalizing (re)divisions of family legacies. Let us turn to examine this contestation more closely.

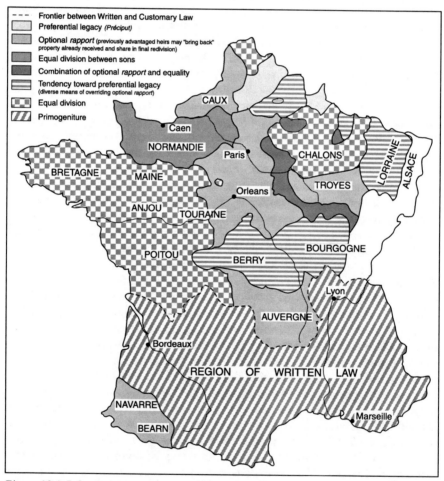

Figure 10.1 Inheritance customs in Old Regime France

Inheritance contestation in family courts: the district of Caen as a case study

The district of Caen encompassed the growing administrative and commercial city of Caen as well as the productive, grain-producing communes in the surrounding area. Although Caen, the departmental seat of the Calvados, participated in the federalist revolt, the district generally favored the Revolution.[20] Caen was chosen for this study above all because it was the judicial heart of Lower Normandy. Normandy provides a particularly good region for assessing the impact of the new inheritance laws on family dynamics and on women's legal activism because its prerevolutionary customs had a very explicit gender bias. According to tradition, Norman families sought above all to preserve and promote the family line: the all-important obligation to maintain family property and unity overrode any individual desires or ambitions. A complex system of customary law reinforced and even reified these practices by placing tight limits on the disposition of property.[21] To sustain the lineage system, families favored sons over daughters. Norman law restricted daughters to a small dowry or a *légitime* portion, paid as annual *rente*, and then excluded them from further claims on the legacies of their parents, siblings, or collateral relatives. Although the custom required brothers to pay *légitimes* to their sisters, fathers were under no legal obligation to offer dowries to their daughters. As the old expressions went, "A father can dower his daughter with a bouquet of roses"; "He owes his daughter a husband and nothing more." The law even limited the generosity of parents with sons towards their daughters: regardless of the number of girls in the family, their total inheritance share could not legally surpass one-third of the parents' property, unless that property fell within the limits of certain cities.[22] In contrast, brothers benefited from equal division of the remaining inheritance, except in the Pays de Caux where primogeniture persisted.[23] Once married, the Norman woman forged an economic unit of survival with her husband: "to make one family ... and be able to eat bread together more easily," as the gardener Nicolas Labbé put it. On occasion, the young woman would move in with her husband's family, although conjugal families were far more common than stem families in Normandy and dominated particularly within the town of Caen.[24] Moreover, even marriage did not entirely fortify the woman's economic position since Norman law prohibited communal marital property and gifts between spouses and since a young woman could expect little financial help from her family of origin. Norman law nonetheless offered widows some minimal protection by tightly limiting the husband's ability to use his wife's dowry and by guaranteeing certain dower rights to widows.[25]

Because of the specific nature of Norman customary law, struggles over revolutionary inheritance reforms took on a particular cast as a battle between brothers and sisters; for purposes of analysis, this trend allows the isolation of female litigants more easily than in the Midi. Yet, while the alignment of sisters versus brothers was especially prevalent in Normandy, the nature of the struggle over parental legacies nonetheless had much in common with conflict in the Midi governed by written law, as well as in areas of primogeniture or preferential legacy in parts of the north, east, and center.[26] As in Normandy, in all of these areas, revolutionary reforms raised the salient question of how family strategies based on obligation and sacrifice for the family line would incorporate a new definition of the individual, especially if that individual were female.

In the Old Regime, family conflicts could fall under the varied jurisdiction of seigneurial or ecclesiastical courts, or – increasingly in the 1700s – under the royal jurisdiction of *prévôtés, bailliages,* and ultimately the parlements.[27] As part of its overhaul of the judicial system, in August 1790 the National Assembly devised a new form of judicial arbitration, known as the family court (*tribunal de famille*), to handle disputes within the family. Originally envisioned as a means of avoiding expensive, public, and time-consuming legal procedures, the family court would deal with conflicts between parent and child, husband and wife, brother and sister, and so on. Its jurisdiction came to include a wide range of matters, including inheritance, divorce, guardianship and custody, detention of unruly children, approval of marriages by minors, and altercations over family property. The family tribunal was essentially a temporary arbitration court: opposing parties would each choose two arbiters, ideally relatives or friends, to represent their interests and come to a mutually agreed upon resolution. If the four arbiters could not agree, they would in turn name a fifth arbiter (*surarbitre*) to break the deadlock. Losing petitioners could appeal their cases to the local district court. The revolutionaries conceived of this system as a family council that would replace the arbitrary decisions of despotic fathers and the costly procedures of corrupt lawyers. Ideally, it should encourage mutual respect, democratic decision-making, and affection within the family.[28]

By and large, the family courts dealt with inheritance cases more than any other issue.[29] In my sample of 219 family court cases in the district of Caen between 1791 and 1796, roughly two-thirds (143 cases) dealt with inheritance.[30] These conflicts fell into three main categories. Contests between siblings made up almost 60 percent of the cases (83 out of 143). A little over a quarter of the cases, 40 out of the 143, involved settling the property rights of widows or, on rare occasions, widowers.[31] In the remaining 23 cases, collaterals or outsiders made succession claims. Property-owning men and women from a wide range of classes made use of the family tribunals. Unfortunately, the records for the district of Caen virtually never give occupational information on the litigants, but the amounts in contestation illustrate the broad social span of participants. While Marie Angélique Roussel and her husband Philippe Despars won 15,728 livres 2 sous from her brothers after a five-month dispute over arrears of her *légitime*, Anne Fontaine and her husband gained a mere 6 livres 1 sou as a yearly income from her brother Jacques as a result of the 17 *nivôse* law, and the widow Geneviève Betourné went to court repeatedly to defend her pathetic paraphernalia of a few handkerchiefs and other odds and ends.[32] In short, all but the poorest segments of society made use of the family courts. The majority of cases dealt with small annual *rentes* of about 50 to 300 livres or with flat sums between 300 and 2,000 livres.[33]

The proceedings of family courts were relatively informal. The four arbiters chosen by the opposing parties generally met at the home of one of the arbiters or at the local inn to hear the presentations of the litigants, review any written materials (such as marriage contracts or brief *mémoires*), listen to witnesses if necessary, and attempt to resolve differences in an amicable fashion. Since cases could be complex and since litigants and arbiters might stonewall or fail to appear, the family tribunal often met more than once. Of the inheritance cases in the district of Caen, about two-thirds were settled in less than two months, while a sixth took two to six months, and another sixth dragged on for even longer.[34] Over the course of the deliberations, one of the arbiters drew up a record of the proceedings in whatever degree of detail seemed appropriate and then eventually registered the final decision with the clerk of the district tribunal at Caen. Except for cases involving the 17 *nivôse* law, these results could in turn be appealed to the district tribunal, which also had the authority to enforce the family tribunals' decisions and sometimes used *huissiers* or even auctioned sequestered goods to force delinquent defendants to pay fellow family members. In appeals cases, the district tribunal also reinforced proper arbitration procedures and overturned only those decisions which clearly flouted revolutionary laws.[35]

Although the creators of the family court system envisioned the arbiters almost exclusively as relatives or neighbors, in the district of Caen, as elsewhere, litigants increasingly chose men with legal training to represent them and decide their cases. In the town of Caen, as in Dijon, Lyon, Montpellier, Rouen, Laon, and Angoulême, a group of *hommes de loi* gradually earned a reputation as specialists in family arbitration.[36] Tie-breaking arbiters (*surarbitres*) and arbiters named by the justice of the peace if necessary were almost always legally qualified men. Critics of the family court system often fingered this dominance of *hommes de loi* as a corrupting influence. One antagonist in Lyon called them "reptiles," "ogres," and "birds of prey who dwell inside cadavers to devour their prey all the more easily." Yet their legal training undoubtedly helped them to sort out the complex web of civil law in the 1790s: while the new legislation governed certain matters, tortuous customary law continued to hold sway wherever it had not yet been replaced or revised. In short, arbiters and judges struggled to interpret and enforce an intricate mosaic of Old Regime and revolutionary law, which only the Civil Code of 1804 would codify.[37]

Largely because they implemented controversial inheritance laws, the family courts fell under considerable criticism, provoking their abolition in 1796, and in the nineteenth century, historians often condemned their practices. But overall, historians who have studied the family tribunals emphasize that they operated relatively efficiently and fairly. As James Traer notes, the family court "was not bound by old jurisprudence and legal formalities, and hence it could and often did render more flexible justice than could be had in the regular court system."[38] Perhaps local authorities agreed: despite their official suppression early in 1796, family tribunals in the Calvados continued to arbitrate some family conflicts until 1799 under the jurisdiction of the new Civil Tribunal.[39]

The flexible procedural style of the family courts had some striking practical effects for women in civil cases. Notably, the particular structure of these courts combined with the complex mixture of new and old laws to allow certain groups of women, sometimes with the help of their husbands, not only to reawaken and settle Old Regime injustices, but also to make new, unprecedented, and successful claims on family property and to enlist the state on their behalf. Furthermore, the courts became forums for negotiating the impact of revolutionary law and ideology on gender dynamics within the home. To make their decisions, the arbiters drew on a fluid combination of cultural norms, new and old laws, and pragmatic considerations.[40] As arbiters and litigants alike strove to untangle custom, Revolution, and family, the court proceedings reveal a fundamental tension over the changed relationship of women to the family and the state. Most crucially, the family tribunals repeatedly made decisions that called into question traditional gender roles and assumptions.

In many cases, women who entered arbitration were essentially defying deeply embedded practices as well as family unity. Obviously, various women had litigated against family members in the Old Regime, but the revolutionary laws had upped the ante by attempting to institute new family norms and behaviors. Since it was no small matter to pit oneself against habitual lineage strategies, women in certain positions in the family were far more likely to undertake litigation. Most frequently, sisters demanded shares of their patrimony, and widows fought to sort out their dotal rights. To justify their bold actions, litigating women sometimes denounced the inequities of traditional customs and above all, cited financial need and/or allegiance to their new nuclear family.[41] It is important to recognize that while the new laws aimed at creating equality for individuals within households, they also validated the nuclear unit in opposition to the family line.[42] Within this realignment of kinship relations, women, especially married sisters, could carve out a stronger position for themselves by winning cases on behalf of their new families. By invoking egalitarian rights within the home and by opposing the dominant prerogatives of the extended family, litigating women moved in practice toward redefining their own status within the household.

Widows and women who were unmarried, separated, or divorced most often represented themselves, though a few enlisted a male family member, a *fondé de pouvoir*, or a *procureur* to present their cases to the arbiters. As in the Old Regime, married women were usually represented legally by their husbands, though many of these women laid out their own arguments during the tribunal sessions. In sibling inheritance disputes, one brother-in-law often acted on behalf of his wife and her sisters, whether married or unmarried. The new courts did not overturn the prerevolutionary practice and assumption that the husband stood as agent for the couple "in his wife's name." For example, when the plaintiff Eléonore Marie married during the course of the tribunal's deliberations, the family court requested that her new husband François Quesnel approve her choice of arbiters. Women never served as arbiters themselves.[43]

Yet, as in the Old Regime, some married women legally represented their own interests or acted as agents or *portresses de pouvoir* for husbands or brothers under attack. For example, the *femme* Lebourg represented her husband's concerns in a contest versus his sister and brother-in-law in 1794. And in a reversal of the typical pattern of a son-in-law taking his wife's father to court over unpaid dowry items, the *citoyenne* Marc represented her husband in a suit against his father.[44] The newness, relative informality, and local nature of family courts may well have made this practice of women representing men more common than before. At other times, however, women fell back on more traditional claims of legal powerlessness to protect their husbands or themselves from the law. In October 1792 Marie Levernieux came to the family court session and argued vociferously on her husband's behalf against his stepmother, but when the tide seemed to turn against them, she suddenly pleaded ignorance and claimed that in his absence, "she could not make any agreements on his behalf."[45] Since the various revolutionary reforms had awakened uncertainty about women's exact legal status, individual women worked this lack of clarity to their own advantage.[46]

But what is most notable in the family court cases is that sisters, with their husbands if they were married, repeatedly defeated their brothers in court, upsetting customary family strategies and encouraging more women to push for legal changes. Of the eighty-three sibling contests, fifty-eight pitted sisters against brothers; sisters clearly won forty-five (78 percent) of these cases and negotiated a compromise in six of the remaining cases. While it is impossible to know how many of them collected their funds, the courts levied serious fines on those who failed to comply, and the district court took action against some delinquents. Many widows also made successful use of family arbitration to settle their dotal rights at their husbands' deaths or even to regain their rightful dotal shares uncollected in the Old Regime. The court structure facilitated the collection of widows' pensions and often acted to safeguard widows' customary rights, including the dower for those already married. In addition, Norman widows without children particularly benefited from the 17 *nivôse* law, which allowed them to receive gifts from their husbands. Immediately following the law, a flood of childless couples expressed their "tender friendship" or "sincere gratitude" by contracting to offer each other mutual gifts as part of their legacies.[47] Yet generally speaking, in Normandy the new laws had a much more striking impact on daughters than on widows.

Early in the Revolution, the family court structure made it relatively simple and inexpensive for sisters to demand arrears on unpaid *légitimes* or, in a few cases, to reopen procedures left over from the *bailliages* or parlement of the Old Regime. Sibling tension over unpaid *légitimes* was endemic in prerevolutionary Normandy, as in other parts of France. As some forty *citoyennes* from Calvados commented in their petition to the National Convention, many unmarried women "lack the bare necessities of life while their brothers, living in abundance, stubbornly deny them not only humanitarian aid but even the small share that the old custom accorded."[48] Numerous family courts met only once and simply asserted the legal claim of a sister on her brother or brothers, ordering them to pay. In some cases, plaintiffs took advantage of the new institution of the family tribunal to open up very old *légitime* claims or more complex Old Regime cases. The *citoyenne* Françoise Eustache *veuve* Lepeinteur successfully took her maternal uncle to family court to reclaim the *légitime* that he owed her mother who had passed away, while the unmarried Thérèse Pépin seized the initiative and represented her sister and two brothers in a fruitful claim to regain their father's legacy, "usurped from them 23 years ago" by an uncle who now had nothing to say in his own defense.[49]

The laws of 5 *brumaire* and, above all, 17 *nivôse* were responsible for many of the contests among siblings, as well as among collateral relatives. Although in most cases the arbiters simply enforced the law without much discussion of its content, the simmering tension over this deeply gendered "trouble in the family" sometimes broke through to the surface as litigants referred to the revolutionary principles underpinning the new inheritance laws. In 1795 the Letourneur sisters argued successfully that "the law of equality without distinction according to sex had been established much earlier" in the Revolution and could not be overturned by later laws revoking retroactive effects. Another triumphant sister taunted her brothers with gleeful reminders of their lost prerogative as sons. In November 1793 when the *fille majeure* Victoire Leprovost led her two widowed sisters Scolastique and Louise in a demand that their brother redivide their paternal inheritance, the brother hedged, dragged his heels, and finally demanded at least to choose his share first. His sisters retorted that "since the new laws had abolished any privileges of the oldest or youngest as well as the privilege of masculinity," the four children should choose their lots by chance; but they taunted him with the offer to choose lots according to birth order. Needless to say, their brother was the youngest. No doubt angered by this last dig, the brother walked out of the arbitration session, refusing to sign while the arbiters pronounced that the drawing of lots would be done by chance in the presence of the *commissaire* of the district.[50]

Although most sisters did not tease their brothers as did the Leprevosts, many were persistent. When the widow Langlouard failed in her first attempt to use the 8 April 1791 law to share the inheritance of the curé Guillot with her brother Thomas Guillot, she declared, "I will persevere," and did, in fact, succeed in a second claim according to the 5 *brumaire* law. On occasion, the family tribunal structure combined with the new laws and the presence of reformist lawyers to encourage the most daring women to make even more radical demands on their brothers. Late in 1794, for example, Angélique Poignaut, recently emboldened or perhaps just impoverished by divorce, requested that the family court force her brother to increase the size of the dowry he had offered her back in 1779. She argued that the annual payment of 130 livres was far less than her *légitime* of 400 livres a year would have been. The arbiters turned down her proposal and expressed alarm at the concept of other divorced women upsetting "family peace" with requests for higher dowries. "The law cannot admit revisions so unjust and so troubling to the tranquility of families," they concluded.[51]

Especially in redivisions ordered retroactively, brothers were understandably reluctant to surrender land that they had already improved or cultivated. They developed a whole repertoire of moves to delay court decisions: lost inventories, contracts, and deeds; no-show arbiters and defendants; and elaborate excuses and ruses became common. Given the instability of revolutionary politics, some hoped to stonewall long enough that the law would be altered or repealed. These maneuvers in turn forced determined plaintiffs to call repeated court sessions and in some cases, to hire legal help. The frustrated Rogne sisters Marie and Marie Jeanne denounced the "trickery" of Norman men who deliberately chose their "best and most stubborn friends" as arbiters to drag out court cases. They suggested that the National Convention authorize commissioners to speed up cases by standing in for missing brothers or arbiters. In addition, testators seeking to favor sons over daughters came up with various means of eluding the law through false sales, forced gifts between siblings, *légitimes* paid in near worthless *assignats*, new forms of marriage contracts, and so on. By and large, however, the family courts were remarkably persistent in implementing the new laws. In cases where brothers dillydallied too long, most arbiters simply made a decision without the brothers ever having appeared.[52]

As they interpreted and carried out the new laws benefiting sisters, the family courts seem to have been keenly aware that restoring legacy rights to daughters as individuals could violate family expectations and disadvantage brothers who had worked on paternal lands. Particularly in settling retroactive 17 *nivôse* cases, some arbiters mitigated the harshness of the law by assessing the value of brothers' or sons' work on their parents' property and reducing the required payments to sisters or widowed mothers accordingly. Family courts sometimes heard the testimony of neighbors or experts to determine these values and did their best to sort out shares of future and past harvests, locations of threshing, and so on. Justice cut both ways: when the brother Vasnier secretly removed all the manure and animal bedding from a piece of contested land, the arbiters calmly waded in to rescue some of the material for his two sisters.[53]

Since the family courts sought to balance the laws mandating equal inheritance with an older moral code of mutual obligation, the women who used family arbitration were most often successful if they could make traditional moral and economic arguments in addition to ones based on revolutionary law. Litigating women who made demands backed by the new laws often also sought to prove that they had fulfilled Old Regime expectations of family duty, but had nonetheless been shortchanged. In the spring of 1794 the unmarried Françoise Faroux had difficulty convincing the arbiters that the 17 *nivôse* law increased her inheritance share, but she finally persuaded them to grant her twenty-nine years in *légitime* arrears by pointing out that she "had lived with her brothers only to increase the goods of the household ... which she had enabled to flourish through her good housekeeping, thrift, and painstaking, beneficial labor ... serving as mother and main servant at the same time."[54]

In some cases, women used arbitration sessions to enforce traditional family duties as well. Daughters of widowed or separated fathers in particular used the court structure to demand their share of maternal inheritance as annual food pensions. The Lemoine twins argued successfully that their father "had a widower's right to their mother's whole fortune, but his first duty was to feed, maintain, and educate his children." In 1794 the arbiters had little patience with a divorced father who alleged that the new inheritance law in fact left him totally "free control over his property" and ended customary obligations. Lemasson contended that "no law obliges me to pay [my daughter] a pension; Article 61 of the 17 *nivôse* decree releases me from even setting aside the customary one-third; ... if I already let her have 200 livres, it was only due to my good will and friendship for her and due to the repeated insistence of the court." His daughter Augustine retorted that she had cared for her father and "never refused all the help he demanded from her." She asserted that "the place of a daughter is to be with her mother" and boldly demanded an even larger pension of four hundred livres. The court concurred with her version of filial duty, noted that the new 17 *nivôse* law did not relieve a father of his conventional responsibilities, and ordered the father to pay his daughter.[55]

As the family courts sorted delicately through the complex mixture of the customary and the new, they faced the difficult demand by the new legislation that they suspend, or at least temper, the established practice of sacrificing daughters to family strategies. Ultimately, though resistance ran deep, in the majority of the cases the arbiters chose the new version of the family over the old one. In arbitration, litigating women clearly benefited from the reformist leanings of some well-placed lawyers in Caen. These men played a crucial role, for example, in interpreting the 8 April 1791 law, which forbade customary exclusions based on sex or birth order. Initially, this law excluded married offspring from benefiting from its provisions and elicited a confused response about the impact of the law on married daughters in particular.[56] The family courts negotiated in practice an issue that petitions and pamplets would raise in theory: should the law favor unmarried women and men over married women, the mothers of families? And even more important for juridical implementation, had Norman married women been automatically excluded by custom or had they renounced their inheritance portion via freely made contracts? In effect, the new law raised the broader question of whether daughters were entitled to equal rights as individuals or should subordinate their interests for the good of the family line.

Litigation provoked by the April 1791 law led family courts directly into debates over the legal rights and status of daughters within families. For example, when arbiters met in March 1793 to determine whether the married sisters Marie and Madeleine LeCreps and their husbands could redivide their paternal inheritance with their brother's widow, the debate turned to the heart of the issue regarding women's status: had they contracted freely or not? The arbiters chosen by the brother's widow asserted that a marriage contract could not be broken without overturning societal order: paradoxically, they wanted to maintain that daughters in fact had exercised individual property rights in the Old Regime. In turn, the sisters' arbiters argued vehemently that the law was now restoring lost equal rights to women. Above all, they contended that daughters had not been free to contract: "The heirs who make contractual agreements are free to agree; the daughter in Normandy has no freedom; she is subordinated to the will of her father; he can endow her or not, she is forced to accept what he offers her." These lawyers pointed out that mothers who gave children to the Republic should benefit from its equality and noted that most Old Regime Norman dowries were small – a notably weak argument in the current case which featured dowries of forty-three thousand livres for each daughter.[57]

Although the LeCreps sisters lost their case, most others were more successful in a reformist legal climate. Four prorevolutionary *hommes de loi* who often served as arbiters in Caen and surrounding communes wrote a 1792 opinion that urged fathers to recognize their daughters' rights to their affection as well as their property:

> We were so accustomed to see our daughters only as a portion, so to speak, of our beings; it was so convenient to send them out of the paternal house with a bouquet of roses, that we cannot resolve without pain to treat them as the equals of their brothers. . . .
>
> By remembering that *by birthright, all the children of the same father merit his affection and his aid equally*, we will convince ourselves that this disposition of *the new law* does not so much offer daughters an additional benefit, as it *restores a right*, which the old law had taken away from them out of contempt for nature.[58]

Even as they argued on behalf of married daughters, these lawyers' words betrayed the pervasive ambivalence at recognizing the "restored rights" of daughters once seen "as a portion, so to speak, of our beings." As one *homme de loi* in nearby Condé-sur-Noireau commented, "The old Norman prejudices do not surrender willingly to the authority of the law when it does not serve their personal interests." Nonetheless, by 1793 many lawyers repeatedly made decisions as arbiters or published briefs that whittled away at those "Norman prejudices." Citizen Lasseret, a frequently employed arbiter in Caen, wrote, "Daughters . . . should have the same rights as their brothers. The outmoded and barbarous laws had forgotten the rights of nature: the new laws, drawn from the bosom of philosophy and reason, have returned them to this agreeable and useful sex."[59] Revolutionary ideology had entered the courtroom and the family.

The family courts provided the forum for individual women to regain these new rights in practice. Sister after sister used the April 1791 or 17 *nivôse* laws to their own advantage. The legal historian Françoise Fortunet has uncovered a similar pattern in Burgundy. In addition, some families repartitioned inheritance shares amicably with the help of a notary and without recourse to the family courts.[60] Moreover, in Normandy, the new inheritance laws and the reformist legal mood also had a side effect that unintentionally worked to many women's advantage. Since the 17 *nivôse* law took the communal marital property system as its model and placed the old Norman dowry guarantees into an uncertain legal status, from 1795 until almost the fall of Napoleon a majority of families abandoned the Norman system and stipulated communal property in their sons' and daughters' marriage contracts. Many others chose a legal separation of goods within marriage, granting women extensive control over their own property. While the intention of parents and notaries was to find systems more in line with the changing legal structures and possibly to free property from some traditional controls, the result was to enlarge many widows' shares and to increase women's control over property. At least some parts of the Midi witnessed that same shift toward communal property in marriage among the artisanal classes.[61]

The family courts did their best to sort out family conflicts and to balance traditional family practices against the revolutionary attempt to guarantee individual liberty and equality within the home. The court records make little direct mention of revolutionary politics, but they reveal how deeply revolutionary ideology and laws demanded changes in existing conceptions of family structure and gender roles. Nervous about such changes, one arbiter commented that family courts "should not carry the Inquisition into families."[62] The workings of the family court also illustrate the instability of revolutionary settlements and help us to understand the growing conservatism of the later 1790s. In fact, family tribunals came under attack in the mid-1790s because of their crucial role in trying to administer the divisive and controversial 17 *nivôse* law. They faced abolition in early 1796 shortly after the convention overturned the retroactive clauses of the 17 *nivôse* law. Under the auspices of the departmental Civil Tribunal, some family courts nonetheless continued to operate in the Calvados, to enforce egalitarian divisions, and to handle some redivisions of properties that had been divided retroactively.[63]

Above all, the courts' negotiations of inheritance law reveal the profoundly ambiguous impact of the Revolution on women. The same radical leaders who sought to limit women's political voice in clubs,[64] simultaneously increased many women's legal leverage within the home and civil society. The new court structure, the influence of reform-minded lawyers, and the new set of laws governing the family created a situation in which many women could step into the legal arena and make unprecedented claims for egalitarian status within the family. Clearly, not all women won in the family courts: some lost their own individual cases; some lost when their husbands, fathers, or children were defeated; some who won retroactive settlements in the family courts would lose them in yet another redivision after 1795. But in inheritance cases, as in many cases involving divorce or paternal authority, the courts and laws allowed women, especially sisters and widows in certain regions, to demand rights that they had not had in the Old Regime. They were able to use the new revolutionary state on their own behalf.

Furthermore, for many women, the act of challenging family practices inspired them to look beyond their individual cases, to rethink the nature of the family, and to question assumptions about gender roles. These women had turned to litigation in a highly politicized climate, in the context of a Revolution that sought to convert women as well as men and stimulated the vocal participation of all its citizens. The political ideology of the Revolution combined with the possibility for greater legal rights within the family to politicize many women and to encourage them to express their demands for family reform. Many women chose to go beyond the local family tribunals and to petition the national legislature, advocating changes in law and family structure. Analysis of these rich sources complements the examination of litigation in court to provide a more complete view of the political as well as legal contestation over family structure on the grassroots level.

Popular petitioning for egalitarian inheritance

Petitions to national legislatures, individual deputies, and committees provide a valuable glimpse into how ordinary people perceived and received the revolutionary reform of the family and how they related to the new politics and the new state. Unlike lawmakers, the vast majority of petitioners had been or were engaged in litigation, so their words represent well the concerns, impressions, and varied political opinions of those most directly involved in the attempt to reconfigure the family. Since the petitions were meant to persuade, they need to be read with care: the authors often embraced a hyperbolic and inflammatory rhetoric. Their engagement in contentious litigation could lead them at times to exaggerate or distort the impact of revolutionary laws on family dynamics. Yet even as they wrote about how family, revolution, and law *ought* to interact, their idealized visions enable us to grasp popular political thinking with much greater depth than the leaner court records allow. Moreover, since their audience consisted of deputies rather than lawyers or fellow family members, petitioners generally voiced their political agendas and visions more explicitly than they had in court.[65]

This section will examine petitions from across France that demanded equal inheritance for women early in the Revolution or defended its implementation, retroactive to 1789, according to the 17 *nivôse* law. Both men and women petitioned on both sides of the issue, but two points need emphasis. First, female petitioners were much more likely than male petitioners to discuss the gender inequities of Old Regime succession practices and to demand their reform. Younger sons from areas governed by Roman law, primogeniture, or preferential legacy appealed for egalitarian divisions in rhetoric often parallel to their sisters', yet they made scant reference to their sisters' plight or to gender injustice. Strikingly, even in regions like Normandy where many husbands would clearly benefit via their wives from the abolition of the customary exclusion of daughters from legacies, very few men petitioned on behalf of their wives' fate or defended the new laws. One female petitioner wrote to the National Convention that they should maintain the egalitarian 17 *nivôse* law because it made even its critics happy: "All the brothers who clamor against this law benefit from it themselves through their wives," she noted in its defense.[66] Numerous Norman husbands sided with their wives' litigation against their brothers on an individual basis, but these men – unlike their wives – rarely made general appeals for gender equity in inheritance. Among men, only the occasional husband or younger brother, some vocal lawyers, and a few popular societies explicitly petitioned to support equal succession rights *for women*. Second, not all women petitioners favored egalitarian inheritance. Some wives and mothers remonstrated against the laws on behalf of newly disadvantaged husbands or sons, as did some who lost out due to changed rules governing gifts between spouses, bequests to non-family members, the ordering of collateral successions, and so on.[67] Since I seek to probe prorevolutionary female politicization in particular, I will draw primarily on petitions written by women who favored egalitarian inheritance. I will explore their moral stances, their uses of revolutionary ideology, their expectations of the state, and above all, their visions of family reform.

In any analysis of petitioning, the question of direct authorship is central. Only ten women clearly signed petitions written on their behalf by a lawyer, husband, or other *fondé de pouvoir*, and I found no evidence of women copying model petitions in favour of female inheritance rights.[68] Overall, the evidence suggests that individual women appealing for equal partition by and large wrote and composed their own petitions. Most petitions by women were poorly written, scribbled in a barely legible hand, and filled with grammatical errors and misspellings. Some petitioners were woefully misinformed and responded to rumors or false interpretations of the complex new laws. Other barely literate petitioners displayed a strikingly good grasp of new and old laws, and the revolutionary press kept them keenly aware of legislative debates and popular opinion in distant regions. For example, in 1795 a poorly written letter from the "young woman Villiers" of the Saône-et-Loire urged the deputies to open "their souls" to the pro-equality appeals "made by a great number of citizens from the department of la Manche."[69] Groups of women also sent collective petitions, occasionally even printed ones, whose authorship is hard to determine. Many communes, especially in the Midi, sent collective petitions that argued for egalitarian partition more generally and were signed by both men and women.

As women, collectively or individually, demanded the reform of inheritance laws or the maintenance of the 17 *nivôse* law, they adopted the revolutionary language of equal rights. In 1795 when an anonymous *calvadosienne* argued in favor of maintaining the retroactive power of the 17 *nivôse* law, she claimed that the law . . . "reestablished the *natural and imprescriptible rights* of the [female] sex. . . . The legislative assembly decreed all men equal in rights in 1789, and women and girls were included in this generic expression" (her emphasis). Writing in the same cause, Jeanne Barinçon of the Aude complained that it had taken the deputies "three years, six months, and 22 days" to restore equal rights by decreeing egalitarian inheritance. Certainly, these rights should be retroactive to 1789 because "a great people who have done everything possible to break their chains and reestablish their rights should enjoy them from the very moment that they rose up against these usurpations."[70]

Repeatedly, petitioners proclaimed that Nature called for equality within the family; both laws and political institutions should work to *restore* this *natural right*.[71] Individuals and groups presented their particular juridical circumstances as violations of equality, which the deputies must feel compelled to repair. For example, in Normandy, throughout the first half of the 1790s, a series of collective all-women petitions adopted this strategy in their appeals for specific laws protecting or increasing their *légitime* shares. The "citoyennes du département du Calvados" asserted, "Our claim . . . cannot be rejected by the defenders of Equality," echoing a similar declaration by the "citoyennes" of Coutances in 1792. The "unmarried women of Saint-Lô" warned the Legislative Assembly that the "immortal Constitution . . . will accomplish the happiness of the French people only once the assembly realizes that the *filles légitimaires* of the former province of Normandy have not yet been the object of your solicitude for the Nation." "At birth nature gave us equal rights to the succession of our fathers," asserted some forty women from the district of Falaise in 1795.[72] Far to the south, a petition from the Lot-et-Garonne, signed by both men and women, grounded its argument particularly eloquently in natural law: they reminded the deputies that the 17 *nivôse* law was "a restoration of the rights of nature. . . . This sublime law does not belong to you, legislators, it is from nature; she alone has dictated it, you have only been her mouthpiece." Individuals echoed this same emphasis on the restitution of rights to forgotten groups: "Your succession laws have not yet spoken about the fate of widows, which means that sacred equality does not yet reign in our republic," observed the *veuve* Gingoir.[73]

Yet, even as they appropriated the principles of natural rights and equality, pro-equality petitioners almost invariably imbued their appeals with a moral critique of the family as well. They seemed acutely aware that the new civil laws posed a challenge to customary family practices and, in particular, to the gender hierarchy within the household. Far from preordaining women's subjection within the nuclear family, liberal rights ideology – when put into practice – in fact led directly to questioning women's traditional subjugation to the family line.[74] And yet, the new ethic of individualism and equality stood in tension with an older validation of mutual contributions to the collective good. In a delicate balancing act, petitioners sought to criticize those customs without surrendering moral ground. As they claimed equal rights within the family, they drew on deep-rooted moral language to fortify the ethical rhetoric of rights and natural law, to lay bare customary injustices, and to validate their proposals for change. They perceived revolutionary politics not simply as a philosophical battle over citizens' rights as individuals, but as a moral struggle over definitions of justice within the collectivity, that is, within the family as well as the nation. Finally, as petitioners reenvisioned the family, contrary to what one might expect, they did not simply assimilate republican domesticity and emphasize women's value as mothers. Rousseau's emphasis on maternal softness or conjugal solicitude held no place in their appeals.[75] Rather, they forged a new vision of the family based on egalitarianism and affection, evenly divided "without distinction according to sex."

From the outset, women petitioning for equal inheritance denounced paternal and fraternal despotism within the family and unmasked the routine surrendering of women to the family interest. Two anonymous women in Rouen fired an opening salvo on this theme with their *Remonstrances des mères et filles normandes de l'ordre du tiers* in 1789: "If we finally accept as an organizing principle that the strong will no longer impose laws on the weak *in the great family of the State*, why would we allow it in our own families? *Why would we remain enslaved by this barbarous Custom which allows the father to sacrifice his daughters* through bad marriages to the puerile ambition of enriching the one who will carry his name? ... On what grounds would we want to maintain these hateful distinctions between children who have an *equal right to paternal tenderness*?" (my emphasis).[76] Female petitioners in Normandy and the Midi amplified these themes by claiming that the Law itself, the "barbarous laws" and "tyrannical customs" of the "feudal" Old Regime had stifled the natural affection and equality within families. It had allowed fathers "to regard their daughters as if they were not their own children" and "to dower them capriciously." Likewise, the old law had encouraged brothers to grow "deaf to the cries of Nature and to the voice of justice." In petition after petition, women demanding equal inheritance wielded revolutionary terminology to denounce "unnatural brothers," who perpetrated a "long and oppressive despotism" and who benefited from "privileges that wounded common rights and equality."[77] They also mastered the age-old imagery of hunger to condemn the gendered basis of misery. Margaret Briançon warned the Convention matter-of-factly that if they repealed the 17 *nivôse* law. "My brother will be a fat rich man and I will have no more bread. ... Representatives, bring about true justice and make equality reign between brothers and sisters." Countless writers contrasted the hardship of sisters with the "opulence," "laziness," and "greed" of (older) brothers, and appealed "in the name of humanity" for a "law that wants all citizens to survive."[78]

Some told individual tales of woe, adopting the heart-wrenching style of novels and printed *mémoires judiciaires* to give particular power to their petitions, to illuminate the unethical nature of prerevolutionary customs, and to move the sensitive hearts of the deputies.[79] The *fille* Anquetil described how her brother had locked her up, accused her of theft, stolen her possessions, chased her out of their house at midnight, and then stalled during an endless court case. The *citoyenne* Galot Thiphaine charged the legislators to consider her specific plight on behalf of the "public good. ... It is by paying attention to a particular case that you can rise to the task of perfecting the general law, for out of the discussion of particular cases are born ... the codes of civilized nations." Others gave more generalized depictions of injustice to emphasize the universality of the wrong and to clarify its gendered dimension. The "citoyennes du Calvados" claimed that the monster of despotism, "crushed by friends of liberty and equality, ... had taken refuge in Normandy, ... for it knew well that it would find almost as many protectors in this region as there are male inhabitants, because they are all interested in keeping the prerogatives that benefited sons to the detriment of daughters."[80]

By explicitly exposing the accepted policy of sacrificing daughters to family lineages, the petitioners clearly articulated in words what their litigation in family courts put into practice: they called into question a whole structure designed to conserve family property and facilitate the establishment of one or several sons. As the *citoyenne* Beaufils *veuve* Lavallé put it, "It was a mania and a prejudice on the part of our fathers pushed to excess to favor the conservation of family goods [*biens propres et de familles*]." She saluted revolutionary laws that had abolished distinctions between property of different origins and made it more difficult for families to keep property within the paternal or maternal line. The *citoyenne* Montfreulle offered a matter-of-fact description: "I was married in 1773 'for a bouquet of roses' to use the Norman expression. That was how girls were married then. Greed was in the air and one often sacrificed the daughters for the happiness of one son."[81] A lengthy printed petition made the point explicit: "Each family (and especially among the class of *cultivateurs*) wanted to see several of their children shine in the Church, Robe, commerce, military, or other arts, and it was the daughters who – out of respect and obedience for their father and mother and out of friendship with their brothers – upheld the work of the father by staying at home and working hard and with care; and their thrift enriched their brothers."[82]

Petitioners laid bare not just the submission of daughters, but also the legal subjugation of wives within marriage. Some women proposed new laws to repair those injustices, which left widows in a tenuous financial position. For example, *veuve* Gouet exposed the lack of legal protection for wives who were "forced by duty and by their state [of marriage] to follow their husbands" into a region governed by a different custom. She demanded legislation to safeguard their property under the new marital regime. Likewise, when the *citoyenne* LeBalleur sent the convention a legally complex request to protect women's dowries at a "just price," she exposed the inequity of marital structures that allowed "a husband, or rather a master" to coerce his wife to comply with the sale of her dower goods: "I raise the veil over marital despotism with regret . . . [but] I claim this natural equity, superior to forms, to texts, to opinions, to circumstances. . . . I am convinced, citizen representatives, that in the name of the French people, you will give my daughters a model of exact justice by decreeing what I demand."[83] By invoking a "just price" and an "equity, superior to forms, to texts," LeBalleur tapped into the resonant language of the moral economy even as she reminded the deputies of their duties within the new nation.

In associating timeworn family practices with tyranny and inequity, female petitioners harped on two themes with strong political and moral resonance: the need to attack egotistical wealth and to restore natural human sentiment. Their protest held particular power because it melded traditional moral judgments with the new revolutionary ethic. In their accounts, they fused popular culture depictions of excessive greed with the Jacobin image of wealth as a crime at once political and immoral. In addition, they adopted the republican ideals of fraternity and *sensibilité*. Jeanne Côme of the Gironde brandished this discourse in a colorful fashion: "Our brother rolls in money, our deceased father made him a fat *procureur* in the old royal justice system here, a notary all round and puffed up with pride." But at her father's deathbed, when she "had scarcely closed his eyes and begun to give vent to the tears and cries of Nature," her oldest brother assembled the family in the next room to reveal that he had tricked their father into leaving everything to him alone. The heartless cupidity of brothers, rather than the radicalism of revolutionary laws, tore the family apart. Catherine Douillat of the Charente-Inférieure accused her brother of being "more attached to money than sensitive to the tenderness that his sister and mother had always shown him." She demanded the maintenance of the "just" 17 *nivôse* law, which "spread equality in families while maintaining unity and peace."[84]

Beyond simply critiquing the existing family system, female petitioners also staked out a positive new vision of the affective family and voiced confidence that the law could regenerate human emotions as well as morality. Petition after petition suggested that the revolutionary laws would not just "restore equality within families," they would also encourage kindhearted ties within households and end "the reign of domination of the weakest by the strongest." Mutual regard within the family was a natural as well as social law, "for, whatever one says about it, it derives from Nature that one father divides all his tenderness, all his cares, the whole product of his work and thrift, among all his children, without distinction according to sex."[85] In the egalitarian family, personal affection and moral behavior would hold more sway than ambition or authority. As the *citoyenne* Bureau from the Midi argued: "The less power the laws accord to despotism, the more power sentiment will have. Announce to fathers that their principal influence should rest only in the authority of their virtues, the wisdom of their lessons, and the demonstration of their tenderness. . . . Then they will be more loved, more respected, and more listened to. . . . What domination loses, filial love will gain."[86] Good laws would cultivate "a just equilibrium" within households in the words of the Delié sisters: "Here, a kind and virtuous wife receives recompense for her work and cares from her grateful and just husband. There, a self-seeking mother is forced to transmit part of her husband's legacy to her children."[87] Far from promoting a simple individualism, petitioners suggested that laws should foster a sense of equitable responsibility within the home. As a new ethic of equality and mutual esteem replaced the old codes of hierarchy and sacrifice, families would be happier as well.

Explicitly drawing links between family and nation, petitioners asserted that reformed families conformed to the wishes of the sovereign people and would underpin the Republic. Equitable inheritance laws fulfilled "the public interest" and "the wishes of the majority of the sovereign people"; they created "twenty-five happy people for each unnatural brother" and "spread joy within families."[88] Some petitioners even suggested that family structures jibed with political forms of government. For example, the *citoyenne* Mallet asserted that the kinship practices of the old custom of Normandy were fitting to a monarchy, but the Republic should have equal inheritance "without distinction according to sex," retroactive to 10 August 1792. Such parallels could be colorful: "They say loudly that you will give us a king if you give heirs back their old prerogatives," warned one petitioner, adding that she might become another Charlotte Corday and use her example to "embolden the cadets and sisters to take justice into their own hands because the law only cared for them for a moment." Indeed, the interests of nation, nature, and morality were one. The young Adelaide Durand argued forcefully that egalitarian partitions enabled unmarried sisters "to marry and to fill that destiny so much in conformity with the wishes of Nature and the interest of the Nation."[89]

Interestingly, petitioners also saw a parallel between affective families and a state governed by transparent and openhearted legislators.[90] Just as petitioners portrayed an idealized world of kind fathers, they importuned the deputies to be morally attuned and sensitive (*sensible*) to all citizens alike and to maintain egalitarian partitions as "a sign of your affection" for all the citizens of the Republic. Declaring their "intimate confidence" in the deputies, some even entreated them as "the fathers of the nation" or as empathetic fathers of families to embrace the egalitarian laws.[91] Some authors added a particular twist: they invited the deputies to step in where their own fathers had failed or gone astray. "Deign to replace our fathers and defend us against the injustice, tyranny, and despotism of the brothers of Normandy," exhorted Jeanne Gallien in 1795: "Don't all your children have an equal right to your tenderness?" Likewise, Josephine Letellier urged the deputies to help her become "wife, mother, and *citoyenne*. . . . Can't I pass into your hands the power my father has over me?"[92]

Most petitioners did not ask their deputies to step so directly into their families, but on some level, they all appealed to the state to validate their independent criticism of family structures. The Revolution did more than supply a discourse and political context for demanding family reform; it became a rival point of authority, an institutional, legal, and moral ally against the traditional family. To align oneself with the nation in demanding family regeneration, to write "in the name of all the *républicaines* of the former province of Normandy," as did the self-proclaimed "Julie . . . *républicaine*," was to find a political lever to balance against the weight of family networks. It was also to exert a certain moral pressure on the deputies to live up to their promises and to heed the words of citizens, "or *citoyennes*," added *veuve* Descages.[93]

Positioning themselves between the traditional family and the new state, pro-equality petitioners set forth their demands and ideal visions. Egalitarian inheritance reform would not tear apart the tightly woven fabric of the family; rather, it would foster a more natural and just reciprocity, based on mutual affection and an ethos of equality between the sexes. Such families would remain true to codes of collective justice and would also constitute the moral fiber of the Republic. Indeed, the state's representatives had a responsibility, as well as an interest, in making laws to reform families in this way.

Conclusion

This exploration of women petitioning on behalf of egalitarian inheritance should contribute to our understanding of the nature of female politicization and feminist demand during the Revolution. For most women, to engage in revolutionary politics was not simply to embrace an entirely new set of principles. Rather, it was a complex balancing act between new and old allegiances. They viewed politics above all as a struggle over justice, over the moral economy of the family and nation. In defining this moral economy, petitioners for egalitarian inheritance appropriated the revolutionary language of equal rights guaranteed by nature and by law. But they fused this overly individualistic rights ideology with deep-rooted moral notions to voice a sometimes radical critique of existing family relations and gender dynamics, to make an appeal for the centrality of affect and reciprocity within family morality, and to link the legal reform of inheritance to the political and moral regeneration of the family and the state. Good laws, they argued, would bring about those goals, and the new nation would become possible only when the rights of women were no longer sacrificed to the family. Just as women litigating in court had used the new laws and institutions to demand greater equality, women petitioning in the same cause enlisted revolutionary politics to validate their claims. Their particular combination of rights ideology with a moral discourse on the family would inform French feminist thinking in the nineteenth century.[94] In the shorter term, its peculiar power in the revolutionary decade would also contribute to provoking the conservatism of the Civil Code.

In fact, the petition warfare and court contestation over inheritance law also offer insights into the backlash against family reform in the years leading up to the Napoleonic Civil Code. Despite frequent debate over civil law issues, the legislators during the Directory revised only the most extreme features of revolutionary civil law. In the case of inheritance laws, they ended retroactive partitions, but left their central provisions intact until the Napoleonic period. But the legislative debates and the conservative popular reaction against inheritance contestation developed themes and resolutions that the Civil Code would embrace. The petitioners who bemoaned the "war between brothers and sisters" and who attacked the egalitarian inheritance laws and their retroactive enforcement wrote in direct reaction to the litigation in court and to pro-equality petitioners. Portraying the ideal family as a source of order and stability, these conservative petitioners made scarce mention of familial affection or equality and defined morality primarily in terms of upholding the family unit, working on its behalf, and soothing its internal disorders. Although family litigation had also pitted brother against brother, many petitioners couched the conflict by and large in terms of gender conflict: they specifically denounced the laws for upsetting the relationship between the sexes and appealed for the reestablishment of patriarchal authority and traditional gender roles. The state should not pass laws that undermined or invaded family unity; rather, it should restore faith in contracts, defend the right to private property, promote strong family lineages, and sharply limit its definition of equality.[95] Their vision of the law reads as a prelude to the spirit of the Napoleonic Code and helps us understand its enactment into law.

Finally, this exploration of inheritance contestation demands that we rethink the argument that the revolutionary attempt to create democratic politics necessarily excluded women from the public sphere and consigned them to a domestic sphere. In fact, the Revolution called into question the nature of the family and its internal dynamics without resolving women's relationship to politics and the family. In practice, the family became an arena of cultural and political conflict, as politics spanned the gamut from the public to the personal. Revolutionary gender politics was riddled with contradictions: the rhetoric of female domesticity stood in tension with the legal recognition of women's civil rights. For, paradoxically, even as revolutionary leaders evoked images of patriotic mothers and closed down women's clubs, they also validated women's individual rights within families and set up legal institutions to enable women as well as men to make claims on family and state. Women were endowed with a limited form of citizenship, as well as a pivotal role in the moral regeneration of society.[96] These changes in law, institutions, and political culture had an ambiguous and complex impact on women. Laws did not pass easily into practice, and the significance of the changes varied immensely according to region, family and social structure, and each woman's individual position within the household. There can be no global assessment of women's experience of revolution. But by asking how some women reacted to these extensive changes and negotiated them to their own advantage, I have suggested that the impact of the Revolution was not simply to relegate women to a "private sphere" separate from the "public sphere" of politics, but rather to create a series of openings, of possibilities for female legal and political activism. These opportunities lay precisely at the hinge between family and nation, and they were particularly apparent in the realm of inheritance practice for sisters and some windows in Normandy and the Midi. These women's actions suggest the complexity of the path toward domesticity that revolutionary culture, law, and institutions simultaneously encouraged and undercut.

NOTES

Source Reprinted in an abridged format from *French Historical Studies* 20 (1997), pp. 597–634.
Acknowledgment Corinne Bléry, Peggy Darrow, Dena Goodman, Lynn Hunt, Mike Lynn, Sarah Maza, and Rod Phillips have all offered helpful suggestions. The author also thanks the participants in the Cornell European History Colloquium, especially Janine Lanza and Steven Kaplan, and the New York Area French History Seminar, especially Tip Ragan and Isser Woloch.

1   Archives nationales (hereafter AN), DIII 33, "Pétition de la citoyenne LeFranc à la Convention nationale, 30 germinal an III" (22 Mar. 1795); AN DIII 274, "Pétition des citoyens Lenoir et Lammarré aux députés du département de la Manche, 1 frimaire an

III" (21 Nov. 1794). They used the French phrase "dépaternalisé, défraternisé, dessocialisé."

2 Jean-Louis Halpérin, *L'Impossible Code civil* (Paris, 1992); Marcel Garaud and Romuald Szramkiewicz, *La Révolution française et la famille* (Paris, 1978); James Traer, *Marriage and the Family in Eighteenth-Century France* (Ithaca, N.Y., 1980).

3 Based on extensive reading of hundreds of civil law petitions to revolutionary legislatures and committees, esp. in AN, series AD II (Archives imprimées), AD XVIIIc (Suppléments aux P-V des Assemblées nationales), C (Addresses à la Convention), DIII (Comité de législation); DXXXIX (Comité de la classification des lois).

4 Dominique Dessertine, *Divorcer à Lyon sous la Révolution et l'Empire* (Lyon, 1981), 159–73; Roderick Phillips, *Family Breakdown in Late Eighteenth-Century France: Divorces in Rouen, 1792–1803* (Oxford, 1980). On inheritance, Margaret Darrow, *Revolution in the House: Family, Class, and Inheritance in Southern France, 1775–1825* (Princeton, N.J., 1989).

5 Leslie Page Moch et al., "Family Strategies: A Dialogue," *Historical Methods* 20 (1987): 115–25; Louise Tilly, "Women's History and Family History: Fruitful Collaboration or Missed Connection?," *Journal of Family History* 12 (1987): 303–15.

6 Dominique Godineau, *Citoyennes tricoteuses: Les Femmes du peuple à Paris pendant la Révolution française* (Aix-en-Provence, 1988); Harriet Applewhite and Darline G. Levy, eds., *Women and Politics in the Age of Democratic Revolution* (Ann Arbor, Mich., 1990); Darline G. Levy, Harriet B. Applewhite, and Mary Durham Johnson, eds., *Women in Revolutionary Paris, 1789–1795* (Urbana, Ill., 1979). Works on religious or counter-revolutionary activists include Suzanne Desan, *Reclaiming the Sacred: Lay Religion and Popular Politics in Revolutionary France* (Ithaca, N.Y., 1990), 197–214; Olwen Hufton, *Women and the Limits of Citizenship in the French Revolution* (Toronto, 1992); and Nicole Vray, *Les Femmes dans la tourmente* (Rennes, 1988).

7 Joan Landes, *Women and the Public Sphere in the Age of the French Revolution* (Ithaca, N.Y., 1988). See also Geneviève Fraisse, *Muse de la Raison: La Démocratie exclusive et la différence des sexes* (Aix-en-Provence, 1989); Madelyn Gutwirth, *The Twilight of the Goddesses: Women and Representation in the French Revolutionary Era* (New Brunswick, N.J., 1992); Sarah Maza, *Private Lives and Public Affairs: The Causes Célèbres of Prerevolutionary France* (Berkeley, Calif., 1993); Joan Scott, " 'A Woman Who Has Only Paradoxes to Offer': Olympe de Gouges Claims Rights for Women," in *Rebel Daughters: Women and the French Revolution*, ed. Sarah Melzer and Leslie Rabine (New York, 1992), 102–20.

8 Critiques include Dena Goodman, "Public Sphere and Private Life: Toward a Synthesis of Current Historiographical Approaches to the Old Regime," *History and Theory* 31 (1992): 1–20; Daniel Gordon, Daniel Bell, and Sarah Maza, "Forum on the Public Sphere in the Eighteenth Century," *French Historical Studies* 17 (1992): 882–956; Jennifer Jones, "Repackaging Rousseau: Femininity and Fashion in Old Regime France," *French Historical Studies* 18 (1994): 939–67, esp. 939–42; Elizabeth Kindleberger, "Charlotte Corday in Text and Image: A Case Study in the French Revolution and in Women's History," *French Historical Studies* 18 (1994): 969–1000; Mona Ozouf, *Les Mots des femmes: Essai sur la singularité française* (Paris, 1995), 347–64.

9 Lynn Hunt, *The Family Romance of the French Revolution* (Berkeley, Calif., 1992); Elizabeth Colwill, "Transforming Women's Empire: Representations of Women in French Political Culture, 1770–1807" (Ph.D. diss., State University of New York at Binghamton, 1991); Ewa Lajer-Burcharth, "David's *Sabine Women*: Body, Gender, and Republican Culture under the Directory," *Art History* 14 (1991): 397–430.

10 *Archives parlémentaires*, 59: 680, 7 Mar. 1793.

11 The deputies made exceptions for existing marriage contracts and for widows and widowers with children. These exceptions would be overridden in January 1793.

12 Children of adultery (*adultérins*) could claim one-third of a regular share of inheritance as a food pension.

13 The 17 *nivôse* law ruled that this small disposable portion could go only to heirs outside the direct or collateral lines. Most gifts (*donations*) were outlawed, and surviving spouses with children had the right to usufruct of no more than half of their partner's property.

14 The Civil Code allowed a disposable portion of one-half in the case of one child or no children; one-third in the case of two children; and one-quarter in the case of three or more children. The law of 4 *germinal an* VIII (25 Mar. 1800) had already increased the size of the disposable portion to an amount dependent on the number of offspring (one-quarter for three children or fewer, one-fifth in the case of four children, one-sixth in the case of five children, and so on). See André Dejace, *Les Règles de la dévolution successorale sous la Révolution (1789–1794)* (Brussels, 1957); Traer, *Marriage and the Family*, 137–90; Halpérin, *Impossible Code*; Jacques Poumarède, "La Législation successorale de la Révolution entre l'idéologie et la pratique," in *La Famille, la loi, l'état de la Révolution au Code civil*, ed. Irène Théry and Christian Biet (Paris, 1989), 167–82.

15 Voltaire, "Coutumes," in *Dictionnaire philosophique*, vol. 5 of *Œuvres complètes* (Paris, 1878), 272, as quoted by Halpérin, *Impossible Code*, 19.

16 In the west, strict equality prevailed, while custom in the Paris-Orléans region generally allowed heirs to choose between keeping gifts (such as benefits set up in marriage contracts) that they had received during their parents' lifetimes or returning those gifts and partaking in the final division at the death of the parent (system of *rapport-option*). Emmanuel LeRoy Ladurie, "Système de la coutume: Structures familiales et coutumes d'héritages en France au XVIe siècle," *Annales: Economies, sociétés, civilisations* 27 (1972): 825–46; Poumarède, "Législation successorale," 180–81; Jean Yver, *Egalité entre héritiers et exclusion des filles dotées, essai de géographie coutumière* (Paris, 1966). On women and Old Regime civil law in regions across France, see Paul Ourliac and Jean-Louis Gazzinga, *Histoire du droit privé français de l'an mille au Code civil* (Paris, 1985).

17 On resistance to new laws, see Joseph Goy, "Transmission successorale et paysannerie pendant la Révolution française: Un grand malentendu," *Etudes rurales* 110 (1988): 45–56; Elisabeth Claverie et Pierre Lamaison, *L'Impossible mariage: Violence et parenté en Gévaudan, XVIIe, XVIIIe, XIXe siècles* (Paris, 1982), 67–73; Alain Collomp, "Tensions, Dissensions, and Ruptures inside the Family in Seventeenth- and Eighteenth-Century Haute-Provence," in *Interest and Emotion: Essays on the Study of Family and Kinship*, ed. Hans Medick and David Warren Sabean (Cambridge, 1984), 145–70, esp. 168–69; and Jean-François Chassaing, "Les Successions et les donations à la fin de l'ancien régime et sous la Révolution," *Droit et cultures* 3 (1982): 85–111, esp. 87–88. On family courts, see Olivier Devaux, "Les Tribunaux de famille du district de Rieux et l'application de la loi du 17 nivôse an II," *Annales de l'Université des sciences sociales de Toulouse* 35 (1987): 135–58, and idem, "A propos de la transmission du patrimoine: La Loi du 17 nivôse an II," in *Propriété et Révolution: Actes du Colloque de Toulouse, 12–14 octobre 1989*, ed. Geneviève Koubi (Toulouse, 1990), 99–108; Marc Ferret, *Les Tribunaux de famille dans le district de Montpellier (1790–an IV)* (Montpellier, 1926); Françoise Fortunet, "Connaissance et conscience juridique à l'époque révolutionnaire en pays de droit coutumier: La Législation successorale," in *La Révolution et l'ordre juridique privé: Rationalité ou scandale? Actes du Colloque d'Orléans. 11–13 septembre 1986*, 2 vols. (Orléans, 1988), 1:359–71; Poumarède, "Législation successorale"; and James Traer, "The French Family Court," *History* 59 (1974): 211–28.

18 Poumarède, "Législation successorale." While the law abolished dowers for those married after its promulgation, the status of dowers for widows married before 17 *nivôse* lay open to diverse interpretation. In Normandy dowers were granted to any widow married pre-17 *nivôse*. Appeals courts ultimately judged that the law did not

suppress existing dowers across France. J. B. Duvergier, *Collection complète des lois, décrets, ordonnances, réglements, et avis du Conseil d'état* (Paris, 1834), 16:381–82. Corinne Bléry, "L'Application du régime matrimonial normand devant la cour de cassation au XIXe siècle" (Mémoire de DEA, Université de Caen, 1988).

19 Anonymous review of François Lanthenas, *Inconvéniens du droit d'aînesse*, in *Courrier de Lyon*, 14–15 Oct. 1789, 313–16, 320–24, quoted in Gary Kates, " 'The Powers of Husband and Wife Must Be Equal and Separate': The *Cercle social* and the Rights of Women," in Applewhite and Levy, *Women and Politics*, 163–80, 168. According to Kates, Madame Roland probably wrote the review. See also Gary Kates, *The Cercle Social, the Girondins, and the French Revolution* (Princeton, N.J., 1985), 115–27.

20 Paul Hanson, *Provincial Politics in the French Revolution: Caen and Limoges, 1789–1794* (Baton Rouge, La., 1989).

21 Jean-Claude Perrot, *Genèse d'une ville moderne: Caen au XVIIIe siècle*, 2 vols. (Paris, 1975), 1:312–19, 364–65; Charles Alline, *De l'ancien régime matrimonial normand et de sa survivance dans la pratique notariale sous le droit intermédiaire et sous le code civil* (Thèse de droit, Université de Caen, 1908), 120–30. Given the control of customary law over the disposal of property, marriage contracts were narrower in scope and less frequently used in Normandy than elsewhere in France. Perrot, "Note sur les contrats de mariage normands," annex in Adeline Daumard and François Furet, *Structures et relations sociales à Paris au XVIIIe siècle*, Cahiers des Annales 18 (Paris, 1961), 95–97.

22 Real property in certain cities (*bourgs*), including Caen, legally qualified as *bourgages*. Daughters could claim an equal share of that property, and widows could claim their *douaire* share of *bourgages* property outright rather than in usufruct only. On *bourgages*, see Ambroise Colin, "Le Droit des gens mariés dans la coutume de Normandie," *Nouvelle revue historique de droit français et étranger* 16 (1892): 427–69, esp. 460–65; Robert Génestal, *La Tenure en bourgage: Etude sur la propriété foncière dans les villes normandes* (Paris, 1900); Perrot, *Genèse d'une ville*, 1:30–31, 318. On daughters' inheritance, see Robert Besnier, "Les Filles dans le droit successoral normand," *Tijdschrift voor Rechtsgeschedenis: Revue d'histoire du droit* 10 (1930): 488–506; Jacqueline Musset, "Les Droits successoraux des filles dans la coutume de Normandie," in *La Femme en Normandie: Actes du XIXe Congrès des sociétés historiques et archéologiques de Normandie* (Caen, 1986), 53–60.

23 Claude Mazauric, "Réflexions sur l'efficacité sociale du droit successoral cauchois à la veille de son abolition révolutionnaire," in *Révolution et l'ordre juridique privé*, 1:345–58. Even in other parts of Normandy, the system de facto favored the eldest son who received his inheritance portion earliest and used it the longest before the egalitarian redivision at the parents' death. David Sabean, "Aspects of Kinship Behaviour and Property in Rural Western Europe before 1800," in *Family and Inheritance: Rural Society in Western Europe, 1200–1800*, ed. Jack Goody, Joan Thirsk, and E. P. Thompson (Cambridge, 1976), 98–110, esp. 106–7.

24 Pierre Goubert, *The French Peasantry in the Seventeenth Century*, trans. Ian Patterson (Cambridge, 1986), 70–81; Perrot, *Genèse d'une ville*, 1:312–17; Hervé LeBras and Emmanuel Todd, *L'Invention de la France: Atlas anthropologique et politique* (Paris, 1981), 13–88. Quotation from Jean-Marie Gouesse, "Parenté, famille, et mariage en Normandie aux XVIIe et XVIIIe siècles," *Annales: Economies, sociétes, civilisations* 27 (1972): 1139–54.

25 The husband could not alienate the real estate portion of his wife's dowry without guaranteeing a specific replacement (*remploi*). A widow had the right to her dowry, to the usufruct of up to one-third of her husband's real estate, and to the simple possession of one-third of his movable goods if they had children, one-half if they had none. Alline, *De l'ancien régime matrimonial normand*, pt. I; Pierre Cinquabre, "Le Statut juridique de la femme en Normandie aux XVIIe et XVIIIe siècles," in *Femme en Normandie*, 43–51; Charles Lefebvre, "L'Ancien droit matrimonial de Normandie," *Nouvelle revue historique de droit français et étranger* 35 (1911): 481–535.

26 Fortunet, "Connaissance et conscience juridique"; Jean Bart, "L'Egalité entre héritiers dans la région dijonnaise à la fin de l'Ancien Régime et sous la Révolution," *Mémoires de la société pour l'histoire du droit et des institutions des anciens pays bourguignons, comtois, et romands* 29 (1968): 65–78; Paulette Poncet-Crétin, "La Pratique testamentaire en Bourgogne et en Franche-Comté de 1770 à 1815" (Thèse de droit, Université de Dijon, 1973), 16–23, 256–71; Darrow, *Revolution in the House*, 167, 240; Devaux, "Tribunaux de famille du district de Rieux"; Ferret, *Les Tribunaux de famille dans le district de Montpellier (1790–an IV)*; Poumarède, "Législation successorale"; Traer, "French Family Court."

27 Traer, *Marriage and the Family*, 32–47; James Farr, *Authority and Sexuality in Early Modern Burgundy* (Oxford, 1995), 90–123; Roland Mousnier, *Les Institutions de la France sous la monarchie absolue*, 2 vols. (Paris, 1974–80), 2:249–408. On Norman seigneurial courts, see Jonathan Dewald, *Pont-Saint-Pierre, 1398–1789: Lordship, Community, and Capitalism in Early Modern France* (Berkeley, Calif., 1987), 251–63.

28 Old Regime family councils often dealt with guardianship: Archives départementales du Calvados (hereafter ADC), 1B 1185, "Délibérations de famille, bailliage de Caen, 1788–89." On pre-1789 arbitration, see Nicole Castan, *Justice et répression en Languedoc à l'époque des lumières* (Paris, 1980), 13–51. On family courts, see Traer, "French Family Court"; Isser Woloch, *The New Regime: Transformations of the French Civic Order, 1789–1820s* (New York, 1994), 307–20; Claudine Bloch and Jean Hilaire, "Nouveauté et modernité du droit révolutionnaire: La Procédure civile," in *Révolution et l'ordre juridique privé*, 2:469–82; Jean-Jacques Clère, "L'Arbitrage révolutionnaire: Apogée et déclin d'une institution (1790–1806)," *Revue de l'arbitrage* (1981): 3–28; Jean Halpérin, "La Composition des tribunaux de famille sous la Révolution, ou les juristes, comment s'en débarrasser?," in *La Famille, la loi, l'état*, 292–304.

29 Devaux, "Tribunaux de famille du district de Rieux," 146–47; Ferret, *Tribunaux de famille*, Traer, "French Family Court," 219–20.

30 My sample includes all the family court cases clearly occurring in the town of Caen and a random sample of cases in communes of the surrounding district. ADC, 3L 608–17, "Sentences arbitrales du district de Caen" (hereafter SA Caen). Families who returned repeatedly to arbitration are counted only once. Also on Caen, see Jean Forcioli, *Une Institution révolutionnaire, le tribunal de famille d'après les archives du district de Caen* (Thèse de droit, Université de Caen, 1932). Forcioli was able to find only seventy-two cases for the district; more records must have surfaced in the reorganization of the archives of the department of Calvados following World War II.

31 Three cases involved both sibling and dowry disputes. Only four of the widowhood cases involved widowers rather than widows.

32 ADC, 3L 616, SA Caen, 17 *fructidor an* III (3 Sept. 1795); ADC, 3L 614, SA Caen, 3 *frimaire an* III (23 Nov. 1794); ADC, 3L 617, SA Caen, 24 *thermidor an* III (11 Aug. 1795).

33 The lack of precise figures, the variety of complex property types, and the vagaries of the *assignat* prevent the calculation of a reliable average of the amounts in contestation. Devaux comes to the same impasse and also finds frequent contestation over relatively small sums in the family courts in the Haute-Garonne ("Tribunaux de famille du district de Rieux," 155). Olwen Hufton estimates that poor families in nearby Bayeux needed three to four hundred livres a year to subsist; manual laborers typically left only about forty livres' worth of material possessions (*Bayeux in the Late Eighteenth Century* [Oxford, 1967], 81–84).

34 I could determine the duration of 122 of the 143 cases: less than two months in 82 cases (67 percent); two to six months in 19 cases (16 percent); six months or more in 21 cases (17 percent).

35 ADC, Registres 3L 618–3L 626, "Tribunal de district de Caen, minutes d'audience, 5 Jan. 1791–23 *fructidor an* III" (9 Sept. 1795). After the abolition of the district court, the Civil Tribunal of the department enforced family court decisions. ADC, 3L 1354, "Tribunal civil du Calvados, minutes d'audience, 28 *brumaire an* IV" (19 Nov. 1795).

36 Only in 1791 did the majority of arbiters lack legal training. See also Forcioli, *Institution révolutionnaire*, 39. Halpérin, "Composition des tribunaux," 298–99; Phillips, *Family Breakdown*, 22–28; Traer, "French Family Court," 215–19; Paul Viard, "Les Tribunaux de famille dans le district de Dijon (1790–1792)," *Nouvelle revue historique de droit français et étranger* 45 (1921): 242–77, esp. 249–56; Devaux, "Tribunaux de famille du district de Rieux"; Ferret, *Tribunaux de famille dans le district de Montpellier*, 103–5.

37 Halpérin, *Impossible Code*, 174–99, quote 183.

38 Traer, "French Family Court," 225; Halpérin, "Composition des tribunaux," 300.

39 ADC, 3L 1334–3L 1338, "Sentences arbitrales, an IV–VIII" (1796–1800), registered by the Tribunal civil du Calvados (hereafter SA Calvados). These arbitration sessions finally stopped calling themselves "tribunaux de famille" by late 1797 and gradually dealt with fewer divorce and inheritance cases. See also Traer, *Marriage and the Family*, 164.

40 For thought-provoking works on how law, cultural norms, and family and individual strategies all affect practice, see Farr, *Authority and Sexuality*; Hendrik Hartog, "Marital Exits and Marital Expectations in Nineteenth-Century America," *Georgetown Law Journal* 80 (1991): 95–129; Thomas Kuehn, *Law, Family, and Women: Toward a Legal Anthropology of Renaissance Italy* (Chicago, 1991).

41 ADC, 3L 614, SA Caen 28 *frimaire an* III (18 Dec. 1794); ADC, 3L 615, SA Caen 23 *ventôse an* III (13 Mar. 1795). Litigators repeatedly justify their actions along these lines in petitions. Examples include AN, DIII 338, "Mémoire de la citoyenne Jeanne Rouillaud femme Mouret au Comité de législation," n.d., c. spring 1795; AN, DIII 147, "Pétition des citoyennes filles en général de la commune de Tourville [La Manche] aux représentants du peuple, 30 germinal an III" (19 April 1795); AN, DIII 35, "Mémoire de la citoyenne Françoise Quesnay femme Lefort à la Convention nationale, reçu 26 fructidor an II" (12 Sept. 1794).

42 Traer, *Marriage and the Family*; Poumarède, "Législation successorale."

43 ADC, 3L 613, SA Caen, 27 *floréal an* II (16 May 1794). Phillips, *Family Breakdown*, 22.

44 ADC, 3L 615, SA Caen 2 *nivôse an* III (22 Dec. 1795); ADC, 3L 615, SA Caen, 29 *ventôse an* III (19 Mar. 1795). For married women "chargées" to represent themselves as plaintiffs, or to represent their brothers, husbands, or son-in-laws, see, for example, ADC, 3L 611, SA Caen, 11 July 1793; ADC, 3L 611, SA Caen, 22 July 1793; ADC, 3L 616, SA Caen, 26 *floréal an* III (15 May 1795); ADC, 3L 617, SA Caen, 22 *brumaire an* IV (13 Nov. 1795); ADC, 3L 615, SA Caen, 25 *ventôse an* III (15 Mar. 1795); ADC, 3L 614, SA Caen, 23 *brumaire an* III (13 Nov. 1794); ADC, 3L 611, SA Caen, 24 Sept. 1793; ADC, 3L 1336, SA Calvados, 8 *ventôse an* VI (26 Feb. 1798). Procurations were often notarized: examples include ADC, 8E 4393 and 8E 3119, "Tabellionage de Caen, Dépôts de Poignaut & Bocave, an IV." On Old Regime female proxies, see Darrow, *Revolution in the House*, 121.

45 ADC, 3L 610, SA Caen, 25 Oct. 1792. On women's uses of legal powerlessness, see Natalie Zemon Davis, *Fiction in the Archives* (Stanford, Calif., 1987); Castan, *Justice et répression*, 233–37, and idem, *Les Criminels de Languedoc: Les Exigences d'ordre et les voies du ressentiment dans une société pré-révolutionnaire (1750–1790)* (Toulouse, 1980), 25–36; Gayle K. Brunelle, "Dangerous Liaisons: Mésalliance and Early Modern French Noblewomen," *French Historical Studies* 19 (1995): 75–103; Yves Castan, "Statuts féminins au XVIIIe siècle d'après les profils exemplaires des plaidoyers en Languedoc," in *Droit, histoire, sexualité*, ed. Jacques Poumarède and Jean-Pierre Royer (Lille, 1987), 169–75; Darrow, *Revolution in the House*, 205.

46 After September 1792, women could witness acts in the *état civil*. See examples beginning in ADC, 5 mi 1 R55, "Etat civil de Caen, mariages et divorces," 1793. For questions and disputes over various aspects of women's ability to witness or make contracts, see AN, DIII 194, "Lettre des administrateurs du département de l'Orne au Comité de législation, 19 *fructidor an* II" (5 Sept. 1794); AN, DIII 147, "Lettre du J. B. Fafrin, membre du conseil général de la commune de Valogne [La Manche] au Comité de

législation, 17 *fructidor an II*" (3 Sept. 1794); ADC, 3L 611, SA Caen, 10 Sept. 1793; ADC, 3L 615, SA Caen, 8 *pluviôse an* III (27 Jan. 1795); ADC, 3L 610, SA Caen, 23 Oct. 1792.

47 ADC, 3L 616, SA Caen, 1 *prairial an* III (20 May 1795); ADC, 3L 616, SA Caen, 15 *prairial an* III (4 June 1795); ADC, 3L 615, SA Caen, 23 *ventôse an* III (13 Mar. 1795); ADC, 3L 614, SA Caen, 8 *brumaire an* III (29 Oct. 1794); ADC, 3L 614, SA Caen, 26 *brumaire an* III (16 Nov. 1794); ADC, 3L 610, SA Caen, 25 Oct. 1792. On mutual gifts, see ADC, 3L 601, "Tribunal du district de Caen, Enregistrement des insinuations des donations entre-vifs, 31 Dec. 1790–an IV" (1796). Despite challenges, the new spousal gifts held up in court.

48 On sisters' inability to obtain their *légitimes* successfully in the Old Regime, see Roger Bataille, *Du droit des filles dans la succession de leurs parents en Normandie, et particulière-ment du mariage avenant* (Thèse de droit, Université de Paris, 1927), 116–56; Henri Basnage, *Commentaires sur la coutume de Normandie*, 2 vols. (Rouen, 1776), 1:394; AN, DIII 32, "Pétition par les citoyennes soussignées du département du Calvados à la Convention nationale," received 3 Mar. 1793.

49 ADC, 3L 614, SA Caen, 21 *frimaire an* III (11 Dec. 1794); ADC, 3L 617, SA Caen, 6 *messidor an* III (24 June 1795). For comparable *légitime* claims in the Pyrénées, see Poumarède, "Législation successorale," 175.

50 ADC, 3L 1334, SA Calvados, 23 *vendémiaire an* IV (15 Oct. 1795); ADC, 3L 612, SA Caen, 20 *brumaire an* II (10 Nov. 1793).

51 ADC, 3L 608, SA Caen, 28 Nov. 1791, sent to the district tribunal for final decision; ADC, 3L 612, SA Caen, 18 *frimaire an* II (8 Dec. 1793); ADC, 3L 614, SA Caen, 29 *brumaire an* III (19 Nov. 1794).

52 ADC, 3L 610, SA Caen, 3–5 Aug. 1792; ADC, 3L 611–12, SA Caen, 21 Feb. 1793–5 *brumaire an* II (27 Oct. 1793); ADC, 3L 610–11, SA Caen, 12 Aug. 1792–28 Mar. 1793; ADC, 3L 615, SA Caen, 17 *pluviôse an* III (5 Feb. 1795). Quotations from AN, DIII 33, "Pétition des citoyennes Marie Jeanne et Marie Rogne au comité de législation, 5 messidor an II" (23 June 1794). See also Alline, *L'Ancien Régime matrimonial normand*, pt. II, 99–174; Devaux, "Tribunaux de famille du district de Rieux," 143–44; Claverie and Lamaison, *Impossible mariage*, 69–71; Goy, "Transmission successorale," 52; Poumarède, "Législa-tion successorale," 175–76. Darrow suggests that in the Tarn-et-Garonne, resistance to the new laws was stronger among the peasantry than among the bourgeois or artisanal classes (*Revolution in the House*, 86–170, 210–47). Decisions without brothers present were frequent, esp. in 1794–95 (ADC, 3L 613–17, SA Caen, 1794–1795).

53 ADC, 3L 612, SA Caen, 27 *floréal an* II (16 May 1794); ADC, 3L 613, SA Caen, 20 *germinal–26 floréal an* II (9 Apr.–15 May 1794); ADC, 3L 617, SA Caen, 8 *fructidor an* III (25 Aug. 1795); ADC, 3L 614, SA Caen, 15 *frimaire an* III (5 Dec. 1794). Petitioners who critiqued the 17 *nivôse* law had particularly argued that sons were shortchanged for years of work on paternal property.

54 ADC, 3L 613, SA Caen, 14 *floréal–27 thermidor an* II (3 May–14 Aug. 1794). See also ADC, 3L 616, SA Caen, 5 *germinal an* II (25 Mar. 1794); ADC, 3L 611, 614–15, SA Caen, 22 Oct. 1793–97 *nivôse an* III (27 Dec. 1794); ADC, 3L 610, SA Caen, 28 Oct. 1792; ADC, 3L 614, SA Caen, 28 *frimaire an* III (18 Dec. 1794).

55 ADC, 3L 610–11, SA Caen, 3 Dec. 1791–1 June 1793; ADC, 3L 613, SA Caen, 11 *fructidor an* II (28 Aug. 1794).

56 AN, ADII 48, AN, DIII 339, and the DIII dossiers for Norman departments in particular contain printed legal briefs and letters from lay citizens, lawyers, and officials regard-ing the impact of the 8 April 1791 law on Norman women. Many complain that neighboring district tribunals do not interpret the status of married women in the same way.

57 ADC, 3L 611, SA Caen, 26 Mar. 1793.

58 AN, DIII 339, *Question de droit: Consultation. De la succession des filles normandes, délibéré à Caen, 22 décembre 1792*, by *hommes de loi* Thome, Regnault, Pelvey, et Chrétien (Caen, 1792). My emphasis.

59 AN, DIII 34, "Pétition du citoyen Grandmaison, homme de loi à Condé-sur-Noireau [Calvados], au citoyen président de la Convention nationale, 4 juin 1793"; AN, ADII 48, " 'Réponse à un mémoire ayant pour titre, mémoire à l'appui de la pétition présentée à la Convention nationale le 24 mai 1793 relative aux decrets rendus sur la succesion *ab intestat*, par Viellard,' par Lasseret, membre du bureau de conciliation de Caen" (Caen, n.d., c. 1793); AN, DIII 33, "Pétition du citoyen Lagranche [de Caen] au Citoyen président, 28 mai 1793"; AN, DIII 145, "Pétition du citoyen Dellebecque [homme de loi à Falaise, Calvados] aux citoyens législateurs, 13 août 1793"; "Pétition du citoyen Desclosets [Falaise] aux citoyens législateurs, 9 juin 1793." Various *mémoires* printed by the Imprimerie J. L. Poisson in Caen and by the Imprimerie Desenne in Paris supported this interpretation of the April 1791 law and married daughters' legacy rights in general.

60 Fortunet, "Connaissance et conscience juridique." On notarized acts, see ADC, 3Q 2172, "Table des successions, Bureau de Caen" (1791–1809). At least one family notarized their decision not to redivide again regardless of changes in law. See ADC, 8E 3118, "Dépôt de Bocave, notaire Pillet, Accord de la famille Mesange, 25 frimaire an IV" (16 Dec. 1795); see also Poumarède, "La Législation successorale," 177.

61 Alline, *L'Ancien Régime matrimonial normand*, 94–193; Darrow, *Revolution in the House*, 247.

62 ADC, 3L 613, SA Caen, 15 *germinal an* III (4 Apr. 1795).

63 The law of 3 *vendémiaire an* IV (25 Sept. 1795) reversed the retroactive portions of the 17 *nivôse* law, allowing for another round of redivisions, although fewer redivisions occurred than one might expect. Halpérin, *Impossible Code*, 261. The family courts conducted a few redivisions: ADC, 3L 615, SA Caen, 21 *vendémiaire an* IV (13 Oct. 1795); ADC, 3L 1334, SA Calvados, 6 *vendémiaire an* IV (28 Sept. 1795), SA Calvados, 22 *brumaire an* IV (13 Nov. 1795), SA Calvados, 9 *brumaire an* IV (31 Oct. 1795), SA Calvados, 27 *nivôse an* IV (17 Jan. 1796); ADC, 3L 1335, SA Calvados, 25 *ventôse an* V (15 Mar. 1797), SA Calvados, 15 *thermidor an* V (2 Aug. 1797). The vast notarial records no doubt contain more redivisions.

64 Suzanne Desan, " 'Constitutional Amazons': Jacobin Women's Clubs in the French Revolution," in *Recreating Authority in Revolutionary France*, ed. Bryant Ragan and Elizabeth Williams (New Brunswick, N.J., 1992), 11–35; Godineau, *Citoyennes tricoteuses*, 166–77.

65 Analysis based on hundreds of petitions sent to the national legislatures, deputies, or various committees. See n. 3. See esp. AN, DIII 338, 339, 361, 382, Comité de législation, and AN, DXXXIX 4–8, Comité de la classification des lois.

66 AN, DIII 143, "Pétition de la citoyenne Jeanne Gallien veuve Barenton aux citoyens représentants, 9 floréal an III" (28 Apr. 1795).

67 Wives and mothers petitioned far more often on behalf of their husbands and sons than husbands and fathers did on behalf of wives and daughters.

68 Model petitions *attacking* egalitarian inheritance laws circulated widely in both the Midi and Normandy, at least in the departments of Lot-et-Garonne, Tarn, Calvados, la Manche, Seine-Inférieure. Model petitions favoring egalitarian inheritance were evidently rare: I found only one, from the Tarn, which favored cadet inheritance without reference to gender. See AN, DIII 338, "Adresse des héritiers rappelés de la commune de ———— à la Convention nationale," n.d., c. 1795.

69 AN, DIII 338, "Pétition de la citoyenne fille Villier aux citoyens législateurs, 16 floréal an III" (5 May 1795).

70 AN, DIII 274, "Pétition anonyme à la Convention nationale," signed "par une calvadosienne qui a été victime de la tyrannie et qui, voyageant actuellement dans le pays de Caux, peut assurer que les voeux qu'elle forme pour le maintien de la loi du 17 nivôse sont ceux de son département et celui de la Seine-Inférieure. Elle cache son nom pour être mieux aportée de dire ce qu'elle pense," 12 *messidor an* III (30 Jun. 1795).

AN, DIII 338, "Pétition de la citoyenne Jeanne Barinçon au citoyen président de la Convention nationale, 26 prairial an III" (14 Jun. 1795).

71 On natural rights ideology, see Michael Sonenscher, *Work and Wages: Natural Law, Politics, and the Eighteenth-Century French Trades* (Cambridge, 1989), 344–54.

72 AN, DIII 32, "Pétition des citoyennes du département du Calvados à la Convention nationale," received 31 Jan. 1793, signed by fifteen women on behalf of "a large number of other *citoyennes* who have declared that they cannot sign and join with us to solicit the same justice"; AN, DIII 144, "Pétition des citoyennes du département de la Manche au citoyen président de la Convention nationale, envoyée de Coutances," 8 Dec. 1792; AN, DIII 146, "Pétition de plusieurs filles de Saint-Lô, La Manche, au Monsieur le Président de l'assemblée législative," 5 Jun. 1792; AN, DIII 338, "Réclamation à la Convention nationale par des citoyennes des communes du district de Falaise [Calvados]," n.d., c. *floréal an* III (May 1795).

73 AN, DIII 338, "Pétition des héritiers rappellés par la loi [du 17 nivôse an II], au Comité de législation," n.d., c. winter–spring 1795, from Lot-et-Garonne, with c. 100 signers. Some of the female signers added, "tant pour moi que pour mes frères xx et xx à l'armée"; AN, DIII 269, "Pétition de la Veuve Gingoir, 15 *fructidor an* II" (1 Sept. 1794).

74 In contrast to Pateman and Landes, I suggest that liberal democratic ideology did not lead by definition to the exclusion of women from politics and to the creation of a separate private sphere. Rather, liberalism caused the issue of women's position within the family to be raised, but left it unresolved. Only through the extensive struggles in practice would the nineteenth-century turn toward domesticity become clear. Cf. Carol Pateman, *The Sexual Contract* (Stanford, Calif., 1988); Scott, " 'A Woman Who Has Only Paradoxes to Offer' "; Landes, *Women in the Public Sphere*. For a suggestive critique of Pateman, see Hunt, *Family Romance*, 201–4.

75 Female petitioners were most likely to invoke the value of marriage and motherhood in their appeals to extend the 8 April 1791 law against customary exclusion of daughters to married as well as unmarried women. See, for example, AN, DIII 34, "Pétition de la citoyenne Duparc, 17 June 1793"; *Les Filles mariées dans la ci-devant province de Normandie, à la Convention nationale* (Paris, 1793). Notably, two other groups were more likely to use maternalist arguments, emphasizing the moral contribution of mothers to the nation: (1) men favoring egalitarian partition rights for women and (2) women *attacking* the laws because of the negative effect on their husbands or sons. See AN, C125, "Pétition des Amis de la Constitution à Caen à l'Assemblée nationale, 22 Jan. 1791"; AN, DIII 338, "Pétition de la citoyenne Varin née LeCoustier aux citoyens représentants" received 6 prairial an III (25 May 1795); AN, DIII 382, "Observations (d'une femme anonyme qui habite dans la ci-devant coutume de Paris) sur le decret du 5 brumaire à la Convention nationale," n.d., c. winter 1794; AN, AD XVIIIc 365, "Pétition au conseil des Cinq Cents: Représentation d'une mère sur la successibilité d'un enfant naturel aux droits légitimes," n.d., c. 1797; AN, DIII 339, "Pétition de la citoyenne Delphine Clerc au comité de législation, 6 floréal an III" (25 Apr. 1795); and "Pétition de Marguerite Lassave, fournière à Toulouse, aux citoyens membres du comité de législation," n.d., c. 1795; AN, DIII 270, "Pétition de la citoyenne Morin, femme de médecin, 15 brumaire an III" (5 Nov. 1794).

76 *Remonstrances des mères et filles normandes de l'ordre du tiers* (Rouen, 1789). On the identity of the authors, see Claire LeFoll, "Les Femmes et le mouvement révolutionnaire à Rouen (1789–1795)" (Mémoire de maîtrise, Université de Haute-Normandie, 1985), 45–46.

77 AN, DIII 75, "Pétition de la citoyenne Elisabeth Lamaire Veuve Potin, aux citoyens représentants, 1 fructidor an III" (18 Aug. 1795); AN, DIII 35, "Pétition de la citoyenne Marie Marguerite Cordier femme Morin au Comité de législation, 8 floréal an III" (27 Apr. 1795); AN, DIII 272, "Pétition d'Adelaide Dorothée Durand, à la Convention nationale," received 2 *ventôse an* II (20 Feb. 1794); AN, DIII 145, "Pétition de la citoyenne Marie Anne Catherine Duquesnoy, fille majeure, au Comité de Législation

fructidor an III" (Aug.–Sept. 1795); AN, DIII 382, "Mémoire (par une femme anonyme) au Comité de législation," n.d.; AN, DIII 338, "Pétition de quatre veuves au Comité de législation, 14 floréal an III" (3 May 1795).

78 AN, DIII 338, "Pétition de la citoyenne Marguerite Briançon aux citoyens représentants, 14 floréal an III" (3 May 1795); "Pétition de la citoyenne Piard Convers aux citoyens représentants, 12 germinal an III" (1 Apr. 1795); AN, DIII 144, "Pétition des citoyennes du département de la Manche au citoyen président de la Convention nationale, 8 décembre 1792"; AN, DIII 75, "Pétition des citoyennes Bonnelly (3 sœurs) au Comité de législation, 16 floréal an III" (5 May 1795).

79 On "sensibilité," Hans-Jürgen Lüsebrink, "L'Innocence persécutée et ses avocats: Rhétorique et impact public du discours 'sensible' dans la France du XVIIIe siècle," *Revue d'histoire moderne et contemporaine* 40 (1993): 86–101; Sarah Maza, *Private Lives*; Hunt, *Family Romance*.

80 AN, DIII 274, "Pétition de la citoyenne M. M. Anquetil aux citoyens représentants, 29 prairial an III" (17 Jun. 1795); AN, DIII 147, "Lettre de la citoyenne Galot Thiphaine aux citoyens représentants," received 3 *messidor an* II (21 Jun. 1794). Her petition won a marginal comment "well done" signed by Merlin de Douai. AN, DIII 32, "Pétition des citoyennes soussignées du département du Calvados à la Convention nationale," received 3 Mar. 1793, signed by 35 women and several Xs; this is one of several collective petitions from groups calling themselves "citoyennes du Calavados."

81 AN, DIII 273, "Mémoire par Marie Magdelaine Montfreulle, envoyé au Comité de législation, 14 messidor an III" (2 Jul. 1795); AN, DIII 34, "Pétition de la citoyenne Beaufils Veuve Lavallé au comité de législation, 9 messidor an II" (27 Jun. 1794).

82 *Les Filles mariées dans la ci-devant province de Normandie au Corps législatif* (Paris, n.d., c. *an* III [1795]).

83 AN, DIII 273, "Pétition de Veuve Gouet à l'Assemblée nationale," 4 Jan. 1792; 'Pétition de la citoyenne Marguerite Jeanne LeBalleur veuve Fiquet au Comité de législation, 14 fructidor an III" (31 Aug. 1795).

84 AN, DIII 338, "Pétition de la citoyenne Jeanne Côme ainée, aux représentants, pères d'un peuple libre, 14 floréal an III" (3 May 1795).

85 AN, DIII 338, "Pétition de Julie Poursent aux citoyens composant le Comité de législation," n.d.; "Pétition de la citoyenne Jeanne Françoise Aumont au Comité de législation, 7 messidor an III" (25 June 1795); *Remonstrances des mères et filles normandes*; AN, DIII 339, "Pétition de la citoyenne Ruette au Comité de législation, 22 ventôse an III" (12 Mar. 1795); AN, DIII 48, *Question relative au décret du 8 avril 1791 sur les successions* (Paris, n.d., c. *an* IV [1796]).

86 AN, DXXXIX 4, "Pétition de la citoyenne CMH Bureau au Comité de législation," received 9 *pluviôse an* III (28 Jan. 1795).

87 AN, DIII 271, "Pétition des citoyennes Julie, Florence, et Cécile Délié au Comité de législation, 28 messidor an II" (16 Jul. 1794). Cf. AN, DIII 143, "Pétition de la citoyenne Létolé aux vertueux représentants, 29 ventôse an III" (19 Mar. 1795); AN, DIII 147, "Pétitions de la citoyenne Galot Tiphaine aux citoyens représentants, 3 & 10 messidor an II" (21 and 28 Jun. 1794).

88 AN, DIII 338, "Pétition de Marie Girard femme Leglize aux citoyens représentants," received 29 *floréal an* III (18 May 1795); AN, DIII 338, "Pétition de la citoyenne Piard Convers aux citoyens représentants, 12 germinal an III" (1 Apr. 1795); AN, DIII 33, "Pétition des citoyennes Marie Jeanne Rogne et Marie Rogne au Comité de législation, 5 messidor an II" (23 Jun. 1794); AN, DIII 146, "Pétition de la citoyenne Marguerite Letellier femme LeMonnier aux représentants, 7 floréal an III" (26 Apr. 1795); AN DIII 338, "Pétition de la citoyenne Heringue aux représentants du peuple français, 10 floréal an III" (20 Apr. 1795).

89 AN, DIII 34, "Pétition de la citoyenne Mallet au citoyen président de la Convention nationale," received 11 *pluviôse an* II (30 Jan. 1794); AN, DIII 338, "Pétition de la fille Villier aux citoyens législateurs, 16 floréal an III" (5 May 1795); AN, DIII 272, "Pétition

d'Adelaide Dorothée Durand, à la Convention nationale," received 2 *ventôse an* II (20 Feb. 1794).

90   On transparency, see Lynn Hunt, *Politics, Culture, and Class in the French Revolution* (Berkeley, Calif., 1984), 42–43, 72–74.

91   AN, DIII 37, "Pétition des citoyennes Levaillant au Comité de législation, 4 prairial an III" (23 May 1795); AN, DIII 33, "Pétition de la citoyenne Marie Françoise LaLoe au Comité des pétitions et de la correspondance, 26 germinal an III" (15 Apr. 1795); AN, DIII 32, "Pétition des citoyennes Alexandre, LeTonneur, et Antine aux citoyens députés, reçue 2 mai 1793"; AN, DIII 338, "Pétition de la citoyenne Varin née LeCoustier aux citoyens représentants"; *Remonstrances des mères et filles normandes de l'ordre du tiers*; AN, DIII 32, "Pétition des citoyennes soussignées du département du Calvados à la Convention nationale," received 3 Mar. 1793, signed by 35 women and several Xs; AN, DIII 272, "Pétition d'Adelaide Dorothée Durand, à la Convention nationale," received 2 *ventôse an* II (20 Feb. 1794). On the ambiguities of antipatriarchal discourse, see Hunt, *Family Romance*, 17–52. Arguably, multiple different "family romances" coexisted in the 1790s. Colin Jones, "A Fine 'Romance' with No Sisters," *French Historical Studies* 19 (1995): 277–87.

92   AN, DIII 143, "Pétition de la citoyenne Jeanne Gallien veuve Barenton aux citoyens représentants, 9 floréal an III" (28 Apr. 1795); AN, DIII 147, "Pétition de Josephine Letellier aux citoyens législateurs, 26 pluviôse an II" (14 Feb. 1794).

93   AN, DIII 382, "Pétition de la citoyenne Julie . . . républicaine au citoyen président de la Convention nationale," received 1 Nov. 1793; AN, DIII 338, "Pétition de la citoyenne Rausan veuve Descages aux citoyens [représentants], 27 floréal an III" (16 May 1795).

94   Karen Offen, "Defining Feminism: A Comparative Historical Approach," *Signs: Journal of Women in Culture and Society* 14 (1988): 119–57; Joan Scott, *Only Paradoxes to Offer: French Feminists and the Rights of Man* (Cambridge, Mass., 1996), esp. 57–89.

95   Based on petitions opposed to equal inheritance. See n. 3.

96   On the paradoxes of women's citizenship in the arena of popular activism (rather than family law), see Dominique Godineau, "Femmes et citoyenneté: Pratiques et politiques," *Annales historiques de la Révolution française* 300 (1995): 197–207; Darline Gay Levy, "Women's Revolutionary Citizenship in Action, 1791: Setting the Boundaries," in *The French Revolution and the Meaning of Citizenship*, ed. Renée Waldinger, Philip Dawson, and Isser Woloch (Westport, Conn., 1993), 169–84.

11

THE PRICE OF LIBERTY

Victor Hugues and the administration of freedom in Guadeloupe, 1794–1798

Laurent Dubois

French colonies may have been on the periphery of French political consciousness, but they were central to its economy. Throughout the eighteenth century, and especially by 1789, the wealth that poured into France from its sugar colonies in the Caribbean was critical to the success of the French economy. After all, whether or not Marie Antoinette ever said anything like "let them eat cake," what is certain is that by 1789 Frenchmen demanded that their bread be sweetened, and the most common and affordable sweetener was sugar. If the supply of sugar dropped, clearly the price and availability of bread would be affected.

Sugar cane, of course, depended upon large plantations based upon Black slavery. Immediately, therefore, the ideals of the French Revolution (as articulated in the Declaration of the Rights of Man and Citizen) collided with the realities of maintaining the stability of the French economy through its empire. It did not take long for French Revolutionaries to realize that their universal aspirations for world-wide liberty would mean a destabilized colonial economy, which in turn would undermine the French economy. These concerns – debated on the floor of the Constituent Assembly in 1789 and 1790, became moot, as one colony, Saint-Domingue, became immersed in a slave rebellion, inspired in no small part by the Declaration of the Rights of Man and Citizen. Soon the rebellion led to civil war, and by the time the National Convention outlawed slavery in 1793, it was too little too late.

Laurent Dubois uses the fascinating case of Victor Hugues, Jacobin Commissioner on the lesser-known island sugar colony of Guadeloupe. Dubois's focus here is as much with ideology as with politics and the economy: he is interested in watching the convergence between Jacobin ideology and colonial slavery. Building on an intriguing analysis of the ideas of Emmanuel Sieyes, author of the important pamphlet, What is the Third Estate?, *Dubois shows that a "republican racism" lay in the midst of Jacobinism since the start of the Revolution.*

* * *

In 1793, a new flag appeared on both sides of the Atlantic. On top of the red, white, and blue of the French Republican tricolor stood three armed men: one white, one mulatto, and one black. In Saint Domingue, Bramante Lazzary, a leader of slave insurgents who had recently allied himself with the Republic, wrote: "There are no more slaves in St. Domingue, all men of all colors are free and equal. . . . Our flag makes clear that our liberty depends on three colors: black, mulatto, and white: we are fighting for these three colors." At about the same time in Paris, a delegation of free coloreds headed by the 110-year-old Jeanne Odo carried a similar flag into the National Convention. The figures on it wore liberty caps and carried pikes, and a motto read, "Notre union fera notre force" ("Our union will be our strength").[1]

This flag represented both the possibilities and limitations of the policies of emancipation and equality that transformed the French empire during the 1790s. It symbolized both an assertion of a common Republican mission, which sought the elimination of racial hierarchies and the transformation of slaves into citizens and soldiers, and a re-inscription of racial difference. In 1796, in the colony of Guadeloupe, the "three colors" of the flag came to represent three racial categories used in creating a series of censuses of unprecedented detail. Like the Republican flag, the censuses brought together the various social groups on the island, enumerating each of them, from the white merchant to the black plantation laborer, with equal detail. Yet, in identifying who lived where, the censuses helped maintain distinctions between citizens, since it aided the administrators who wished to force ex-slaves to stay and work on the plantations where they had been slaves. The censuses therefore exemplified the contradictions of the administration of Guadeloupe, where, as in other post-emancipation societies, freedom was both granted and retracted in a complex struggle over the meaning of citizenship.[2]

The struggle over slavery during the 1790s transformed the meaning of citizenship and presaged the later struggles over the political and legal rights of the colonized. The period was a turning point in the history of French empire, when the elimination of slavery created an imperial nation-state in which the same laws were applied in the metropole and the colonies. This new order presented a sharp contrast not only to the previous French colonial order and to the British empire but also to the United States, where slavery and abolition coexisted within one nation. Its radical implications were felt far and wide, as were those of its bloody reversal in the early 1800s, which led to the birth of Haiti in 1804 and to the end of a major French presence in the Americas. The period also left another, less-well-known inheritance. The regimes of emancipation, notably that of Victor Hugues in Guadeloupe, developed new forms of governance that combined an antiracist and emancipatory agenda with forms of labor coercion and racial exclusion. These regimes helped shape a form of Republican racism that was central to the functioning of the French empire of the nineteenth and twentieth centuries, in which the promise of political assimilation was routinely deferred because the colonized were incapable of exercising the rights of citizens.[3]

From the first years of the French Revolution, slaves throughout the French Caribbean organized insurrections, often mobilizing around rumors that the metropole had decreed emancipation but that local officials were resisting its application. Ultimately, these insurrections made necessary and conceivable the alliance between slave insurgents and Republican officials. In Saint Domingue, starting in 1791, with organization that had bewildered the whites who became its victims, slaves had destroyed nearly a hundred plantations across the most prosperous section of France's most prosperous colony. They defeated the confident attempts to end their insurrection and transformed themselves into a credible military force that ultimately became the salvation of the Republic in Saint Domingue. A parallel process took shape in Guadeloupe. In April 1793, when hundreds of slaves rose up in Trois-Rivières and killed twenty-three whites, they justified their actions to the officials of the island as an attack against the royalist conspiracies of their masters. "We have come to save you," they told the whites; "we want to fight for the republic, the law, the nation, order." Instead of punishing them, Republican whites and *gens de couleur* accepted their version of the events and called for the formation of a slave army to defend the island from attack.[4]

Such alliances formed the foundation for the abolition of slavery. In Saint Domingue in June 1793, pressured by slave insurgents, many of them allied with Spain, and threatened by an English invasion made more likely by the increasing defection of white planters, the Republican commissioner Léger Félicité Sonthonax offered liberty and citizenship to those slaves who would serve as soldiers of the Republic. Strengthened by these new recruits, Sonthonax was able to hold off the royalists on the island, and in August 1793 he broadened his offer for individual liberty into a blanket emancipation. In February 1794, representatives elected in Saint Domingue brought news of the successes of Sonthonax's decrees to the National Convention. One of them, Dufay, eulogized the slaves-turned-soldiers who presented themselves to the commissioners and announced: "We are black, and French . . . we will fight for France, but in return we want our freedom." He argued that it was sound policy "to create new citizens for the Republic in order to oppose our enemies." Moved by his speech, another deputy demanded the immediate abolition of slavery, and the National Convention quickly voted a law decreeing "that slavery is abolished throughout the territory of the Republic; in consequence, all men, without distinction of color, will enjoy the rights of French citizens." A year later, Sonthonax warned that, if France abandoned Saint Domingue, "the last place where the flag of the Republic would fly would be that defended by an army of blacks." He continued: "The Blacks are the true sans-culottes of the colonies, they are the people, and only they are capable of defending the country."[5]

The years of conflict in Saint Domingue drove many whites to leave the colony, including a man named Victor Hugues. The son of a baker from Marseille, Hugues became a sailor and traveled to the Americas, working as a merchant throughout the Caribbean before acquiring a shop in Port-au-Prince.

Sometime during 1791 or 1792, his shop was burned down, and his brother was killed. He left the colony and in October 1792 arrived in Paris, where he made connections among the Jacobins and was named the judge of the revolutionary tribunal of the port town of Rochefort. In February 1794, because of his revolutionary credentials and his experience in the Antilles, Hugues was one of three commissioners appointed by the Jacobin *Comité du Salut Public* (which essentially ruled France at the time) to carry the decree of emancipation to Guadeloupe. Hugues led the Republican troops in an assault on the British-held island in June 1794, and he quickly became the most powerful administrator on the island. Between 1794 and 1798, Hugues turned the island into the Republican stronghold of the eastern Caribbean, sending armies of French *sans-culottes* and slaves-turned-citizens against the British. As Robin Blackburn has noted, Hugues's regime has received little attention from historians, despite its military importance and political impact. Auguste Lacour's classic *Histoire de la Guadeloupe*, published in the mid-nineteenth century, drew on the experiences of the white planter families that suffered during Hugues's regime to portray him as a tyrannical and brutal Jacobin. Lacour's work served as the basis for the only existing biography of Hugues, published in 1932 by Georges Sainte-Croix de la Roncière, which celebrated Hugues's military accomplishments even as it reiterated Lacour's vision of his regime. It also inspired Alejo Carpentier's novel *El siglo de las luces*, perhaps the best-known account of this fascinating historical figure, which made Hugues's story an allegory of the spiraling contradictions of the Revolution itself.[6]

Hugues's mission was to create a new society where virtue, rather than race, would be the basis for social advancement and where legal equality would form the bedrock of the constitutional order. But for Hugues, as for other administrators at the time and later, emancipation raised serious philosophical, political, and economic problems: how could slaves, who had consistently been denied all legal and social rights, become citizens ready to use and defend these rights? And how could the colonial plantation economy, deemed central to the economy of France, be maintained? Hugues confronted the problem posed by the transition from slave to citizen, and from slave labor to free labor, through a combination of liberation and repression. He limited the rights of the ex-slaves, invoking the needs of the endangered nation to argue that, since ex-slaves were incapable of being full citizens, it was their responsibility to serve the nation according to their particular, and limited, capacities.

Hugues put into practice the ideas of gradualist abolitionists, whose conception of postemancipation citizenship combined a universalist discourse of racial equality with new forms of racial exclusion. Understanding Hugues's regime, therefore, requires, first, an engagement with those thinkers of the French Revolution who grappled both with the broad definition of Republican citizenship and with the particular problem of transforming slaves into citizens. The thought of the Abbé Sieyès, the Marquis de Condorcet, and Julien Raimond best exemplify the foundation upon which Hugues built his approach to slave emancipation in Guadeloupe. Each argued in favor of certain kinds of restrictions on citizenship; Raimond and Condorcet explicitly identified such restrictions as vital for the peaceful and successful transition from slavery to freedom. As he sought to apply these strains of Republican and abolitionist thought in Guadeloupe, however, Hugues was constrained by the context of war against the British and by the actions of the ex-slaves of the island. These "new citizens" struggled to fulfill their own vision of liberty, which often led them to resist his labor policies. The social world of Guadeloupe – like that of other postemancipation societies in the Americas – took shape through this complex struggle over the meaning of freedom.[7] The study of the roots and trajectory of Hugues's regime, and of the ex-slaves who molded it, highlights how social conflicts in the Caribbean shaped the broader Republican engagement with citizenship, race, and labor.

What is the citizen? The title of the politically prophetic pamphlet published in 1789 by the Abbé Sieyès, *What Is the Third Estate?*, begged this question. Sieyès's pamphlet – and the actions of the summer of 1789 that instituted many of its suggestions – helped produce the modern idea of the French nation. Sieyès, a radical priest who was to become a central figure in the Revolution and later in the rise of Napoleon Bonaparte, asked, "Where do we find the nation?"; his response was that the nation was the people. The people were the heart of the nation, and only political equality could create a legitimate and representative government. Fundamental political equality should override – though not eliminate – social inequality. Sieyès's powerful script for the assertion of democratic power over privilege nevertheless allowed for multiple exclusions from active participation in national affairs. The citizen, in Sieyès's view, had to be both productive and economically independent to be trusted with the direction of the nation. Nobles were therefore excluded, as were "vagabonds and beggars," servants and "any person under the domination of a master, or a nonnaturalized foreigner." "Political liberty," wrote Sieyès, "has its limits, just as civil liberty has."[8]

During the early years of the French Revolution, the representatives of the National Assembly limited access to full citizenship in multiple ways. Women were categorically excluded from voting. The idea that only the wealthy were independent enough to be capable and disinterested political actors led to the distinction between the "active" citizen – who could fully participate in the political process by voting and being elected – and the "passive" citizen – who remained protected by the laws of the Republic but was not qualified for direct political participation. The Terror represented a continuing battle over the terms of national belonging and the meaning of responsible citizenship. Although the distinction between "active" and "passive" citizenship was destroyed, accusations of treason and anti-Republicanism increasingly became the basis for a severing of the accused citizen from the political body. The figure of the "foreigner" – initially the beneficiary of a hospitality inspired by the universalist project of the Republic – increasingly became subject to the politics of identification and exclusion. The boundaries of citizenship could expand, notably via slaves in the Antilles in the years leading up to emancipation; but they could also contract, as happened under the regime of Hugues, through arguments about the incapacity of certain people to be citizens. Ideologies of political equality were layered with discussions of the intellectual and social qualifications necessary for the practice of citizenship.[9]

Sieyès, whose major argument in *What Is the Third Estate?* was that labor was the key indicator of political belonging, directly contradicted this position elsewhere. In his *Ecrits Politiques*, he distinguished between the "Two Nations" within France, arguing that the laboring classes should be passive participants in the nation and that those with "some sort of affluence" were more fit to rule. In confronting the difficult question of how to create a society in which the degrading yet necessary state of the laborer coexisted with the successful functioning of a democracy, Sieyès was driven to a surreal racial solution. Through the interbreeding of "negroes" and different "species of monkeys," he envisaged the creation of new-species of laborers, "a strong race (six to eight feet tall) for hard labor . . . a middle-sized race (three to four feet tall) for domestic details . . . a small race (from twelve to fifteen inches) for petty services and amusement." These new laborers would be trained and commanded by "negroes," and the "heads of production" would be white. "However extraordinary, however immoral this idea may be at first glance," he wrote, "I have meditated on it for a long time, and you will find no other means, in a large nation especially in very warm and very cold countries, to reconcile the directors of work with the simple instruments of labor."[10]

Sieyès's diagnosis and solution echoed the situation already in place between metropolitan and colonial France. Two nations did exist. One was at its center, the other was consigned to its margins, where labor was organized on the kind of racial hierarchies Sieyès imagined. The legal structures of the two nations differed profoundly, and this difference was justified by the idea that the colonies' role was to produce commodities that brought prosperity to the metropole. During the colonial debates of the early years of the Revolution, pro-slavery advocates defended this situation, arguing that the colonies, because of their distance, climate, and different population, needed a separate and local constitution. In opposing this view, the *Société des Amis des Noirs* (Paris's abolitionist club, founded in 1787) and their gens de couleur allies argued that the colonies were an integral part of the nation and could be governed only through universal Republican principles that gave free individuals of all colors (though not slaves) the right to citizenship.[11] The abolition of slavery first in Saint Domingue and then in France in 1794 represented the victory of this argument and the creation of new terms of juridical and political equality between metropole and colony. As Sieyès's proposal suggests, however, there was room within the concepts of political liberty and equality for the exclusion of certain "auxiliaries" who would labor for the nation without being citizens. Indeed, in Sieyès's utopia, the existence of an inferior race of slaves actually made possible the proper functioning of political culture. In this imagined solution lay the foundation for the actions of administrators like Hugues who, without the benefit of genetic engineering, sought to achieve feats of profound social engineering in Antilles.

Sieyès merely hinted at the massive problem of reconciling economic inequality with political participation – a problem explored in detail in the work of the Physiocrats of the eighteenth century, who as part of their agenda had pursued a critique of slave labor as immoral and economically inefficient. The pressure of marronage and other forms of slave resistance in the colonies incited ever increasing concern with the untenability of slavery as a social and economic system. During the 1780s, antislavery discourse became increasingly important among prominent figures such as the Comte de Mirabeau (whose brother had been a governor of Guadeloupe), the Abbé Grègoire, the Marquis de Lafayette, and the Marquis de Condorcet. Influenced by the broader Atlantic debates about slavery, and by the experiences of emancipation in the northern United States, these thinkers drew in particular on the work and political example of the British abolitionists. Although convinced that slavery was a moral wrong and should be eliminated, these thinkers debated the central question of how the slaves, used to the arbitrary and brutalizing order of slavery, were to be transformed into free individuals who could actively participate in the legal and economic order of society.[12]

In 1781, the Marquis de Condorcet – who was to become one of the founding members of the French Société des Amis des Noirs – published a work called *Réflexions sur l'esclavage des nègres*, which dealt directly with the question of how to convert slaves into citizens. Condorcet's thought and political activity had a profound impact on the broad development of French Republicanism, and his work on slavery reflects his preoccupation with the question of how individuals were to be transformed into responsible citizens. In his *Réflexions*, Condorcet issued a powerful attack on slavery. His opening "Epitre Dédicatoire aux Nègres Esclaves" lamented that the slaves, who he always considered his brothers and his equals, would never read his work. More than a decade before Sonthonax, Condorcet asserted the superiority of the colonial slaves to the violent and decadent planters: "If you were to search for a man in the American islands, you would not find him among the whites." Like Montesquieu before him, Condorcet systematically and satirically undermined pro-slavery arguments. "The reasoning of the politicians who believe that the slavery of the *Nègres* is necessary," he wrote, "reduces itself to this: *Whites are miserly, drunken, and sordid, so the Blacks must be enslaved.*"[13]

Condorcet's work stands out among eighteenth-century French abolitionist texts for its sustained discussion of how slavery could be abolished without causing a revolution in the colonies. He proposed the gradual abolition of slavery and the gradual integration of slaves into the state of political and economic freedom. Masters would be forced to emancipate all slaves born after a certain date at the age of thirty-five. These slaves, starting at the age of eighteen, would be granted a modicum of legal subjecthood: they could file complaints against their masters for ill-treatment, for instance, and the state would have the right to take a slave from an abusive master. Condorcet claimed that, if his plan was followed, slavery would be entirely abolished in sixty-six years, and most slaves would be freed within thirty or forty; meanwhile, the colonial economy would continue functioning as before, since the ex-slaves would be gradually integrated as free workers without a sudden shock to the social system.[14]

This gradual solution was necessary, argued Condorcet, because "most of the *Nègres* are very stupid," not through any fault of their own, but because of how they had been "degraded by the outrages of their masters, cut down by their severity, [and] corrupted by their example." Given the experience of slavery, Condorcet wondered: "Are these men worthy enough for us to place in their hands their happiness and the government of their family? Are they not in the case of those unfortunates who have, through barbarous treatment, been deprived of their reason?" Though the *natural* rights unjustly taken from the slaves had to be returned to them, the case for granting *political* rights was not as compelling. Any law that refused rights to "a citizen or a foreigner" was in principle unjust, but in certain cases the interests of the victims of oppression, and the need to maintain public tranquillity, could justify a cautious approach to the application of such just principles. "If there exists a kind of certainty that a man is incapable of exercising his rights, and that if his rights are granted to him, he will abuse them [by acting] against others, or will use them to his own advantage, then a society can look upon him as having lost his rights, or never having acquired them." If the slaves "because of their lack of education, and the stupidity contracted through slavery by the corruption of their morals (the necessary result of the influence of their masters)" had become "incapable of fulfilling the duties of free men," then it would be reasonable for the legislator to "treat them as men who have been deprived by misery or sickness of a portion of their faculties" – at least until such time as "the experience of liberty has returned to them what slavery has taken away." Granting the ex-slaves full rights would inevitably expose them "to the risk of hurting others, or harming themselves," and an initial limitation of rights was "simply a way of making sure that the destruction of the abuses takes place in such a way as to assure that freedom will more certainly be the foundation for happiness." Since "before placing the slaves in the ranks of free men, the law must assure itself that in this new quality they will not trouble the security of the citizens," a gradual granting of rights would be a justifiable way of protecting the larger society from the violence and chaos that could be unleashed by those who were emerging from the violence of slavery.[15]

Condorcet argued that generations of slavery had systematically destroyed the natural impulses for improvement and the moral foundations of virtue; ending slavery thus required a complex transformation of the slaves' identities. The philosophical problem of how to fix a long-standing moral wrong, which had corrupted both the slaves and slaveowners of the Caribbean for centuries, weighed on Condorcet, who thought a sudden social transformation might lead to massive upheaval and bloodshed. Condorcet "feared that the *Nègres*, accustomed to obeying only force and whim, will not be contained, in the beginning, by the same laws as the whites" and worried "that they will form crowds, and give themselves over to theft, to individual vengeance, and to a vagabond life in the forests and the mountains." In addition, "disorders will be fomented by the *Blancs*, who will try and use them as a pretext to obtain the re-establishment of slavery." Therefore, "it will be necessary to subject the *Nègres*, in the beginning, to a severe discipline, regulated by laws." The process, wrote Condorcet, would have to be placed in the hands of "a man who is human, firm, enlightened, and incorruptible, who will be indulgent towards the rapture in which this change of status will plunge the *Nègres*, without leaving them with the hope of impunity, and who will disdain the gold of the whites, their intrigues and their menaces."[16] Condorcet's description of such an "incorruptible" administrator was prophetic of – and perhaps a direct influence on – the regime of Victor Hugues. Indeed, the commissioner used the same arguments as Condorcet when he argued that, given the incapacity of the ex-slaves, it was right to limit their rights to prevent "disorders" in Guadeloupe.

There are more immediate and obvious links – though again no proof of direct influence – between Hugues's ideas and those proposed by the *homme de couleur* lawyer Julien Raimond in a 1793 pamphlet called *Réflexions sur les véritables causes des troubles et des désastres de nos colonies*. From the beginning of the Revolution, Raimond argued that the gens de couleur had the right to political equality, and after the slave insurrections in Saint Domingue in 1791 he presented them as a propertied class who could be a bulwark against the slave insurrections. His activity helped bring about the decree on political equality of gens de couleur passed in the National Assembly in April 1792.[17]

Raimond's 1793 address argued that the best way for France to maintain its hold on its threatened colony of Saint Domingue was to create a strong bond between the slaves and the Republic. In contrast to Sonthonax, who was at the time busy on the other side of the Atlantic creating such an alliance through immediate and general abolition, Raimond believed that the preservation of the Republic depended on a gradual transition to freedom through which the slaves would be regenerated as virtuous and moral citizens. He laid out his plan through a speech that he proposed could be given to the slaves, and particularly the slave insurgents, of Saint Domingue. "Your souls," Raimond announced, "long oppressed by the debasement of vigorous punishment, have been degraded; slavery has snuffed out the divine fire that produces and maintains the virtues that are necessary for man and are indispensable for the state of sociability." "The powerful and generous nation" of France wished to help the "abandoned men" of the colonies. But to do so, he told the slaves, the nation had to "uproot the vice from your souls" and plant there "the seed of virtue necessary for the new state destined for you." For this, however, "it is necessary that you stay for a certain time under the tutelage of those who are responsible for improving your condition; for it is only by developing the habit of practicing what the law requires of you that you will show yourselves worthy of the happiness which it will bring to you." Raimond outlined the "qualities necessary for the state of liberty and equality": absolute respect for the property of others, love of work ("for those who do not work, either to procure their needs or to conserve their property, soon become a charge to society, its shame and its scourge"), and moral conduct. Because of "the defects of the laws that have reigned over you until now," the slaves lacked these qualities.[18]

Different laws would produce different subjects. To inculcate the requisite capacities in the slaves, Raimond recommended a process of gradual self-purchase, where the slaves, using the money they made during their one free day of the week, could buy additional days of freedom from their masters until they were entirely free. According to Raimond, this system would allow those who worked hard and developed the virtues necessary for freedom to buy themselves and to set an example for other slaves. In this way, society would slowly be transformed as slaves became responsible, hardworking, independent citizens who, as consumers "of certain commodities," would gain the virtues necessary for the "state of sociability." Raimond emphasized to the slaves that "in order to be equal to the free, you will have to work, once you have procured your liberty, to procure all the objects of luxury and convenience that distinguish the free from the slave." If the ex-slaves neglected the work of cultivating "the rich commodities of the colony," then "the nation will have nothing to exchange with you, and will no longer bring to these countries all the necessary objects that can give you the joys to which you aspire." Indeed, work would be the duty of the slaves who, once freed, should always remember "the boons you have received from the nation." They would have a responsibility to pay back the nation for the gifts it had granted them, "and there is no better way to prove your gratefulness than by always continuing to make, through your work, the soil of the colonies productive, in order to obtain a large quantity of commodities, whose production will always turn to your advantage."[19]

As an homme de couleur, Raimond had a particular and personal insight into the complexities of the transition from slavery to freedom. His vision of emancipation, although parallel in certain ways to the gradualism of others, was more radical because it applied the Jacobin idea that all citizens had a primary, and even transcendent, responsibility for the preservation of the nation.[20] Although he was given the responsibility of granting universal and immediate, rather than gradual, emancipation, Victor Hugues applied many of Raimond's arguments and suggestions in Guadeloupe. Both thinkers believed that the slaves did not truly deserve freedom. Once the nation had followed its universal principles in decreeing emancipation, Hugues argued, the ex-slaves had to show that they deserved the citizenship they had been granted. They were indebted to the generous Republic, and their particular debt brought with it particular responsibilities. Their obligations were not those common to all citizens of the French nation; they were specific to those citizens who had until recently been property, and who had, as property, helped produce vital commodities for the nation. Like all good citizens, the ex-slaves should be willing to sacrifice anything for the larger good of the nation; and their history dictated that their patriotic role would be to cultivate the soil as laborers. Their old condition determined the meaning of their new rights; they were free, but they had to pay for their freedom through the limitation of their liberty.

That was the "price of Liberty" to which Hugues repeatedly referred as he subjected the ex-slaves to a peculiar kind of social contract in which their duty as citizens was to work to produce the staples – sugar, coffee, and cotton – of the colonial economy. In his regime, a certain tenuousness remained in the freedom that was to be granted; on some level, the nation would reserve the right to retract what it had given. To be a new citizen meant to be free, to be a part of the nation like all other citizens, but to have a particular role tied to a past condition. New converts to the nation, the ex-slaves would carry the mark of the generosity that freed them. And they would be responsible for not disappointing the needy Republic that had made them citizens.

When the flotilla of Republican soldiers led by Victor Hugues arrived off the coast of Guadeloupe in June 1794, they encountered a well-fortified island occupied by British and French royalist troops. Nevertheless, in a military action that was touted in France as an example of the almost superhuman qualities of the sans-culottes, the French common soldiers – joined by the slaves they freed – managed to rout the British forces and take back the northeastern half of the island known as Grande-Terre. In celebrating the victory two months later, Hugues praised the "*Citoyens noirs* who, thankful for the blessings granted them by the French nation, have shared in our victories by fighting for Liberty." He counseled these new citizens to follow the example of their metropolitan brothers-in-arms, the sans-culottes, "who will always show you the path to victory, and will consolidate with you your liberty and that of your children." All of them, concluded Hugues, using a Jacobin formulation that filled the speeches and declarations of the National Convention at the time, had shown themselves "WORTHY OF THE NATION."[21]

The early Republican victory depended on the key weapon of war Hugues had brought: the abolition of slavery. As soon as they disembarked on June 2, the French troops announced the decree of emancipation, prompting large numbers of freed slaves to join the attack against the British. A few days later, after taking the island's economic capital, Pointe-à-Pitre, the commissioners issued a proclamation calling on "citizens of all colors" to volunteer to fight against those who had made the citizens of Guadeloupe "without distinction" into a "people of slaves." The new citizens responded in droves, flooding into Pointe-à-Pitre from the surrounding plantations. Some, like the leper Vulcain, became officers owing to a policy that rewarded those who brought other recruits with them when they joined the army.[22]

In a report he wrote several weeks later to the Comité du Salut Public, Hugues said of the former slaves: "Many have taken up arms and shown themselves worthy of the fight for Liberty." His decision to create battalions composed of sans-culottes of all colors, he wrote, was a success. "This mix has had the best possible effect on the former slaves. I have granted them the same pay as the troops from France. They exercise twice a day and are flattered to be treated like our brothers the sans culottes, who, thanks to my constant fraternal exhortations, respect the former slaves as much as is possible." Hugues praised the ex-slaves' behavior in battle: "The Black Citizens, our new brothers, have shown on this occasion what the spirit of Liberty can accomplish; out of men previously brutalized by slavery, she made heroes." So, with the arrival of emancipation, the freed slaves were finally accepted as Republican soldiers who could help in the crucial battle for the preservation and expansion of the Revolution. Yet, within the new order predicated on equal treatment, a hierarchy of value remained. Hugues was skeptical of what could be expected of the black soldiers; he tempered his praise of them by adding, at the end of his report, that "the blacks alone, without Europeans, will never fight well."[23]

In the next years, Guadeloupe became the stronghold of the Republic in the Eastern Caribbean. Armies composed of a majority of ex-slaves conducted an extensive war against the British, attacking Grenada and Saint Vincent and conquering Saint Lucia. In the military arena, the principles of racial equality announced by the abolition of slavery were fully applied. Before emancipation, slaves had most clearly expressed their demands for citizenship through military action; after emancipation, the army combined the national service demanded of ex-slaves with meritocratic advancement touted by Republicans. In 1796, of the approximately forty-six hundred soldiers in the garrison of Guadeloupe, only 20 percent had arrived from France, and more than 50 percent were ex-slaves. The following year, an estimated thirty-six hundred soldiers comprised similar proportions of Europeans and ex-slaves. These numbers, however, did not include the many soldiers who fought in the service of the French Republic elsewhere in the region, like the Black Caribs of Saint Vincent. There might have been as many as eleven thousand such soldiers at the height of the campaigns. Although whites were overrepresented among the officer corps, some ex-slaves, such as the former maroon Joseph Ignace and a number of gens de couleur, notably the Martinican Louis Delgrès, achieved high positions in the military hierarchy. When Bonaparte sought to reestablish slavery in Guadeloupe and Saint Domingue in 1802, these officers and many of their soldiers organized to resist the return to the old order.[24]

The army was not the only institution that provided rich opportunities for ex-slaves. Hugues encouraged (and in fact invested his own money in) the arming of corsairs that roved the eastern Caribbean attacking and capturing British merchant ships and neutral ships heading toward enemy islands. The sailors, many of them ex-slaves, received a portion of the loot in payment for their service. As early as 1794, thirty such corsairs were based in Guadeloupe and, during the next three years, captured eight hundred ships. An estimated thirty-five hundred ex-slaves worked as sailors, and many empowered women in Basse-Terre to handle their proceeds. The corsairs used rifles "cut down to ten or twelve inches" to make "boarding guns," bayonets cut in half to make daggers, and straps taken from ammunition boxes to make belts for swords. Through the corsair trade, ex-slaves ranged far and wide in the greater Caribbean, spreading the message of emancipation and developing new connections throughout the region. Meanwhile, the port towns of Guadeloupe thrived through the loot that poured into them, and whites and blacks mixed as they participated in the new economy. Building on the foundations of the economic independence they had developed within slavery, women participated in the burgeoning commercial activity, and some were able to acquire property in towns such as Basse-Terre. Ex-slaves were employed by the Republic unloading ships in the harbor and working as carpenters and masons, whereas others worked as salaried bakers and fishermen. In contrast to the limited possibilities available to the ex-slaves on the plantations, the towns presented opportunities for rapid social change, and many of the new citizens migrated to them in search of the meaningful application of their newly acquired rights.[25]

For Hugues, military service was one simple and edifying way for the new citizens to serve the nation. More difficult was the problem of what rights would accompany the citizenship granted to the majority of the laboring population of the island. In instituting his regime, Hugues had little help from the metropole. When the National Convention enthusiastically decreed emancipation in February 1794, Georges-Jacques Danton had warned that the generosity of the Republic should not "exceed the boundaries of wisdom" and recommended that rather than sending the news directly to the colonies the matter be forwarded to the Comité du Salut Public and the *Comité des Colonies*, "to bring together the means to make this law useful for humanity without endangering it."[26] The Comité de Salut Public named Hugues commissioner, but neither they nor the Comité des Colonies provided him with any detailed framework for the institution of emancipation. Hugues therefore left France with little more than a description of his daunting mission: to free the slaves, maintain plantation production, and prosecute the war against the British. In announcing and attempting to control the effects of emancipation after his arrival in Guadeloupe, Hugues's directives trumpeted the universal justice of slave emancipation as one chapter in the epic of revolutionary liberation. But they also quickly put in motion a set of pragmatic policies that limited the roles of the freed slaves and sought to contain the effects of freedom. As he struggled to impose his vision of emancipation on the recalcitrant ex-slaves of Guadeloupe, Hugues constructed an administration that uniquely applied Republican and abolitionist thinking to the problem of transforming slave labor to free labor.

During its first days in Guadeloupe, the new Republican administration published the emancipation decree of the National Convention with an explanation of what the new law would demand of both whites and ex-slaves. "CITIZENS," it announced, "a republican government accepts neither chains nor slavery, and therefore the National Convention has just solemnly proclaimed the liberty of the negroes and confided the execution of this law to the commissioners it has delegated for the colonies." These commissioners had been given the responsibility of establishing "an administration both generally and individually committed to guaranteeing the property already held by some, and the product of the work and industry of others." The happiness of "CITIZENS of all colors" depended on the new law; but, to make it function, "the white citizens must kindly offer, in fraternity, and with reasonable wages, work to their black and colored brothers; and the latter must also learn and never forget that those who have no property must provide, through their work, for their own subsistence and that of their family, as well as to the support of their nation." The proclamation ended with a threat: "CITIZENS, you have become equal in order to enjoy happiness and to share it with all others; the person who oppresses his co-citizen is a monster who must be banished from the social world."[27]

In the next days, as freedom was declared throughout Grande-Terre, the idealized picture of whites and blacks working together for the nation was quickly undermined. The ex-slaves, celebrating their newfound freedom, were probably skeptical of administrators and masters (now supposedly co-citizens) who asked them to stay on their plantations and keep working for "reasonable wages." Reportedly, some took food from the plantations. The commissioners reacted with a decree emphasizing that the end of slavery signified no alteration in property rights. The proclamation was explicitly addressed to the ex-slaves and was to be read and posted on all plantations; plantation owners and managers were to report the response of the ex-slaves back to the commissioners. It declared: "The National Convention, through its decree of 16 Pluviôse, has granted you the highest of blessings: liberty . . . her intention, in smashing your chains, was to grant you greater happiness by allowing you to enjoy your rights." The commissioners, however, had been "pained to learn" that, since liberty had been decreed, "depredations" had been committed in the countryside, where manioc trees had been cut and bananas stolen "for no reason, with the simple intention of hurting the owners." Given the situation of the colony, the commissioners insisted the preservation of property – particularly provisions – was vitally important. "Therefore we expressly forbid all citizens of whatever color to touch the provisions of the habitations, such as maniocs, bananas, corn, etc., without the express permission of the owner." The punishment for those who violated this law was severe; ex-slaves who took "the said provisions with malevolence" would be "declared outlaws and punished with death as traitors who have consorted with the enemies of the Republic."[28]

The proclamation went beyond asserting the continuing property rights of the ex-masters to make theft not only a crime against the owner but an act of treason against the nation. Provisions grown on plantations were declared fundamental to the island's security in the context of war. The state's commissioners were responsible for administering agriculture and labor for the profit of the nation and in the service of its expansionist Republican project. The state's claim to control the agricultural production of the island had particular power since more than half of the plantations on the island were the property of the state, owing to Republican laws that sequestered the property of émigrés or counter-revolutionaries. Hugues's decree made theft a crime against the state, sending individual ex-slaves who stole from the planation to the tribunals that he had set up. In so doing, he set the terms for a broader policy of state control over the economic and social destinies of all the ex-slaves on the island.

Victor Hugues expressed his disappointment at the behavior of the ex-slaves in a letter written the day after the proclamation was released. Hugues noted: "We proclaimed the decree on the liberty of the Negroes, but far from providing us with resources this decree steals them from us, because of the lack of education among our brothers in the colonies; nonetheless it is to be hoped that careful and severe measures will make them feel the price of Liberty." He added that "the black Citizens do not yet know the price of Liberty, and are using it only to steal and destroy."[29] The behavior of the new citizens continued to dissatisfy Hugues, who on June 20, 1794, issued a new "Proclamation to the Black Citizens." In a tone that echoed that of Raimond in his 1793 speech, Hugues's decree cast the refusal of ex-slaves to fulfill their assigned roles as treason against the Republic:

> The Republic, in recognizing the rights that nature gave you, did not intend to release you from the obligation of working for what you need to live. He who does not work deserves only disdain and must not profit from the blessings of our regeneration; we must assume, with good reason, that the lazy survive only by pillaging.
>
> Since all citizens cannot be employed in the defense of the colony, it is indispensable that those who are not incorporated into the armed forces go to work cultivating the land and planting food as quickly as possible.
>
> In fact, Citizens, he who sacrifices his pain and his sweat to provide food to his co-citizens deserves just as much a reward as he who sacrifices to defend them. In consequence, Citizens, we invite and require those of you who are not incorporated into the army to return to the plantations where you previously lived, and to work there without respite planting potatoes, yams and other edible roots. We promise to protect you and to pay you for your work; but if, against our will, some of you refuse to respond to our invitation, we will declare you traitors, in the name of the Republic, and punish you to the full extent of the law. We order the municipality to use the armed forces to break up the mobs and force the black citizens to return to their respective plantations to plant provisions.[30]

Hugues's regime outlined two ways for the *Citoyens Noirs* to pay the "price of Liberty": through service as soldiers or as *cultivateurs*, as the exslave field laborers on the plantations were called. He cast both of these roles as responsibilities required by Republican citizenship. But, especially for the cultivateurs, their possibilities in the new society were to be defined by their continuing work on the plantations. The labor of the ex-slaves, much like that of slaves, was to be mobilized and controlled from above; now, however, the benefit of their labor was to accrue, not to individual masters, but to the nation. The island existed to support the nation and its Republican project, and the ex-slaves had their assigned role, one that constrained them inside the structures emancipation had in principle shattered.

Hugues's view of the ex-slaves was complex, rooted both in his past as a slaveowning white in Saint Domingue and in his passionate (though ultimately short-lived) belief in Jacobin ideology. His writings on the behavior of the ex-slaves vacillated between enthusiasm for the freed slaves' potential and dis-appointment at their failure to fulfill it. In interpreting the failures he saw, he quickly turned to racialized characterizations of the Africans' capacities to be citizens; yet, he consistently returned to the argument that education and social reform could transform the ex-slaves into citizens. His uncertainty suffused a report he wrote to the Comité du Salut Public a month after the release of his June 20 proclamation. "The blacks who, by ignorance, never think about tomorrow, consume all the provisions but refuse to plant," he complained. Yet, he added, "it is not that they would keep doing so if we could talk to them on all the plantations; but there are too few of us to send the kind of preachers they can trust; there is no way they can grant their trust to the people of this land." In a pessimistic vein, he noted that "having spent twenty years in the colonies and having always owned negroes, I had always feared what would happen if they were to be set free." He admitted more optimistically that in general the ex-slaves had "shown themselves deserving of liberty by their behavior, avoiding thievery and laziness – vices innate among those enslaved by the degradation in which they are kept – and they have not carried themselves to extremes against their former masters." Although they had pillaged a great deal, he added, they had "limited themselves to that."[31]

Hugues's regime was profoundly ambivalent. He believed the symbols and ideals of Republicanism could produce an equal and just society. In July 1794, he requested thousands of *cocardes* – the small tricolor symbols that Republicans pinned to their clothes – to be sent for the new citizens to replace the expensive locally made ones he had been using. He also requested new banners to repre-sent his army regiments, in which the majority of troops were black. "These are little stimulants which produce great things," he added.[32] Yet, even if he meant to dress the ex-slaves in the colors of the Republic, he would not invest them with all the rights to which citizens were entitled. For the next four years, this deeply divided logic would be the foundation for Hugues's regime as it sought to con-tain the aspirations of its new citizens.

In the wake of emancipation, ex-slaves had flocked to the towns of Guadeloupe, testing their freedom, seeking opportunities, and leaving the plantations abandoned. It was not until October 1794, after he had finally reconquered all of Guadeloupe, that Hugues consolidated the piecemeal efforts to stop this process through an islandwide labor directive aimed at forcing the ex-slaves to continue working on the plantations. Most of the "citizens of the countryside," Hugues claimed, had "deserted their plantations to take refuge in the city, where, unconcerned about the public good, they wallow in laziness, hide from the public authorities, and give themselves up to all kinds of secret brigandage in order to survive." Although on the state plantations there were huge quantities of coffee that needed to be picked, a great deal of it was "lost each day due to the negligence or the bad faith of those destined to harvest them." Hugues therefore commanded all those "who usually work during the harvest," whether they lived in the city or in the countryside, to return to their coffee plantations. To this specific directive he added a general order for all those who were not employed for the public good to return to the plantations where they had previously lived, whether they had been taken over by the state or were still in private hands. He promised that the cultivateurs would be given a salary for their work. But he clearly understood that this promise was not enough to inspire them to submit to the order. He reiterated that any refusal of his orders, and all actions that encouraged the abandonment of work, were to be severely punished as crimes of counterrevolution and treason.[33]

Hugues sent to all the plantation managers appointed by the state a document describing how plantation labor was to be conducted. At five o'clock, all the cultivateurs were to be woken up and gathered together; they were to be led in singing "La Marseillaise," followed by cries of "Vive la République!" The conducteurs (drivers) would direct the cultivateurs to work, "still singing, with that naive and lively happiness which must animate the good child of the nation." Apparently, the general good required childlike simplicity and expressive cheerfulness. The manager was to visit the houses and demand explanations from all those who were not working and to determine whether their excuses were legitimate. Work breaks were set from eight to half past eight in the morning for breakfast, and from half past eleven to two o'clock for lunch. Work was to stop at dusk. If, "when the good of the plantation requires it," additional work was needed for the mills or for other reasons, "we are persuaded that all will work like true Republicans." The managers were to report regularly to Hugues and to note those cultivateurs who were particularly industrious. A new song, to the tune of "La Marseillaise," was written and taught to the ex-slaves. It thanked the "infinite being that men adore / under different names and through different religions," for "shattering the chains of captivity everywhere." "In making man in your image," one of the choruses began, "you made him free like you / trying to enslave him / is therefore to attack the law." With its echoes of the Robespierrean rituals of worship dedicated to the "Supreme Being," the song encouraged gratitude and deference to the Republic that performed God's will through the benevolent authoritarianism of its representative, Victor Hugues.[34]

Uninspired by this song or by Hugues's arguments about the responsibilities of the ex-slaves, many cultivateurs continued to leave the plantations rather than submit to the new order. In May 1795, the commissioner of the commune of Anse-Bertrand wrote: "No matter what I do to secure all citizens on their respective plantations, nothing works." He noted that the cultivateurs from one plantation had simply left for the towns: "Yesterday, again, five or six from this plantation left without permission, carrying baggage and weapons and heading for Port de la Liberté, or the bourg of Abymes. All of the ateliers (workers) disperse when we talk to them of work, and each day a considerable number are missing." If Hugues did not provide remedies, the official wrote, soon "all the plantations will be abandoned." In the same month, on the Champ-d'Arbaud – the park at the center of Basse-Terre – Hugues's officials stopped a "mass of citoyennes who were watching the troops march" and others who had taken up residence with the garrison of the town and brought them back to their plantations, which they once again immediately abandoned. Hugues had, the month before, sent a circular describing how "citoyennes *noires*, living on the plantations, refuse to work the land on the pretext that they were formerly only employed in purely domestic occupations" and threatening these recalcitrant workers with deportation if they continued to maintain such pretensions. The changes in the populations on certain plantations between 1793 and 1796 suggest the significant extent of the exodus among the ex-slaves.[35]

Hugues sought various practical solutions to encourage the ex-slaves to keep working on the plantations. In some areas, he noted in a March 1795 proclamation, the laborers on the plantations continued taking Sundays as a day of rest; in others that had adopted the new Republican calendar, workers took the tenth day of the week, the *décadi*, as their day off. To establish a uniform policy on the plantations, Hugues granted all workers the *nonedi*, the ninth day of the week, as a day for "personal affairs," and the décadi as a day of rest. The new system, based on the Republican calendar, aimed to help the "free citizens . . . forget everything that reminds them of their time of servitude."[36] Yet, while asserting the need to erase the past of slavery, Hugues kept the cultivateurs laboring without pay, so that their two free days were the only time they could work for their own profit. Although an improvement from having one day of seven to themselves and a contribution to the autonomy of the cultivateurs in the cultivation of their own plots of land, the order still severely limited the personal freedom of plantation workers. Writing to Etienne Laveaux, the commissioner in charge of Saint Domingue, Hugues defended his regime by declaring: "All the citizens have been treated equally, and they all carry a love of the good, of the nation, and of work which we have seeded within their hearts; but the lazy of all colors have been punished, for in a laboring society how can we accept that some men live at the expense of others?" As with ineffective or libertine soldiers, Hugues punished "the *cultivateur* who abandons his work in order to vagabond" about the island, and by this measure he managed to pay all the soldiers and the civil servants with the profits that continued to come from the plantations.[37]

In the middle of 1795, Hugues, who was operating in isolation from the metropole, sent three commissioners to Paris to report on the state of the colony and request instructions on how to proceed. In their description of Guadeloupe, these commissioners argued that, because of inadequate guidelines, the project of slave emancipation had remained fundamentally incomplete. Although they were sent to represent Hugues, and in many ways they reiterated his views, they also argued that his failure to pay the cultivateurs was his regime's fundamental "vice." It was only natural, they suggested, that many "Black Citizens" abandoned their plantations after emancipation, since "men who were used to seeing their sweat and their energy absorbed by a greedy master" would logically "associate the ideas of Liberty [with] those of rest" and would be "swept away by the enthusiasm produced in them by the spectacle of their broken chains and the fall of their tyrants." Although Hugues had been successful in forcing many of the ex-slaves back onto the plantations, their interests were fundamentally separated from those of the propertyowner because the only "indemnity" the cultivateurs received for their work was "the fruit of their gardens." Only a free-labor market could resolve this problem by combining the self-interest of the slaves with the larger interests of the colonial economy. Explicitly referring to the writings of those "who have for many years studied the behavior and the character of the blacks," the three commissioners argued that only through wage work and through education could the ex-slaves be taught "to know their rights, to use them with moderation, to defend them with passion," and, ultimately, to "contract the virtuous habits extinguished in them by slavery and barbarism."[38]

Even as his representatives argued that economic reform was the necessary next step in the transformation of the colonies, Hugues was already disavowing the project of granting equality and full freedom to the ex-slaves. In part, Hugues was simply incorporating the politics of the new Directory Regime, which in mid-1795 created a constitution that replaced the National Convention with two parliamentary houses overseen by an executive council. The Clubs, revolutionary tribunals, and institutions of direct democracy that had been the hallmark of the Jacobin regime were dismantled and, significantly for the colonies, the previous hard-line policies on émigrés were softened.[39] In November 1795, when Hugues issued an invitation to those whites who had fled Guadeloupe for the United States to return to the island, he sought to entice them by explicitly describing how he had restricted the rights of the ex-slaves. Although the point of his administration had been to "erase the miseries of our co-citizens in Guadeloupe by drawing a curtain across all that had happened before our arrival," the "blacks" had been given only "that portion of liberty that could be accorded to unfortunates who have barely surpassed the limits of instinct." The subjugation of these new citizens was, he argued, justified because equality was not absolute, and citizens had to be treated differently according to their moral and intellectual capacities. "We have never believed that a rascal was the equal of an honest man, that a brute, or a drunk, thanks to equality can enter and sit at the patriarchal banquet of an honest family; that the wife of a virtuous citizen could be compared to a prostitute". As a result, "people have been protected . . . property has been respected . . . the agriculture is just as it was three years ago: there are no idlers, no vagabonds."[40]

Though Hugues incorporated some of the terms of the Directory regime, he also explicitly rejected the orders to apply the new 1795 constitution. It threatened to dismantle the foundation of his regime – the Jacobin idea that a state involved in a state of war with external and internal enemies had the right to demand certain kinds of loyalty, and labor, from its citizens. "The Constitution which offers so many advantages in France presents only difficulties in these lands," he wrote to the minister of the colonies in November 1795. "Apply it here, and tomorrow there will be no more colonies." He argued that the situation in Saint Domingue, where the overzealous application of principles of social equality had invited laziness among the ex-slaves and violence against their former masters, highlighted the successes of his regime. If the Directory forced him to loosen control over the population, similar events would occur in Guadeloupe: "Who will be able to contain 90,000 strong and robust individuals, embittered by long suffering, terrible tortures, and horrible punishments? Who will be able to contain the natural ferocity of the Africans when it is compounded with their desire for vengeance?"[41]

Anything but the regime of coercion he had instituted, Hugues argued to the minister, would destroy the colony. Recapitulating the familiar arguments used to defend slavery before emancipation, Hugues wrote that, in the Caribbean, where it was easy for a man to provide himself with his basic needs, there was no natural compulsion to work. "He has no needs, clothes are useless to him, indolence and laziness are his ultimate happiness, and he is inspired by none of the passions that can motivate men to work. . . . There is nothing more painful than agricultural work in the colonies, there is no wealth in the world that can recompense the *cultivateur* for his pains, under this burning sun." The only way to get work out of the cultivateurs, therefore, was constraint. This need not be as cruel as the constraints of ancien régime slavery. "We understand by constraint," Hugues wrote, "only those methods that conform to the principles of the constitution, which will prevent the *cultivateur* from remaining in his inactivity." But, Hugues argued, this kind of coercion was fundamentally opposed to the constitution of France. "*Is this the spirit of the Constitution?*" he asked. "How can I, Minister, reconcile the Constitution with orders you have given: *make severe regulations for cultivation*, you say. . . . If we follow the spirit of the Constitution and give liberty to a man who only needs ten days out of the year to procure himself all he needs to live for a year without taking away from society, it is against the spirit of the same Constitution to subject a man, through regulations, to work for others." It was, Hugues argued, possible to govern Guadeloupe only through a particular set of laws that were different from those of the metropole.[42]

Hugues was at an impasse, unable to reconcile principles of liberty with the exigencies of colonial production. Free labor would not solve the problem, he suggested, because no salary would be worth the painful, degrading labor demanded of the cultivateurs. Without the threat of force, the ex-slaves would choose other means of survival, and the colonial economy would crumble. To learn how to be free, they had to be forced to work. Only then could the moral stain of generations of slavery be removed; only then could the ex-slaves become citizens. "It is only by degrees, through education, through the needs and even the vices of Society that we can bring these unfortunates to the state that the Government calls them towards." He had begun this process by putting "the most intelligent of the blacks" in "civil and military positions," where they could learn to "enjoy the liberty which will turn to their advantage and to that of the government." But the road, he suggested, would be long.[43]

The 1795 French constitution stipulated that those who had "defended the nation" in the armed forces had the right to vote without paying poll taxes. In Guadeloupe, therefore, the large number of black soldiers were technically eligible to participate in primary elections. Hugues explicitly rejected any possibility of such participation, however, on the basis that blacks had no independent will of their own and were therefore incapable of responsible political participation. Allowing ex-slaves to vote, argued Hugues in December 1795, had brought chaos and destruction to Saint Domingue and sealed the fate of the colony, which was "lost for all of the powers of Europe." He noted prophetically that "the greatest folly our government can commit is to try to reestablish control over" Saint Domingue and that to do so "we would have to sacrifice a huge number of men and almost all of the existing population."[44] Hugues claimed that only his policies could prevent Guadeloupe from falling prey to the chaos and violence that had enveloped Saint Domingue. "The *Noirs* are freer here than in St. Domingue," he wrote condescendingly, "they suffer no bad treatment, *they depend only on the Government*, and not on their former masters: they are fat and happy, and they love and cherish the whites because the leaders of the colony are men who deserve to be *cherished*." Hugues emphatically dismissed the possibility of organizing primary elections that included blacks. "I have not felt it necessary to assemble the *peuple noir* to name representatives, I will never do it: honor and my conscience will not permit me to. I will not play games with what is most sacred to society. No." He was defiant about his refusal, boasting that he "who reestablished order . . . who maintained the work of the manufacturers, will never burn this all down under the *vain* word of liberty."[45]

Despite his rejection of the metropole's orders, Hugues was not replaced, perhaps because he was still considered too valuable to France's conflict with Britain in the Caribbean. He continued to refine the techniques of control at his disposal. During 1796 and 1797, Hugues ordered local administrators to list all the citizens in their respective communes by name, age, race, and occupation. Employing the racial categories black, white, and red, the administrators generated statistics based on race as well as sex and occupation. Hugues's administration had assumed a task previously the responsibility of slave masters, who in private inventories had listed their slaves' names, their market value, and often their African nation of origin or their status as "creole." As state administrators took responsibility for managing and disciplining the laborers of the island, they also took on the task of identifying and enumerating them. The terms of the census were different in some ways – the notation of African or creole origins was replaced with a system that identified people by color – either "white," "black," or "red" (the category that replaced "mulatto"). Yet, there were also important continuities. The census forms included a column for "observations," and certain of those termed cultivateurs were described as *divaguant* ("rambler") – a new term for an old practice that remained a mechanism for resistance: marronage.[46]

Hugues doggedly continued to defend his policies in Guadeloupe as a positive middle ground between slavery and anarchy. In October 1797, he rebutted arguments for the reestablishment of slavery that were beginning to circulate in the metropole and in Guadeloupe. Referring to Guadeloupe's blacks, he announced: 'We are far from sharing the opinion of those who want to return them to slavery. . . . The danger would be as great in one extremity as in the other. . . . It is a dangerous to allow them to enjoy a great Liberty as it would be to submit them to a rigorous slavery." In terms that had changed little in two years, Hugues argued that coercion was necessary in a colony where "the land is nothing, and arms are everything." He reiterated his view that the French constitution was impracticable in the colony, even if all of its inhabitants united to support it. The ex-slaves were simply not intelligent enough to enjoy the rights of French citizens. Guadeloupe was still intact owing to Hugues's policies, but, if mistakes were made there as they had been in Saint Domingue, it could become "a theatre of carnage and blood, like the coast of Africa which is inhabited by the most barbarous of peoples." Hugues probably knew that his rule was soon to end, as accusations against his "tyrannical" regime, such as those delivered to the parliament in Paris in 1797 by an administrator who had served under him in Guadeloupe, grew stronger. He summarized his successes as fighting both "the despotism of the former masters and the exaggerated pretensions of the former slaves." He consoled himself with the thought that, "if we have been unable to change the hearts of men, we have at least contained their passions."[47]

Hugues's governance of Guadeloupe ended in 1798. By that time, the commissioner had many enemies. Perhaps the most ferocious were Guadeloupean planters who had suffered profoundly from his regime and dearly wished to see him ousted so that they could take back the plantations that he had nationalized. Yet, his regime was also out of step with defenders of emancipation such as Etienne Laveaux, who had served for many years in collaboration with Toussaint Louverture in Saint Domingue. In 1797 and 1798, Laveaux dominated the formation of colonial policy in Paris, advocating the strengthening of the "system of absolute unity" in which the same laws were applied in the metropole and the colony. Hugues's refusal to apply the 1795 constitution was a direct challenge to this vision, so, in 1798, the Directory regime sent a new agent, the General Desfourneaux, to assume the governance of Guadeloupe. When he arrived in November 1798, Desfourneaux, fearing that Hugues would not step down, quickly arrested him and sent him away from the island.[48]

Desfourneaux was right to fear insurrection, not so much from Hugues but from his defenders on the island. Indeed, as Hugues was being deported, large crowds of new citizens gathered to listen to speakers who argued that the point of Desfourneaux's mission "was to take freedom away from the negroes and to put them back in the state they were in before the arrival of Citizen Hugues." The speakers, according to one witness, gave Hugues a "pompous eulogy" describing his attachment to the blacks and called on the crowd to join an insurrection to prevent his departure from the island. In another town, a speaker told a similar crowd that Hugues "had brought liberty and was the only one who could conserve it." After Hugues's departure, Desfourneaux faced and repressed a series of conspiracies among former slaves in the towns and among white and black soldiers in the army. During his short rule, which lasted until early in 1800, he organized elections on the island, though the electors were all propertyowners and included only a few wealthy gens de couleur and no common soldiers. He introduced new measures that required paying cultivateurs, and they were at least partially put into effect. Yet Desfourneaux, like those administrators sent by the Consulate a year later, maintained the essence of the system put into place by Hugues, forcing the former slaves to work on their plantations and seeking to limit their movement throughout the island.[49]

The liberator of the slaves of Guadeloupe – whose arrival in 1794 with the decree of emancipation and the guillotine necessary to apply it was imaginatively dramatized in the opening scene of Carpentier's *Siglo de las luces* – returned to a much-changed France. As part of a broader movement against the earlier policies of the Revolution, arguments in favor of the reestablishment of slavery were gaining ground. Within a few years, Hugues's often articulated argument that it was impossible to incorporate the slaves into the political life of the Republic became the prevailing position in the metropolitan government. In 1802, as a prelude to the reestablishment of slavery, Bonaparte decreed a separation between the laws of the metropole and the laws of the colonies. Perhaps thinking of Hugues's portrayal of Guadeloupe as a place where the ex-slaves had been forced to continue laboring on the plantations, Bonaparte noted in his "secret instructions" to General Charles Victor Emmanuel Leclerc that, after the destruction of the autonomous regime of Toussaint Louverture, "all blacks will live in Saint-Domingue as they do today in Guadeloupe." As he faced an increasingly dire situation in Saint Domingue late in 1802, Leclerc sought a savior who was "knowledgeable as a military man and as an administrator" and had a "great character." He suggested "a man little known in France, but known to the English because of his good conduct in Guadeloupe: Victor Hugues." Instead, Hugues was sent to Guyana, where he oversaw the reestablishment of slavery in 1802.[50]

Despite its many restrictions, Hugues's regime, and the mobilization of armies of ex-slaves upon which it had depended, had provided many opportunities for the new citizens and transformed the social landscape of Guadeloupe. Taking advantage of the legal freedom he had brought, the new citizens affirmed and extended economic rights and familial connections that they had developed and maintained in bondage. They filled the Etat Civil registers and the notary registers of Guadeloupe, leaving documents that testify eloquently to the ways they solidified and improved their material circumstances. Tenuous holds on property became official through contracts; weddings and the documentation of family genealogies assured inheritance from parents to children. The ex-slaves clearly understood the importance of official records, which was well illustrated by the way cultivateurs assimilated new arrivals from Africa – the human "cargo" from English ships captured by French corsairs. In groups of three or four, new citizens from the plantations brought these Africans to the municipal offices of Basse-Terre and gave them new, French names. They did so in registers of births, marking their social existence, their "rebirth" into the Republic. And, in so doing, they described the new arrivals as "from the coast of Africa," marking their origin instead of their "race."[51]

The experience of freedom created the foundation for the resistance against metropolitan authorities that developed in 1801. When the commissioner Jean-Baptiste Raymond de Lacrosse, sent by Bonaparte to Guadeloupe, threatened the policies of racial equality in the armed forces, black soldiers defended their rights. Citizens of the towns and cultivateurs, mobilized by the increasing hints that the metropolitan governments intended to reduce them once again to slavery, joined the soldiers. In October and November 1801, an uprising spread across the island; black soldiers expelled Lacrosse. A number of prominent hommes de couleur led by the officer Magloire Pélage took over the administration of the island. In May 1802, Pélage welcomed the Richepanse expedition, which had been sent from France at the same time as the Leclerc expedition with instructions to reestablish slavery. Yet, the rapid disarmament of black troops by the French signaled the intention of the expedition, and many black soldiers who had long been suspicious of the intentions of the metropole gathered under the leadership of Louis Delgrès to fight back. After being pushed out of Basse-Terre, the insurgents, who had been joined by many thousands of women and men from the plantations, retreated to a plantation at Matouba, on the flanks of the Souffrière volcano. Delgrès ordered the plantation mined with barrels of powder, and, when he saw that defeat was imminent, he gave the order to light the wicks; a huge explosion shattered the plantation, killing hundreds, along with the advance guard of the French troops. In the next months, the majority of the people of Guadeloupe were forced to return to slavery, while those who resisted were executed or deported. More than ten thousand died in the conflict. The events in Guadeloupe in turn helped reinvigorate the struggle against the French in Saint Domingue. Indeed, as they fought on the flanks of Matouba in 1802, the insurgents flew a French tricolor flag with the white ripped from it, a prelude to the flag of the independent Republic of Haiti two years later.[52]

Hugues's legacy is complex and contradictory. As the commissioner of the island of Guadeloupe, he brought emancipation to the island and led the Republican campaigns against slavery. The brief experience of freedom, and its reversal in 1802, profoundly marked the history of the island and the political culture through which Guadeloupeans continued to interpret and confront their place within the French empire.[53] Yet, by developing strategies of racial exclusion within the Republican framework, Hugues also contributed to the reversal of freedom by providing a counterpoint to the extremes of Saint Domingue. He was a pioneer of the strategies of Republican racism that would be at the heart of the French colonial enterprise in the Antilles and, later, in Africa and Indochina. Both in Guadeloupe and in these other realms of the French empire, it was conceivable, and even intended, that certain educated and assimilated members of the colonial population might become citizens with full political rights. Yet, for the most part, citizenship was deferred, granted through a slow process that would transform tradition-bound colonial subjects into independent citizens.[54] The particularity of the Caribbean, both during the 1790s and 1848, was that the evil that had to be undone in the formation of citizens was the product of the European colonial venture itself. Hugues, like others throughout the Americas then and afterward, sought to confront and overcome the legacy of the history of slavery, and, as he did so, he found himself caught in the web of that history, unable to emancipate himself. It is this failure, perhaps, that makes his little-known story so familiar.

NOTES

Source Reprinted in an abridged format from *The William and Mary Quarterly*, 3rd Ser., 56 (April 1999), pp. 363–392.

Acknowledgment This article was first presented as a paper at the CEPIC seminar at the Institut d'Etudes Politiques in Paris, May 1997; I received useful comments from the participants, notably Eric Bleich, Daniel Cohen, Lucien Jumeau, and Patrick Weil. While I was in Paris, Carlo Celius also contributed to the development of my ideas by generously showing me some of his work. I subsequently presented the piece as a working paper to the 1997 International Seminar in the History of the Atlantic World at Harvard University, where the responses of David Armitage, Bernard Bailyn, Saliha Belmessous, and Andrew O'Shaughnessy helped me continue my revisions. At the University of Michigan, Frederick Cooper, Fernando Coronil, Paul Eiss, Setrag Manoukian, David Pedersen, Steven Pierce, Rebecca Scott, and Katharine Brophy Dubois all contributed in important ways to the development of this article.

1 For Bramante Lazzary's letter, dated Aug. 30, 1793, see Archives Nationales (hereafter cited as AN) DXXV 23, 231, letter 98. For the delegation led by Jeanne Odo, see Florence Gauthier, "Le rôle de la députation de Saint-Domingue dans l'abolition de l'esclavage," in Marcel Dorigny, ed., *Les abolitions de l'esclavage: de L. F. Sonthonax à V. Schileher, 1793, 1794, 1848: actes du colloque international tenu à l'Université de Paris VIII, les 3, 4, et 5 février 1994* (Paris, 1995), 200–11.

2 For the censuses, discussed below, see Archives Nationales, Section Outre-Mer (hereafter cited as ANSOM) G1 500–04.

3 For a discussion of the Haitian Revolution in the broader context of colonial history, see Frederick Cooper and Ann Laura Stoler, eds., *Tensions of Empire: Colonial Cultures in a Bourgeois World* (Berkeley, Calif., 1997), 2. For an examination of "Republican racism" in a different context, see David R. Roediger, *The Wages of Whiteness: Race and the Making of the American Working Class* (New York, 1991).

4 For the revolt of Trois-Rivières and the argument that slave insurgents in Guadeloupe and throughout the Caribbean gave new content to the universal language of rights, see Laurent Dubois, *Les Esclaves de la République: l'histoire oubliée de la première émancipation, 1789–1794* (Paris, 1988). See also part 1 of Dubois, "A Colony of Citizens: Revolution and Slave Emancipation in the French Caribbean, 1789–1802" (Ph.D. diss., University of Michigan, 1998). For the most detailed history of the political conflicts between whites, gens de couleur, and slaves in Guadeloupe during the period 1789–1794, see Anne Pérotin-Dumon, *Etre patriote sous les tropiques: la Guadeloupe, la colonisation et la Révolution (1789–1794)* (Basse-Terre, Guadeloupe, 1985). For a discussion of the importance of rumors in the development of slave resistance during the period, see Julius Sherrard Scott III, "The Common Wind: Currents of Afro-American Communication in the Era of the Haitian Revolution" (Ph.D. diss., Duke University, 1986); and David Patrick Geggus, "Slavery, War, and Revolution in the Greater Caribbean, 1789–1815," in David Barry Gaspar and Geggus, eds., *A Turbulent Time: The French Revolution and the Greater Caribbean* (Bloomington, Ind., 1997), 1–50.

5 See Carolyn E. Fick, *The Making of Haiti: The Saint Domingue Revolution from Below* (Knoxville, Tenn., 1990), esp. 159–63. For an account of Sonthonax's role in the transformation of Saint Domingue, see Robert Louis Stein, *Léger Félicité Sonthonax: The Lost*

Sentinel of the Republic (London, 1985). For the abolition of slavery in the National Convention, see J. Mavidal and E. Laurent et al., eds., *Archives Parlementaires de 1787 à 1860; recueil complet des débats législatifs et politiques des chambres français . . ., première série (1787 à 1799)*, vol. 84 (Paris, 1962), 276–85; see also Gauthier, "Le rôle de la députation de Saint-Domingue." For Sonthonax's speech, see "Sonthonax, ci-devant Commissaire Civil, Delegué a Saint Domingue, à la Convention Nationale," 2 Fructidor an II, AN, AD VII, 20A.

6 See A[uguste] Lacour, *Histoire de la Guadeloupe*, 2 vols. (Basse-Terre, Guadeloupe, 1858); the biographical details on Hugues are in 2:280–81. See also Georges Sainte-Croix de la Roncière, *Victor Hugues, Le Conventionnel* (Paris, 1932). Robin Blackburn comments on the lack of studies on Hugues's regime in *The Overthrow of Colonial Slavery, 1776–1848* (London, 1988), 262. Alejo Carpentier's novel *El siglo de las luces* (1962) was translated as *Explosion in a Cathedral* (New York, 1963); on Carpentier's use of Lacour, see Carmen Vasquez, "Dans le sillage de Victor Hugues et de son temps," in Jacqueline Baldran et al., eds., *Quinze Études autour de El Siglo de las Luces de Alejo Carpentier* (Paris, 1983), 85–97.

7 Thomas C. Holt's work on Jamaica provides a fascinating parallel case, which has been crucial in developing my account of Hugues's regime; see Holt, *The Problem of Freedom: Race, Labor, and Politics in Jamaica and Britain, 1832–1938* (Baltimore, 1992).

8 William Sewell, *A Rhetoric of Bourgeois Revolution: The Abbé Sieyès and What Is the Third Estate?* (Durham, N.C., 1994), 137–47.

9 Olivier Le Cour Grandmaison, *Les Citoyennetés en révolution, 1789–1794* (Paris, 1992); Pierre Rosanvallon, *Le sacre du citoyen: Histoire du suffrage universel en France* (Paris, 1979); Sophie Wahnich, *L'impossible citoyen: L'étranger dans le discours de la Révolution Française* (Paris, 1997). For parallel discourses of political incapacity in England, see Uday S. Mehta, "Liberal Strategies of Exclusion," *Politics and Society*, 18 (1990), 427–54.

10 Sieyès, quoted in Sewell, *Rhetoric of Bourgeois Revolution*, 153–54. Here Sieyès echoes Charles Secondat, Baron de Montesquieu's argument in his *De l'Esprit des Lois . . .* (1748) that, because of the exigencies of labor in certain extreme climates, slavery may be justified by "natural reason" even if it is a crime against "natural law."

11 On the debates surrounding the citizenship of gens de couleur during the early 1790s, see Yves Bénot, *La Révolution française et la fin des colonies: essai* (Paris, 1989).

12 See Michèle Duchet's classic work, *Anthropologie et Histoire au siècle des lumières* (Paris, 1988); see also Daniel P. Resnick, "The Société des Amis des Noirs and the Abolition of Slavery," *French Historical Studies*, 7 (1972), 558–69. On the broader context of abolitionist thinking, see David Brion Davis, *The Problem of Slavery in the Age of Revolution, 1770–1823* (Ithaca, N.Y., 1975); and Gordon K. Lewis, *Main Currents in Caribbean Thought: The Historical Evolution of Caribbean Society in Its Ideological Aspects, 1492–1900* (Baltimore, 1983), chap. 4. For an interesting argument about the impact of abolitionist thought, and its contradictions, on the regime of Toussaint Louverture and the subsequent "Haitian social contract," see Carlo Celius, "Le contrat social haïtien" (unpublished).

13 Jean-Antoine-Nicolas de Caritat, Marquis de Condorcet, *Réflexions sur l'esclavage des Nègres* (Paris, 1788), i, 17. On the broader context of Condorcet's thought, see Keith Michael Baker, *Condorcet: From Natural Philosophy to Social Mathematics* (Chicago, 1975).

14 Condorcet, *Réflexions*, 33–45.

15 Ibid., 11–16.

16 Ibid., 28–33.

17 Julien Raimond, *Réflexions sur les véritables causes des troubles et des désastres de nos colonies . . . adressees à la Convention Nationale* (Paris, 1793). See Bénot, *La Révolution Française*; and David Patrick Geggus, "Racial Equality, Slavery, and Colonial Secession during the Constituent Assembly," *American Historical Review*, 94 (1989), 1290–308.

18 Raimond, *Réflexions*, 19–21. I am indebted to Carlo Celius for pointing out the existence and importance of this text; he discusses Raimond's influence on Toussaint Louverture and his 1801 constitution in "Le contrat social haïtien."

19 Raimond, *Réflexions*, 26. Raimond also argues that the slaves need to develop sexual morality and form patriarchical families to be good citizens, an argument common to later abolitionist thought; see Myriam Cottias " 'L'oubli du passé' contre la 'citoyenneté': troc et ressentiment à Martinique (1848–1946)," in Fred Constant and Justin Daniel, eds., *1946–1996: cinquante ans de départementalisation outre-mer* (Paris, 1997).

20 My thanks to an anonymous reviewer for the *William and Mary Quarterly* for pointing out these particularities in Raimond's thought.

21 The original French for this expression is "*Vous avez bien merité de la patrie.*" See "Le Commissaire Délégué ... aux Republicains des armées de terre et de mer de la République, actuellement à la Guadeloupe," 1 Thermidor An 2 (July 19, 1794), ANSOM C7A 47, 18. Soon after the arrival of the Republicans in Guadeloupe, one of the commissioners, Pierre Chretien, died of fever. The second commissioner, Lebas, remained on the island, occasionally signing certain directives, but, faced with the overbearing Hugues, he seems to have had a minor role in developing the policies on the island. I therefore identify all the proclamations of the regime as those of Hugues, although some were also cosigned by Lebas.

22 Lacour, *Histoire*, 2:307–15; "Les Commissaires Délégués ... à tous les Citoyens," 20 Prairial an 2 (June 8, 1794), ANSOM C7A 47, 9.

23 Hugues to the Comité du Salut Public, 4 Thermidor An 2 (July 22, 1794), ANSOM C7A 47, 20–25.

24 See Jacques Adélaïde-Merlande, *Delgrès, ou, La Guadeloupe en 1802* (Paris, 1986), 37–48; and Louis-François Tigrane, "Historie méconnue, histoire oubliée que celle de la Guadeloupe et son armée pendant la période révolutionnaire," *Revue Historique*, 571 (Juillet–September 1989), 167–86. On the French campaigns in the eastern Caribbean, see Michael Duffy, *Soldiers, Sugar, and Seapower: The British Expeditions to the West Indies and the War against Revolutionary France* (Oxford, 1982); and David Barry Gaspar, "La Guerre des Bois: Revolution, War, and Slavery in St. Lucia, 1793–1838," in Gaspar and Geggus, eds., *A Turbulent Time*, 102–30. On the parallel battles in Saint Domingue, see Geggus, *Slavery, War, and Revolution: The British Occupation of Saint Dominque, 1793–1798* (Oxford, 1982). For Ignace, see Roland Anduse, *Joseph Ignace, Le Premier Rebelle: 1802, la révolution antiesclavagiste guadeloupéenne* (Paris, 1989).

25 For the numbers of corsairs and captures, see Tigrane, "Histoire méconnue," 180–81. For Victor Hugues's involvement in the arming of corsairs, see Archives Départementales de la Guadeloupe (hereafter cited as ADG) Bonnet 2E2/41 (2Mi193), 8 Thermidor An 6 (July 26, 1798); see also ANSOM, C7A 48, 158–212, for the registers of his dealings with the British, much of which revolved around captured ships. For a description of the weapons used on the corsairs, see the Report of General Pélardy, 18 Vendémiaire An 10 (Oct. 10, 1801), ANSOM C7A 55, 207–09. On the broader conflicts over the corsairs, see H.J.K. Jenkins, "Franco-British Disagreement regarding American Commerce in the Eastern Caribbean, 1793–1798," *Revue française d'histoire d'outre-mer*, 73, no. 3 (1986), 257–65. For two examples of sailors' leaving their loot in the hands of women in Basse-Terre, see ADG, Bonnet 2E2/41, 11 Messidor An 6 (June 29, 1798), 30 Prairial An 6 (June 18, 1798), 11 Thermidor An 6 (July 29, 1798). For the changing social landscape of Basse-Terre during this period, see Dubois, "A Colony of Citizens," chap. 8.

26 See Madival and Laurent et al., eds., *Archives Parlementaires*, 84:284.

27 "Extrait du procès-verbal de la Convention Nationale ...," 19 Prairial 1794 (June 7, 1794), ANSOM C7A 47, 8.

28 "Les Commissaires Délégués ... aux habitans de campagnes de toutes les couleurs," 25 Prairial an 2 (June 13, 1794), ANSOM C7A 47, 10.

29 "Nous Commissaires … au … Comité de Salut Public," 26 Prairial An 2 (June 14, 1794), ANSOM C7A 47, 12–13.

30 "Les Commissaires Délégués … aux Citoyens Noirs," 2 Messidor An 2 (June 20, 1794), ANSOM C7A 47, 14.

31 "Victor Hugues aux Comité du Salut Public," 4 Thermidor An 2 (July 22, 1794), ANSOM C7A 47, 20–25.

32 "Victor Hugues aux Comité du Salut Public," 5 Thermidor An 2 (July 23, 1794), ANSOM C7A 47, 31.

33 "Extrait du registre des délibérations du conseil général de la commune du Port de la Liberté," 29 Vendémiaire An 3 (Oct. 20, 1794), ANSOM C7A 47, 117. At the time, approximately 50% of the plantations in Guadeloupe were sequestered and therefore under direct state control. The rest of the plantations were administered by the owners. For the censuses, see ANSOM, G1 501.

34 Lacour, *Histoire*, 2:384–86. For the celebration of the "Supreme Being" in France under Robespierre, see Mona Ozouf, *Festivals and the French Revolution* (Cambridge, Mass., 1988).

35 Lacour, *Histoire*, 2:390–92; Dubois, "A Colony of Citizens," chap. 7.

36 "Arrêté sur les journées de travail," 23 Ventôse An 3 (Mar. 13, 1795), ANSOM C7A 48, 8.

37 "Les Commissaires Délégués … au Citoyen Laveaux," 19 Messidor An 3 (July 7, 1795), ANSOM C7A 48, 17–18.

38 "Les envoyées des commissaires … au près du Comité du Salut Public," 22 Thermidor An 3 (Aug. 9, 1795), ANSOM C7A 48, 72–76.

39 On the metropolitan colonial policies of the Directory, see Bernard Gainot, "La constitutionalization de la liberté générale sous le Directoire," in Dorigny, *Les abolitions de l'esclavage*, 213–29. For a broad account of the Directory Regime, see Lynn Hunt, David Lansky, and Paul Hanson, "The Failure of the Liberal Republic in France, 1795–1799: The Road to Brumaire," *Journal of Modern History,* 51 (1979), 734–59.

40 "Proclamation aux Citoyens Français des Isles du Vent actuellement aux Etats-Unis," 27 Brumaire An 4 (Nov. 18, 1795), ANSOM C7A 48, 34.

41 "Les Commissaire Délégués aux Ministre de la Marine et des Colonies," 22 Thermidor An 4 (Aug. 9, 1796), ANSOM C7A 49, 43–45.

42 Ibid.

43 Ibid.

44 "Le Commissaire Délégué au Ministre de la Marine et des Colonies," 20 Frimaire An 5 (Dec. 10, 1796), ANSOM C7A 49, 61–63.

45 "Extrait d'une lettre de Hugues à Fourniols deputé de la Martinique," 26 Frimaire An 5 (Dec. 16, 1796), ANSOM C7A 49, 65–66.

46 For the censuses, see ANSOM G1 501–04. See also Dubois, "A Colony of Citizens," pt. 2, for details on how they were administered and the complications involving racial identification within the censuses.

47 "Les Commissaires Délégués au Ministre de la Marine et des Colonies," 4 Brumaire An 6 (Oct. 25, 1797), ANSOM C7A 49, 228–29. For the attacks on Hugues, see "Le Citoyen Jastram, Député de la Guadeloupe au Conseil des Cinq Cents, à ses con-citoyens," AN, AD VII, 21C, 57, which details the "tyranny" of his regime in Guadeloupe. For an example of a pamphlet that argued for a return to slavery, see the anonymous *De la nécessité d'adopter l'esclavage en France: 1. Comme moyen de prospérité pour nos colonies; 2. Comme punition pour les coupables; 3. Comme ressource en faveur des indigents* (Paris, 1797).

48 On Laveaux, see Gainot, "La constitutionalization"; for his reference to a "system of absolute unity," see "Discours prononcé par Laveaux, sur l'anniversaire du 16 Pluviôse An 2," Corps Législatif, Conseil des Anciens, Bibliothèque Nationale. On the deportation of Hugues, see Lacour, *Histoire*, 3:1–7, which describes how he was

forced onto a boat in the harbor of Basse-Terre and let loose a string of insults in his native Provençal.

49 For pro-Hugues speeches, see the Depositions of Duchamps and Duchesne, 13 Frimaire An 7 (Dec. 3, 1798), AN, AF III, 209, dossier 954. For the end of Hugues's regime and the policies of Desfourneaux, see Laurent Dubois, "The Promise of Revolution: St. Domingue and the Struggle for Autonomy in Guadeloupe," in David Patrick Geggus, ed., *The Impact of the Haitian Revolution in the Atlantic World* (Columbia, S.C., forthcoming).

50 Bonaparte's quote is taken from "Notes pour servir aux instructions a donner au Capitaine Général Leclerc"; Leclerc's is from his letter of 29 Fructidor An X (Sept. 16, 1802). Both are reprinted in Paul Roubier, ed., *Lettres du Général Leclerc, commandant en chef de l'armée de Saint-Domingue en 1802* (Paris, 1937), 235, 269.

51 For the naming of the new arrivals from Africa, see, for example, ANSOM EC Basseterre 10 (Births, 1797), nos. 64, 65, 71–73.

52 For an account of the fighting in 1802, see Adélaïde-Merlande, *Delgrès*. On the flag, see General Ménard's report, ANSOM C7A 21–37, 28–30. In the letters he wrote from Saint Domingue in 1802, General Leclerc repeatedly complained that the news of the brutal reestablishment of slavery in Guadeloupe had turned the tide of the conflict in Saint Domingue. In September 1802, for instance, he wrote: "As soon as the news of the re-establishment of slavery in Guadeloupe arrived, the insurrection, which up until then had only been partial, became general; I could not confront it on all sides, and I was obliged to abandon certain points which have suffered." See Roubier, ed., *Lettres*, 229 (other examples are on 200, 256).

53 This period is one of the roots of the differences in politics and culture, often commented on in the French Antilles, between Guadeloupe and Martinique. For a powerful evocation of the continuing presence of this history, particularly that of the reestablishment of slavery on the island, see Daniel Maximin's novel. *L'Isolé soleil* (Paris, 1981), which was translated as *Lone Sun* (Charlottesville, Va., 1989).

54 For a detailed examination of the workings of exclusion from citizenship in the 20th-century French empire, see Gary Wilder, "Subject-Citizens and Interwar France: Negritude, Colonial Humanism, and the Imperial Nation-State" (Ph.D. diss., University of Chicago, forthcoming). See also Alice L. Conklin, *A Mission to Civilize: The Republican Idea of Empire in France and West Africa, 1895–1930* (Stanford, Calif., 1997).

INDEX

283